SUPPORTING & STRENGTHENING FAMILIES

Methods, Strategies and Practices

Carl J. Dunst,
Carol M. Trivette, and
Angela G. Deal, EDITORS

Brookline Books • Cambridge, Massachusetts

Library of Congress Cataloging-in-Publication Data

Dunst, Carl J.
Supporting & Strengthening Families: Methods, Strategies, and Practices by Carl J. Dunst, Carol M. Trivette, and Angela G. Deal
p. cm
Includes bibliographical references.
ISBN 0-914797-94-8
1. Handicapped children—Home care—United States. 2. Handicapped children— United States—Family relationships. 3. Family social work—United States. I. Trivette, Carol M. II. Deal, Angela G. III. Title IV. Supporting and Strengthening Families.
HV888.5.D87 1994
362.82'0973—dc20   93-50893
                                                                                         CIP

10 9 8 7 6 5 4 3

Reprinted, 1995.

If you want to order this book call or send a letter to:
BROOKLINE BOOKS
P.O. Box 1046, Cambridge, MA, Tel (617) 868-0360 Fax (617) 868-1772

TABLE OF CONTENTS

PART V: EFFECTIVE HELP-GIVING PRACTICES

PART VI: GENERAL CONCLUSION

PREFACE

The publication of our first book *Enabling and Empowering Families: Principles and Guidelines for Practice* was the culmination of six years of research, model-demonstration, and clinical practice with an eye toward a better understanding of the best ways to promote and enhance child, parent, and family development. In the intervening years, we have continued to study the environmental conditions and social contexts best suited for strengthening individual and family functioning.

This first volume of *Supporting and Strengthening Families: Methods, Strategies and Practices*, includes articles that describe our current thinking about working effectively with families. The second volume, *Supporting and Strengthening Families: Research Findings and Intervention Outcomes*, includes articles that describe the results from studies which specifically tested hypotheses central to tenets set forth in Volume 1.

This volume elaborates on the themes addressed in *Enabling and Empowering Families* and introduces new themes that have emerged as our understanding of how best to support families has progressed.

The theme that family-centered assessment and intervention practices ought to be needs-based and consumer-driven is both reinforced and extended. Although needs-based practices have been recently criticized as being a deficit approach, such criticism seems both unwarranted and misguided. If a professional identifies what he or she believes to be family needs, thus implying and inferring weaknesses, that can be construed as a deficit perspective. However, needs identified by a family constitute a particular kind of strength, and as our work has found, intervention practices that are responsive to what a family establishes as its priorities and goals will have more positive influences and consequences on child, parent, and family functioning because the family is more likely to embrace them.

Second, the theme that *all* families have existing strengths as well as the capacity to become more competent, permeates the contents of each and every chapter in the book. Moreover, the contention is made that building on strengths rather than correcting weaknesses cannot but be a more productive approach to working with families. We have repeatedly found that this approach to working with families results in better interactions between a family and professionals, and in better outcomes for the family and its members.

Third, we elaborate further on the theme that mobilization of both informal and formal sources of support increases the likelihood that family needs can be adequately met. Resource-based intervention practices are introduced as a particular way of conceptualizing and mapping a broad range of supports and resources onto individual family-identified needs. Resource-based practices look toward a variety of community people, programs, and organizations as sources of support, rather than depending solely on professionals and the services they provide (service-based approaches) as the source of support for meeting family needs.

Fourth, the proposition that it matters as much *how* professionals assist families in mobilizing resources as it does *which* supports are mobilized is reinforced by the results of studies completed since *Enabling and Empowering Families* was published. Extensive work on identifying the key features of effective helpgiving, and relating these characteristics to family outcomes, has led us to an increased understanding of, and rationale why, it is important to interact with families in empowering ways. This theme is addressed in terms of the characteristics of effective helpgiving practices in general, and those aspects of family-centered case management practices and parent–professional collaboration and partnerships more specifically.

Fifth, our major and primary emphasis on family empowerment as an outcome of successful intervention efforts is reiterated. A new and expanded perspective of empowerment is offered as a framework for differentiating between processes used to create opportunities for people to use existing competencies as well as acquire new skills (enabling experiences) and the outcomes and benefits associated with such experiences (empowering consequences). A criticism levied against the idea of empowerment espoused in *Enabling and Empowering Families* has to be with people's misunderstanding of the term as it is defined in most dictionaries and our use of the term as a psychological and phenomenological construct. The model described in this book hopefully clarifies these misunderstandings.

In addition, two other themes play a prominent role in our elaboration of a family-centered approach. The first has to do with the *context* of working with families. We propose that this context ought to be family support programs that specifically aim to enable and empower people by enhancing and promoting individual and family capabilities in ways that support and strengthen family functioning. Effective family support programs are characterized by guiding beliefs and principles that constitute a family-centered philosophy about working with children, their parents, and other family members. We argue that the underpinnings of family support programs are more consistent with family-centered assessment and intervention practices than are more traditional human services models and practices. Indeed, we would say that traditional human services models and practices are a major deterrent to becoming family-centered because such models and practices tend to reinforce entrenched thinking about the methods and goals of professionally-centered assessment and interventions.

The other new theme has to do with a conceptual and operational distinction between treatment, prevention, and promotion models of intervention, and the contention that empowering children, parents, and families can be best achieved by adopting promotive and competency-enhancing intervention strategies. The model we describe directly addresses a long-standing controversy waged between human services practitioners who claim that people with problems ought to take priority in receiving treatment services, and prevention enthusiasts who argue that resources are best spent deterring the onset of problems and disorders. We resolve this controversy by arguing that *all* people can benefit from efforts to enhance and promote their competencies and capabilities, and that by doing so, human functioning is supported and strengthened.

The thread that ties all of these themes together is a particular approach for conceptualizing and describing the *processes* for developing and implementing Individualized Family *Support* Plans (IFSPs). The choice of the term *support* rather than *service* is intentional, and reflects our belief that service-based approaches to intervention are both limited and limiting. We reiterate the contention throughout the book that the IFSP process rather than the product itself is the most important part of working with families. It is the process which leads one from needs identification to resource mobilization in ways that have empowering consequences and family strengthening influences.

The contents of this book provide a blueprint for developing and implementing family-centered assessment and intervention practices. This first volume of *Supporting and Strengthening Families* represents our second generation thoughts about the key characteristics of family-centered assessment and intervention practices if such practices are to have optimal positive benefits.

The book is divided into five major sections. Section I includes an overview of the family-centered assessment and intervention model that has evolved from our work with families. This section also includes a description of an empowerment model that defines and operationalizes both the processes and outcomes that ought to be realized from use of the model. Section II details both the aims and principles of family support programs, and the characteristics and consequences of human services intervention models consistent or inconsistent with these aims and principles. The call for adoption of enhancement and promotion models is advanced because only these kinds of models can produce optimal effects. The particular approach we have adopted for developing and implementing IFSPs is described in Section III. As noted above, the model and framework we have developed structures the processes used to mobilize resources to meet family needs in ways that have empowering consequences. Section IV includes detailed information about the needs-based, strengths-based, and resource-based components of our family-centered model. The description of each component is followed by a chapter that describes one particular way of assessing needs, strengths, and supports, respectively, and includes empirical evidence demonstrating the relationship between these model components and other aspects of parent and family functioning. The final section includes a number of chapters that describe the particular kinds of helpgiving practices that will most likely produce empowering outcomes. The specific characteristics of effective helping are described from three different but related perspectives, and data are presented demonstrating that helpgiving practices consistent with effective helpgiving characteristics are related to self-efficacy appraisals in ways highly consistent with the empowerment model that undergirds all aspects of our family-centered model.

Collectively, the 18 chapters in this book describe and elaborate upon a social systems approach for supporting and strengthening families that has evolved over the past 10 to 12 years. To the extent that readers find the contents and ideas we have presented useful in their own work, the goal we set for ourselves will have been realized. Additionally, we hope that our particular way of conceptualizing family-centered assessment and intervention practices will reorient human services policy in ways that truly result in program activities supporting and strengthening family functioning.

ACKNOWLEDGMENTS

The completion of this book was made possible with the help of many friends and colleagues. First and foremost, we would like to extend special thanks to the staff of the Family, Infant and Preschool Program and the many families who participated in the development and validation of the model and practices described in this book. We would like to specifically acknowledge, with much gratitude, Barbara Pollock, Benny Hudgins, Cora Hudgins, Debbie Kantner, Donald Kantner, Gail Harrison, Ginna Wheatley, Kathleen Paget, Lauren Starnes, Lisa Shetts, Lola Harrison, Nancy Gordon, Nancy Watts, Renne Harrison, Sherra Vance, Tammy Moss, Theresa Rounds, and Wilson Hamer who helped with the field-testing of the family-centered model. Pat Condrey and Norma Hunter typed numerous versions of the book, and their patience and assistance are greatly appreciated. Thanks is also extended to Mary Brown, Jane Powell and Renee Campbell for typing different versions of several chapters. The data analysis and graphics were completed by Deborah Hamby, Sherra Vance and Norma Hunter. Their help is appreciated as well. Carol Berardelli, Wendy Jodry and Sandy Prins read several versions of galley proofs, and their careful editing and feedback has been invaluable. Lastly, special thanks is extended to J. Iverson Riddle, M.D., Director, Western Carolina Center, for his continued support and encouragement throughout the process of developing the methods and procedures described in this book.

The work reported in this book was supported, in part, by grants from the Illinois Planning Council on Developmental Disabilities (89-1517); National Institute of Child Health and Human Development, Mental Retardation and Developmental Disabilities Branch (HD23038); National Institute of Mental Health, Prevention Research Branch (MH38862); North Carolina Children's Trust Fund (C1130, C1912, C7753, C9514); North Carolina Council on Developmental Disabilities; North Carolina Department of Human Resources, Research and Evaluation Section (83527); U.S. Department of Education, Office of Special Education Programs (G008530078, H024C80023); U.S. Department of Health and Human Services, National Center for Child Abuse and Neglect (90CA124602); and U.S. Department of Health and Human Services, Administration on Developmental Disabilities (90DD0113, 90DD0144). This support is greatly appreciated; without which the model could not have been developed and research on various aspects of the model completed.

We would also like to thank the following publishers for permission to reprint material in this book:

Deal, A., Dunst, C. J., & Trivette, C. M. (1989). A flexible and functional approach to developing Individualized Family Support Plans. *Infants and Young Children. 1* (4), 32-43. Reprinted with permission of Aspen Publishers, Inc., © 1989.

Dunst, C. J., & Leet, H. (1987) Measuring the adequacy of resources in households with young children. *Child: Care, Health and Development, 13*, 111-125. Reprinted with permission of Blackwell Scientific Publications Ltd. © 1987.

Dunst, C. J., & Trivette, C. M. (1989). An enablement and empowerment perspective of case management. *Topics in Early Childhood Special Education, 8* (4), 87-102. Copyright 1989 by PRO-ED, Inc. Reprinted by permission.

Dunst, C. J., Trivette, C. M., Davis, M., & Cornwell, J. (1988). Empowering families of children with health impairments. *Children's Health Care, 17* (2), 71-81. Reproduced with permission of the Association for the Care of Children's Health, 7910 Woodmont Avenue, Suite 300, Bethesda, MD 20814.

Dunst, C. J., Trivette, C. M., & LaPointe, N. (1992). Toward clarification of the meaning and key elments of empowerment. *Family Science Review, 5* (1/2), 111-130. Reprinted with permission of The Consortium of Family Science Departments © 1992.

Dunst, C. J., Trivette, C. M., & Thompson, R. (1991). Supporting and strengthening family functioning: Toward a congruence between principles and practice. *Prevention in Human Services, 9* (1), 19-43. © By The Haworth Press, Inc. All rights reserved. Reprinted with permission. For copies of this work, contact Marianne Arnold at The Haworth Document Delivery Service (Telephone 1-800-3-HAWORTH; 10 Alice Street, Binghamton, N.Y. 13904). For other questions concerning rights and permissions contact Wanda Latour at the above address.

CONTRIBUTORS

Kimberly Boyd, M.S.W., Developmental Specialist, Child and Family Studies Program, Allegheny-Singer Research Institute, Pittsburg, PA.

Jeffri Brookfield, Ph.D., Research Scientist, Child and Family Studies Program, Allegheny-Singer Research Institute, Pittsburg, PA.

Janet Cornwell, Ph.D., Director of Early Childhood Education, Research for Better Schools, Philadelphia, PA.

Michelle Davis, Human Service Coordinator, Family Resource Program, Family, Infant and Preschool Program, Western Carolina Center, Morganton, NC.

Angela G. Deal, M.S.W., Executive Director of the Burke Partnership for Children, Morganton, NC.

Hope Leet Dittmeier, M.R.C., Coordinator of Community Resource Development, R.E.A.C.H. of Louisville, Inc., Louisville, KY.

Carl J. Dunst, Ph.D., Professor of Psychiatry, Medical College of Pennsylvania (Allegheny Campus) and Senior Research Scientist, Allegheny-Singer Research Institute and Allegheny General Hospital, Pittsburg, PA.

Deborah W. Hamby, B.S., Research Associate, Center for Family Studies, Western Carolina Center, Morganton, NC.

Charlie Johanson, M.A., Director of Chugiak Children's Services, Inc., Chugiak, AK.

Nancy LaPointe, M.A., Public Relations/Research Assistant, Colon Polyp Prevention Study for the American Cancer Society, Richmond, VA.

Donald W. Mott, M.A., Coordinator, Family Resource Program, Family, Infant and Preschool Program, Western Carolina Center, Morganton, NC.

David Sexton, Ph.D., Professor and Chair, Department of Special Education and Habilitative Services, University of New Orleans, New Orleans, LA.

Rebekah B. Thompson, M.A., Psychological Associate, RHA, Health Services, Cleveland, NC.

Carol M. Trivette, Ph.D., Director of the Family, Infant and Preschool Program and the Center for Family Studies, Western Carolina Center, Morganton, NC.

I

INTRODUCTION

The two chapters in this introductory section lay the groundwork for this volume. The first chapter describes a family systems framework for assessing and intervening with families in ways that have competency-enhancing and strengthening influences. The second chapter presents a unified framework for conceptualizing and operationalizing empowerment notions. The material in both chapters serve as the foundation for a set of family-centered methods and practices for identifying family needs, supports and resources for meeting needs, and family capabilities for mobilizing supports.

The material presented in Chapter 1 is a synopsis of principles and guidelines described in <u>Enabling and Empowering Families</u> *(Dunst, Trivette & Deal, 1988). The reader is referred to this book for a detailed presentation of the specifics of the family-centered model. The material presented in Chapter 2 provides an updated perspective of the meaning and key characteristics of empowerment that has emerged from our efforts to translate an empowerment philosophy into practice as part of implementing the family-centered model. Taken together, both chapters provide an empirically-based rationale for the family-centered approach to assessment and intervention elaborated upon in the other chapters of the book.*

CHAPTER 1

Enabling and Empowering Families

Carl J. Dunst, Carol M. Trivette & Angela G. Deal

THE PURPOSE OF THIS CHAPTER is to present an overview of a particular approach for identifying family concerns and needs, intrafamily and community resources for meeting needs, and family strengths and capabilities for mobilizing supports and resources. The model is derived substantially from systems theory and human ecology, where environmental forces are viewed as a major determinant for shaping the need and desire for different kinds of aid and assistance.

The need or desire for different kinds of resources and supports represents at least one set of conditions that led Bronfenbrenner (1975, 1979) as well as others (Dunst, 1985; Dunst & Trivette, 1988a, 1988d; Foster, Berger, & McLean, 1981; Hobbs et al., 1984; Stoneman, 1985; Zigler & Berman, 1983) to argue that successful human services practices are more likely to be those that employ an ecological framework and intervene in ways that produce broad-based family system changes. A basic premise of social systems theories is that different social settings and their members are interdependent, and that events and changes in one unit reverberate and produce changes in other social units. More specifically, there is "concern for the progressive accommodations between a growing human organism and its immediate environment, and *the way in which this relation is mediated by forces emanating from remote regions in the larger physical and social milieu*" (Bronfenbrenner, 1979, p. 3, emphasis added).

Consequently, the behavior of a child, his/her siblings, parents, and other family members may be affected by events in settings in which the person may not even be present.

There is both theoretical and empirical evidence to support the contention that needs (aspirations, goals, personal projects, etc.) are at least one major *set of forces* that shape the behavior of different family members, and that needs are often generated by events and circumstances both within and outside the family unit (Dunst & Leet, 1987; Dunst & Trivette,1988a; Fisher, Nadler, & DePaulo, 1983a; Garbarino, 1982; Little, 1983; Palys, 1980). Moreover, there is evidence that lack of consensus between what professionals and families see as needs often sets the occasion for both conflict and a family's failure to follow professionally prescribed regimens. The latter is often interpreted by professionals as resistant, uncooperative, and noncompliant behavior (Merton, Merton, & Barber, 1983). However, what may be viewed as either oppositional or apathetic behavior may have less to do with contempt for professional opinion and more to do with lack of consensus regarding the nature of the presenting problem, the need for treatment (medical, educational, therapeutic, etc.), and the course of action that should be taken. As noted by Merton (1976), people that occupy different positions in a social structure (client vs. professional, low SES vs. middle SES, etc.) tend to differ in terms of what constitutes individual and family needs,

The material in this chapter is abstracted from C.J. Dunst, C.M. Trivette, & A. G. Deal (1988), *Enabling and Empowering Families*. Cambridge, MA: Brookline Books. Reprinted by permission from the publisher.

and therefore how one should allocate time and energy to meet those needs.

The various chapters in this book both describe and elaborate upon a strategy proposed by Dunst, Trivette, and Deal (1988) and Hobbs et al. (1984) in terms of the goal of family-centered assessment and intervention practices from a social systems perspective of human development. According to these investigators, the goal of family-centered intervention is to identify family needs, locate the informal and formal resources and supports for meeting those needs, and help families use existing capabilities as well as learn new skills in order to mobilize needed resources. If this can be done in a way that makes a family more competent and better able to mobilize intrafamily and extrafamily resources, which in turn positively influences child, parent, and family functioning (see especially Dunst, 1986b; Dunst & Trivette, 1987a, 1988c), the family will have become empowered *par excellence*. Because the major focus of our assessment and intervention efforts is to enable and empower families in a way that makes them more competent and better able to mobilize resources, we begin with a brief description of what we mean when we use the term empowerment to place the material described in this book in proper perspective. A detailed examination of the meaning and key elements of empowerment is presented in Chapter 2.

A SOCIAL SYSTEMS PERSPECTIVE OF EMPOWERMENT

Empowerment implies that many competencies are already present or at least possible.... Empowerment implies that what you see as poor functioning is a result of social structure and lack of resources which make it impossible for the existing competencies to operate. It implies that in those cases where new competencies need to be learned, they are best learned in a context of living life rather than in artificial programs where everyone, including the person learning, knows that it is really the expert who is in charge. (Rappaport, 1981, p. 16)

This set of assertions includes three conditions that we believe reflect the way in which we need to think about helping relationships and empowerment practices. First, it states that people are already competent or that they have the capacity to become competent. This is what we refer to as a *proactive* stance as part of helping relationships. Second, it states that the failure to display competence is not due to deficits within the person, but rather the failure of social systems to create opportunities for competencies to be displayed or learned. Creating opportunities for competence to be displayed or learned is what we refer to as *enabling* experiences. Third, it implicitly states that the person who is the help-seeker (learner, client, etc.) must attribute behavior change at least in part to his or her own actions if one is to acquire a sense of control necessary to manage family affairs. This is what we mean when we say a person is *empowered*.

Collectively, these three assertions provide a framework for viewing empowerment from a broader-based social systems perspective suggesting the importance of the help-giver's behavior as part of enabling and empowering families. Consequently, *it is not simply a matter of whether or not family needs are met, but rather the manner in which needs are met that is likely to have empowering consequences.* The methods and strategies described in this book are designed to help professionals engage in help-giving exchanges that increase the likelihood of a family becoming empowered through efforts to meet needs.

MAJOR FEATURES OF THE FAMILY-CENTERED MODEL

The family-centered assessment and intervention model described in this book is characterized by eight, interrelated features that collectively form the foundation for a particular approach to working with families. The eight features are:

1. Adoption of a social systems perspective of families that suggests a new and expanded definition of intervention (Dunst, 1985; Dunst & Trivette, 1988a).
2. Movement beyond the child as the sole focus of intervention, toward the family as the unit of intervention (Hobbs, 1975; Hobbs et al., 1984).
3. Major emphasis upon empowerment of families as the goal of intervention practices (Rappaport, 1981, 1987).
4. A proactive stance toward families that places major emphasis upon promotion of growth producing behavior rather than treatment of problems or prevention of negative outcomes (Dunst & Trivette, 1987a).
5. Focus on family, and *not* professionally identified needs and aspirations as the primary targets of intervention (Dunst & Leet, 1987).
6. Major emphasis on identifying and building upon family capabilities as a way of strengthening family functioning (Hobbs et al., 1984).
7. Major emphasis upon strengthening the family's personal social network and utilizing this network as a primary source of support and resources for meeting needs (Gottlieb, 1983).

8. A shift and expansion in the roles professionals play in interactions with families and the ways in which these roles are performed (Slater & Wikler, 1986; Solomon, 1985; Trivette, Deal, & Dunst, 1986).

SOCIAL SYSTEMS PERSPECTIVE

A social systems perspective views a family as a social unit embedded within other formal and informal social support systems and networks. It also views these different social networks as interdependent where events and changes in one unit resonate and, in turn, influence directly and indirectly the behavior of individuals in other social units. A social systems perspective also considers events within and between social units as supportive and health promoting to the extent that they have positive influences on family functioning. Collectively, these various relationships provide a basis for proposing a social systems definition of intervention as the *provision and/or mobilization of supports and resources by members of a family's informal and formal social network that either directly or indirectly influences child, parent, and family functioning.* This type of social systems perspective of families and intervention is reflected in the following quote taken from Bronfenbrenner (1979) in terms of parenting tasks:

(W)hether parents can perform effectively in their child-rearing roles within the family depends on the *role demands, stresses, and supports emanating from other settings....*Parents' evaluations of their own capacity to function, as well as their view of their child, are related to such external factors as *flexibility of job schedules, adequacy of child care arrangements, the presence of friends and neighbors who can help out in large and small emergencies,* the quality of health and social services, and neighborhood safety. The availability of supportive settings is, in turn, a function of their existence and frequency in a given culture or subculture. This frequency can be enhanced by the adoption of public policies and practices that create additional settings and societal roles conducive to family life. (p. 7, emphasis added)

FAMILY AS UNIT OF INTERVENTION

The family, and not the child, as the unit of intervention recognizes the fact that the family system is comprised of interdependent members, and that by strengthening and supporting the family unit and not just the child, the chances of making a significant positive impact upon *ALL* family members is enhanced considerably. Enabling parents to meet the needs of all family members is valued because to do so promotes the acquisition of different kinds of competencies, which, in turn, makes parents better able to have the time, energy, and resources necessary for enhancing the well-being and development of other family members. As noted by Hobbs et al. (1984):

> (F)amilies are the critical element in the rearing of healthy, competent, and caring children. We suggest, however that families–all *families-cannot perform this function as well as they might unless they are supported by a caring and strong community, for it is community (support) that provides the informal and formal supplements to families' own resources.* Just as a child needs nurturance, stimulation, and the resources that caring adults bring to his or her life, so, too, do parents–as individuals and as adults filling socially valued roles (for example, parent, worker)–need the re-

sources made possible by a caring community if they are to fulfill their roles well. (p. 45, emphasis added)

EMPOWERMENT OF FAMILIES

The ability of families to manage life events effectively, as well as gain mastery over their affairs, requires that we empower families to become competent and capable rather than dependent upon professional helpers or helping systems. This is accomplished by creating opportunities for families to acquire the necessary knowledge and skills to become stronger, and better able to manage and negotiate the many demands and forces that impinge upon them in a way that promotes individual and family well-being. Deriving pleasure and gratification in seeing others become competent and capable is a fundamental attribute of a helping professional who is a proponent of an empowerment philosophy. To the extent that we do not recognize and explicitly consider empowerment of families as the goal of intervention, we are more likely to fool ourselves into believing that we have done a good job, when, in fact, we have lost an opportunity to enable and empower the family, and perhaps have even created dependencies by engaging in noncontingent helping (Skinner, 1978).

As Rappaport (1981) has so aptly pointed out, most of what we do in the name of helping is usurping rather than empowering:

> (T)he pervasive belief that experts should solve all of (the help-seeker's) problems in living has created a social and cultural iatrogenesis which extends the sense of alienation and loss of ability to control (one's) life....This is the path that the social as well as the physical health experts have been on, and we need to reverse this trend. (p. 17)

PROACTIVE PROMOTION

A proactive approach to helping relationships views families–*all* families–in a positive light, and places major emphasis upon promoting the acquisition of self-sustaining and adaptive behaviors that emphasize growth among all family members and not just an individual child. Acceptance of individual differences is valued because "It encourages a more productive approach to intervention in which we do not try to change children (and their families) but instead try to build on the strengths that they bring to the program" (Zigler & Berman, 1983, p. 895). A proactive approach focuses on family strengths and capabilities in a way that supports and strengthens family functioning. To the extent possible, the focus of all intervention efforts is on promoting the acquisition of knowledge and skills that makes the family more competent, thus strengthening family functioning. In contrast to treatment strategies that *correct* problems or disorders and prevention strategies that *decrease the risk* of problems or disorders (both of which are deficit oriented), a promotion approach to working with families emphasizes positive targets as the goal of intervention, not the alleviation or reduction of negative outcomes. The major characteristics of this element are perhaps best reflected in Carkhuff and Anthony's (1979) definition of helping restated in terms of a family focus:

> Helping is the act of *promoting* and *supporting* family functioning in a way that *enhances* the acquisition of competencies that permit a greater degree of *intrafamily* control over subsequent activities.

FAMILY NEEDS AND ASPIRATIONS

The focus on family-identified, not professionally-identified needs and aspirations as the primary targets of intervention, recognizes the family's rightful role in deciding what is most important and in the best interest of the family unit and its members. According to Hobbs (1975), "The foresighted professional person knows that it is the parent who truly bears the responsibility for the child, and the parent cannot be replaced by episodic professional service" (pp. 228-229). Responsive and truly individualized interventions address the needs and aspirations of the family by promoting the family's ability to identify and meet their needs in a way that makes them more capable and competent. This approach to working with families in terms of the relationship between the help-seeker's and help-giver's roles as part of social support interventions was stated in the following way by Pilisuk and Parks (1986):

> The (family) defines the need for service. (A) need for assistance is not assumed until the (family) has set forth such a need. This request for assistance might originate with one individual or with the...(family) system.... (T)he social support facilitator helps the (family) crystallize the (concern). (pp. 162-163)

FAMILY STRENGTHS

All families have strengths and capabilities. If we take the time to identify these qualities and build upon them rather than focus on correcting deficits or weaknesses, families are not only more likely to respond favorably to interventions, but the chances of making a significant positive impact on the family unit will be enhanced considerably. A major consideration as part of strengthening families is promoting their ability to use existing strengths for meeting needs in a way that produces positive changes in family functioning. According to Garbarino (1982):

The crucial property of families, and systems in general, is that the whole and its parts must be able to (achieve their aspirations) for both to continue. A family "works" when its members feel good about the family, *when their needs are being met*, and the development of relationships flow smoothly. (p. 72, emphasis added)

SOCIAL SUPPORT AND RESOURCES

A family's personal social network generally has a wealth of support and resources that can be used to meet needs and attain aspirations; yet there is a tendency for professionals to supplant or replace natural support systems with professional services. To the extent possible and appropriate, major emphasis is placed upon strengthening and building natural support systems that create positive, proactive linkages between the members of the family's support network. This is not to imply that all needs can or should be met by informal support sources. The intent of this feature of our approach is not to usurp or supplant natural sources of support when they can be mobilized as a way of meeting needs. According to Hobbs et al. (1984), meeting family needs "do(es) not necessarily require the involvement of formal service bureaucracies, but rather (can be accomplished by) helping parents look toward more primary kinds of social support, such as family members, kinship groups, neighbors, and voluntary associations" (p. 50). To the extent that this is possible, it should be the focus of intervention efforts. The importance of doing so is reflected in Gottlieb's (1983) observations:

When people recognize that they (have needs), they (generally) consult family members, friends, workmates, and neighbors, calling upon them for ad-

vice about *community resources that are best matched to their needs.* (p. 210)

PROFESSIONAL ROLES

Meeting the individualized needs of families requires not only a shift and expansion in the roles professionals assume in interactions with families, but also a significant change in the ways in which these roles are performed. According to Rappaport (1981), the ability to empower and strengthen families in a way that makes them more competent and capable "requires a breakdown of the typical role relationship(s) between professionals and community people" (p. 19). Partnerships are valued over paternalistic approaches because the former implies and conveys the belief that partners are capable individuals who become more capable by sharing knowledge, skills, and resources in a manner that benefits all participants as a result of the cooperative arrangement. As noted by Dunst (1985), helping relationships

that utilize partnerships avoid viewing (individual and family) differences as deficits that have some pathological origins that must be "treated" as an illness. Rather, differences arising from intra- and extra-family influences are seen as conditions that *generate needs that can best be met by mobilizing resources that allow these needs to be met and thus strengthen families.* (p. 171, emphasis added)

The above set of eight considerations collectively form the basis of the assessment and intervention model briefly described below and elaborated upon in Dunst, Trivette, and Deal (1988). These distinct but interrelated maxims serve as guidelines and principles for the conduct of a family-centered approach to empowering families to meet their needs in ways that are growth producing. The *conceptual and philosophical underpinnings* of our model are reflected in the social systems, family as unit of intervention, empowerment, and proactive orientation that we have adopted in our work with families. The *operational and application-in-practice aspects* of the model are reflected in the needs and aspirations, family strengths, supports and resources, and professional roles (help-giving behavior) features of the model.

OPERATIONALIZATION OF THE FAMILY-CENTERED MODEL

Figure 1-1 graphically shows the four operational components of the model and relationships among the components. Family needs and aspirations, family strengths and capabilities (family functioning style), and social supports and resources are seen as separate but interdependent parts of the family-centered assessment and intervention process. The help-giving behaviors used by professionals are seen as the ways in which families are enabled and empowered to acquire and use competencies to procure support and mobilize resources for meeting needs. Needs and resources, family strengths and capabilities, and supports and resources may be thought of as sets of interlocking gears, whereas help-giving behaviors may be thought of as the mechanism for aligning the gears in a way that makes the parts of the system optimally efficient.

The operationalization of the process may be described in the following manner:

1. Family needs and aspirations are first identified in order to determine what a family considers important for individual and family well-being.

2. The unique ways in which the family system operates are identified in order to determine how the family typically deals with life's trials and tribulations, and what aspects of the family system are "working well."

3. The family's personal social network is "mapped" onto individual and family needs to identify existing and potential sources of aid and assistance that can be procured and mobilized to meet needs and to achieve aspirations.

4. The optimal alignment and integration of the three parts of the family system occurs, in part, by the help-giving behaviors (professional roles) that are employed as part of the assessment and intervention process.

The model is best described as a *dynamic, fluid process* that is continually operationalized *each and every time a help-giver interacts with a family*. The ability to carry out our assessment and intervention model is a *craft* that can be learned if one is willing to devote the time and energy to master the necessary material, and

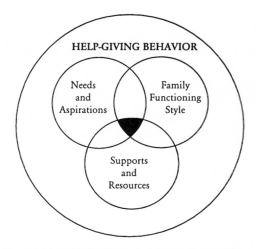

Fig. 1-1. Four Major Components of the Family-Centered Assessment and Intervention Model.

practice and perfect the skills needed to work effectively with families (see especially Dunst, Trivette, & Deal, 1988). Learning, practicing, and perfecting the craft should result in the help-giver acquiring a set of skills and competencies that permit him or her to promote a family's ability to mobilize supports and resources to meet needs and attain aspirations in ways that are both enabling and empowering.

ASSESSMENT AND INTERVENTION PRINCIPLES

Four substantive principles guide the implementation of the family-centered model. These principles are:

1. To promote positive child, parent, and family functioning, base intervention efforts on family identified needs, aspirations, and desires.
2. To enhance successful efforts toward meeting needs, use existing family functioning styles (strengths & capabilities) as a basis for promoting the family's ability to mobilize resources.
3. To insure the availability and adequacy of resources for meeting needs, place major emphasis upon strengthening the family's personal social network and promote the utilization of untapped, but potential, sources of community aid and assistance.
4. To enhance a family's ability to become more self-sustaining with respect to meeting their needs, employ help-giving behaviors that promote the family's acquisition and use of competencies and skills necessary to mobilize and secure needed resources.

Each of these principles states a pragmatic relationship that specifies an *outcome* and the *action* that has the greatest probability of achieving the end or goal. These principles, or general rules, form the basis of a technological model

for linking theory and research to practice (Brandstadter, 1980). The rationale for these principles are described next and elaborated upon in subsequent chapters in the book.

The first principle states that the greatest impact on child, parent, and family functioning is most likely to occur when interventions are based upon the needs, aspirations, and desires a family considers important. This principle is based upon evidence that establishes a clear relationship between needs (desires, aspirations, personal projects, etc.) and a number of aspects of family functioning, including well-being and adherence to professionally prescribed regimens (see Chapter 8).

The second principle states that persons are more likely to be successful in efforts toward realizing desires, reaching aspirations, and meeting needs if we build upon (strengthen and support) the things the family already does well as a basis for mobilizing resources. This principle is derived from evidence regarding the capabilities that constitute family strengths, and how family functioning style affects the ability to deal with normative and nonnormative life events as well as promotes growth in all family members (see Chapter 10).

The third principle states that informal support networks are a primary source of resources for meeting needs, and to the extent possible, one should build and strengthen natural support systems as a major way of meeting needs. This principle is based upon evidence that shows the most powerful benefits of support are realized if aid and assistance comes primarily from informal sources (see Chapter 12).

The fourth principle states that the family's use and acquisition of competencies for mobilizing resources is most likely to occur when professionals employ help-giving behaviors that create opportunities for family members to display existing competencies and become better able to meet their needs. This principle is derived from evidence which demonstrates that different ways of helping have differential effects on the help-seeker's ability to become more self-sustaining (see Chapters 14 & 17).

LEARNING AND PERFECTING THE CRAFT

As previously noted, our approach to working with families is best described as a *dynamic, fluid process*. The division of the overall assessment and intervention process into separate components is done primarily for heuristic reasons. Needs and aspirations, family strengths and capabilities, and supports and resources are seen as interdependent aspects of family functioning. The extent to which they are optimally integrated depends upon the ways in which the help-giver enables and empowers families (see Figure 1-1). In practice, the four components considerably overlap and the majority of activities within each component are implemented in a parallel and integrated rather than a sequential fashion. Collectively, the operatives within each component define a process that can be used to operationalize the principles in a way that promotes a family's ability to meet needs through mobilization of intrafamily and extrafamily resources.

Learning the *craft* and using it to enable and empower families, requires that help-seeker/help-giver exchanges have certain characteristics if they are to be optimally effective with respect to promoting the abilities of families to meet their needs. These characteristics are briefly described next.

1. The heart of the process for enabling and empowering families is the *relationship* established between the help-seeker and help-giver. Accordingly, the help-giver must develop a relationship with the family in which he or she becomes a trusted confi-

dant. Remember that each and every contact with the family counts toward establishing a help-seeker/help-giver relationship that eventually evolves into a partnership. It is a partnership that creates the medium for effective work with families.

2. Effective *communication* is the name of the game. The principal way to establish partnerships with families is to communicate in a way that individual members and the family unit are treated with dignity, respect and trust. Emphasis should be placed upon active and reflective listening techniques as a way of understanding and supporting families.

3. *Honesty* is the first and foremost requirement of effective communication and partnerships. Each and every interaction with the family must include a clear statement about the purpose of the exchange, what will be asked, and how the information will be used. We have found repeatedly that if one is "straight forward" and "up front" with families in a way that communicates a sincere caring and interest in the well being of all family members, families will in return be open and honest.

4. Effective help-giving requires *understanding* of the families' concerns and interests and not minute details about every aspect of the family's life. By restricting attention to what is important to families (needs, concerns, projects, etc.), information gathering becomes focused rather than inclusive.

5. Emphasis should be placed upon *solutions* rather than the causes of family situations. Effective interactions that are both positive and proactive focus on identifying choices and options for meeting needs rather than placing blame upon or looking for reasons why things are not as they ought to be.

6. Effective help-giving encourages and promotes movement from concerns to needs to *actions* as rapidly as possible. As little time and energy as possible is devoted to problem talking and negative discussions. Rather, one should create interactive exchanges in which listening promotes help-seeker sharing, sharing promotes help-giver understanding, understanding promotes help-seeker and help-giver exploration, and exploration promotes help-seeker action and competence.

7. *Confidentiality* must be maintained and preserved at all times. The help-giver must communicate to the help-seeker that what is shared during interactions will be held in strictest confidence. If the information is to be shared or discussed with others (e.g., team members), this must be made explicitly clear to the family. It must also be made explicitly clear that no information will be shared with others without the family's permission.

A METAPHOR FOR CONCEPTUALIZING THE ASSESSMENT AND INTERVENTION PROCESS

The process of enabling and empowering families can be thought of as a system of interlocking gears (needs and aspirations, family strengths and capabilities, supports and resources) that must be properly aligned if motion and energy are to be passed from one gear to another. Each gear in the system serves a specific function, which when properly adjusted generates energy and power that makes the parts of the whole contribute to optimal efficiency.

The dynamic processes that make up the (family) system can be likened to those on a touring bike when, at any given time, one gear plays a more important role, but it is still the particular alignment among all gears that generates momentum, speed, energy, and power. The latter set of characteristics are primarily influenced by two factors: the terrain (developmental course) that is being traversed (by the family) and the capabilities necessary for the family to drive the system forward in a positive direction.

Conceptualizing the interrelationship among needs and aspirations, strengths and capabilities, and resources and supports as an interlocking set of gears which forms a system that generates energy and power requires a shift in how help-givers work with families. The goal is not for the help-giver to take control of the system and define the family's developmental course. Rather, the goal becomes one of promoting the family's ability to negotiate alignment of the gears comprising the system in a way that makes the system operate as efficiently as possible. The remainder of this book includes numerous descriptions, approaches, and examples of the ways in which we have translated this model into practice.

CHAPTER 2

Meaning and Key Characteristics of Empowerment

Carl J. Dunst, Carol M. Trivette & Nancy LaPointe

THE TERM *empowerment*, and the meaning it embodies, has broadly and collectively been used to describe a wide array of individual- and group-centered participatory endeavors directed at influencing a sense of control over important life events. Empowerment, in its broadest sense, has been used as a framework for devising a particular way of addressing a broad range of social, economic, and political concerns (Swift, 1984). The "idea" of empowerment (Rappaport, 1984) strongly suggests the need for a paradigmatic shift in how human needs and concerns are viewed, how one would address concerns and desires, and how one would operationalize outcome indicators related to successful efforts to empower people.

The call for adoption of empowerment as an ideology, guiding both theory and practice, has been championed by a diverse number of behavioral and social scientists and practitioners in equally diverse fields. The idea of empowerment can now be found in the literatures of *community psychology* (Rappaport, 1981, 1987), *organizational psychology* (Belasco, 1990), *participatory research* (Whitmore & Kerans, 1988), *education* (McGrew & Gilman, 1991), *early childhood intervention* (Dunst, 1985), *family support* (Cochran & Woolever, 1983; Weiss, 1990), *business and management* (Conger & Kanungo, 1988), *help-giving* (Biegel, 1984; Dunst, 1987), *family-centered intervention* (Dunst, Trivette, & Deal, 1988), citizen *participation*

(Wandersman & Florin, 1990), *public policy* (Berger & Neuhaus, 1977), *medical* (Fox, 1989), *social work* (Solomon, 1985), and *speech pathology* (Damico & Armstrong, 1990/91). The idea of empowerment, and its implications for practice, has served as a major force challenging entrenched thinking about the capabilities of people and the roles they can play in shaping their own destinies.

Although empowerment terminology is now part of the everyday lexicon of social and behavioral scientists and practitioners, there is surprisingly very little consensus regarding either the meaning or parameters of the construct. Empowerment has been construed as being *diverse* with respect to its form, level, and context.

Its *form* differs in as many ways as the notion has been described, operationalized, and practiced (e.g., Conger & Kanungo, 1988; Rappaport, Swift, & Hess, 1984; Whitmore & Kerans, 1988; Zimmerman & Rappaport, 1988). As illustrated later, the term empowerment has been used in six different ways, each depicting discernible dimensions of the construct.

Its *level of analysis* differs in terms of the focus of efforts to empower people. The term has been used to describe empowerment of individuals, groups, organizations, and communities (Rappaport, 1984; Whitmore & Kerans, 1988; Zimmerman, 1990a). Its *context* differs by as many real or perceived settings

The material in this chapter is reprinted from the *Family Science Review*, 1992, 5(1/2), 111-130, with permission from the publisher.

and contexts that persons and groups experience in everyday life (Bronfenbrenner, 1979), and by the assertion that empowerment takes on different forms in different contexts (Rappaport, 1981, 1984, 1987).

When one considers the fact that empowerment has been used in at least six different ways at multiple "levels of analysis"across varied contexts and situations, it is easy to understand why Rappaport (1984) contended that "Empowerment (needs to be) viewed...as a process of infinite variety" (p. 3).

The complexity of the issue may be taken even further. Zimmerman (1990b) has challenged empowerment enthusiasts to consider the *interaction* between the forms, levels, and contexts of empowerment, and argues persuasively that the failure to consider their interrelations may impede advances in the ability to understand and operationalize the construct. The above contentions are some of the reasons which make it difficult to be precise about the meaning of empowerment and its manifestations. Nonetheless, the usefulness of the construct, and especially its continued contributions to theory and practice, is dependent in part on having as precise an idea as possible regarding the meaning of empowerment, and a better understanding of its parameters and key elements. The challenge is doing so while maintaining the contributions inherent in the diversity of the construct.

The major purposes of this chapter are to: (a) describe and illustrate the various uses (forms) of the term empowerment and (b) propose a unified framework for capturing the diverse meanings of the construct. We achieve these purposes by taking full advantage of the burgeoning literature on empowerment in diverse fields, and integrating notions and themes central to each. The unified framework that we propose provides at least one way of being more precise about the meaning of

empowerment while, at the same time, preserving the role diversity plays in explicating the utility of the construct. The usefulness of the framework is illustrated with data gathered as part of a study designed to learn more about the meaning of empowerment from the perspective of people involved in a family support and early intervention program, and which employed empowerment notions for guiding program practices (Dunst, 1985; Dunst & Trivette, 1987a; Dunst, Trivette, & Deal, 1988).

DEFINITIONS OF EMPOWERMENT

A good starting point for understanding the diverse meanings of empowerment is to examine the different ways the term has been defined. However, as cautioned by one authority, "Empowerment is a little bit like obscenity; you have trouble defining it but you know it when you see it" (Rappaport, 1985, p. 17). This observation highlights why it is difficult to find a generally agreed upon operational definition of the term.

Thomas and Velthouse (1990) made the observation that "empowerment has no agreed-upon definition.... Rather, the term has been used, often loosely, to capture a family of somewhat related meanings" (p. 666). Table 2-1 provides several definitions found in the contemporary empowerment literature, their sources, and a list of key terms and elements that each source seems to emphasize. (See Dunst, 1986b, for a listing of definitions of empowerment found in earlier literatures.) A content analysis of the definitions, together with other information provided in the cited sources, finds that despite their diversity, the differing definitions have a number of explicit and implicit commonalities. The first is the emphasis on *mastery and control* as the outcome or goal of efforts to empower. The

Table 2-1. Examples of Differing Definitions of Empowerment

Definitions of Empowerment	Source	Key Terms
An interactive process through which people experience personal and social change, enabling them to take action to achieve influence over the organizations and institutions which affect their lives and the communities in which they live.	Whitmore & Kerans (1988)	Interactive process, enable(ment), action, influence.
A process of enhancing feelings of self-efficacy among organizational members through the identification of conditions that foster powerlessness and through their removal by both formal organizational practices and informal techniques of providing efficacy information.	Conger & Kanungo (1988)	Process, self-efficacy, fostering conditions, efficacy information.
Process by which individuals gain mastery or control over their own lives and democratic participation in the life of their community.	Zimmerman & Rappaport (1988)	Process, mastery, control, participation.
An international, ongoing process centered in the local community, involving mutual respect, critical reflection, caring, and group participation, through which people lacking an equal share of valued resources gain greater access to and control over those resources.	Cornell Empowerment Group (1989)	Process, mutual respect, caring, participation, control.

second is the emphasis on the *processes* and experiences that create or produce empowerment. The third is the emphasis on *intrapersonal and interpersonal behavior* that moderates and mediates mastery and control. The fourth is the *interactional relationship* between the processes and outcomes of empowering experiences. And the fifth is the implicit assertion that efforts to empower are *guided by a set of beliefs* that uniquely define the construct as an ideology.

Our reading of the empowerment literature has led us to conclude that there are identifiable key elements and common parameters central to the construct, but that there have generally been inadequate attempts to differentiate between and organize the different empowerment notions. These observations led us to a review, integration, and interpretation of the empowerment literature in a way that was designed to contribute to our increased understanding of the construct.

DIVERSE USES OF THE TERM EMPOWERMENT

Besides Rappaport's (1981, 1984, 1985, 1987; Zimmerman & Rappaport, 1988) evolving characterization of empowerment and its implications for theory and practice, there have been surprisingly few attempts to bring clarity to the diverse uses of the construct. The one exception is a recent study by Cornish and Conway (1991). They utilized a clustering model for organizing the different ways in which the construct has been used, including a listing of the essential features and components that define each cluster.

Our review and synthesis of the empowerment literature found that the term has been used in at least six diverse but interrelated ways. As both a phenomenological and behavioral construct, one finds descriptions and discussions of empowerment as *philosophy, paradigm, process, partnership, performance,* and *perception*. In order to bring clarity to the meaning of empowerment, we begin with a brief description of the key elements for each dimension together with examples of how these elements have been used by theorists, researchers, and practitioners. The relationship between the different forms of empowerment, and the integration of the six dimensions into a unified framework, are described after the parameters are defined and illustrated.

EMPOWERMENT AS PHILOSOPHY

Descriptions of *empowerment as philosophy* can be found in the writings of Clark (1989), Rappaport (1981), and Dunst and his colleagues (1985, 1987; Dunst & Trivette, 1987a; Dunst, Trivette, & Deal, 1988). These different discussions attempt to delineate the *principles* and beliefs that uniquely define a philosophy of empowerment. For example, the principles described by Clark (1989) address specific assumptions that he argues need to be embraced by health care (as well as other) practitioners as part of redesigning health care programs and practices. Similarly, the Cornell Empowerment Group (1989) has developed a viewpoint of empowerment based on a set of 10 assumptions, including the postulates that all people have strengths, diversity should be positively valued, and society must be organized to provide people choices and the power to exercise choices.

Rappaport (1981) argues that empowerment is an *ideology* that demands adoption of certain assumptions about the capabilities of people, the locus of adaptive and maladaptive behavior, and the strategies best adopted for enhancing and promoting competence. Dunst and his colleagues (Dunst & Trivette, 1987a; Dunst, Trivette, & Deal, 1988) used Rappaport's ideological perspective to delineate three *guiding principles* of an empowering philosophy. These are:

1. All people have existing strengths and capabilities as well as the capacity to become more competent,

2. The failure of a person to display competence is *not* due to deficits within a person but rather the failure of social systems to provide or create opportunities for competencies to be displayed or acquired, and

3. In situations where existing capabilities need to be strengthened or new competencies need to be learned, they are best learned through experiences that lead people to make self-attributions about their capabilities to influence important life events.

The translation of this philosophy into practice has been accomplished in a number of ways. For example, Dunst, Trivette, and Deal (1988) describe a system of family-centered intervention practices that use these philosophical principles as premises for identifying family concerns and desires, strengthening family capabilities, building supportive resource networks to meet family needs, and adopting help-giving roles that promote and enhance family help-giving. In a specific field-test of the implications of this philosophical stance, Dunst et al. (1989) demonstrated that in cases where the above principles guided nearly *all* aspects of program practices, unempowered families from very poor backgrounds with limited resources gained the ability to mobilize social support networks to meet their needs.

EMPOWERMENT AS PARADIGM

Empowerment as paradigm has been discussed extensively by Rappaport (1981, 1984, 1987). Paradigms are models that have formal *properties and characteristics*, and therefore permit one to operationally define and differentiate between sets of properties that are uniquely associated with different world views (Reese & Overton, 1980).

Empowerment as paradigm has been contrasted with the assumptions and properties of both paternalism (Swift, 1984) and prevention (Rappaport, 1981, 1987). More recently, Dunst, Trivette, and Thompson (1990; Chapter 4) described the basic differences between treatment, prevention, and promotion models, and how empowerment defined as a philosophy, process, and outcome is theoretically and procedurally congruent primarily with promotion models.

The framework proposed by Dunst, Trivette, and Thompson (1990) specifically describes and delineates the unique properties and characteristics of three different "intervention" models. In this description of the three models, promotion and empowerment models are viewed as fully compatible since their presuppositions are logically consistent (Reese & Overton, 1980). According to these investigators, promotion models are best characterized as having a *mastery and optimization* orientation, in contrast to treatment and prevention models that are problem-oriented and aim to correct or deter negative outcomes. Additionally, promotion models place major emphasis on the development, enhancement, and elaboration of people's *competencies and capabilities* (Bond, 1982), particularly those that increase a *sense of control* over important aspects of life (Rappaport, 1981). Such an approach is also considered *proactive* because it gives primacy to anticipatory actions that support and strengthen individual and group functioning (Cowen, 1985). Promotion efforts are *strengths-based* as well, and assume all people have existing capabilities and the *capacity to become more competent* (Rappaport, 1981). Accordingly, by building on strengths rather than rectifying weaknesses, people become more adaptive in not only dealing with diffi-

cult life events, but in achieving growth-oriented goals and personal aspirations. A comparison of these properties with the characteristics of the definitions of empowerment delineated above finds that they are fundamentally identical.

Empowerment as paradigm gives specificity to the defining characteristics of the construct as well as provides a lens through which to view the properties in a circumscribed manner. Additionally, the paradigmatic features provide a basis for contrasting empowerment models with other, incompatible models or world views of behavior and development, so as to be able to appreciate procedurally and practically the unique aspects of a paradigm of empowerment.

EMPOWERMENT AS PROCESS

A number of theorists and practitioners argue that primacy be given to *empowerment as process* (Cornell Empowerment Group, 1989; Whitmore, 1991). Whitmore (1991) has gone so far as to say that process is the most important aspect of defining and operationalizing empowerment with respect to the application of the construct.

In its most general sense, process refers to the *means to an end*. Means, however, is often quite difficult to specify because "processes that facilitate empowerment are fluid and difficult to articulate" (Whitmore, 1991, p. 4). Rappaport (1984) stated this in the following way: "The content of the process is of infinite variety and as the process plays itself out among different people and settings the end products will be variable and even inconsistent with one another. The inconsistency is in the ends rather than in the process; yet the *form of the process will also vary*" (p. 3, emphasis added). While acknowledging these claims, it is nonetheless possible to be a bit more precise about the implicit meaning of process.

More specifically, empowerment as process refers to the full range of experiences, encounters, occurrences, and events that *afford* people opportunities to use existing capabilities as well as learn new competencies (see especially Rappaport, Swift, & Hess, 1984). Dunst and his colleagues (Dunst & Trivette, 1987a; Dunst, Trivette, & Deal, 1988) label process experiences *enabling opportunities*, whereas Conger and Kanungo (1988) label such experiences *enabling conditions*. Mecklem (1989) argued that process is in fact more correctly thought of as *enablement*, and that there are many types of enabling experiences than can be employed for supporting and strengthening functioning.

The work of Dunst and his colleagues has included the identification and application of enabling experiences for promoting and enhancing the capabilities of people. The benefits of these efforts have been demonstrated in a number of different ways (see e.g., Dunst, 1991; Dunst, Trivette, Davis, & Weeldreyer, 1988; Dunst, Trivette, Gordon, & Pletcher, 1989; Dunst & Vance, 1989). For example, in a project specifically designed to strengthen the parenting capabilities of teenage mothers, these investigators employed opportunities to interact with care givers known to use effective nurturing behaviors as an enabling experience (Dunst & Vance, 1989). The participants were found to increase their use of different styles of nurturing behaviors as a function of their ongoing exposure to these learning opportunities.

The use of the term *enable* to describe empowerment as process has intuitive appeal. The notion of enabling opportunities is consistent with the belief that varied experiences can be empowering, and clearly distinguishes learning opportunities from their consequences, a distinction that is often made in terms of describing empowering *process* and

outcome variables (Whitmore, 1991), but which is rarely adequately attended to either in theory or practice (see Zimmerman, 1990a; Zimmerman & Rappaport, 1988, for exceptions).

EMPOWERMENT AS PARTNERSHIP

Empowerment as partnership refers to the characteristics of *interpersonal transactions* that influence and are influenced by enabling experiences and the effects of these experiences. The use of empowerment as an interpersonal construct has been described in a number of ways, including *relational power sharing* (see Conger & Kanungo, 1988) and *proactive helping style* (Dunst, 1987). Most theorists and practitioners have described these transactional relationships as participation and participatory involvement, although these terms fail to capture the richness of different person–person, person–group, and group–group encounters. Partnerships seems to be a better term for capturing the key characteristics of such encounters.

The use of empowerment as partnership is underscored by a number of important interpersonal characteristics, including reciprocity, open communication, mutual trust and respect, shared responsibility, and cooperation. Collectively, these characteristics define the key elements of collaboration and partnerships (Dunst & Paget, 1991; Dunst, Johanson, Rounds, Trivette, & Hamby, 1992, Chapter 16). Additionally, recent work by Dunst and his colleagues (Dunst & Paget, 1991; Dunst, Johanson, Rounds, Trivette, & Hamby, 1992) on the relationship between effective helping styles and partnerships finds that there is considerable overlap in the characteristics that define each interpersonal relationship. Furthermore, this research has shown that the transactional behaviors that are associated with effective helping and partnerships are highly related to a sense of control over life events, whereas the opposite is true with respect to the effects of paternalistic styles of helping (Dunst, Trivette, Davis, & Weeldreyer, 1988).

The importance of partnership relationships and transactions as part of participatory activities was noted by Rappaport (1984) who stated: "Empowerment may be the result of programs designed by professionals, but more likely will be found in those circumstances where there is either *true collaboration* among professionals and the supposed beneficiaries, or in settings and under conditions where professionals are not the key actors" (p. 4, emphasis added). With respect to parent–professional partnerships, for example, Dunst and Paget (1991) noted that the balance of power in such relationships ought to belong to the "senior" partner– namely the parents, since they rightfully possess decision-making power concerning their child's behavior and development.

EMPOWERMENT AS PERFORMANCE

Descriptions of *empowerment as performance* focus specifically on the knowledge and skills that are strengthened or learned as a result of enabling opportunities and interpersonal transactions. Performance refers to an array of behavioral capabilities that are observable and contribute to an emerging sense of control (Bandura, 1986). Personal capabilities, behavioral traits, competence, critical thinking, flexibility, cohesion, and collective action are the varied terms used most frequently to describe empowerment as performance (Thomas & Velthouse, 1990; Whitmore & Kerans, 1988). The fact that there has been very little specificity regarding the behaviors that constitute empowerment as performance is not surprising. According to Rappaport (1984), the manifestations of empowerment are likely to be

different among different people in different contexts, even varying in the same person over time (Zimmerman, 1990a).

A number of investigators who have studied empowerment as performance provide hints about the multitude of behavioral competencies that are legitimate behavioral indicators of empowerment (Rappaport et al., 1984). Dunst, Trivette, Gordon, and Pletcher (1989), as part of an evaluation of a project designed to help people build supportive resource networks, operationally defined empowerment as the ability to initiate resource exchanges *independently* with other social support network members (without the assistance of a professional) in order to procure desired resources. The findings from this study showed that there were significant increases in the ability to engage in independent exchanges as a function of repeated enabling experiences.

EMPOWERMENT AS PERCEPTIONS

Empowerment as perceptions has been used extensively to describe a wide array of *attributions and beliefs* that reflect a *sense of control* or influence people have with respect to varying aspects of their behavior. The study of empowerment as perceptions has included a variety of phenomenological beliefs as outcomes, including constructs such as personal control, locus-of-control, efficacy expectations, self-efficacy, self-esteem, personal power, intrinsic motivation, political efficacy, political control, and cultural awareness. Collectively, these terms describe the types of attributions people make in response to efforts to produce desired effects and outcomes (Lord & Farlow, 1990; Zimmerman, 1990b; Zimmerman & Rappaport, 1988), where "the confluence of these (various) areas of perceived control is hypothesized to represent *psychological empowerment*" (Zimmerman & Rappaport, 1988, p. 727, emphasis added). Research has shown that these various attributions both influence and are influenced by empowering processes, interpersonal transactions, and behavioral capabilities (Bandura, 1977, 1978, 1986).

A focus on empowerment as perceptions reflecting an increased sense of control has been tested in a number of studies conducted by Dunst (1991) and Dunst and Vance (1989) on empowerment. For example, in one study designed to promote the flow of child care resources to families, Dunst (1991) found that enabling experiences that encouraged active participation of parents in all aspects of the resource building process produced greater changes in self-efficacy compared to interventions that emphasized professional-resource mobilization.

Table 2-2 summarizes the major dimensions and key elements of the various uses of the term empowerment. This way of organizing and structuring the diverse forms of empowerment captures the essence of the construct, at least, as it has been used by theorists

and practitioners in the contemporary literature on the topic. The framework presented in Table 2-2 provides a particular vantage point for understanding what social scientists and practitioners *mean* when they use the term empowerment. Except for Rappaport (1981, 1987), and more recently Cornish and Conway (1991), we are not aware of any other discussions on empowerment that have taken into consideration all six dimensions simultaneously.

A UNIFIED FRAMEWORK

Our multidimensional framework may be taken one step further by postulating the conceptual relationships that apparently exist between the six components. Figure 2-1 shows a model for proposing how we would initially hypothesize the major relationships between the six dimensions of empowerment based upon our reading and synthesis of the published literature. According to this model,

Table 2-2. Major Dimensions, Key Elements, and Exemplars of Empowerment		
Dimensions	Key Elements	Exemplars
Philosophy	Principles	Presumed Capabilities of People, Valuing Diversity
Paradigm	Properties	Strengths-Based, Proactive, Mastery Orientation
Process	Enabling Experiences	Learning Opportunities and Events
Partnership	Collaboration	Mutual Respect, Shared Decision-Making, Cooperation
Performance	Behavioral Capabilities	Knowledge, Skills, Personal Growth, Affiliate Behavior
Perceptions	Attributions	Self-Efficacy, Personal Control, Self-Esteem, Locus-of-Control, Political Efficacy

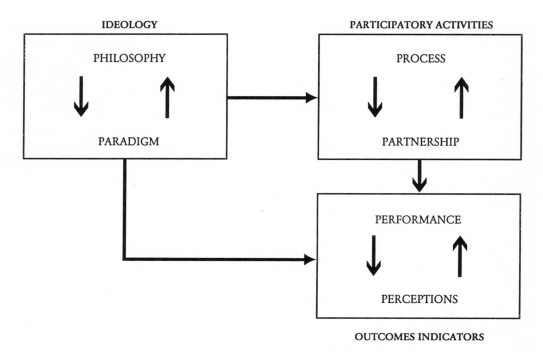

Fig. 2-1. A Model for Depicting the Major Relationships Between the Key Elements of Empowerment.

philosophy and paradigm are considered highly related and major contributors to an empowerment ideology. Taken together, both are hypothesized to have both direct and indirect influences on each of the other dimensions. Process and partnerships are considered two separate but related dimensions of participatory activities, and both are seen as determinants of performance and perceptions. Performance and perceptions are seen as highly related, and taken together are seen as outcome indicators of efforts to empower.

Although the relationships between the different dimensions are depicted as being related primarily in a unidirectional manner, the direction of influences would be expected, to a certain degree, to be bidirectional. For example, increases in self-efficacy resulting from participatory experiences would be expected to result in efforts to increase association with people who have provided opportunities for such perceptions to be shaped and strengthened.

We recognize that we risk criticism for suggesting how the dimensions may be related, given the complexity and diversity of the empowerment construct. We offer this model in the spirit of discussion, and hope that it will stimulate further advances in understanding how the dimensions might be related, how the relationships might be empirically investigated, and what implications the proposed linkages have for translating the construct into practice. Findings from our own research, described below, illustrate that the relationships depicted by the model, to a large degree, are supported by empirical evidence, thus providing credence to how we have initially "linked" the six dimensions.

The way in which we have organized and structured the various uses of empowerment may be taken one step further by incorporating two other components into the model: *unit* and *context* of empowerment. As previously described, unit refers to the focus of who is empowered, and context refers to the situational aspects and characteristics of empowerment.

LEVELS OF ANALYSIS

It is generally acknowledged that empowerment differs at a number of levels of analysis (Rappaport, 1984; Whitmore & Kerans, 1988; Zimmerman, 1990b). Its application has been described primarily in terms of four levels: individuals, groups, organizations, and communities. At the individual level, empowerment focuses on promoting participatory behavior, skill acquisition, and differing forms of self-efficacy attributions (self-esteem, efficacy attributions, etc.) leading to an increased sense of personal control. At the group level, empowerment enhances cohesiveness, collective problem-solving skills, affiliate behavior, and joint feelings of efficacy and control. "Organizational empowerment includes shared leadership, and opportunities to develop skills, expansion, and effective community leadership. Empowered communities comprise empowered organizations, including opportunities for citizen participation in community decision making" (Zimmerman, 1990b, pp. 169-170).

The multiple levels of analyses at which empowerment may be studied and practiced expands the meaning of the construct when considered in light of what has already been said about the dimensions (uses) that empowerment notions embody. Further elaborations on the framework are possible, and necessary, when one recognizes the fact that empowerment also differs as a function of context (see especially Rappaport, 1981, 1984, 1987).

CONTEXT

Despite the diversity of the construct, there is general agreement among social scientists that empowerment differs as a function of context, and takes on different forms at different levels of analysis (see Rappaport et al., 1984). Context, however, has generally been defined rather loosely and in an atheoretical manner. The types of advances Zimmerman (1990b) has called for with respect to understanding the contextual bases of empowerment are not likely to be realized unless more attention is given to a precise definition of context. Moreover investigations must focus on the theoretical and empirical relationships that exist between different contexts.

A helpful way of defining *context* is to use Bronfenbrenner's (1979) notion of four embedded and interrelated ecosystems for specifying person–environment transactions. Ecosystems are collections or communities of interrelated settings that, taken together, define differing types of settings. The four ecosystems that make up Bronfenbrenner's framework include the microsystem, mesosystem, exosystem, and macrosystem.

Microsystems are the contexts and immediate settings in which individuals have day-to-day experiences and learning opportunities that affect behavior and development. These settings include, but are not limited to, places where people live and work, the people who are present in these settings, and the things that are done by individuals separately or together with other people in these settings. Person- environment and person–person interactions are considered the most important aspects of microsystems, and it is the nature of these interactions, both real and perceived, that contribute to a person's evolving conception of the world and his or her role in influencing experiences and events, including a sense of control (balance-of-power in Bronfenbrenner's terms).

Mesosystems are defined as the interrelationships between two or more settings that people *directly* experience and in which they are active participants (e.g., home & work). The experiences within settings, and the relationships between settings, are seen as conditions that can either promote or impede development depending upon the nature of the experiences. In principle, for example, environments and settings in which people are active participants and which provide a variety of enabling experiences would be expected to contribute to an enhanced sense of control (see Bronfenbrenner, 1986).

Exosystems are contexts and settings that a person is never "an active participant but in which events occur that affect, or are affected by, what happens in that setting" (Bronfenbrenner, 1979, p. 237). The linkages that exists between exosystems and what people experience in both micro- and mesosystems, although indirect, nonetheless can have powerful influences on people's behavior; as demonstrated by the Clarence Thomas confirmation hearings concerning his appointment to the Supreme Court.

Macrosystems refer to the relationship and general organization among settings that directly and indirectly link micro-, meso-, and exosystems, and the degree to which *consistencies* in beliefs and ideologies across settings have cumulative and interactive effects on people's behavior. For example, if the different settings people experience directly and indirectly are consistent with an empowerment ideology, one would hypothesize that the sense of control people acquire and feel ought to be maximized.

Bronfenbrenner's (1979) "blueprint" for defining and studying setting effects would seem especially valuable for advancing our knowledge with respect to the contextual bases of empowerment. This or a similar framework would serve researchers well in terms of defin-

ing settings, and studying how contextual variables influence and are influenced by a person's emerging sense of control over events in various environments.

Figure 2-2 shows a unified framework for depicting the dimensions, contexts, and units of empowerment. The framework yields a 96 cell matrix depicting every combination of the three major features of empowerment. On the one hand, the framework provides a basis for being more precise about what one is referring to when talking about empowerment; for example, by describing, studying, and practicing empowerment with respect to process within mesosystems at the group level of analysis. On the other hand, the framework provides a particular way of structuring efforts to conduct research on empowerment where "pieces of the empowerment puzzle" are systematically investigated. A modest attempt to accomplish the latter is described next to illustrate the usefulness of the unified framework.

UTILITY OF THE UNIFIED FRAMEWORK

The utility of both the material we have presented and the framework we have proposed is illustrated in the final section of this chapter from recent research aimed at understanding the meaning of and multidimensional aspects of empowerment. More specifically, we were interested in the relationships between help-giving styles of professionals as mediators of the sense of empowerment experienced by people being provided help as part of their involvement in a social action program.

PARTICIPANTS

The participants were 74 mothers of young

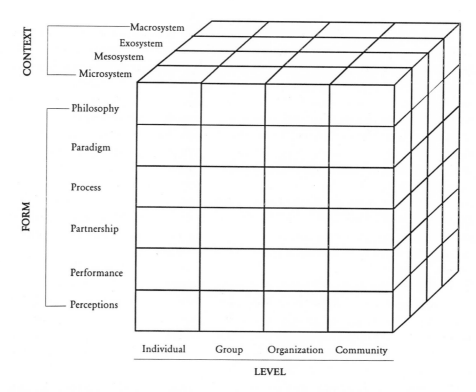

Fig. 2-2. A Unified Framework for Depicting the Dimensions, Context, and Units of Empowerment.

children involved in an early intervention and family support program guided by an empowerment philosophy (Dunst, 1985; Dunst, Trivette, & Deal, 1988). The mothers had a mean age of 32.53 years (SD = 7.36) and had completed an average of 12.22 years of school (SD = 2.24). The majority of the mothers (76%) were married, and just over half (58%) worked outside the home either full- or part-time. The mean gross monthly family income of the participants was $1488 (SD = 691). Nearly three-quarters (73%) of the sample were from the three lowest socioeconomic stratum using the Hollingshead (1975) system for determining social class.

PROCEDURE

The subjects completed two self-report scales: the Professional Helpers Characteristics Scale (HCS; Trivette & Dunst, 1990) and the Parent Empowerment Survey (PES; LaPointe, Trivette, & Dunst, 1990). Both instruments were developed specifically as part of a line of research examining the meaning, determinants, and outcome indicators of empowerment. The HCS asks a respondent to indicate the extent to which a particular professional help-giver displays a range of help-giving beliefs, attitudes and behaviors (see Dunst, Trivette, Davis, & Weeldreyer, 1988) in interactions with the respondent, whereas the PES asks a respondent to indicate the extent to which he or she feels a sense of control over different life events. Both instruments are self-report measures, and all items are rated on 5-point scales that tap different degrees-of-empowerment as experienced by the respondents.

The HCS includes 28 items, half of which measure four dimensions of empowerment (philosophy, paradigm, process and partnership) as defined above. Coefficient alpha for the full scale is .93, and for the items measuring the four empowerment dimensions, alpha is .86. The PES includes 32 items, 21 of which measure two or more aspects of performance and perceptions as defined above and which were expected to be related to help-giving styles as measured by the HCS. Coefficient alpha for the full scale is .93, and for the 21 items measuring performance and perceptions, alpha is .92.

DATA ANALYSES

The data were analyzed in several ways specifically for the purpose of illustrating the usefulness of the unified framework presented in this chapter. First, the items were rank-ordered with respect to the percentage of the sample that strongly agreed that an item reflected a sense of empowerment. Second, we computed scores (sum of the ratings of the items) measuring each of the six empowerment dimensions, and calculated the correlations between the scores to ascertain the degree to which the different dimensions were related as hypothesized (see Figure 2-1). Third, we organized the data according to different social and physical contexts to establish whether the "strength" of a sense of control was similar or different across settings.

RESULTS

Rank-ordering results. Table 2-3 shows the rank ordering of the 20 items that the respondents most frequently indicated reflected a strong sense of control. Several noteworthy findings are evident from inspection of the results. First, each of the major empowerment dimensions were represented among these items. That is, the pattern of responses showed that the

sample indicated all the dimensions of empowerment contributed to a heightened sense of control. Second, the distribution of the items shows that each dimension assumes a relatively equal degree of importance. That is, all the dimensions of empowerment (except for the paradigm items) were rated by the sample as reflecting a sense of control. Collectively, the rank-order data shows that empowerment, as assessed by the respondents, was viewed as a multidimensional construct with each dimension contributing proportionally to the meaning of empowerment and a sense of control.

Correlational results. Table 2-4 shows the correlations between the measures of the six empowerment dimensions. With the exception the paradigm dimension, the relationships between all the indices were significant beyond the .05 level. These results are consistent with our expectations, thus indicating that these particular key elements of empowerment covaried in a highly predictable manner.

According to the model described earlier (see Figure 2-1), substantial covariation would be expected between the pairwise dimensions measuring ideology (philosophy and paradigm), participation (process and partnership) and the outcome indicators (performance and perception). The correlations between these pairwise measures are underlined in Table 2-4, and as can be seen, there was substantial covariation between the corresponding indicators of the "superordinate" dimensions.

Based upon the model postulated earlier, one would also expect substantial covariation between the measures contributing to the superordinate dimensions. Multiple (canonical) correlations were computed to ascertain whether such covariation existed. The multiple correlations between the ideology measures and both the participation ($R = .71$, $p < .001$) and outcome indicator ($R = .46$, $p < .005$) measures were significant as expected.

Table 2-3. Rank Ordering the Items Rated as Strong Indicators of Empowerment

Rank	Abbreviated Description of the Scale Items	% of Sample	Empowerment Dimensions					
			Philosophy	Paradigm	Process	Partnership	Performance	Perception
1.5	Professionals view parents in a positive light	81	●					
1.5	Professionals do not treat parents as the cause of the problem	81		●				
3.0	Knowing that one can find somebody to care for a family member	76					●	
4.0	Feeling good about oneself because of important accomplishments	74						●
5.0	Positive feelings associated with "doing a good job"	73						●
6.0	Finding exactly the type of child care parent wants	72					●	
7.5	Professionals view parents as capable of learning new skills	71	●					
7.5	Professionals helping parents find solutions to their problems	71				●		
9.0	Parent's ability to influence the quality of child care	70					●	
10.0	Knowing about health services in the community	70					●	
11.5	Professionals encouraging parents to make their own decisions	68			●			
11.5	Professionals working together with parents	68				●		
14.0	Professionals share all relevant information with parents	67			●			
14.0	Professional's beliefs about family capabilities	67	●					
14.0	Professionals helping parents learn new skills	67			●			
16.5	Past efforts at successfully dealing with family problems	65						●
16.5	Believing in one's abilities to make good things happen in life	65						●
18.0	Professionals focusing on parent strengths	63		●				
19.0	Good feelings associated with past parenting efforts	61						●
20.0	Professional's emphasis on helping parents learn new skills	60				●		

Table 2-4. Correlations Between the Measures of the Six Empowerment Dimensions

Scales/Empowerment Dimensions	Number of Items	PH	PA	PR	PT	PM	PC
Help-Giving Scale:							
Philosophy (PH)	3	–	.61****	.61****	.66****	.40****	.42****
Paradigm (PA)	3		–	.54****	.49****	.16*	.15*
Process (PR)	4			–	.68****	.19**	.27***
Partnership (PT)	3				–	.29***	.29***
Parent Empowerment Scale:							
Performance (PM)	9					–	.79****
Perception (PC)	12						–

*p<.08; **p<.05; ***p<.01; ****p<.005.

Similarly, the multiple correlation between the participation and outcome indicator measures was significant as well (R = .31, p < .05). These findings, together with the results presented above, demonstrate that the different dimensions of empowerment as described in this chapter and as measured in our study, are interrelated both conceptually and empirically.

Setting results. The extent to which a sense of empowerment differed as a function of inter- and extra-personal settings was assessed by examining the sample's responses to the items on the HCS and PES scales from a different vantage point. On an a priori basis, the items on the two instruments were organized into 10 groups, each measuring a sense of control with respect to different social and physical settings. The groupings to the greatest extent possible were based on ecological settings and contexts as typically conceptualized by social systems theorists (Bronfenbrenner, 1979; Garbarino, 1982).

A two-step data analysis scheme was used to ascertain similarities and differences in the sense of control reported by the respondents in the different settings. Analysis-by-inspection was first used to determine discernible patterns in the data. The findings are presented in Figure 2-3. Visual inspection of the results showed that the findings clustered into four contextual groups: microsystem environments, interpersonal structures, personal social networks, and community resources.

Second, a within group ANOVA was used to assess whether the analysis-by-inspection was substantiated empirically. The average score for the items included in each group was used as an estimate of the "degree of control" in each grouping. A 4 Within Context ANOVA was significant, F(9, 621) = 19.94, p < .001, indicating that reported sense of control did vary as a function of these particular social and physical settings. Pairwise post-hoc comparisons between the mean scores for the four contexts all were significant beyond the .01

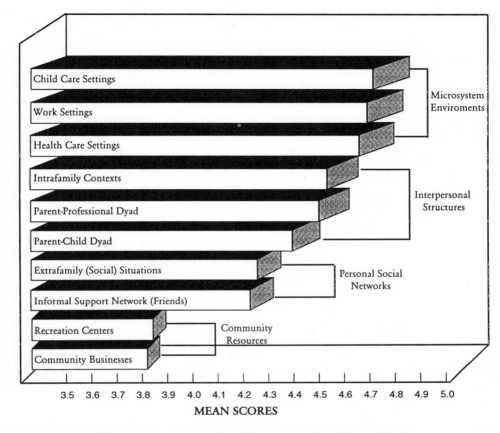

Fig. 2-3. Mean "Degree of Control" Scores Found in Different Social and Physical Settings.

level, demonstrating that setting was in fact an important determinant for understanding the sense of control people feel when reflecting upon the meaning of empowerment.

SUMMARY AND CONCLUSION

The purpose of this chapter was to review and synthesize what is known from the empowerment literature as well as propose a framework for specifying the key elements of empowerment. We found, based upon our review, that empowerment has been described as philosophy, paradigm, process, partnership, performance, and perception. A concep-

tual model depicting the relationships among the six components was proposed and subsequently validated. The description of empowerment was taken several steps further by incorporating two other components into our proposed model: unit and context of empowerment. Findings from our own research provided preliminary evidence supporting the way in which we conceptualized empowerment as a behavioral construct.

The framework described in this chapter has special utility for defining and structuring program practices that aim to support and strengthen family functioning. On the one hand, the framework provides guidance about those conditions that are best suited for pro-

moting adoption of an empowerment philosophy, and on the other hand, a test of the
framework yielded evidence to indicate that
helping behaviors consistent with an empowerment philosophy contribute to families'
assessment of control over different kinds of
supports and resources. As noted by Rappaport
(1981), the ability to empower and strengthen
people in ways that make them more capable
"requires a breakdown of the typical role

relationships between professionals and community people" (p. 19). The framework described in this chapter provides at least one
way of thinking about what kinds of changes
seem necessary if program and help-giving
practices maximize competency enhancing
effects. The four chapters in Section V (Effective Help-giving Practices) describe many of
the specifics of empowering help-giving practices.

II

FAMILY SUPPORT PROGRAMS

The likelihood of family-centered models and practices being successful, to a large degree, is influenced by the <u>context</u> in which the model and practices are implemented. The two chapters in this section include information strongly suggesting that this context ought to be <u>family support programs.</u> As described in Chapter 3, the aims and principles of family support programs contrast sharply with those of more traditional human services programs. The argument is made in Chapter 4 that supporting and strengthening family functioning within the context of family support programs is best achieved using promotion, rather than either treatment or prevention models, for guiding program development and structuring intervention practices.

In addition to delineating the aims and principles of family support programs, this section includes a description of a model integrating the key elements of the family-centered assessment and intervention practices described in Chapter 1 and the empowerment framework presented in Chapter 2. A number of challenges facing program builders and practitioners who desire to become more family-centered within the context of family support programs are also listed. Taken together, the contents of this section place family-centered practices within a broader-based program context that must be considered if models and practices are to have empowering consequences and family strengthening influences.

CHAPTER 3

Aims and Principles of Family Support Programs

Carl J. Dunst & Carol M. Trivette

T HE CURRENT INTEREST in family support programs as social interventions aimed at supporting and strengthening family functioning has a short but rich history (Kagan, Powell, Weissbourd, & Zigler, 1987). Both political and contemporaneous social changes have been a major impetus for the development of a number of different kinds of family support initiatives. Both grass roots and government sponsored family support activities have been initiated in the United States (Moroney, 1986; Weissbourd, 1987a; Weissbourd & Kagan, 1989), Australia (Edgar, 1988, 1989; O'Brien, 1988; Wolcott, 1989), Canada (Anglin & Glossop, 1987) and Europe (De'Ath, 1988, 1989). The purposes of this chapter are to: (1) describe the aims and principles of family support programs to illustrate how such programs differ from more traditional human services programs and (2) to describe the implications of these principles for practice. The challenges that policy makers, program builders, and practitioners face as part of developing family-centered human services practices are also presented.

AIMS OF FAMILY SUPPORT PROGRAMS

Although there is no single accepted definition delineating the aims and goals of family support programs, several descriptions can be found which share common elements. According to Kagan and Shelley (1987),

> Family support efforts are directed at reforming existing policies and practices so that major institutions will improve family functioning by their support...(and)...empower (people) to act for their own good and the good of their immediate community. (p. 8)

Similarly, Zigler and Berman (1983) stated that the aim of family support programs is "not to provide families with direct services, but to enhance parent empowerment—to enable families to help themselves and their children" (p. 901). Dunst (1990b) defined family support programs as "efforts designed to promote the flow of resources and supports to families in ways that strengthen the functioning and enhance the growth and development of individual family members and the family unit" (p. 1). He also noted that family support programs conduct interventions in ways that have empowering consequences, and thus make families and their members more capable and competent. Another definition offered by Weissbourd and Kagan (1989) states that "Family support programs provide services to families that empower and strengthen adults in their roles as parents, nurturers, and providers" (p. 21).

This chapter is an extended version of a paper presented at the Sixth Annual Conference of the Australian Early Intervention Association, Melbourne, Australia, September 1990.

Each of these definitions as well as others found in the family support program literature (see Dunst, Trivette, & Thompson, 1990; Kagan, et al., 1987; Powell, 1988; Weiss & Jacobs, 1988a) share a common theme; namely, that family support programs place primary emphasis on the *strengthening* of individual and family functioning. This emphasis is reflected in the careful selection of terms like improve, enhance, promote, nurture, enable, and empower to describe the *goals* of intervention efforts. Stated differently,

the aims of family support programs are to enable and empower people by enhancing and promoting individual and family capabilities that support and strengthen family functioning.

KEY TERMS AND CHARACTERISTICS

This definition includes a number of key terms that deserve both comment and elaboration. The term *enable* is used in a specific sense to refer to opportunities that are afforded individual family members and the family unit in order that they may use existing competencies, as well as learn new competencies necessary to mobilize resources to meet needs or achieve aspirations. The term *empower* refers to both the behaviors and the beliefs that reflect a family's sense of master and control over important aspects of its life. The term *enhance* and *promote* are used very specifically to mean the facilitation of prosocial and positive aspects of behavior that strengthen a sense of mastery and empowerment. The term *family capabilities* refers to the knowledge, skills, and competencies that families use to mobilize resources to meet needs, achieve aspirations, and fulfill family functions. And finally, the terms *supporting* and *strengthening* family functioning refer to outcomes of human services practices resulting from efforts

to enable and empower individual family members and the family unit. A major feature of accomplishing the aims of family support programs is the utilization of a broad range of community people and supports as resources for meeting needs and empowering families. The community context of family support is briefly described next.

FAMILY SUPPORT PROGRAMS AND A SENSE OF COMMUNITY

A common feature of most family support programs is the emphasis given to the importance of *community support*. Family support programs recognize the fact that families are embedded within a broader-based community, and that it is this community which is a major source of support and resource for meeting needs. In their description of the meaning of community, Hobbs and his colleagues (1984) stated that

a community is an immediate social group that promotes human development.... In communities, individuals experience a sense of membership, influence members of the group and are themselves in turn influenced by others, have personal needs fulfilled, and share a psychologically and personally satisfying connection with other people.... Community basically involves the coming together of people around shared values and the pursuit of common cause. (p. 41)

A sense of community, in turn, promotes the exchange of resources and supports that constitute the range of aid and assistance necessary for enhancing and maintaining individual, family, and community well-being. Bronfenbrenner (1979), for example, noted that

(W)hether parents can perform effectively in their child-rearing roles within the family depends upon the role demands, stresses, and supports emanating from (community) settings.... The availability of supportive settings is, in turn, a function of their existence and frequency in a given culture or subculture. (p. 7)

Promoting and enhancing the present and future well-being, growth, and development of individual family members and the family unit are the major goals of family support programs as well as supportive communities. However, not all social action programs and human services interventions achieve this aim. One needs only look to the social welfare systems in our country to see that provision of resources in and of itself is not necessarily supportive and competency-enhancing (see especially Albert, 1988; Moroney, 1986). A number of family support movements, however, break with dependency-forming practices.

CONTEMPORARY FAMILY SUPPORT MOVEMENTS

There are now a number of major family support efforts that collectively aim to support and strengthen families, albeit from different perspectives using different approaches, but having very similar assumptions.

The first and most influential movement can be traced to the self-help and grassroots efforts that emerged in the late 1960s and early 1970s (Weissbourd, 1987a). This approach is best reflected by the efforts of the Family Resource Coalition, an organization of nearly 3,000 family support programs dedicated to the development of community-based programs for supporting and strengthening fam-

ily functioning (Weissbourd & Kagan, 1989; Zigler & Black, 1989). The Family Resource Coalition and the types of diverse programs it represents are bonded together by the following set of assumptions:

1. All families need support, regardless of economic status or specific concerns. Most parents want to be good parents no matter what their resources are. The varying kinds of support provided by family resource programs are determined by the needs of the parents and are responsive to the culture and social characteristics of the communities in which the families live.

2. The availability of social networks, mutual aid and peer groups, is essential to the family's ability to enhance a child's development.

3. Information on child development, obtained both formally and informally, assists families in their child rearing roles.

4. Support programs increase the family's ability to cope rather than provide a system on which families become dependent. Support builds on the strengths that the whole family and individual family members already have. The confidence that parents acquire through family support enables them to manage their own lives and participate in shaping the environment in which they live.

5. Providing support during the first years of a child's life serves a preventive function. Early and continuing support is aimed at strengthening the family unit and preventing family dysfunction.

6. Since families are part of a community, their needs cannot be met in isolation from it. Support is provided in the context of community life and through links with community resources (Weissbourd, 1987a, p. 53).

A second movement is represented by the efforts of state governments to establish policies and programs that aim to support and strengthen *all* families of young children (Weiss, 1989). These efforts break with public service tradition in which human services are rendered only to those judged "most needy" or "at greater risk" for poor outcomes. According to Weiss (1989), these government initiatives "provide prevention services to enhance parenting and strengthen families and communities as contexts for human development" (p. 33). Such state-sponsored family support initiatives illustrate how some states view their roles and responsibilities in supporting and strengthening family functioning. To a large degree, these programs are based upon the following program elements delineated by Weiss and Jacobs (1988b; pp. xx-xxi):

1. They demonstrate an ecological approach to promoting human development in that they foster child and adult growth by enhancing both the family's childrearing capacities and the community context in which childrearing takes place.
2. They are community-based and sensitive to local needs and resources, even when they have a federal or state sponsor.
3. They provide services in each of the domains typically included within the concept of social support: *information* (e.g., child health and development and parenting information), *emotional and appraisal support* (e.g., empathy, feedback, and reinforcement to adults in parenting roles and access to other parents), and *instrumental assistance* (e.g., transportation and referrals to other services).
4. They emphasize *primary and secondary prevention* of various child and family dysfunctions.

5. They represent innovative and *multilateral* (as opposed to exclusively professional) approaches to service delivery through such means as peer support, creative use of volunteers and paraprofessionals, and the promotion of informal networks.
6. They underscore the *interdependent* relationship between family and community (including both formal and informal supports) while at the same time framing this relationship so as to reinforce and respect the family's role and prerogatives.

A third movement is represented by the family-centered and community-based efforts espoused by the U.S. Department of Health and Human Services (Brewer, McPherson, Magrab, & Hutchins, 1989; Gittler, 1988; Nelkin, 1987; Shelton, Jeppson, & Johnson, 1987). This movement aims to mobilize the necessary supports and resources needed by families of health-impaired and medically fragile children and adolescents. It is underscored by the following elements of family-centered care:

1. Recognizing that the family is the constant in a child's life, while the service systems and personnel within those systems fluctuate.
2. Facilitating family/professional collaboration at all levels of health care, including the care of an individual child; program development, implementation, and evaluation; and policy formation.
3. Honoring the racial, ethnic, cultural, religious and socioeconomic diversity of families.
4. Recognizing family strengths and individuality and respecting different methods of coping.
5. Sharing with families, on a continuing

basis and in a supportive manner, complete and unbiased information.

6. Encouraging and facilitating family-to-family support and networking.

7. Understanding and incorporating the developmental needs of infants, children, and adolescents and their families into health care delivery systems.

8. Implementing comprehensive policies and programs that provide emotional and financial support to meet the needs of families.

9. Designing accessible health care systems that are flexible, culturally competent, and responsive to family-identified needs (Johnson, 1990).

A fourth movement is represented by contemporary early intervention practices as established by the P.L. 99-457 Education of the Handicapped Act Amendments of 1986. The Part H Program of the Act established an early intervention discretionary program specifically to meet the needs of infants and toddlers with special needs and their families by enhancing the capacity of parents to effectively perform their child rearing roles (U.S. House of Representatives Report 99-860). P.L. 99-457 gives parents of children with special needs and those at risk for disabilities a central role in specifying which types and forms of early intervention are best suited to the families' individual life styles and desires. McGonigel (1991, p. 9), recently enumerated the following set of principles for implementing early intervention practices in a family-centered manner:

1. Infants and toddlers are uniquely dependent on their families for their survival and nurturance. This dependence necessitates a family-centered approach to early intervention.

2. States and programs should define "family" in a way that reflects the diversity of family patterns and structures.

3. Each family has its own structure, roles, values, beliefs, and coping styles. Respect for and acceptance of this diversity is a cornerstone of family-centered early intervention.

4. Early intervention systems and strategies must honor the racial, ethnic, cultural, and socioeconomic diversity of families.

5. Respect for family autonomy, independence, and decision making means that families must be able to choose the level and nature of early intervention's involvement in their lives.

6. Family/professional collaboration and partnerships are the keys to family-centered early intervention and to successful implementation of the IFSP (Individualized Family Service Plan) process.

7. An enabling approach to working with families requires that professionals reexamine their traditional roles and practices and develop new practices when necessary-practices that promote mutual respect and partnerships.

8. Early intervention services should be flexible, accessible, and responsive to family-identified needs.

9. Early intervention services should be provided according to the normalization principle-that is, families should have access to services provided in as normal a fashion and environment as possible, and which promote the integration of the child and family within the community.

10. No one agency or discipline can meet the diverse and complex needs of infants and toddlers with special needs and their families. Therefore, a team approach to planning and implementing the IFSP is necessary.

A fifth movement is represented by efforts in the mental health field to develop family support programs. According to the Federation of Families for Children's Mental Health (1992), family support is a constellation of formal and informal services and tangible goods that are defined and determined by families. "Whatever it takes" for a family to care for and live with a child or adolescent who has an emotional, behavioral or mental disorder constitutes the focus of intervention. It also includes supports needed to assist families to maintain close involvement with their children who are in out-of-home placements, and help families when their children are ready to return home.

According to the Federation, the following principles ought to guide the provision of services to children and families:

1. Decisions must be based on a family's preferences, choices, and values and not on administrative expediencies.
2. Families must be recognized as the primary resource and decision makers for their child.
3. Families must have access to a flexible, affordable, individualized array of supports, services, and material items that provide "whatever it takes" to maintain themselves as a family.
4. The family's strengths, including the social networks and informal supports already available to and within the family, should be the foundation upon which new supports are designed or provided. Furthermore, if (but only if) the family wishes it, family support services should help to expand and strengthen the informal resources available to the family.
5. Support services must be culturally and geographically sensitive and able to meet the diverse needs of families.
6. Family supports must be affordable, well-

coordinated, accessible, and available to all families who need them, when and how they need them.

A sixth movement is now represented by more than 40 states that have family support initiatives for persons with developmental disabilities and their families (Knoll et al., 1990; Taylor, Knoll, Lehr, & Walker, 1989). This movement has nearly a 20 year history, but was spurred on by P.L. 100-113, the Developmental Disabilities Assistance and Bill of Rights Act of 1987. This law has one of the strongest statements in support of family-oriented initiatives (U.S. Senate Report 100-113). As noted in the Senate Report, efforts emanating from the Bill and Act:

> focus on the capabilities, competencies, and preferences as well as the needs of persons with disabilities and emphasize the *important role the family and members of the community* can play in enhancing the lives of persons with disabilities, especially when necessary support services are provided. (pp. 1-2, emphasis added)

An added impetus to this movement was the *Statement in Support of Families and Their Children* issued by the Center on Human Policy (1986) which specified that the following principles should guide public policy toward families of children with developmental disabilities and the actions of states and agencies when they become involved with families:

1. All children, regardless of disabilities, belong with families and need enduring relationships with adults. When states or agencies become involved with families, permanency planning should be a guiding philosophy.

2. Families should receive the supports nec-
    essary to maintain their children at home.
    Family support services must be based on
    the principle "whatever it takes." In short,
    family support services should be flexible,
    individualized, and designed to meet the
    diverse needs of families.

3. Family supports should build on existing
    social networks and natural sources of sup-
    port. As a guiding principle, natural sources
    of support, including neighbors, extended
    families, friends, and community associa-
    tions, should be preferred over agency pro-
    grams and professional services.

4. Family supports should maximize the
    family's control over the services and
    supports they receive. Family support ser-
    vices must be based on the assumption
    that families, rather than states and agen-
    cies, are in the best position to determine
    their needs.

5. Family supports should support the en-
    tire family. Family support services should
    be defined broadly in terms of the needs
    of the entire family, including children
    with disabilities, parents, and siblings.
    Family support services should encourage
    the integration of children with disabili-
    ties into the community. Family support
    services should be designed to maximize
    integration and participation in commu-
    nity life for children and disabilities.

6. When children cannot remain with their
    families for whatever reason, out-of-home
    placement should be viewed initially as a
    temporary arrangement and efforts should
    be directed toward reuniting the family.
    Consistent with the philosophy of perma-
    nency planning, children should live with
    their families whenever possible.

7. When families cannot be reunited and
    when active parental involvement is ab-
    sent, adoption should be aggressively pur-

sued. In fulfillment of each child's right to
a stable family and an enduring relationship with one or more adults, adoption
should be pursued for children whose ties
with their families have been broken.

8. While a preferred alternative to any group
    setting out-of-home placement, foster care
    should only be pursued when children
    cannot live with their families or with
    adoptive families. After families and adop-
    tive families, children should have the
    opportunity to live with foster families.

FAMILY SUPPORT PRINCIPLES

Collectively, the one feature that makes the
above family support movements different from
other social interventions is the fact that they
are underscored by adherence to family support
principles. Family support principles are statements of beliefs about how supports and resources ought to be provided to families. Taken
together, a particular set of principles represents a *philosophy* about family-centered intervention practices (Dunst, 1990a, 1990b). To the
extent that a program operates in ways consistent with a set of principles, it would receive
"high marks" as a *family support program*.

More than a dozen sets of family support
principles can now be found in the family
support program literature, including those
listed above (Center on Human Policy, 1986;
Child Welfare League, 1989; Dokecki, 1983;
Family Resource Coalition, 1987; Hobbs et
al., 1984; Musick & Weissbourd, 1988; Nelkin, 1987; Ooms & Preister, 1988; Roberts,
1988; Shelton, Jeppson, & Johnson, 1987;
Smith, 1987; Weiss & Jacobs, 1988b;
Weissbourd, 1987b; Weissbourd & Kagan,
1989; Zigler, 1986; Zigler & Black, 1989).
According to Weissbourd (1987b), these principles are the characteristics that make family

support programs unique, and distinguish these programs from other human service initiatives.

An aggregation and categorization of the various collections of family support principles finds that they can be conveniently organized into six major sets of principles (Dunst, 1990b). Collectively, these sets of principles provide a framework for assessing whether policies or practices, or any other aspect of a program (e.g., staff roles and responsibilities), show a *presumption toward* "family-centeredness" in ways that are likely to support and strengthen family functioning. The six sets of family support principles include:

1. Enhancing a Sense of Community
2. Mobilizing Resources and Supports
3. Shared Responsibility and Collaboration
4. Protecting Family Integrity
5. Strengthening Family Functioning
6. Proactive Human Services Practices

Table 3-1 lists the major characteristics of the principles that comprise each set. A detailed description of the major elements of each set of principles is described next.

ENHANCING A SENSE OF COMMUNITY

The *Enhancing a Sense of Community* principles emphasize efforts that "promote the coming together of people around shared values and the pursuit of common cause...where people concern themselves with the well-being of all people and not just those who are most needy or hold some special status" (Hobbs et al., 1984, p. 46). Weiss and Jacobs (1988b), for example, noted that family resource programs are grass-roots, community-based efforts that are sensitive to the local needs and resources of all people. Similarly, Weissbourd (1987b) stated that family resource programs "recognize a need for interaction and support, and

understand that the ability to relate to others" (p. 49) enhances *interdependencies and mutually beneficial exchanges* among community members. Family resource programs recognize that in a strong community there is both *reciprocity* and *mutual support* among its members, and that family resource programs aim to enhance a *sense of community* that reflect strong, interdependent ties among people (Moroney, 1987). Zigler (1986) noted, for example, that family resource programs are "valuable in fostering communication, exchanging information, and giving individuals a *sense that they are members of a caring unit*" (p. 10, emphasis added). Strong communities, in turn, increase the availability of needed supports and resources, and enrich the community environment for families and their members.

MOBILIZING RESOURCES AND SUPPORTS

The *Mobilizing Resources and Supports* principles describe the conditions which create opportunities for *building* and *mobilizing* social support networks in ways that enhance the flow of necessary resources so families have the time, energy, knowledge, and skills to carry out family functions, particularly parenting responsibilities (Hobbs et al., 1984). Principles in this category emphasize the *building* and *strengthening* of informal support networks, and the provision of resources and supports in ways that are *flexible, individualized*, and *responsive* to the changing needs of families. Scholars and practitioners almost uniformly agree that building and strengthening informal support networks are at the heart of the family resource movement (e.g., Center on Human Policy, 1986; Smith, 1987; Weissbourd, 1987b; Zigler & Black, 1989). On the one hand, those who endorse this tenet recognize the wealth of resources that already exist within a family's personal social network, and on the other hand, recognize the fact that

Table 3-1. Major Categories and Examples of Family Support Principles	
Category/Characteristics	Examples of Principles
Enhancing A Sense of Community: Promoting the coming together of people around shared values and common needs in ways that create mutually beneficial interdependencies	Interventions should focus on the building of interdependencies between members of the community and the family unit. Interventions should emphasize the common needs and supports of all people and base intervention actions on those commonalities.
Mobilizing Resources and Supports: Building support systems that enhance the flow of resources in ways that assist families with parenting responsibilities	Interventions should focus on building and strengthening informal support networks for families rather than depend solely on professional support systems. Resources and supports should be made available to families in ways that are flexible, individualized, and responsive to the needs of the entire family unit.
Shared Responsibility and Collaboration: Sharing of ideas and skills by parents and professionals in ways that build and strengthen collaborative arrangements	Interventions should employ partnerships between parents and professionals as a primary mechanism for supporting and strengthening family functioning. Resource and support mobilization interactions between families and service providers should be based upon mutual respect and sharing of unbiased information.
Protecting Family Integrity: Respecting the family's beliefs and values and protecting the family from intrusion upon its beliefs by outsiders	Resources and supports should be provided to families in ways that encourage, develop, and maintain healthy, stable relationships among all family members. Interventions should be conducted in ways that accept, value, and protect a family's personal and cultural values and beliefs.
Strengthening Family Functioning: Promoting the capabilities and competencies of families necessary to mobilize resources and perform parenting responsibilities in ways that have empowering consequences	Interventions should build upon family strengths rather than correct weaknesses or deficits as a primary way of supporting and strengthening family functioning. Resources and supports should be made available to families in ways that maximize the family's control over and decision-making power regarding services they receive.
Proactive Human Services Practices: Adoption of consumer-driven human services-delivery models and practices that support and strengthen family functioning	Service-delivery programs should employ promotion rather than treatment approaches as the framework for strengthening family functioning. Resource and support mobilization should be consumer-driven rather than service provider-driven or professionally prescribed.

mobilizing and utilizing community support networks as sources of resources decreases the likelihood of dependency on professional and formal human services systems as sources of all or even most of a family's resources. As noted by Weissbourd and Kagan (1989), "Such (informal) support increases a family's ability to cope and foster independence and mutual interdependence in contrast to dependence" (p. 23).

SHARED RESPONSIBILITY AND COLLABORATION

The *Shared Responsibility and Collaboration* principles emphasize the sharing of ideas, knowledge, and skills between families and family resource program staff in ways that encourage *partnerships* and *collaboration* as the mechanism for resource mobilization and community building. A call for a revision in the role of traditional relationships between service providers and community people has been voiced on a number of fronts (Dunst & Paget, 1991; Rappaport, 1987; Weissbourd & Kagan, 1989). According to Musick and Weissbourd (1988), service providers who "view themselves as partners with parents.... reduce dependence on professionals and re-emphasize the capability of individuals and the power of peer support, mutual aid, and social networks" (p. 5). The use of *mutually agreed upon roles* in pursuit of a common goal creates not only the types of collaborative relationships between parents and professionals that are the essence of partnership arrangements, but are also the conditions that will likely have mutually empowering consequences in both partners (Dunst & Paget, 1991). As noted by Oster (1984), "It behooves all of us...to develop a forum where parents and professionals can share the valuable and hard won knowledge that each possesses" (p. 32).

PROTECTING FAMILY INTEGRITY

The *Protecting Family Integrity* principles emphasize efforts to buffer the family unit from: (a) intrusion upon the family's *personal and cultural values* and beliefs by "outsiders" and (b) abuse and neglect of individual family members and the family unit by provision of supports and resources that reduce the likelihood of risk factors functioning as precipitators of maltreatment (Hobbs et al., 1984). On the one hand, this two pronged emphasis acknowledges and values a family's personal and cultural belief systems, and on the other hand, recognizes the family's need for supports and resources necessary for enhancing

healthy family functioning. As noted by Ooms and Preister (1988), interventive efforts that are sensitive to a family's personal values and beliefs demand that

> Policies and programs recognize the diversity of family life....The diversities that need to be taken into account include different types of family structure; different stages of the family life cycle; different ethnic, cultural, racial and religious backgrounds; socio-economic differences; and differing community contexts. (p. 11)

Similarly, "Policies are valued that recognize the importance of parental rights to the maintenance of the family unit but that stop short of allowing these rights to work to the significant detriment of individual family members" (Hobbs et al., 1984, p. 52). Many family support scholars note that adherence to the *Protecting Family Integrity* principles increases the likelihood of fostering healthy, stable relationships among family members (e.g., Hobbs et al., 1984; Musick & Weissbourd, 1988).

STRENGTHENING FAMILY FUNCTIONING

The *Strengthening Family Functioning* principles emphasize opportunities and experiences that permit the family and its members to become capable of mastering a wide range of developmental tasks and functions. Family support scholars and practitioners universally advocate for the position that family resource programs should identify and *build on family strengths* rather than correct weaknesses or cure deficiencies (e.g., Family Resource Coalition, 1987; Musick & Weissbourd, 1988; Weissbourd, 1987b; Zigler, 1986; Zigler & Black, 1989). This principle attempts to reverse previous human service practices based upon deficit and "cultural difference" approaches to addressing human concerns. Additionally, there is near universal acceptance that primacy be given to *promotion and enhancement* of family competencies and capabilities as the way to support and strengthen family functioning (Zigler & Berman, 1983; Zigler & Black, 1989). As noted by Hobbs et al. (1984),

> policies [and practices] are valued that create conditions or provide services enhancing parental competency especially in relation to intrafamily and extrafamily factors that influence child rearing. Such policies (and practices) improve the knowledge, skill, and decision-making capacity of parents in dealing with family developmental issues, such as pregnancy and childbirth, children's growth and developmental tasks, children's health and nutrition, family needs for child care provision because of parental work responsibilities, and children's entry into school. (p. 49)

The foci of principles that emphasize the strengthening of family functioning are considered by many as the cornerstone of family resource programs. *Enabling experiences* and *empowering consequences* are seen, respectively, as the processes and outcomes that derive from the operationalization of principles that aim to support and strengthen family functioning (Dunst & Trivette, 1987a; Hobbs et al., 1984; Zigler & Berman, 1983).

PROACTIVE HUMAN SERVICES PRACTICES

The *Proactive Human Services Practices* principles specify human services models and approaches that are most likely to produce outcomes consistent with the aims of family resource programs. By far, most scholars and practitioners have called for the use of *prevention* and *promotion* models rather than treatment models for guiding human services practices (Dunst, Trivette, & Thompson, 1990; Family Resource Coalition, 1987; Musick & Weissbourd, 1988; Weiss & Jacobs, 1988b; Weissbourd, 1987a; Weissbourd & Kagan, 1989; Zigler, 1986; Zigler & Black, 1989). Preventive interventions deter or hinder the occurrence of problems or disease, and occur prior to the onset of negative functioning in order to reduce the incidence or prevalence of poor outcomes (Dunst, Trivette, & Thompson, 1990; Hoke, 1968; Zautra & Sandler, 1983). Promotive interventions enhance and optimize the development of positive functioning, and focus on the acquisition of competencies and capabilities that strengthen functioning and adaptive capacities (Dunst, Trivette, & Thompson, 1990; Hoke, 1968; Rappaport, 1981, 1987; Zautra & Sandler, 1983). Additionally, adoption of *resource-based* and *consumer-driven* approaches to intervention are seen as ways of insuring: "The empowerment of parents, an ability to control their lives and to become involved in shaping their environments...a frequent outcome for those participating in support programs" (Weissbourd & Kagan, 1989, p. 23). This not only necessitates but demands adoption of *holistic* intervention practices that clearly emphasize an ecological, social systems perspective of human development (Bronfenbrenner, 1979).

Collectively, the principles in each of the above categories represent, at a minimum, the *essential elements* of family support programs considered necessary for human service policies and practices to have family strengthening influences. Dunst (1990b) has recently developed six checklists that can be used to ascertain whether social interventions are consistent with the aims of family support programs. Each checklist includes five principles, stated as a series of questions, that can be used by program builders and practitioners to stimulate discussion and dialogue about the ways in which policies and practices influence various aspects of family functioning. The principles and their associated questions serve as *criteria* and a set of *standards* against which policies and practices may be judged. Affirmative answers to the majority of questions may be taken as evidence that a policy or program shows a *presumption toward* the aims of family resource programs.

IMPLICATIONS FOR PRACTICE

The integration of the family-centered approach described in Chapter 1, the empowerment model described in Chapter 2, and the family support principles described above, suggests a bold approach to developing family support program policies and practices. A "call for" new service-delivery models has been voiced by a number of family support program advocates (Brewer et al., 1989; Cohen et al., 1989; Dokecki & Heflinger, 1989; Knoll et al., 1990; Moroney, 1986; Rappaport, 1981, 1987; Shelton et al., 1987; Weissbourd, 1990; Weissbourd & Kagan, 1989).

The implications of the material described thus far for program development and human services practices is described next specifically in terms of a *model* for conceptualizing community-based family support programs and the *challenges* program builders and practitioners face in translating the model into practice. The material presented in both sections provides a framework for developing family support activities, and judging the extent to which such activities are consistent with the characteristics considered the key elements of successful family support programs.

PROGRAM DEVELOPMENT MODEL

Figure 3-1 depicts a framework that incorporates the various features of a family-centered model and family support principles into a single coherent program model. The figure shows the "flow of influences" from family-identified needs to the types of outcomes that would be realized if practices were implemented in ways consistent with the intent of both family support principles and an empowerment philosophy. Collectively, the components of the model shown in the figure include those program characteristics that would provide enabling opportunities and empower program participants by enhancing and promoting individual and family capabilities that support and strengthen family functioning–the aim of family support programs.

The seven components of the model shown in Figure 3-1 are briefly described next to illustrate their implications for family support program development and implementation. Some of the major challenges that program builders and practitioners face in implementing the model are enumerated following the description of seven components:

1. *Family Support Principles.* Programs that are underscored by a broad-based set of family support principles are more likely to result in a consumer-driven, empowerment philosophy that guides all other aspects of program development and implementation (see e.g., Dunst 1990b). Family support principles that guide program practices provide standards against which other aspects of program decisions, actions, and practices can be judged. For example, a principle which states that "information should be shared with families in a complete and unbiased manner" provides a standard for judging whether or not any particular program practice is true to this stated belief. The importance of having an explicit list of family support

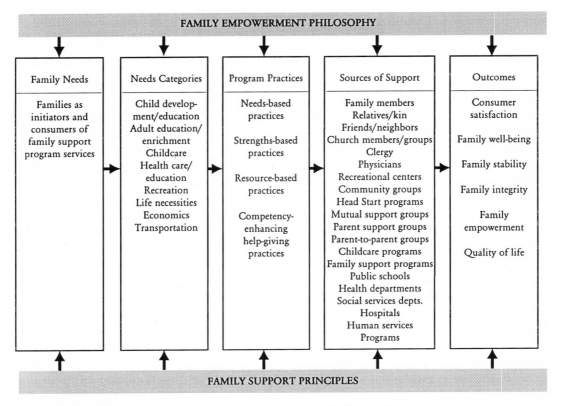

Fig.3-1. A Model for Depicting the Key Components of a Family-Centered Support Program.

principles cannot be overstated. On the one hand the principles constitute a program's philosophy, and on the other hand provide concrete benchmarks for judging whether program staff "walk the talk."

2. *Family Empowerment Philosophy.* Family-centered support principles have as a major focus a family empowerment program philosophy. An empowerment philosophy places families in pivotal roles in all aspects of program development and implementation, including, but not limited to, identification of those characteristics of program policies and practices that are most likely to result in provision of resources and supports that meet family identified needs. An empowerment philosophy requires a shift in how families are viewed and how professionals define their roles and responsibilities as part of helping relationships (Rappaport, 1981, 1987). Dunst, Trivette, and LaPointe (1992; Chapter 2) recently synthesized the literature on empowerment, and found that the use of the term is underscored by empowerment as a *philosophy and ideology*, and when operationalized, contributes to program participant competence and a sense-of-control over important life events and circumstances. An empowerment philosophy, for example, states that *all* people have existing strengths and capabilities as well as the capacity to become more com-

petent; the failure of a person to display competence is *not* due to deficits within a person but rather the failure of social systems and organizations to provide or create opportunities for competencies to be displayed or acquired; and in situations where existing capabilities need to be strengthened or new competencies need to be learned, they are best learned by actively participating in knowledge and skill acquisition that lead people to make self-attributions about their capabilities to influence important life events (Dunst & Trivette, 1987a; Dunst, Trivette, & Deal, 1988; Rappaport, 1981). Such a philosophy has far reaching implications for how human service programs deliver resources and supports to families.

3. *Family Needs.* Family support programs, to the maximum extent possible, employ consumer-driven intervention practices. This requires a shift away from prescribing solutions to family problems and concerns, and expecting families to adhere to such prescriptions, toward intervention practices that respond to what families consider the resources needed for normal community life. According to Weissbourd (1987b), *all* families, regardless of socio-economic status or other family characteristics, have diverse needs that can be met by family support programs. Although a family's specific need for resources and supports will differ depending upon many family circumstances, it is nonetheless possible to think of needs as being determined or influenced by two different, broad sets of conditions: (1) Needs that are ongoing and change very little on a day-in and day-out basis, and (2) needs that vary as a function of changes in a family's situation, whether anticipated or unanticipated.

The need for financial resources to pay for food and shelter is an example of the first type of need. The need for information about a job placement and the need for emotional support in response to the sudden death of a family member are examples, respectively, of anticipated and unanticipated needs that occur as a function of changes in a family's life situation. Family-centered assessment and intervention practices that are consumer-driven attempt to be responsive to both the ongoing and changing needs of families, and such practices fully recognize and address family concerns in both areas of needs.

4. *Needs Categories.* Responsive family support programs are ones that recognize the broad-based, individualized, and changing needs of families, and are ones that employ practices that assist families in identifying resources that are best suited to a family's unique life style. The ability to adequately identify a family's needs, as well as resources for meeting needs, necessitates that one have a good idea about what all families are likely to require for stable functioning, individual and family growth, and day-to-day coping and well-being. A number of program developers and practitioners have organized needs into broad categories for guiding needs identification and resource mobilization practices. The reader is referred to Dunst, Trivette, and Deal (1988), Hartman and Laird (1983), and Trivette, Deal, and Dunst (1986) for useful lists of these kinds of needs categories. The list provided by Dunst, Trivette, and Deal (1988) includes the following 12 groups of needs:

- Economic Needs
- Adult Education Needs
- Physical and Environmental Needs

- Child Education and Intervention Needs
- Food and Clothing Needs
- Child Care Needs
- Medical and Dental Care Needs
- Recreational Needs
- Employment and Vocational Needs
- Emotional Needs
- Cultural and Social Needs
- Transportation Needs

Chapter 7 includes an elaborated list of examples of the kinds of resources that are often required by families in each of these needs categories.

5. *Program Practices.* Family support programs that are family-centered are ones that employ needs-based practices, strengths-based practices, resource-based intervention practices, and competency-enhancing help-giving practices as part of promoting the flow-of-resources to families in ways that are competency-enhancing and supportive (see Sections IV & V). Needs-based practices are ones that place families in a *pivotal role* in defining the focus of intervention practices. Strengths-based practices are ones that build on existing family capabilities as well as promote family acquisition of competencies that lead to empowering consequences. Resource-based practices are ones that look to a wide range of community people, groups, organizations, agencies, and programs for resources and supports for meeting family needs. Competency-enhancing help-giving practices are ones that focus on solutions rather than causes of problems, promotion of family capabilities, and the strengthening of family functioning. The latter was perhaps best said by Maple (1977) who stated that in traditional helping relationships "the rescuer

becomes the 'star.' (In competency-enhancing help giving) your goal as helpers is not to learn how to become a star, but rather to help people become the 'star' in some aspects of their lives" (p. 7). Family support programs that employed the four types of practices listed in Figure 3-1 as part of delivering services and resources would be considered a very strong support initiative.

6. *Sources of Support.* Family support programs that employ resource-based intervention practices recognize a wide range of community people, groups, organizations, programs, and agencies as potential sources of support for meeting family needs, and work toward making such sources viable resource options. Figure 3-1 lists some, but certainly not all, the sources of support which are potentially available to families. Expanded lists and descriptions of potential support sources can be found in Dunst (1985), Dunst, Trivette, and Deal (1988), Kagan et al. (1987), Turnbull, Summers and Brotherson (1986), and Weiss and Jacobs (1988a). Employing resource-based intervention practices recognizes that *all* people have resources that might be of benefit to others (see Dunst, Trivette, Gordon, & Pletcher, 1989), and that such resources become viable support sources when they are explicitly targeted as resources for meeting needs. A rule-of-thumb that ought to be followed in mobilizing resources to meet family needs is not to use a professional source of support when a more informal source of support exists for meeting needs. In this way, resource and support network building will not become overly professionalized.

7. *Outcomes.* The development and implementation of family support programs that operationalize activities in each of the above components in the ways de-

scribed, ought to result in a broad range of positive outcomes among families participating in these programs. Those listed in Figure 3-1 are ones most often mentioned by the families participating in human services programs (see e.g., Dunst, Trivette, Starnes, Hamby, & Gordon, 1993). Similar outcomes have been reported in our other work (see Dunst & Trivette, 1988a, 1988c, 1989; Dunst, Trivette, & LaPointe, 1992) as well as by others (see especially Dunst, Trivette, & LaPointe, 1992; Rappaport et al., 1984).

The model shown in Figure 3-1 and briefly described here provides at least one way of conceptualizing a program structure that explicitly considers a broad range of program development considerations. Formulating a model, however, is only the first step. Translating the model into day-to-day practice in ways that are consistent with the key elements of family support programs is obviously the next step. Doing so is not without its problems as we describe next.

CHALLENGES IN PROGRAM IMPLEMENTATION

Program builders and practitioners face many challenges in developing and implementing family support programs in ways consistent with the model just described. The list that follows addresses a number of major obstacles which stand in the way of building community-based family support programs that are characterized by the key elements of family support initiatives. These challenges are enumerated next as a basis for providing program builders and practitioners a set of questions that can be posed and answered as part of program development and implemen-

tation activities. To the extent that the questions are answered in the affirmative, one would conclude that program development and implementation was proceeding in ways consistent with family support principles and family-centered practices. The particular challenges that we list are ones that repeatedly emerge from efforts to understand how to build and evaluate family support programs. Many of the challenges are similar to ones described by others interested in family support and community-based human services programs (Dokecki & Heflinger, 1989; Dunst, Trivette, & Thompson, 1990; Kagan et al., 1987; Knoll et al., 1990; Powell, 1988; Singer & Irvin, 1989; Taylor et al., 1989; Weiss & Jacobs, 1988b; Weissbourd, 1990; Weissbourd & Kagan, 1989; Zigler & Black, 1989; Zimmerman & Rappaport, 1988).

1. *Does the program activity or practice employ consumer-driven approaches to identifying family needs as opposed to using professionally-driven and prescriptive practices.* The major challenge that program builders and practitioners face with respect to adoption of consumer-driven assessment and intervention practices is taking the time to listen and understand family concerns from a family's own perspective. Too often, professionals want to "jump in" and solve problems for families rather than employ practices that assist families in identifying their own needs. Doing so is inconsistent with a family-centered approach to assessment and intervention.

2. *Does the program respond to the broad-based needs of families rather than focus on a single type of support?* Differences in family backgrounds, circumstances, desires, etc. will almost certainly result in diversity in what families identify as their needs. Needs-based intervention practices mean being

responsive to all family concerns; it does not necessarily mean being everything to every family. Successful family support programs do not dismiss what families deem important; rather they assist families in learning about community resources that can address such concerns.

3. *Does the program activity or practice provide families the necessary information to make informed, competent decisions as opposed to having professionals make decisions for families?* One challenge faced by practitioners as part of providing information to families so they can make informed, intelligent decisions, is sharing relevant information completely and in ways that it is understandable. So often you hear, as we did from practitioners in a recent study (Dunst, Trivette, Starnes, Hamby, & Gordon, 1993), that the reason information is not shared is because certain families are not assumed competent enough to understand it. Such a belief and practice is inconsistent with an empowerment philosophy.

4. *Does the program activity or practice recognize and build upon family strengths as a way of strengthening family functioning rather than attempt to correct weaknesses?* The major challenge here is the recognition that all people and families have strengths and capabilities, and that by building upon these capabilities as part of mobilizing resources for meeting needs, the chances of being successful are enhanced considerably. If one assumes an individual or family has no strengths, practitioners are more likely to do for families rather than help families do for themselves, and an opportunity to promote competence will have been lost. Moreover, such a practice is more likely to contribute to a dependency of the family on the program staff,

an outcome inconsistent with the goals of family support programs.

5. *Does the program activity or practice promote collaboration and partnerships between families and professionals rather than employ paternalistic practices for building resource networks for meeting needs?* The major challenge faced by practitioners with regard to this concern is building *true* collaboration between professionals and families, where each makes meaningful contributions to the process of identifying needs and mobilizing resources to meet needs. Helping relationships built upon *mutual* trust, respect, honesty, and caring will most likely produce the greatest positive effects.

6. *Does the program activity or practice provide resources and supports to families in ways that are flexible, individualized, and family-centered rather than provide services to families at the convenience of programs and practitioners?* The challenge faced by program builders and practitioners alike is the shift away from "standard operating procedures" toward a model that molds and shapes program practices to the evolving and changing needs of families, and the provision and mobilization of resources and supports that are responsive to family concerns and desires. Despite the fact that flexible and individualized service provision are considered a cornerstone of family support programs, so often families are made to fit into how a program is organized and operated rather than the other way around. Such a practice is inconsistent with a family-centered approach to intervention.

7. *Does the program activity or practice emphasize the delivery of supports and resources in the communities in which a family lives rather than provide services primarily in centralized locations?* One major challenge as part of

the delivery of program services in a community-based manner is blending the provision of human services into the everyday lives of children and their families so that they are supportive of normal community life. This means "breaking up" institutionalized and entrenched service-delivery systems and reorganizing program operations so that they are part of a community and do not simply involve delivery of service in the community. Doing so is the "acid test" for assessing the "community-centeredness" of a family support initiatives.

8. *Does the program activity or practice encourage the use of resource-based approaches rather than only service-based solutions for meeting family needs?* This challenge has to do with strengthening informal support networks and existing community resources for meeting family needs rather than only looking to professionals as sources of supports. Overcoming this obstacle seems simple enough on the surface, but it is perhaps the single most difficult challenge facing family support program builders and practitioners. This is the case because there is a long history that has reinforced a belief that professionals are the only or the primary source of support for meeting the needs of families. Dispelling this belief and recognizing the richness of communities as sources of supports must be a major emphasis as part of building successful family support initiatives.

9. *Does the program activity or practice promote adoption of empowering help giving as opposed to paternalistic help-giving practices?* This challenge has to do with changing professionals' views about their roles and responsibilities as part of helping relationships. At the most basic level this means not doing for families but rather

helping families to learn to promote the flow of resources to meet their needs. At a more complex level, it means use of helping practices that truly provide choices, and adoption of practices that support families' decisions regarding what is needed for normal community life.

10. *Does the program activity or practice encourage adoption of promotion models over either prevention or treatment models for guiding program development and day-to-day human services practice?* The major challenge here is movement beyond efforts to forestall or overcome negative outcomes toward enhancement of positive aspects of functioning. Supporting and strengthening individual and family functioning is not likely to be realized, unless program practices specifically focus on promotion of a broad range of behavior capabilities and competencies–the goal of an empowerment orientation toward family support.

These 10 considerations are by no means the only challenges that face family support program builders and practitioners. They are, however, considerations that are data based, and derived from the findings of a study examining family support initiatives (Dunst, Trivette, Starnes, Hamby, & Gordon, 1993). Program builders and practitioners who successfully address these challenges, and who are able to overcome the obstacles and move toward practices consistent with the intent of family support principles would most certainly be heralded as innovators *par excellence*.

SUMMARY AND CONCLUSION

Effective family-centered assessment and intervention practices require a major shift in the ways in which human services practitioners have traditionally conceptualized and rendered resources and services to families. Both the aims and principles of family support programs provide at least one framework for making such a shift. Developing program practices and delivering services, supports, and resources in ways consistent with family-centered policies is an ongoing endeavor in contrast to establishing policy which is a much more static process. It is not uncommon to find a "drift" away from the intent of policy as program builders and practitioners get caught-up in day-to-day demands and expectations that rob them of the time and energy to "stay on track." The material presented in this chapter provides a framework for creating a vision about what a program ought to look like, and to the extent that day-to-day practices show a presumption toward consistency with family support principles, a program would be judged favorably as a successful family support initiative.

Supporting and Strengthening Family Functioning: Toward a Congruence Between Principles and Practice

Carl J. Dunst, Carol M. Trivette & Rebekah B. Thompson

THE EMERGING INTEREST in family support programs as the context for supporting and strengthening family functioning represents a significant departure from the ways in which human services practitioners have traditionally rendered services and resources. In contrast to traditional human services practices where interventions are typically provided following the onset of some problem or difficulty, family support programs are "oriented toward preventing families' and children's problems rather than toward treatment" (Weissbourd & Kagan, 1989, p. 21). Family support programs are to a large degree based upon the presupposition that the prevention of parent and child problems will result in the strengthening of family functioning. But is this a valid assumption?

The two major theses of this chapter are as follows: (1) the *absence* of psychological or physical problems does not necessarily mean the *presence* of positive functioning, and (2) the *prevention of problems* by family support programs does not necessarily guarantee the *strengthening of family functioning*. It is our contention that the use of prevention models for guiding intervention practices in family support programs is inconsistent with the aim of strengthening family functioning. We argue that only the use of promotion and enhancement models increase the likelihood that people will become more capable and competent as a result of intervention efforts.

Evidence to support this contention is aggregated and presented in this chapter.

The chapter is divided into four sections. In the first section we briefly examine the major characteristics and aims of family support programs, and a particular set of principles upon which these programs are based. In the second section we describe the major characteristics and features of treatment, prevention, and promotion models, and describe the limited, problem reduction perspective of both treatment and prevention models, and the expanded, growth-enhancing perspective of promotion models. In the third section we review available evidence which indicates that the absence of poor functioning cannot be equated with the presence of positive functioning. This evidence is used to support the two theses presented above. In the last section we integrate the material on family support principles, human development models, and the empirical evidence regarding the absence-presence of negative and positive aspects of functioning. We argue that there is a greater congruence between the aims of family support programs and the characteristics of promotion models, than there is between the goals of family support programs and prevention models. We conclude this final section with a discussion of the implications of the material presented in the article for refining and "fine-tuning" practices in family support programs.

This chapter is based upon an article appearing in *Prevention in Human Services*, 1991, *9* (1), 19-43. Reprinted with permission from the publisher.

CHARACTERISTICS OF FAMILY SUPPORT PROGRAMS

It is generally recognized that the aims and assumptions of family support programs are different from those of other types of family-oriented, service-delivery programs (e.g., Kagan, Powell, Weissbourd, & Zigler, 1987; Zigler & Black, 1989). These differences are derived from a number of distinctive characteristics that make family support programs unique in both their aims and guiding principles (see Chapter 3).

AIMS OF FAMILY SUPPORT PROGRAMS

According to Kagan and Shelley (1987),

Family support efforts are directed at reforming existing policies and practices so that major institutions will improve family functioning by their support...(and)...empower (people) to act for their own good and the good of their immediate community. (p. 8)

Similarly, Zigler and Berman (1983) stated that the aim of family support programs is "not to provide families with direct services, but to enhance parent empowerment to enable families to help themselves and their children" (p. 904). Dunst (1989) defined family support programs as "efforts designed to promote the flow of resources and supports to families in ways that strengthen the functioning and enhance the growth and development of individual family members and the family unit" (p. 1). He also noted that family support programs conduct interventions in ways that have empowering consequences, and therefore aid families and their members in becoming more capable and competent. Yet another definition has been offered by Weissbourd and Kagan (1989): "family support programs

provide services to families that empower and strengthen adults in their roles as parents, nurturers, and providers" (p. 21).

Each of these definitions share a common theme; namely, family support programs place primary emphasis on the *strengthening* of individual and family functioning. This emphasis is reflected in the careful selection of terms like improve, enhance, promote, nurture, enable, and empower to describe the *processes* and *outcomes* of intervention efforts. Stated differently, the aim of family support programs is to enable and empower people by enhancing and promoting individual and family capabilities that support and strengthen family functioning.

At first glance, this definition may not seem new or novel. Upon reflection, however, it is quite radical. It suggests a significant change and shift in the ways in which we both conceptualize and operationalize intervention practices (Rappaport, 1981; Seeman, 1989). This shift is reflected to a large degree in the guiding principles of family support programs.

FAMILY SUPPORT PRINCIPLES

Over a dozen sets of family support principles can now be found in the literature (Center on Human Policy, 1986; Dokecki, 1983; Family Resource Coalition, 1987; Hobbs, et al, 1984; Musick & Weissbourd, 1988; Nelkin, 1987; Roberts, 1988; Shelton, Jeppson, & Johnson, 1987; Smith, 1987; Weiss & Jacobs, 1988b; Weissbourd, 1987b; Weissbourd & Kagan, 1989; Zigler, 1986; Zigler & Black, 1989). According to Weissbourd (1987b), these principles make family support programs unique, and distinguish these principles from other human service initiatives. Many of these principles share common features that make clear the presuppositions of efforts to support and strengthen family functioning.

An aggregation and categorization of the

different family support principles can be conveniently organized into six major categories. These include: Enhancing a sense of community, mobilizing resources and supports, shared responsibility and collaboration, protecting family integrity, strengthening family functioning, and human service practices. The reader is referred to Chapter 3 for a detailed description of family support principles in each of these categories. There is little doubt that family support principles not only differentiate family support programs from traditional human service programs, but also suggest new and novel ways of addressing human development concerns and rendering resources to meet family needs. Close inspection of the principles, however, show some to be contradictory and inconsistent in their assumptions, methods, and outcomes.

By far, most family support scholars and practitioners have called for the use of prevention rather than treatment models for guiding human service practices (Family Resource Coalition, 1987; Musick & Weissbourd, 1988; Weiss & Jacobs, 1988b; Weissbourd, 1987b; Weissbourd & Kagan, 1989; Zigler, 1986; Zigler & Black, 1989). Such models emphasize the prevention of family problems and negative outcomes as opposed to treatment following the onset of pathology or crisis. A prevention approach is viewed as *the* alternative to human services practices where interventions almost always occur following a hardship or difficulty, which only increases the likelihood of a paternalistic solution to the problem (Rappaport, 1981, 1987; Swift, 1984). By intervening before problems manifest themselves, it is argued, the need for professional assistance with many of life's difficulties are eliminated or at least significantly reduced.

The contradiction that is the focus of this chapter is the incongruence between the emphasis on the enhancement of the positive aspects of family functioning and adoption of prevention models as the interventive approach for achieving the aims of family support programs. The implicit assumption that a preventive approach will result in the strengthening of functioning, as we shall see, cannot be supported either conceptually or empirically. It is this evidence that we use as a basis for arguing that promotion rather than prevention models be employed by family support programs as the framework for guiding interventive actions to strengthen family functioning.

HUMAN SERVICES INTERVENTION MODELS

In this section we describe both the limited, problem-reduction perspective of different prevention models as well as the expanded, growth-enhancing perspective of promotion models. We begin by contrasting two systems for classifying human services intervention models —illustrating the pitfalls of one and the strengths of the other— for intervention practices in general and those specific to family support programs.

The classification system of disease prevention advanced by the Commission on Chronic Illness (1957) —categorizing prevention as either primary or secondary— has been used widely for categorizing interventive efforts based on the onset and timing of preventive actions. Primary prevention refers to actions taken *prior to* the onset of a disease or problem aimed specifically at reducing or eliminating the likelihood of a disorder. Secondary prevention refers to actions taken *after* a disease or problem has been identified, but *before* it has caused disability or suffering. Subsequent to the development of this classification scheme, the term tertiary prevention was added and applied widely to describe intervention efforts designed to reduce the negative consequences of a disease and disability *following their onset.* Tertiary prevention is most commonly used to describe actions that are considered treatment in nature.

Discussions abound regarding the utility of a prevention scheme for structuring human service intervention practices (e.g., Cowen, 1985; Lamb & Zusman, 1979). A complete analysis of the pros and cons of this framework is beyond the scope of this chapter. We point out, however, that all three types of prevention, by definition, aim to avert or forestall negative outcomes or their consequences, and again by definition, do not necessarily have anything to do with the enhancement of positive aspects of functioning. Herein lies the potential pitfall of the tripartite classification scheme, and the danger of its use by family support programs.

About a decade after the tripartite prevention scheme had been developed, Hoke (1968) proposed an alternative framework for categorizing interventive aims and methods that is derived from a completely different orientation and perspective. This framework provides a basis for conceptually and operationally distinguishing between problem-oriented and competency-enhancement models of intervention. It also provides a framework for empirically testing the validity of the argument that absence of poor functioning does not necessarily mean the presence of positive functioning. According to Hoke (1968), both prevention and treatment models have disease-buffering underpinnings, whereas promotion models have health-enhancement orientations. He noted:

(T)he philosophy of promotive medicine goes beyond the goal of protecting people's health and preventing harm or disease.... (M)edicine has had two primary orientations: curing disease and preventing disease. Actually these are but two aspects of a single orientation–disease orientation.... Health and disease have been regarded as polar opposites with health being the absence of disease....Promotive medicine views health...as a developmental process involving multi-level responses to a total environment (where) healthy responses are *life enhancing.* Promotive medicine seeks to promote healthy, positive, adaptive responses. (pp. 269- 270)

A similar distinction between treatment, prevention, and promotion models is presented in the Surgeon General's (1979) report *Healthy People.* Others, as well, have noted the underlying differences between, and implications of, differing models of intervention (e.g., Bond, 1982; Danish & D'Augelli, 1980). This is especially true regarding the differences between prevention and promotion. Klein and Goldston (1977), for example, noted that

Prevention is directed toward reducing the incidence of a highly predictable undesirable consequence. The term should not be used interchangeably with 'promotion of mental health' or 'improving the quality of life' (p. vii).

According to Bond (1982), "(Prevention) presumes that disaster is impending in our lives and that our efforts should be focused upon its diversion.... Protecting ourselves from negative influences is, at most, a narrow perspective on the course of growth and well-being" (p. 5).

Although there are clear differences between prevention and promotion models, there is controversy over whether these are in fact different approaches to intervention.

The introduction of promotion as a procedurally and methodologically distinct intervention model posed a dilemma for prevention enthusiasts. Proponents of the tripartite prevention scheme were quick to argue that promotion is a special case of primary prevention (e.g., ADAMHA, 1981; Edelman & Mandle, 1986; Jason & Bogat, 1983; L'Abate & Young, 1988), but such a leap of reasoning seems faulty. There is considerable evidence indicating that prevention and promotion approaches differ considerably in their assumptions, presuppositions, and processes so as to make them conceptually and procedurally distinct. Rappaport (1981), for example, argued persuasively that the enhancement of competence and a sense of personal control is derived from a set of assumptions and beliefs at variance with the prevention of poor functioning. Similarly, Zautra and Sandler (1983) contrasted and illustrated the differences between models that focus on the prevention of distress compared to models that emphasize optimization of functioning. They noted that adoption of either model would be expected to produce quite different outcomes. Others as well have noted the fundamental differences in the underlying assumptions of promotion and prevention models and their implications for practice (e.g., Bond, 1982; Danish & D'Augelli, 1980, Hoke, 1968; Sanford, 1972; Seeman, 1989).

THREE MODELS OF INTERVENTION

Available material indicates the existence of three contrasting models of intervention–treatment, prevention, and promotion–each of which has distinctive characteristics and differential features (Cowen, 1985; Dunst, 1987; Dunst & Trivette, 1987a, 1988c; Hoke, 1968; Rappaport, 1981, 1987; Rappaport, Swift, & Hess, 1984; Stanley & Maddux, 1986; Zautra & Sandler, 1983). The term *intervention* is used broadly to mean a planned effort to alter or influence the course of development in an anticipated direction. The unique characteristics of the three models are shown in Table 4-1, and are described next.

Each of the models defines intervention quite differently. *Treatment* is defined as the management and provision of care (assistance, help, etc.) in order to eliminate, or minimize the negative effects of a disorder, problem, or disease. Interventions focus on the remediation or amelioration of an aberration or its consequences. *Prevention* is defined as the deterrence or hindrance of a problem, disorder, or disease. Interventions occur prior to the onset of negative functioning in order to reduce the incidence or prevalence of negative outcomes. *Promotion* is defined as the enhancement and optimization of positive functioning. Interventions focus on the acquisition of competence and capabilities that strengthen functioning and adaptive capacities.

Table 4-1 also shows the major features of the three intervention models and some of the outcomes that would be expected using each model. The three models are characterized by features that collectively represent the major emphasis and underlying assumptions of the interventive approach. Either implicit or explicit adoption of the differential characteristics would in turn be expected to produce differing outcomes that manifest themselves in the cognitive, behavior, and social-affective domains (Bond, 1982; Seeman, 1989).

Treatment model. The treatment model is perhaps best characterized as *corrective* in its orientation. Primary emphasis is typically placed on the *reduction* of negative effects associated with an identifiable problem or disability. The treatment model is *counteractive* in the sense that interventive actions attempt to overcome, or at least, neutralize the

Table 4-1. The Major Characteristics of Treatment, Prevention, and Promotion Models			
Characteristics	**Treatment**	**Prevention**	**Promotion**
Definition	Management and provision of care following the onset of a disorder, disease, disability, or problem	Deter, hinder, or forestall the occurence of problems or negative functioning	Enhance, bring about, and optimize positive growth and functioning
Intervention Focus	Remediation or amelioration of a disorder or disease or the consequences of associated problems	Avoidance or reduction in the prevalence or incidence of negative outcomes	Facilitate competence by enhancing capabilities that strengthen functioning
Differential Features	"Corrective" Orientation Reduction of Negative Effects Counteractive Deficit-Based	"Protection" Orientation Deter Occurrence of Negative Outcomes Reactive Weakness-Based	"Mastery" Orientation Develop Adaptive Capabilities/Competencies Proactive Strengths-Based
Examples of Outcomes	"Fragility" Appraisals Stress Reduction Elimination of Dysfunctional Behavior Minimization of Disability Complications	"Life-Threatening" Appraisals Stress Prevention Avoidance of Maladaptive Functioning Averting Disease	"Self-Efficacy" Appraisals Enhance Psychological Well-Being Enhancement of Adaptive Functioning Sense of Personal Control

effects of the presenting disorder or disability. This approach is *deficit-based* since it specifically targets the reduction or elimination of actual or inferred deficiencies of a person. This would be expected to result in *fragility appraisals* by the "patient" who must be treated for his or her condition or problem. That is, a person receiving treatment would likely see himself or herself as handicapped or weakened by the condition even if the disability or its consequences are not minimized or subdued. Other types of outcomes one would expect using treatment models include problem reduction, elimination of dysfunctional behaviors, correction of aberrations, and the minimization of complications and deterioration in functioning.

Prevention model. The primary orientation of the prevention model is *protection* against either actual or perceived events that are likely to result in negative reactions or outcomes. Major emphasis is placed on the *deterrence* or

forestalling of otherwise negative consequences (Cowen, 1985). This is accomplished by "reducing and/or coping with harmful or otherwise threatening events...(using)...*defense* as the primary orientation" (Zautra & Sandler, 1983, p. 39, emphasis added). Cowen (1985) characterized interventive actions that assume this stance as *reactive* because they attempt to avert problems and "short-circuit otherwise probably negative psychological effects" (p. 34). This approach is *weakness-based* since it presumes that people are basically vulnerable, and need to be protected or buffered from potentially damaging situations. Preventive actions based upon these characteristics communicate, sometimes implicitly and sometimes explicitly, that life is full of troubles, and life events constitute threats to one's health. Consequently, one would expect to see people make *life-threatening appraisals* in response to interventive actions that are preventive in orientation (Zautra & Sandler, 1983). A person participating in an intervention that takes this orientation will likely come to believe that he or she has a need to protect oneself from potentially or presently unnerving threats. Interventions that aim to deter negative outcomes would be expected to produce results like stress and anxiety circumvention, avoidance of maladaptive functioning, thwarting of distress or disease, and the warding off of other harmful reactions.

Promotion model. In contrast to treatment and prevention models that are both problem-oriented, the promotion model is best characterized as having a *mastery and optimization* orientation. Major emphasis is placed on the development, enhancement, and elaboration of a person's *competencies and capabilities* (Bond, 1982), particularly those that increase a sense of control over important aspects of one's life (Rappaport, 1981). Cowen (1985) called this approach *proactive* because it gives primacy to actions that support and strengthen functioning. Promotion efforts are *strengths-based* because they assume all people have strengths or the capacity to become competent (Rappaport, 1981). Moreover, by building on strengths rather than rectifying deficits, people become more adaptive in not only dealing with difficult life events but in setting growth-oriented goals and achieving personal aspirations. Operationalization of these characteristics conveys the message that people, *all* people, have the capacity to better themselves. Therefore, promotive interventions are likely to evoke *self-efficacy appraisals* (Rappaport, 1981; Zautra & Sandler, 1983; Stanley & Maddux, 1986). That is, a person participating in promotion interventions will likely come to believe that he or she has the capacity to master a wide range of development tasks and functions if afforded certain opportunities to learn. Other types of outcomes one would expect as a result of promotive interventions include enhanced

well-being and health, better adaptive functioning and social competence, and other positive indicators of personal and family growth and development.

The classificatory framework of intervention practices proposed by Hoke (1968) and elaborated upon in this chapter represents an alternative to the tripartite prevention scheme that has dominated thinking in the human services arena. This alternative framework considers prevention and treatment models more alike than different, and considers promotion and prevention models more different than alike. This contention is similar to positions advanced by Bond (1982), Danish and D'Augelli (1980), Rappaport (1981, 1987), Seeman (1989), and Zautra and Sandler (1983), but is different than that of Cowen (1985) who considered both prevention and promotion approaches alternative pathways to the same outcomes. Corroborative evidence from diverse but conceptually coherent lines of research converges to support our argument that the absence (prevention) of problems cannot be taken to mean the presence (promotion) of positive aspects of functioning. Relevant research studies are examined next.

RELATIONSHIPS BETWEEN POSITIVE AND NEGATIVE ASPECTS OF HUMAN FUNCTIONING

An implicit assumption underlying preventive interventions is that the absence of problems (negative functioning, stress, etc.) may be taken as evidence for the presence of positive functioning. This position is derived, in part, from yet another assumption in which health is considered a continuous variable with the absence of disease at one end of the continuum and the presence of healthy functioning at the other end of the continuum (see Antonovsky, 1981). This notion of health has been historically associated with Western thought (Seeman, 1989), and is a view that has been implicitly woven into the fabric of both treatment and preventive interventions. This perspective differs considerably from the definition of health formulated by the World Health Organization (WHO, 1964) in which health is not considered merely the absence of disease but the presence of complete physical, mental, and social well-being.

Empirically, if the position that health is a continuous variable is correct, one would expect to find evidence demonstrating strong *interdependencies* (covariation) between the absence of poor functioning and the presence of positive functioning (or vice versa), whereas the position advanced in this chapter with regard to the relationship between prevention and promotion models posits *independence* between negative and positive functioning. Investigative interest in the interdependence-independence relationships between psychological phenomenon has more than a 100-year history (see e.g., Beebe-Center, 1932). In recent years there has been renewed interest in the relationships between positive and negative aspects of functioning by investigators using instruments and measurement procedures that include specific sets of negative functioning items and specific sets of positive functioning items (Bradburn, 1969; Dunst, Trivette, Jodry, Morrow, & Hamer, 1988; Kammann & Fleet, 1983; Kanner, Coyne, Schaefer, & Lazarus, 1981; Orden & Bradburn, 1968; Reich & Zautra, 1983; Trivette, Dunst, Morrow, Jodry, & Hamer, 1988). Data from such scales allow direct tests of the interdependence-independence hypothesis. The findings from studies that have used these instruments yield corroborative evidence demonstrating that the positive and negative aspects of functioning are much more independent than interdependent, and that positive and negative aspects of functioning are differentially related to other aspects of functioning in a predictable manner.

INDEPENDENCE-INTERDEPENDENCE RELATIONSHIPS

The most extensive evidence supporting the independence hypothesis comes from studies of well-being, in which measures of both positive and negative affect are obtained from the same individuals and the nature of the relationship between the two types of affect discerned (e.g., Beiser, 1974; Harding, 1982). The results of these investigations were extensively reviewed and scrutinized by Diener (1984) who concluded that the *"absence of negative affect is not the same as the presence of positive affect"* (pp. 547, 549, emphasis added). In those studies in which negative and positive affect have been statistically correlated, a shared variance interpretation of the findings also supports the independence position. If the absence of problems is not associated with the presence of positive functioning, one would expect a very small amount of shared variance between the two functioning measures. Examination of the correlations between positive and negative affect show that only about 30% of the variability in one dimension of affect is related to variability in the other dimension (e.g., Brenner, 1975; Kammann, Christie, Irwin, & Dixon, 1979).

In our own research we have obtained positive and negative well-being measures (Bradburn, 1969; Bradburn & Caplovitz, 1965) on quite different samples of parents and prospective parents (pregnant women, parents of preschoolers with disabilities, and parents of young children without developmental delays), and consistently find very little covariation between negative and positive affect. The average amount of shared variance between these two well-being indices in five separate studies is only 7% (range = 3 to 12%), indicating that positive and negative affect are mostly independent aspects of psychological functioning.

Besides well-being, the independence between the negative and positive aspects of functioning has been studied in other behavioral areas as well. Orden and Bradburn (1968), for example, found only 20% shared variance between marital happiness and marital tensions. Similarly, Beiser (1974) found only 2% shared variance between negative affect and pleasurable feelings, and Watson and Pennebaker (1989) found that the absence of health complaints was only minimally related to positive health status. As noted by Rappaport (1990), "in studies of health, when high scores on indicators of wellness may indicate health, low scores do not necessarily indicate illness" and vice versa.

An interesting line of research by Kanner and his colleagues (Kanner, Coyne, Schaefer, & Lazarus,1981; Kanner, Feldman, Wein-berger, & Ford, 1987), studying the relationship between daily hassles and daily uplifts, provides evidence that the presence of irritating and frustrating day-to-day demands is only minimally related to their counterparts– uplifts (e.g., day-to-day experiences that are positive and desirable). In our own research using the Personal Assessment of Life Experiences Scale (Trivette et al., 1988) with expectant mothers, data similar to that obtained by Kanner et al.(1981) on hassles and uplifts were gathered in which judgments were made by respondents regarding whether different life events represented either positive or negative experiences. An analysis of the frequency of occurrence of positive and negative events showed less than 1% shared variance between the two measures. This finding indicated that the absence of negative life experiences did not necessarily mean that a person was experiencing positive life experiences.

Finally, in yet another part of our own

research, the relationship between the use of *reactive* and *proactive* coping strategies has been examined using the Personal Assessment of Coping Experiences Scale (Dunst et al., 1988) with a sample of pregnant women. Reactive strategies are ones used in response to difficult or stressful life events, and proactive strategies are ones used to evoke or prolong pleasurable or desirable life experiences. The shared variance between the total number of proactive and reactive coping strategies used by the subjects is only 9%, and the shared variance between the use of a range of different proactive and reactive techniques across different life events is only 14%.

Collectively, available evidence strongly demonstrates that positive and negative aspects of behavior are relatively independent, and that the absence of negative or unpleasant functioning does not mean the presence of positive or pleasurable behaviors.

DIFFERENTIAL RELATIONSHIPS IN BEHAVIOR FUNCTIONING

There is also a rich database showing that positive aspects of functioning tend to be related to other aspects of positive but not negative functioning, and that negative aspects of functioning tend to be related to other negative but not positive aspects of functioning (see Diener, 1984). Warr, Barter, and Brownbridge (1983), for example, found positive affect significantly correlated with desirable but not undesirable life events, and found negative affect significantly correlated with undesirable but not desirable life events. Similarly, Kanner et al. (1981) found daily hassles significantly related to negative but not positive affect, and daily uplifts significantly related to positive but not negative affect. In another relevant study, Harding (1982) reported significant correlations between physical and psychological indices of symptomatology and negative affect, but found no relationship between the absence of symptomatology and positive affect.

In our own research examining the differential relationships between positive and negative aspects of functioning, we have found similar results. In a study of pregnant women, for example, we found that use of proactive coping strategies was significantly correlated with positive but not negative affect, and use of reactive coping strategies was more highly cor-related with negative compared to positive affect. In addition, we found that negative life experiences were highly related to use of reactive coping strategies but were unrelated to positive coping techniques, and that positive experiences were highly related to use of proactive coping strategies but were unrelated to negative coping techniques.

Taken together, data regarding the differential relationships between sets of positive and negative functioning measures bolster the contention that absence of problems cannot be considered an index for the presence of positive aspects of functioning.

INDEPENDENT CONTRIBUTIONS OF NEGATIVE AND POSITIVE FUNCTIONING

Yet another set of findings provide further evidence that positive and negative aspects of functioning operate relatively independently, and make separate, incremental contributions to the relationship between positive and negative functioning as predictor variables, and other behavioral measures, as dependent variables. In the studies described next, hierarchical multiple regression techniques were used in which negative functioning was entered into the analysis first followed by the positive functioning measure. This strategy provides a way of assessing the extent to which negative aspects of functioning make contributions to the variability in other as-

pects of functioning. It also provides a way of discerning the contributions that positive aspects of functioning make to enhanced functioning beyond that accounted for by negative behavior functioning.

Kanner et al. (1987), using hassles and uplifts as independent measures and a set of seven adaptational measures as outcomes (e.g., depression, self-worth), found that in nearly every analysis, hassles accounted for a significant amount of variance in the outcomes, and uplifts accounted for additional significant amounts of variance in the outcome measures. In a similar study, Reich and Zautra (1983), used demands and desires as predictor variables and quality of life, positive and negative mood, and symptomatology as outcome measures. They found, for two separate samples of subjects, that demands accounted for significant amounts of variance in all eight sets of analyses, and desires accounted for additional significant amounts of variance in 6 of the 8 analyses.

In several investigations conducted in our own laboratory in which we had positive and negative functioning measures that could be used as independent measures, we conducted the same analyses as performed by Kanner et al. (1987) and Reich and Zautra (1983). In a study of parents of preschool aged children without handicaps, we found that both negative and positive affect made significant, incremental contributions to both anxiety and depression. As expected, negative affect was associated with higher levels of anxiety and depression, whereas the opposite was true for the relationship between positive affect and the two dependent measures. In a study of pregnant women also conducted in our laboratory, negative affect was associated with less intimacy and personal relationships, whereas positive affect was significantly related to the enhanced intimacy.

In this same study of pregnant women, a

particularly compelling set of findings was produced in the regression analyses of the relationship between reactive and proactive coping strategies and five dimensions of social support (frequency of contacts with personal network members, dependability of network members, frequency of use of social support, emotional ties with network members, and satisfaction with support (Dunst & Trivette, 1988b). In none of the analyses were reactive coping techniques related to any of the support measures, but in all of the analyses proactive techniques were significantly related to greater levels and amounts of social support.

SUMMARY

In summary, available evidence indicates that the absence of negative functioning or problems cannot be considered a necessary condition for arguing that a person's behavior will reflect positive functioning. Extrapolating from this evidence, a strong case can be made for the argument that the prevention of poor outcomes will not necessarily result in enhancement and strengthening of positive functioning. Certainly, comparative studies of the differential effects of promotion versus prevention interventions would provide a more direct test of the two major tenets presented in the introductory section of this chapter. But also certainly, the evidence argues against the position that strengthening of functioning has necessarily taken place when one prevents negative outcomes.

CONCLUSIONS

In the first section of the chapter, we pointed out that family support programs aim to support and strengthen functioning in ways that have empowering consequences. We noted, however, an apparent contradiction with the implied relationship between this aim and the call for use of prevention models as the interventive strategy for achieving the goals of such programs.

In the second section of the chapter, we described the differences in the assumptions and presupposition of treatment, prevention, and promotion models. In the third section, we reviewed evidence to support the argument that the absence (prevention) of negative outcomes could not be equated with the presence (promotion) of positive aspects of functioning.

When one considers the information presented in the first section of this chapter in relationship to the information presented in the second and third sections, one begins to see that there is a greater congruence between the aims of family support programs and the goals of promotion models than there is between the respective goals of family support programs and prevention models. Both theoretically and empirically, evidence indicates a need to "rethink" at least some of the assumptions of family support programs.

There is one major implication from the material in this chapter. If one aim of family support programs is to support and strengthen family functioning, this is more likely to occur if practitioners adopt promotion models for structuring interventive actions. Our rationale is simple. The evidence points to the differentially produced positive effects that are likely to accrue from use of promotion and enhancement actions.

As the family support movement continues to grow and break new ground, it is incumbent upon scholars and practitioners to critically examine and scrutinize their efforts to be sure what they believe is congruent with what they do. In this chapter we have taken a first step in that direction.

III

INDIVIDUALIZED FAMILY SUPPORT PLANS

The two chapters in this section describe a particular approach for developing Individualized Family Support Plans (IFSPs). Chapter 5 describes the development of IFSPs within the context of the family-centered model outlined in Chapter 1 (see Dunst, Trivette, & Deal, 1988). Step-by-step procedures for conceptualizing and operationalizing the IFSP process are described in Chapter 6. Both chapters include examples of portions of actual IFSPs that have been developed in our work with families.

An important consideration addressed in both chapters is the fact that the process of developing and implementing IFSPs is substantially more important than is the product. This is often an overlooked (and sometimes ignored) consideration, and is at least one reason why human services practitioners and programs lose sight of the intent and purpose of developing and implementing family support plans. Effective and efficient IFSPs are ones that promote and enhance the process of identifying family needs and mobilization of resources and supports to meet needs. The IFSP product is simply the tool for documenting what happened and ascertaining whether or not efforts to mobilize resources and supports were successful. It is of paramount importance that one continually remind himself or herself that process rather than product should guide the development of IFSPs that are flexible and responsive to each family's unique circumstances.

CHAPTER 5

A Flexible and Functional Approach to Developing Individualized Family Support Plans

Angela G. Deal, Carl J. Dunst & Carol M. Trivette

Constructing any type of building begins with some idea of what the structure will look like and what purpose it will serve. Architects take such ideas and use them to design and draw up plans for the building. These architectural drawings are the blueprints that builders depend upon for erecting the structure. Without the benefit of blueprints, the completed building may not be or do what the originator had in mind.

Building family support programs as well begins with some idea of what the programs ought to look like and what purposes they should serve (Dunst, Trivette, & Deal, 1988; Hobbs, Dokecki, Hoover-Dempsey, Moroney, Shayne, & Weeks, 1984; Kagan, Powell, Weissbourd, & Zigler, 1987; Pooley & Littell, 1986). The architects of such programs formulate plans that guide program development and implementation. These plans serve as blueprints for building support systems and mobilizing community resources that will result in the intended outcomes. Without the benefit of blueprints, program building efforts may not have anticipated impacts.

The approach to developing and implementing IFSPs described in this chapter is based upon principles and guidelines for practice designed to support and strengthen family functioning (Hobbs et al., 1984). It has been developed within the context of a consumer-driven family-centered model of assessment and intervention (Dunst, Trivette, &

Deal, 1988). The process for developing IFSPs is designed to be both flexible and functional in order to be continually responsive to the concerns and needs expressed by families. The format for writing IFSPs is flexible and functional to insure that the plan reflects accurately the transactions that occur between the members of family's social network designed to mobilize resources to meet needs.

A FAMILY-CENTERED ASSESSMENT AND INTERVENTION MODEL

The family-centered model and the IFSP process are based upon a set of conceptual underpinnings and principles for practice that guide resource mobilization to meet family needs. This model is briefly described next to place the approach to developing IFSPs in proper perspective.

CONCEPTUAL BASES

The implementation of the assessment and intervention model is guided by a number of beliefs that emphasize a proactive, highly responsive approach to working with families. First, major emphasis is placed on both enabling and empowering families (Dunst, 1986a, 1987, 1988; Dunst & Trivette, 1987a, 1988c). Enabling families means creating opportunities for family members to become more com-

This chapter appeared in *Infants and Young Children*, 1989, *1*(4), 32-43. Reprinted by permission of the publisher.

petent, independent, and self-sustaining with respect to their abilities to mobilize their social networks to get needs met and attain desired goals (Hobbs et al., 1984). For example, assisting families in meeting needs provides experiences and opportunities for acquiring skills that should prove useful as part of future efforts to obtain resources to meet new needs and challenges. Empowering families means carrying out interventions in a manner in which family members acquire a sense of control over their own developmental course as a result of their efforts to meet needs (Dunst, 1987; Rappaport, 1981; Rappaport, 1987). That is, as families experience success in accessing resources, confidence in their own abilities to handle future challenges is greatly enhanced.

Second, major emphasis is placed on strengthening both families and their natural support networks, and neither usurping their decision-making power, nor supplanting their personal social support networks with professional services (Hobbs et al., 1984). Strengthening families means supporting and building upon the things the family already does well as a basis for promoting and encouraging the mobilization of resources among the family's personal social network members (Stinnett & DeFrain, 1985b).

Third, major emphasis is placed on enhancing families' acquisitions of a wide variety of competencies that permit them to become capable of meeting needs through mobilization of their support networks. Enhancing the acquisition of competencies means providing families with the necessary information and skills for them to become more self-sustaining and thus better able to promote personal well-being, as well as have positive influences in other areas of family functioning (Dunst, 1985, 1986c; Dunst & Trivette, 1987a, 1987b, 1988c, 1988d). Enabling, empowering, and strengthening families constitute the major goals of the family-centered assessment and intervention process.

PRINCIPLES FOR PRACTICE

The family-centered assessment and intervention model is based upon four principles derived from a converging body of empirical and clinical evidence (Dunst, Trivette, & Deal, 1988) regarding the essential components and elements of effective helping (Dunst, 1987; Dunst & Trivette, 1987a, 1988c).

Principle 1. Base intervention efforts on family identified needs and aspirations in order to have the greatest positive influences on child, parent, and family functioning.

This principle states that the greatest impact on child, parent, and family functioning is most likely to occur when interventions are based upon the needs, aspirations, and desires that a family considers important, and thus deserving of time and energy. It is based upon evidence that establishes a functional relationship between needs (desires, aspirations, personal projects, etc.) and a number of aspects of family functioning, including well-being and adherence to professionally prescribed regimens (Dunst, Leet, & Trivette, 1988). One theme that has surfaced repeatedly as part of both our research and clinical experience is that interventions implemented in response to family identified needs are more likely to have second and higher order influences (Bronfenbrenner, 1979) on a number of aspects of parent, child, and family functioning (Dunst, 1986b; Dunst & Trivette, 1987b, 1988a).

Principle 2. Build upon existing family strengths and capabilities (family functioning style) as a basis for promoting the family's ability to mobilize resources in order to enhance successful efforts toward meeting needs.

The second principle is derived from evidence regarding the capabilities that constitute family strengths, and how family functioning style influences the ability to deal effectively with normative and non-normative life events and promotes growth in all family members (Dunst, Trivette, & Deal, 1988). The importance of this step in the intervention process cannot be stressed enough. Another theme that has evolved from our work with families is that knowledge of family strengths and capabilities provides the basis for building upon the things a family already does well, and that doing so is more likely to result in the family's investment of time and energy to mobilize resources.

Principle 3. Strengthen the family's personal social network as well as promote utilization of untapped sources of aid and assistance in order to insure the availability and adequacy of resources for meeting needs.

The third principle states that informal support networks are the primary source of resources for meeting needs, and to the extent possible, one should build and strengthen natural support systems as a major way of meeting needs. This principle is based upon evidence that shows the most powerful benefits of support are realized if aid and assistance comes primarily from informal sources (Dunst & Trivette, 1988a, 1988d). Our experience tells us that many human services practitioners fail to consider the full range of social support options available to families, and the tendency to "overprofessionalize" services to children and their families. A rule of thumb to follow in mobilizing resources to meet needs is never provide aid or assistance that the family can obtain from sources of support closer to the family unit.

Principle 4. Employ help-giving behaviors that

promote the family's acquisition and use of competencies and skills necessary to mobilize and secure resources in order to enhance the family's ability to become more self-sustaining with respect to meeting its needs.

The fourth principle states that the family's use and acquisition of competencies for mobilizing resources is most likely to occur when professionals employ help-giving behaviors that create opportunities for family members to display competencies and become better able to meet their needs. The ability to attain this goal is guided by a proactive approach to working with families, a shift and expansion in the roles professionals employ in working with families, and a set of guidelines that are both enabling and empowering (Dunst, Trivette, & Deal, 1988). This principle is derived from evidence which demonstrates that different ways of helping have differential effects on a person's ability to become more self-sustaining (Dunst & Trivette, 1987a, 1988c). Another consistent theme that has surfaced repeatedly as part of both our research and clinical experiences with mobilizing resources to meet family needs is that it is not just a matter of whether needs are met, but rather the manner in which mobilization of resources and support occurs that is a major determinant of empowering consequences (Dunst, 1986b; Dunst & Trivette, 1987a, 1988c). To be both enabling and empowering in a way that promotes a family's capabilities and competencies, the family must be actively involved in the process of identifying and mobilizing resources, and interventionists must derive personal and intrinsic gratification and enjoyment from seeing others become more capable and competent (Maple, 1977).

Figure 5-1 graphically shows the four operational components of the model and relationships among the components. Family needs and aspirations, family strengths and

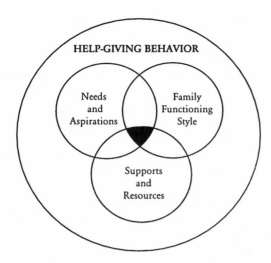

Figure 5-1. Four Major Components of the Family-Centered Assessment and Intervention Model.

capabilities (family functioning style), and social support and resources are seen as separate but interdependent elements of the assessment and intervention process. The help-giving behaviors used by professionals are seen as the ways in which families are enabled and empowered to acquire and use competencies to procure supports and to mobilize resources for meeting needs.

The process of enabling and empowering families can be thought of as a system of interlocking gears (needs and aspirations, family strengths and capabilities, support and resources) that must be properly aligned if motion and energy are to be passed from one gear to another. Each gear in the system serves a specific function, and when properly adjusted generates energy and power that makes the parts of the whole contribute to optimal efficiency.

The dynamic processes that make up the family system can be likened to those on a touring bike where, at any given time, one gear plays a more important role, but it is still the particular alignment among all gears that

generates momentum, speed, energy, and power. The latter set of characteristics are primarily influenced by two factors: the terrain (developmental course) that is being traversed by the family and the capabilities necessary for the family to drive the system forward in a positive direction.

Conceptualizing the interrelationship among needs and aspirations, strengths and capabilities, and resources and support as an interlocking set of gears which forms a system that generates energy and power requires a shift in professionals' work with families. The goal is not for the professional to take control of the system and define the family's developmental course. Rather, the goal becomes one of promoting the family's ability to negotiate alignment of the gears comprising the system in a way that makes the system operate as efficiently as possible.

WRITING FLEXIBLE AND FUNCTIONAL IFSPs

The family-centered assessment and intervention model described above has been used to develop both a process and format for developing and writing IFSPs. The process is intended to be continually responsive to the changing needs of children and families. The format for developing and implementing IFSPs is both flexible and functional, and it is designed as a blueprint for capturing the details of what is accomplished as part of mobilizing resources to meet family needs.

As part of our efforts to help families identify their needs and mobilize resources for meeting needs, we have found it useful to distinguish between static and fluid intervention plans as a basis for proposing a more flexible and functional approach for developing and implementing plans to meet family-level needs. A static plan is one that does not permit or at least discourages frequent changes and modifications once goals, methods, and outcomes have been specified. In contrast, a fluid plan is one that not only permits but encourages frequent modifications as a result of the changes that occur in a family, including the situations that influence family behavior, and any other conditions that affect child and family functioning. A fluid plan is one that is responsive to the changing needs of families, and therefore is both flexible and functional.

GUIDING PRINCIPLES

The process of developing IFSPs is guided by a number of principles that enable, empower, support, and strengthen family functioning. The principles are based upon conceptual and pragmatic considerations described elsewhere (Dunst, 1985; Hobbs et al., 1984; Shelton, Jeppson, & Johnson, 1987).

1. *Development of the IFSP is done within the context of collaboration and partnerships between the family and human services practitioners.* Collaboration means working together toward a common goal. Partnerships means the pooling of resources which are used in pursuit of some common or joint interest. Collaborative and partnership arrangements between the family and human services practitioners increase the likelihood that, as a team, mobilization of resources will occur in a manner that achieves stated intentions because of shared responsibility (McGonigel & Garland, 1988).

2. *Any and all information included in the IFSP is done so with the explicit permission and authorization of the family.* The content of the IFSP need not be intrusive or violate confidentiality if the family, as architect

of the IFSP, retains final decision-making power with respect to its content. This principle recognizes the family's rightful role to decide what is important for the family unit and individual family members, and that the family alone bears the responsibility for deciding its developmental course to the extent that the well-being and rights of all family members are protected. The human services practitioner helps the family make informed decisions by providing whatever information, aid, assistance, etc. is necessary for the family to choose what it considers is in its best interest (Dunst & Paget, 1991).

3. *The development and revision of the IFSP should be responsive to the broad-based needs of families, although no human services practitioner or program should be expected to offer support to meet all family needs.* This principle includes two important interrelated elements of effective helping. The first pertains to the fact that any and all concerns and needs of families must be attended to by the human services practitioner, otherwise one is likely to communicate a lack of interest and concern regarding family needs. "To be effective (in work with families), service providers must want to hear what parents have to say and must be truly interested in understanding the family's concerns and needs" (Stoneman, 1985). The second pertains to a major role human services practitioners must play in interactions with families. Although no one person or program should provide or be expected to provide all the resources and services to meet family needs, human services providers should nonetheless *assist* families in learning about and accessing needed resources. To assist families, one *links* them with other support systems which they can then mobilize to procure

needed resources. Human services practitioners who perform this function help families become more knowledgeable about resources and service options; create opportunities for families to make informed decisions about the assets and limitations of different options; link families with desired resources and services, and promote and enhance the family's acquisition of competencies necessary to mobilize resources to meet needs.

4. *Both the development and implementation of the IFSP should emphasize promotion of the competence of the family and interdependence with members of the family's community.* Competence refers to the capacity to identify needs, to assess options for meeting needs, and mobilize resources required to support and strengthen family functioning. Interdependence refers to the joint efforts among family members and between the family and members of its formal and informal social network designed to promote well-being and strengthen the functioning of all network members. Unless needs are met in a way that promotes acquisition of a family's knowledge and competencies so that there are discernible changes in the family life and its personal social network, the interventions can not be considered truly successful.

These four basic, but far reaching principles guide the process of developing and writing IFSPs. The particular format that has evolved from our work which guides the development and implementation process is described next.

A FORMAT FOR WRITING IFSPs

The IFSP form is divided into two parts. Part A includes the following background information: (1) the name of the human services practitioner who will function in a number of roles intended to empower families with the knowledge and skills necessary to identify needs and mobilize resources, (2) a statement of the child's strengths and current levels of functioning, (3) a statement of the family's unique strengths and intrafamily resources, and (4) a cumulative record of the specific services, programs, community agencies, and other community supports and programs that the child and family has previously employed or is currently using to access resources to meet needs.

Part B of the plan is the "working" document that guides needs specification and resource mobilization. It includes: (1) a list of family identified needs, aspirations, desires, etc. in order of priority, (2) a series of statements regarding the sources of support and resources that will be mobilized to meet needs, (3) a series of statements regarding the actions that will be taken by the family and human services practitioner to mobilize resources, and (4) procedures for evaluating the extent to which needs are met.

The information that is gathered as part of writing the IFSP is shown in Table 5-1. The *Background Information* section includes data and descriptors useful for depicting unique features of both the child and family and the support systems used to meet child and family needs. Space is provided for recording the child and family's name and the name of the human service practitioner, child behavior and development (strengths and capabilities, current levels of functioning), family functioning style (strengths and capabilities, intrafamily resources), and community support services (informal, formal). The *Intervention Plan* section provides the framework for describing what is to be accomplished; who is going to do what to mobilize resources, what is to be done to attain

Table 5-1. Framework for Developing Individualized Family Support Plan	
Background Information	Intervention Plan

Identifying Information
  A. Child/Family's Name
  B. Human Services Practitioner
	Needs
	  A. Child
	  B. Siblings
	  C. Parents
	  D. Family

Child Behavior and Development
  A. Strengths and Capabilities
  B. Current Levels of Functioning
	E. Other
	
	Sources of Support/Resources
	  A. Intrafamily
	  B. Informal

Family Functioning Style
  A. Strengths and Capabilities
  B. Intrafamily Resources
	C. Community
	  D. Formal
	
	Course of Action
	  A. Family
	  B. Human Services Practitioner

Community Support Services
  A. Informal
  B. Formal
	Evaluation
	  A. Goal Attainment
	  B. Satisfaction

stated intentions, and how effective actions were in accomplishing outcomes.

The particular *Intervention Plan* section of the IFSP described here is physically formatted in a 28cm x 43cm "booklet" that allows the human services practitioner to keep a running account of the needs, sources of support, and actions taken to mobilize resources to meet needs (see Figure 5-2). The process of writing the plan consists of the following five steps:

1. *Record the date on which the need was identified.* Family identified needs and desires are recorded continuously as they are identified during interactions with family members. They are simply listed on the IFSP in order of priority which reflects the family's desire to take actions necessary to meet needs. Recording needs in this fashion provides a cumulative record of the particular projects and aspirations that constituted the targets of intervention by the family and service provider. The sim-

plicity of this recording system insures that *all* concerns are documented since no elaborate plan need to be written at this or any point in the IFSP process.

2. *Write the needs statement in terms of both what is to occur (process) and what is expected to be accomplished (outcome) as a result of actions to obtain needed resources.* Needs, goals, aspirations, desires, etc. are written as *in order to* statements so they are functionally based and easily understood. Something is done *in order to* have something else achieved or attained (e.g., Mother will obtain additional information about "John's" genetic disorder in order to learn more about its implications for future development). We have found that both child- and family-level needs can easily be stated in this format. All needs statements are phrased in proactive, competency-enhancing outcomes to reflect the positive stance taken toward children and families. It has been our experience that regard-

less of the need or specific family situation, *ALL* needs can be stated in this manner.

3. *Specify the source(s) of support that will be used to obtain needed resources and the particular aid or assistance that will be procured from each source.* The individual(s) or support system(s) who will be accessed to obtain needed resources (aid, assistance, advice, etc.), and the particular help or aid that they will provide are listed as succinctly as possible (e.g., Dr. Will B., Genetic Counseling). To the extent appropriate, the sources of support/resources that are listed include individual family members, personal social network members, and community and formal support systems.

4. *Specify the actions that will be taken to mobilize the support sources to obtain needed resources.* The "steps" that will be taken to mobilize resources to meet needs are listed for both the family and human services practitioner. The actions are stated in terms of what will be done by each "partner" to actualize the plan. Doing so emphasizes shared responsibility (partnership) between the family and human services practitioner. Our experience tells us that by stating what each partner will do, the likelihood of resource mobilization occurring in a timely manner is increased considerably.

5. *Evaluate progress toward resource mobilization in terms of both goal attainment and family satisfaction.* The method for evaluating the effectiveness of the IFSP assesses the degree to which both actions result in resource mobilization (i.e., goal attainment) and the family's satisfaction with the process and outcome. Each and every contact with the family (face-to-face, phone, etc.) can be used to evaluate progress toward resource mobilization and goal attainment. The family is simply asked whether or not they have had the opportunity to do "so-and-so," and how they feel about goal attainment and/or progress toward the stated intentions. The following rating scale is used for assessing the effectiveness of implementation efforts for each needs statement:

Child_____Parent_____ Human Services Practitioner_____										
Date	Need/Outcome Statement	Source of Support/Resource	Course of Action	Evaluation Date						

Fig. 5-2. The Physical Layout of the Intervention Plan Section of the Individualized Family Support Plan.

1.... No longer a need, goal, or project.
2.... Situation unchanged; still a need goal, or project.
3.... Implementation begun; still a need, goal, or project.
4.... Outcome partially attained or accomplished.
5.... Outcome accomplished or attained, but not to the family's satisfaction.
6.... Outcome mostly accomplished or attained to the family's satisfaction.
7.... Outcome completely accomplished or attained to the family's satisfaction.

This simple and relatively straightforward evaluation scheme has proved to have general utility for assessing the effectiveness of the IFSP without the need to develop separate evaluation criteria for each outcome statement.

CASE EXAMPLE

Table 5-2 shows an example of both a child-level and family-level needs statement that is written in the format just described. The examples are taken from an actual IFSP written with a mother who recently became separated from her husband. The mother has a 3-year-old daughter and a 20-month-old daughter, and is pregnant with her third child. The family became involved in our program because the youngest child has a visual impairment. A total of 16 needs were identified and addressed during a four-month intervention period. The examples shown in Table 5-2 are representative of the general foci of the collaborative efforts between the family and human services practitioner. The child-level need was identified by the mother because of her concern about not being able to carry "Sara" as her pregnancy progressed. Sara's ability to pull-to-stand and independently cruise around the room increased within two months after

the need was first identified. The family-level need was identified because the family, already living in a crowded apartment, would need additional space once the new baby was born. At the present time, the mother and human services practitioner are continuing to pursue options to meet this particular need.

BENEFITS AND IMPLICATIONS

The development of the IFSP process described in this chapter evolved within the context of a number of model demonstration programs and special projects designed to identify the best ways to support and strengthen family functioning. Both the families and staff who have participated in the development and field testing of the IFSP have reported numerous benefits that are not realized when less flexible and more static approaches are used to developing intervention plans. Several of the comments made by *staff* who have used the IFSP process and written format have included the following:

- "This approach provides a picture of the partnership relationship between families and professionals."
- "It actually documents what really is important to the family."
- "It keeps me focused on the things that are going on with the family."
- "This approach makes it clear who is in control of making decisions about what is needed by the child and family."

The families who agreed to participate in the field testing of the IFSP approach have reported personal benefits as well. Several of the comments made by these *families* have included:

- "It makes me feel like I'm really accomplishing things for my family."
- "This approach helps me focus on the

Table 5-2. Illustrative Examples of Individualized Family Support Plan Activities

Child-Level Activity	Family-Level Activity
1. Needs Identification	**1. Needs Identification**
2/1/88 S. will be provided increased opportunities to cruise along furniture to promote independent walking	3/1/88 Family will explore alternative housing opportunities in order to find larger accommodations for the mother, the children, and new infant
2. Source of Support and Resources	**2. Source of Support and Resources**
Mother-Physically arrange apartment to encourage cruising Human services practitioner-Provide information regarding intervention strategies Family and friends- Provide encouragement to S. to cruise while providing child care	Family, friends, and neighbors-information about available apartment or house to rent Newspaper-Classified section on house or apartment rentals Local reality company-Listing of rental housing Public Housing Authority-Information regarding eligibility and availability of public housing
3. Course of Action	**3. Course of Action**

Mother
  A. Position furniture so S. can reach without obstacles
  B. Place toys with sound just beyond S.'s reach to encourage her
  C. Verbally encourage S. to cruise and praise for her attempts
  D. Demostrate strategies for family and friends regarding methods to encourage S. to cruise
 	
Human services practitioner
  A. Discuss intervention strategies with mother regarding arrangement of furniture and techniques to encourage cruising
  B. Provide feedback to the mother as she demonstrates techniques
  C. Demonstrate strategies to other family and friends, as requested by mother
	Mother
	  A. Ask extended family members, friends, and neighbors about their knowledge of available rental housing
	  B. Obtain local newspaper and review listings for available rental housing
	  C. Call local realty company to inquire about listings or available housing for rent
	
	Human services practitioner
	  A. Will call Public Housing Authority to obtain eligibility information and availability of housing
	  B. Share information with family

4. Evaluation	**4. Evaluation**
2/15/88 Progress proceeding (3)* 3/01/88 Partially attained (4) 3/15/88 Mostly attained (6) 4/01/88 Accomplished	3/15/88 Situation unchanged (2) 4/01/88 Progress proceeding (3) 5/10/88 Partially attained (4)

* See text for explanations of ratings.

things that my family can do and not what we cannot do."
- "It helps me see who the people are that can help me when I need it."
- "This plan changes as my family's needs change."

Collectively, these comments reflect the fact that our approach to developing and writing IFSPs yields practical and personal benefits that otherwise might not be realized using other approaches to developing family-level intervention plans. We are currently completing an empirical investigation designed to document the increased efficiency of our IFSP process compared to the static framework that had been used prior to the implementation of the more flexible and functional approach to developing and writing family support plans. The results from this study should provide additional support concerning the usefulness of developing IFSPs in the manner described in this chapter.

The IFSP approach to identifying and meeting family needs described in this chapter has been found to be particularly effective in our work with families, and represents at least one viable system for developing, implementing, and evaluating family support plans. To be effective in work with families, we must be both flexible and functional in the ways in which we identify family concerns and interests and intervene to meet needs. Family support plans *MUST* reflect this flexibility and functionality if human services practitioners are to be continually responsive to changes in the family system. Family-level intervention plans that meet these criteria can serve as blueprints for supporting and strengthening family functioning. As both architects and builders, the family and human services practitioner can go about building support systems to meet needs in ways that enhance parent, family, and child competence. To the extent that these outcomes are realized, the intervention efforts may be considered effective.

CHAPTER 6

A Family-Centered Approach to Developing Individualized Family Support Plans

Carl J. Dunst & Angela G. Deal

FAMILY-CENTERED assessment and intervention practices place major emphasis on supporting and strengthening family functioning as part of developing Individualized Family Support Plans (IFSPs). It is important to note what is and is not a *family-centered* assessment practice. It *does not* mean assessing marital relationships, family dynamics, family stress or dysfunctional patterns, or any other aspects of the family system that generally falls within the purview of family therapy (e.g., Minuchian, 1974). It *does* mean assessing child and family needs and family strengths and capabilities related to meeting those needs. It also means assessing needs and strengths from a family's perspective with assistance and guidance from professionals. Additionally, it means the use of a needs-based rather than categorical or service-based approach to assessment and resource mobilization (Hobbs, 1975), and a positive and proactive rather than a pathological or deficit approach to assessment and service delivery (Dokecki & Heflinger, 1989; Hobbs et al., 1984).

These various features of a family-centered approach indicate a need to make a major shift in the ways in which we have typically assessed and intervened with children and their families (see e.g., Dunst, Trivette, & Deal, 1988). One approach for making such a shift is described in this chapter. This approach has evolved from efforts that aims to support and strengthen family functioning using family-centered assessment and intervention practices (e.g., Deal, Dunst, & Trivette, 1989; Dunst, 1987, 1989; Dunst & Leet, 1987; Dunst & Trivette, 1989; Dunst, Trivette, & Deal, 1988; Dunst, Trivette, & Mott, 1990; Trivette, Dunst, Deal, Hamer, & Propst, 1990).

A FAMILY-CENTERED MODEL FOR ASSESSING FAMILY NEEDS, SUPPORTS AND STRENGTHS

The model described in this chapter states that the goals of assessment and intervention are: (1) to identify family needs, (2) locate the informal and formal supports and resources to meet these needs, and (3) help families identify and use their strengths and capabilities to obtain required resources in ways that strengthen family functioning (Dokecki & Heflinger, 1989; Dunst, Trivette, & Deal, 1988; Hobbs et al., 1984). This simple and rather straightforward model helps focus assessment specifically on identification of family needs, supports and strengths that can be used to meet those needs, and not on any other aspect of family functioning.

OVERVIEW OF THE MODEL

The cornerstone of the family-centered model is the Individualized Family Support Plans (IFSP). An IFSP is a blueprint for guiding resource mobilization designed to meet child and family needs. The model includes eight elements that, taken together, lead to the development and implementation of IFSPs in ways that should have family strengthening and empowering consequences (Hobbs et al., 1984; Rappaport, 1981, 1987). The eight elements are:

1. *Family Concerns*: Areas of interest or importance related to the well-being and functioning of the family unit or individual family members (e.g., Parental concerns about the implications of their child's disability on future development).

2. *Family Needs*: Judgments regarding the desire or necessity for resources that will be responsive to concerns (e.g., Request for professional opinion about the child's likelihood of making developmental progress).

3. *Outcome Statement*: A statement of what will be done to procure a resource or support (process) in order to meet the identified need or concern (outcome) (e.g., Parents will schedule a developmental assessment in order to obtain information necessary to understand their child's potential for developmental progress).

4. *Resources and Supports*: Types and source of assistance, advice, information, etc. necessary to address needs and respond to concerns (e.g., Early childhood professional will conduct a child assessment and provide information to the family about the child's developmental prognosis).

5. *Courses of Action*: Steps that will be taken in order for the family to obtain necessary resources and supports to meet needs (e.g., Parents will contact an early childhood professional to schedule an assessment. Parents will share their knowledge of their child's development with the early child-

hood professional. Parents and professional will collaboratively participate in the child's assessment. Professional will share opinion about implications for future progress. Parents and professional will discuss and identify appropriate intervention targets.)

6. *Family Strengths*: Knowledge, skills, and capabilities of the family unit and individual family members that are used to identify needs and procure necessary resources and supports to meet needs (e.g., Parents will describe their desire and reasons for wanting a developmental assessment of their child).

7. *Partnership*: Collaboration between a family and a professional using agreed upon roles to obtain necessary resources and supports (e.g., Pooling developmental assessment information [professional] and knowledge of the child [parent] in order to decide upon appropriate intervention targets).

8. *Evaluation*: Determination of the extent to which resources and supports were obtained and to the family's satisfaction (e.g., Whether or not the assessment process yielded information and guidance that the family felt adequately addressed their concerns and desires).

Figure 6-1 shows the relationship between these eight elements, how those elements are put into writing as part of an IFSP *(outcome statements, resources and supports, courses of action)*, how evaluation of interventive actions feed back and influence changes in family concerns/desires, and how enhancement and promotion of family competence (empowerment, sense-of-control, self-efficacy, well-being, etc.) feed back and strengthen family functioning.

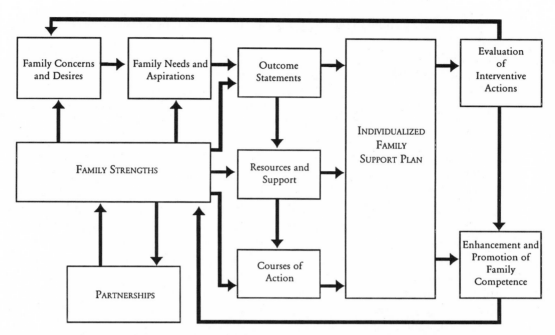

Fig. 6-1. Family-Centered Intervention Model for Developing Individualized Family Support Plans.

FAMILY STRENGTHS

Family strengths are viewed as the most fundamental element of the model, and, as defined above, include the knowledge, skills, and competencies of a family as manifested in the cognitive, attitudinal, and behavioral domains (Seeman, 1989). More concretely and specifically, family strengths include the capabilities of individual family members and the family unit as demonstrated vis a vis the ability to recognize concerns, identify needs, specify desired outcomes, mobilize resources, and take action to procure support and resources. In addition to influencing the ability to identify needs and mobilize resources to meet needs, family strengths are in turn influenced by at least two other aspects of the assessment and interventive process. First, partnerships between families and professionals are seen as a primary context for (a) assisting families to recognize their capabilities and (b) creating opportunities for families to use existing com-

petencies as well as learn new skills that can be used to mobilize resources to meet needs. Second, enhancement and promotion of family competence from successful efforts at mobilizing resources are seen as the mechanisms for further strengthening of family functioning leading to empowering consequences.

Other considerations that need to be taken into account as part of making family-centered assessment and intervention practices strengths-oriented include the following:

1. First, it must be recognized that all families have strengths and that these strengths are unique and depend upon the family's beliefs, cultural backgrounds, ethnicity, socio-economic backgrounds, and so forth.
2. Second, the failure of a family or individual family member to display competence must not be viewed as a deficit within the family system or family member, but rather the failure of social systems

and institutions (e.g., human services programs) to create opportunities for competencies to be displayed or learned.

3. Third, work with families must be approached in ways that focus and build on the positive aspects of functioning, rather than seeing families as being "broken" and always "needing to be fixed."

4. Fourth, a shift must be made away from the use of either treatment or prevention models toward the adoption of promotion and enhancement models which are more consistent with the aim of strengthening family functioning (Dunst, Trivette, & Mott, 1990; Stanley & Maddux, 1986; Zautra & Sandler, 1983).

5. Fifth, the goal of intervention must not be seen as "doing for people" but rather strengthening functioning in ways that make families more capable and competent and less and not more dependent upon professionals for help (Dunst, 1987; Maple, 1977).

PRAGMATIC CONSIDERATIONS

Several additional features and characteristics of our approach to assessment and intervention should be briefly mentioned to place our model in proper perspective.

1. First, the model is designed to be a *responsive, flexible, and fluid process* for gathering, exchanging, and employing information for the purpose of identifying family needs and strengths and the resources to meet needs. It is unrealistic to expect that a necessary understanding of a family's situation can be obtained from a single or even several contacts with a family. Assessment and intervention practices need to be flexible, fluid and everchanging so as to be responsive to the changing needs of a family. This means, for example, that

IFSPs must be able to be continually revised and updated on an ongoing basis in response to changes in a family's situation.

2. Second, the process is *highly individualized*, and is shaped by the family's desires and priorities for their child and their family as a whole. Both assessment and intervention practices are driven by family concerns and priorities (Dunst & Leet, 1987; Dunst, Leet, & Trivette, 1988), and focus on those aspects of family life and functioning determined as important by the family itself. Concretely, this means that assessment and intervention practices are shaped by a family's situation rather than a family being made to "fit" predetermined and static assessment and intervention processes.

3. Third, the approach to assessment and intervention *values and accepts* a family's personal and cultural beliefs. Assessment and intervention practices are done in a way that respects the family's cultural background, the family's willingness to want to share information, the family's desire to participate in the intervention process, etc. Full disclosure of why information is being requested, how it will be used, who will be privied to assessment and intervention information, etc. is done at the very outset, and is continually reiterated as a way of insuring that the assessment and intervention process does not become either reactive or intrusive.

We have described elsewhere principles-for-practice that guide implementation of the family-centered assessment and intervention process (Deal, Dunst, & Trivette, 1989; Dunst, Trivette, & Deal, 1988; Trivette et al., 1990). Johnson, McGonigel and Kaufmann (1989) describe as well helpful principles underlying the IFSP process. The reader is referred to these sources for a discussion of other important considerations as part of family-centered assessment and intervention practices.

ASSESSMENT AND INTERVENTION PRACTICES

The material presented in this section is intended to serve as a framework for guiding assessment and intervention practices leading to the development and implementation of family-centered IFSPs. Major emphasis is placed upon the procedural understanding of each element necessary to link assessment, intervention, and evaluation practices. Implementation of the model as depicted in Figure 6-1, and as described next, is intended to have enabling and empowering consequences and family strengthening influences (see Dunst, Trivette, & Deal, 1988; Dunst, Trivette, & Mott, 1990).

FAMILY CONCERNS

Areas of interest and importance to individual family members and the family unit are what generally bring people to the attention of professionals. These matters are often manifested as "concerns." Concerns are operationally defined as the perception or indication of a discrepancy between *what is* and *what ought to be*. That is, there must be an awareness on the part of a family and its members that their situation is sufficiently different from what they want it to be so as to seek assistance from others or take action or see the need for help or assistance. Bradshaw (1972) and McKillip (1987) both discuss the different types of situations that lead people to indicate that things are "not as they want them to be" (see also Dunst, Trivette, & Deal, 1988).

Concerns may be either reactive or proactive. *Reactive concerns* are ones mani-

fested in response to life events that produce problems, worries, difficulties, "troubling feelings," and so on (e.g., parents reactions to being informed that their child has a developmental disability). *Proactive concerns* are ones manifested in anticipation of what a family wants or desires in order to "make things better" (e.g., parents wanting to share their experiences with other parents so the latter have "first hand" information about what it has meant to parent a child with a disability).

Elsewhere we discuss the usefulness of the notion of *personal projects* as one way of placing more emphasis on proactive concerns as part of family-centered assessment and intervention practices. Little (1983) defined personal projects as a "set of interrelated acts extending over time, which is intended to maintain or attain a state of affairs foreseen by the individual" (p. 276). Personal projects include any activity, event, or goal that is *viewed as important enough for an individual to devote his or her time and energy*. Personal projects include such things as securing employment, graduating from school, gaining parenting experience, aspirations for oneself, child or family, or any other goal or outcome that is deemed personally important to a person. We find the idea of "personal projects" particularly appealing because it moves the focus of family-centered assessment and intervention beyond rectification of problems toward a competency enhancing, growth producing emphasis (Dunst, Trivette, & Mott, 1990).

Identification and clarification of family concerns and priorities is the first and perhaps most important step in any effective helping process (Dunst, 1987). This requires that one take the time and energy necessary to listen to what a family has to say about their situation. Remember that the word listen includes the same letters as the word silent! Therefore, it is important that one learn active, reflective, and empathic listening skills so as to be able to identify family concerns (see especially Carkhuff & Anthony, 1979; DeVito, 1989; Garrett, 1982b). In our own research, for example, families report that effective helpers are ones who take the time to *listen* and *understand* what bothers, worries, is important, etc. to the family (Dunst, Trivette, Davis, & Weeldreyer, 1988). The reader is referred to Gordon (1987, pp. 139-157) for a detailed set of communication facilitation techniques that are useful for learning effective listening skills.

The following are examples of concerns that might be raised by families:

1. Parents are concerned that their pediatrician sees their child's development as delayed.
2. Mom is worried that the preschool teacher will not know how to read her son's signs of discomfort or fatigue.
3. Parents are eager for their child to attend a summer camp, but are quite concerned about the long bus ride everyday to and from camp.
4. Parents wonder what will be options for higher education and living away from home for their child with physical disabilities.
5. Dad hopes that his son, who has a significant hearing loss, will be able to play on the local soccer team with other children his age.
6. Parents want their child with special needs to attend preschool with other children in their neighborhood, but there are no integrated programs available.
7. A single mom would like to begin college, working toward a nursing degree, but has no help with child care or the expenses of attending school.
8. Parents want their child to begin to eat regular table foods.

9. Parents wonder "Is our child able to see?"
10. A family's present house is too small and rent continues to increase.

FAMILY NEEDS

A need is a judgment or indication that a resource (information, advice, assistance, etc.) is required or desired in order to achieve a goal or attain a particular end (e.g., "I need to know more about what I can do to help my child. Where can I get information and advice about teaching my child to walk?"). It is unfortunate that the word "need" has taken on negative connotations in the human services fields. Its negative use is generally employed within the context of describing people as "needy." Such use "gives the message" that a person or family is *deficit* in some way. If I as a professional say that someone needs something, my contention implies that a person is weak or deficient. But if a person with concerns recognizes the need for a resource to address concerns, such recognition is a *strength*. Herein lies one difference between needs-based vs. prescriptive approaches to assessment and intervention practices. *Needs-based interventions are responsive to the individualized desires, aspirations, wants, and so on from the family's and not the professional's perspective.*

The process of identifying and defining family needs may be conducted through use of interviews, observations, or need-based assessment scales, or a combination of these strategies. All three methods provide a basis for gathering information about needs from the family's unique perspective of their situation. The combined use of these strategies increases the likelihood that the family's concerns and priorities will be identified in ways that are respectful of the family's choice of involvement in the assessment and intervention process. The reader is referred to Carkhuff and Anthony (1979), Dunst, Trivette, and Deal

(1988), Garrett (1982b), and Gordon (1987) for descriptions of the various methods and techniques that can be used to identify family needs.

Any interaction or contact with a family (phone call, office interview, home visit, etc.) can be used as a basis for understanding family priorities and identifying unmet needs. Several steps should be taken into consideration as part of the needs identification process. First, the purpose of the contact should be made explicitly clear and the family's consent obtained. Second, where the assessment will take place and who will participate should be decided in collaboration with the family. Third, prior to the conduct of the assessment, the purpose should be reiterated and a full explanation of how the results will be used provided to the family. Lastly, sufficient time should be allotted to the needs identification process in order to gain a perspective of the "bigger picture," including what has led to the family's current situation as well as the complexities of their present concerns. Adherence to these simple considerations insures that assessments are done in a helpful, proactive manner rather than being reactive or intrusive.

The following are examples of family needs:

1. Parents want to learn ways of teaching their child appropriate behavior on shopping trips so the entire family can go to the mall.
2. Grandmother wants to learn how to give tube feedings so she can feel confident keeping her grandson with her.
3. A single mother wants to get to know other single mothers with children with special needs.
4. Parents want to know what they can be doing at home to prepare their children for transition to preschool.
5. An older sibling is interested in learning ways to teach her brother during playtime.
6. Dad wants to take evening classes at the community college in electrical contracting in order to get a better paying job with better working hours.
7. Parents want information on how to help their child develop skills needed for eating regular table foods.
8. Mom feels a professional consultation on the child's visual abilities would be helpful.
9. Family wants information on other housing options that would fit the family budget.

OUTCOME STATEMENTS

Identification of family concerns and translation of concerns into needs are followed by written *outcome statements* that become the "heart" of an IFSP. According to Maple (1977), "good" outcome statements are "specific enough to generate action and to determine progress toward the goal" (p. 47). That is, outcome statements are action-oriented with the action specifically stated in relationship to a desired goal.

Operationally, an outcome statement specifies both what is to occur (process) and what is expected to be accomplished (outcome) as a result of actions to obtain needed resources. Needs, goals, and aspirations are written as *in order to* statements so they are functionally-based, easily understood, and promote translation of needs into action steps. That is, something is done in order to have something else achieved or attained. We have found that both child- and family-level needs can easily be stated in this format. It has also been our experience that nearly all outcomes can be stated in positive, growth-producing terms to reflect a positive stance toward children and families. The reader is referred to Dunst,

Trivette, and Thompson (1990) who describe the expanded benefits of enhancement- and promotion-based intervention practices compared to the limited, problem-reduction perspectives of both treatment-based and prevention-based interventive actions (see also Chapter 4).

The following are several examples of outcome statements:

1. Child will use a pointing gesture in order to request desired food at mealtimes.
2. Mother will obtain additional information about her child's genetic disorder in order to learn more about its implications for future development.
3. Child will play with toys adapted for use with an Ablenet switch during afternoon playtime in order for Mom to have time to prepare dinner.
4. Parents will participate in the assessment and intervention planning process to help decide appropriate classroom goals for their child.
5. Parents will contact other parents to discuss the pros and cons of purchasing a motorized wheelchair for a preschooler.
6. Child will drink small amounts from a cup held by mom during breakfast in order to learn to use a cup independently.
7. Child will use the sign for "drink" independently during daily routines to indicate his desire for something to drink.
8. Child will activate a tape recorder attached to his wheelchair to indicate his need to go to the bathroom.
9. Parents will exchange transportation to the grocery store for babysitting from their neighbor in order to have a few hours free each week for themselves.
10. Child will eat 2 or 3 different types of mashed table foods at each meal in order to adjust to more texture in the food.
11. Parents will take child for an ophthalmological evaluation in order to determine her visual abilities.
12. Parents will gather information on housing options in their community in order to consider the possibilities of buying a house.

RESOURCES AND SUPPORTS

Once needs have been identified and translated into outcome statements, the next step is to identify sources of support and resources for meeting needs. *Personal social network mapping* is used to accomplish the goal of identifying sources of support and resources for meeting needs. The persons and institutions with which a family and its members come in contact–either directly or indirectly–are referred to as the family's *personal social network*, and it is this network that is the primary source of support to families and individual family members (Cohen & Syme, 1985b). For each need/outcome statement, the range of options for meeting needs are identified and their viability as sources of support and resources determined. A simple rule of thumb is followed in network mapping: *Potential sources of support are mapped for each need/outcome statement separately so as to focus the resource and support identification and mobilization process.* By doing so, the human services practitioner gathers information specifically and only in relationship to family-identified needs. This insures that the identification of resources and supports does not become intrusive.

In mapping sources of support and resources, it must always be remembered that the assessment and mobilization of support and resources should be done within the context of the family system and the family's indicated need for support (see Dunst & Trivette, 1990). Thus, a determination of indicated need for aid and assistance is the first and fundamentally most important part of social support interventions, and *all* intervention efforts must be based on these family identified needs if they are to be successful in affecting parent, family, and child functioning (Pilisuk & Parks, 1986).

Another consideration involving the assessment and mobilization of support and resources has to do with the range of personal social network members available to a family. It should be remembered that *informal* support network members (spouse/partner, relatives, friends, neighbors, other parents, self-help groups, etc.) as well as *formal* support network members (e.g., human services practitioners) constitute sources of support and resources for meeting needs. To the extent possible and appropriate, major emphasis should be placed upon identification and use of informal personal network members as sources of support and resources for meeting family needs. So often, we overprofessionalize all types of interventions in human services programs, which only interferes with and precludes opportunities to build and strengthen more natural family and community support (Hobbs et al., 1984).

The following are examples of resources and sources of support that constitute some but certainly not all possible sources of aid and assistance:

1. *Child care for 1-3 hours twice a week.* (Possible sources of support: grandparents, neighbor, college student, trained respite provider, babysitting co-op and mother's morning-out program.)
2. *Information on motorized wheelchair.* (Possible sources of support: medical equipment vendor, physical therapist, parents of a child with a motorized wheelchair.)
3. *Financial support for medical equipment, baby formula and diapers.* (Possible sources of

support: grandparents, church members and Children's Special Health Care Services.)
4. *Information about teaching a child to communicate.* (Possible sources of support: human services practitioner, language therapist, instructional video.)
5. *Literacy training.* (Possible sources of support: community college, department of social services special project.)
6. *Integrated recreational program for special needs children.* (Possible sources of support: YMCA swimming program, community recreation center, exercise classes for tots.)
7. *Life necessities: Food, clothing, etc.* (Possible sources of support: community resource exchange program, friends and relatives, Salvation Army.)

COURSES OF ACTION

This element specifies the actions that will be taken to mobilize the support sources to obtain needed resources. The steps that will be taken to access resources to meet needs are listed for both the family and human services practitioner. The actions are stated in terms of what will be done by each partner to actualize the plan. Doing so emphasizes shared responsibility (see *Partnership* element below) between the family and human services practitioner. Our experience indicates that by stating what each partner will do, the likelihood of resource mobilization occurring in a timely manner is increased considerably.

The steps that are listed as courses of action need not include detailed descriptions of precisely what will be done to mobilize resources to meet needs. Rather, action steps should be stated succinctly and serve as *prompts and reminders* about what needs to be done to actualize the IFSP. The following are examples of action steps that might constitute appropriate courses of action for a family to obtain information about child care options in order to make an informed decision about choices for child care that are responsive to the family's unique situation:

Step 1. Parents will list people they already know who might provide child care.

Step 2. Human services practitioner will provide information about other child care options in the family's community.

Step 3. Parents and human services practitioner will examine all child care options to determine which sources of support represent viable choices.

Step 4. Parents will contact potential child care providers and assess whether or not it is appropriate to pursue as potential sources of child care.

This rather straightforward approach to developing courses of action provides enough information to structure implementation of the IFSP; yet, is simple enough to significantly reduce "paperwork" demands on both the family and human services practitioner.

Other examples of courses of action include the following:

1. During weekly appointments the communication specialist will show parents ways of encouraging the child's use of words. Parents will use the suggestions provided during daily routines at home to encourage the child's talking.
2. Parents will make a list of their goals for their child at preschool and share these during the planning meeting with the preschool teacher. The preschool teacher will share her ideas on possible learning goals based on her screening of the child. Together, parents and teacher will identify initial learning objectives for the child's time at preschool.
3. Parents will identify people they know who could assist in building a ramp onto

their house. Human services practitioner will share names and telephone numbers of civic clubs who do volunteer service projects. Parents will decide which options(s) to pursue to getting assistance with the ramp.
4. Human services practitioner and parents will assess child's current eating abilities during a mealtime session in the home. Human services practitioner will provide information on adding texture to the child's favorite foods (bananas, scrambled eggs, etc.). Parents and grandparents will give child one or two bites of mashed table foods each meal, increasing the number of bites by two or three each meal.
5. Parents will contact child's pediatrician to secure names of pediatric ophthalmologists and schedule an evaluation with the physician of their choice. Parents will prepare questions they have related to their child's vision as well as questions regarding the implications of the test results. Parents will take child for evaluation and have their questions answered. Parents will share results with human services practitioner, who will assist the family in developing an appropriate intervention plan based on the test results.

FAMILY STRENGTHS

The family strengths portion of family-centered assessment and intervention practices is designed to identify and acknowledge those qualities, beliefs, competencies, skills, etc. that a family can use to: (a) recognize concerns and identify needs, (b) translate needs into outcome statements, (c) identify sources of support for meeting needs, (d) develop courses of action to mobilize resources, and (e) take action to translate plans into action steps. That is, *family strengths include both the knowledge and skills that a family has at their disposal to contribute and participate in each part of the assessment and intervention process.* For example, a simple and straightforward way to recognize and acknowledge family strengths as part of resource mobilization and actualizing the IFSP is to elicit from the family descriptions of (a) what has already been done to mobilize resources to meet needs and (b) what the family feels comfortable doing either alone or in collaboration with others as part of actualizing the steps listed in the *Course of Action* section of the IFSP. What a family has already successfully done to mobilize resources to meet needs constitutes strengths, and what a family is willing to learn in order to acquire new competencies (or build on existing competencies) to mobilize resources also constitutes strengths. The process of identifying, acknowledging, and promoting use of family strengths need not be anymore complicated.

Despite the simplicity of this approach to family strengths assessment and intervention, building and supporting family strengths requires a major shift in how families and family functioning are viewed and assessed. Trivette et al. (1990) lists five principles for making this shift:

> First, it must be recognized that *all* families have strengths. Second, the failure of a family to display competence must not be viewed as a deficit within the family system, but rather the failure of social systems to create opportunities for competencies to be displayed or learned. Third, work with families must be approached in ways that focus and build on the positive aspects of functioning, rather than families being seen as "broken" and "needing to be fixed." Fourth, (we must) adopt promotion and enhancement models (of intervention) in order to

increase the likelihood of strengthening family functioning. Fifth, the goal of intervention must be the strengthening of functioning in ways that make families less and not more dependent upon professionals for help. (p. 21)

Collectively, these five considerations suggest an alternative to the deficit, reactive approach that has dominated the ways in which both child-and family-level assessments and interventions have traditionally been conducted in the human services fields.

The following are examples of family strengths:

1. Family members' knowledge of the child's abilities, preferences and temperament that they are able to share with professionals.
2. Family members' abilities to identify their concerns, goals, hopes, aspirations for the child's growth and development.
3. Family members' abilities to specify what would be helpful in meeting needs, achieving goals, alleviating concerns, etc.
4. The family's knowledge of people within their social network who might supply needed resources for meeting needs.
5. The ability to negotiate for needed resources with persons within their personal network.
6. Abilities to access resources from formal community agencies.
7. Abilities to sustain supportive relationships with others who provide needed resources (e.g., reciprocate exchanges of resources).
8. The ability to take information, techniques, etc. provided by others and use it to promote the development of the child.
9. The ability of family members to communicate and work with each other to accom-

plish tasks and projects of importance to the family.

10. A shared sense of commitment to the tasks and projects that are of importance and a congruence about what is important.

11. Knowledge of the rules, values, and beliefs that guide family members' behavior.

12. The ability to problem-solve ways for getting resources to meet needs.

13. Use of a variety of coping strategies for dealing with life events.

14. The ability to be flexible and adaptable in the assignment of roles family members need to perform in meeting needs.

15. The ability to keep a balance between the use of internal family resources and asking for help from others outside the family.

PARTNERSHIPS

Partnerships between parents and professionals are seen as the primary context for developing and implementing IFSPs. Operationally, a parent–professional partnership is defined as an association between a family and one or more professionals who function collaboratively using agreed upon roles in pursuit of a common interest or goal (Dunst & Paget, 1991).

Partnerships are characterized by certain features that make them different than other types of cooperative endeavors. First, partners recognize the benefits of a collaborative arrangement, openly agree to pool their respective resources (knowledge, skills, etc.), and cooperatively agree to work toward mutually agreed upon goals or interests. Second, partnerships are built upon mutual loyalty, trust, and honesty, and involve full disclosure of any and all information affecting the joint effort. Honesty, trust, and commitment are the backbone of any effective helping relation-

ship, and are, as well, absolutely necessary for partnerships to be effective (see Chapter 1). Third, to the extent that the well-being and rights of all family members are protected, the family alone bears responsibility for deciding its goals and course of development (Hobbs et al., 1984). In parent–professional partnerships, a major duty and responsibility of the professional is to provide all necessary information to assist the family to evaluate different options so that the parents can make *intelligent and informed decisions* regarding their child and family. The final decision, however, about what goals and interests should be pursued, and what courses of action will be taken to attain stated intentions, rests solely with the "senior" partners; namely the parents.

Practically, parent-professional partnerships are manifested vis a vis collaborative efforts between a family and human services practitioner in terms of the mutual sharing of information about potential sources of resources, joint implementation of actions required to mobilize resources to meet needs, feedback regarding each partner's contributions to the collaborative endeavor, etc. Use of partnerships as a primary means for supporting and strengthening family functioning insures or at least increases the likelihood that the family-centered assessment and intervention process is being implemented as intended.

Several examples of collaborative arrangements are as follows:

1. During an assessment process, the family shares their knowledge of the child's abilities and the professionals share knowledge gained from evaluations, observations, etc.

2. In addressing a parent's need for daycare, the parent identifies people within her

personal network who could provide care and the professional shares information about licenced daycares in the community and what to look for in a daycare program.

3. In preparing for a medical consultation, the professional assists the parent in identifying questions to ask and accompanies the parent to the consult appointment. The parent interacts directly with the medical professional and gets questions answered.

4. During a physical therapy session, the therapist demonstrates handling techniques and gives the parent feedback on her use of the techniques. The parent takes the information and skills in handling and uses them within daily routines with the child.

5. The human services practitioner shares knowledge of feeding techniques. Family members draw from their knowledge of the child and utilize the techniques offered to provide opportunities for the child to develop skills in eating table foods.

6. Parents share their knowledge of their child's abilities as part of participating in ophthalmological evaluation. The medical professional conducts an evaluation and provides an interpretation of results. The human services practitioner collaborates with parents and physician in developing ways to promote the child's visual abilities based on the test results.

7. The human services practitioner provides information about community resources that may be able to assist the family in exploring various housing options. The parents contact the appropriate agencies (Housing Authority and FHA) to begin gathering information about housing options. The human services practitioner

and parents pool information and develop a plan to secure the family's desired housing.

EVALUATION

Progress toward resource mobilization is evaluated as part of the assessment and intervention process in terms of both goal attainment and family satisfaction. The method for evaluating the effectiveness of the IFSP assesses the degree to which: (a) actions result in resource mobilization and goal attainment, and (b) the family is satisfied with the process and outcome. Each and every contact with the family (e.g., face-to-face, phone) can be used to evaluate progress toward resource mobilization and goal attainment. The family is simply asked whether or not they have had the opportunity to take particular actions, and how they feel about both goal attainment and progress toward the stated intentions. The information provided by the family is used to assign a rating to the family's description of their situation. The following rating scale is used for assessing the effectiveness of implementation efforts for each need outcome:

1.... No longer a need, goal, or project.
2.... Situation unchanged; still a need, goal, or project.
3.... Implementation begun; still a need, goal, or project.
4.... Outcome partially attained or accomplished.
5.... Outcome accomplished or attained, but not to the family's satisfaction.
6.... Outcome mostly accomplished or attained to the family's satisfaction.
7.... Outcome completely accomplished or attained to the family's satisfaction.

This simple and relatively straightforward evaluation scheme has proven useful for as-

Date / #	NEED/ OUTCOME STATEMENT	SOURCE OF SUPPORT/ RESOURCES	COURSE OF ACTION	FAMILY'S EVALUATION	
				Date	Rating
11-06-90 / 13	Natasha will contact SSI to see if Willie would qualify for benefits in order to help with family finances.	Natasha-skills in gathering information Human Services Practitioner (HSP)-help making a list of concerns Social Security-information on SSI eligibility	During weekly visits, HSP and Natasha will make a list of questions to ask about SSI. Natasha will call Social Security to get information on eligibility and decide if she wants to apply for benefits.	11-20-90 12-04-90 12-16-90	4 6 7
11-13-90 / 14	Natasha will talk with preschool staff in order to feel better about Willie going there.	Natasha-ability to talk with the teachers HSP-help in making list of concerns Preschool-safe place for Willie to play	During weekly home visits, HSP and Natasha will list concerns about Willie's safety at school. Natasha will schedule a time to talk with Willie's teachers about her concerns and then decide about letting Willie return to school.	11-20-90 12-04-90	4 7
12-04-90 / 15	Willie will use signs for "no, eat, drink and more" at home and school to let others know what he wants.	Natasha-ability to use signs and teach Willie HSP-information on signing Preschool-use of signs	During weekly visits, HSP will share information on signing. Natasha and Family will use signs with Willie and teach him. Natasha will tell the school what signs she is working on so they can use them, also.	12-07-90 01-08-91	3 4
12-11-90 / 16	Family will use time-out chair when Willie tantrums or bites to help him learn better behaviors.	Natasha and Family-skill in using time-out HSP-information and encouragement on using time-out	During weekly visits, HSP will review how use of time-out is working and offer suggestions, as needed. Family will use the chair at home when Willie tantrums or bites (setting timer for 2 minutes).	12-17-90 01-08-91	3 3

Fig. 6-2. Example of a Portion of a Completed IFSP (Example A).

sessing the effectiveness of the IFSP without the need to develop individualized evaluation criteria for each outcome statement. Several examples of how this evaluation system is used as part of assessing progress toward mobilization of resources to meet needs are provided next.

The following are examples of evaluative criteria that represent each level of the rating scale:

1.... A parent telephones to say that she has

been laid off from her job, therefore her goal of pursuing different child care is no longer a priority.

2.... During a contact, a family indicates that they are still interested in getting information on seating equipment, but a family illness has precluded their beginning to make calls about this.

3.... The family indicates that they have begun giving the child opportunities to use a spoon during mealtimes, but their goal of the child beginning to use the spoon to

Date / #	NEED/ OUTCOME STATEMENT	SOURCE OF SUPPORT/ RESOURCES	COURSE OF ACTION	FAMILY'S EVALUATION Date	Rating
	Child's Name: Matthew	Family's Name: Wilson	Staff Member: S. Vance	IFSP#: 1	Page#: 2
9-13-90 / 5	Kay will look into getting a stroller in order to be able to get out with the baby.	Kay-$20 saved for stroller Human Services Practitioner (HSP)-help in problem solving Baby's Father-?money Baby's Grandfather-?money	During weekly visits, Kay and HSP will talk about how to get help with buying stroller. Kay will check prices of new and used strollers. She will talk with the baby's father and her father about helping with the cost of a stroller.	09-20-90 10-01-90 10-10-90	3 6 7
9-20-90 / 6	Kay will try getting babysitting jobs to earn money to get the brakes fixed on the car.	Kay-skills in caring for children HSP-encouragement	Kay will talk with neighbors, friends and family about wanting to babysit or provide after-school care. Will run an ad in newspaper. HSP will provide support and encouragement during weekly contacts. Will post a sign at work for Kay.	10-01-90 10-10-90	3 3
10-01-90 / 7	Kay will check into the HRD program as a posibility of getting her GED and job placement.	Kay-skills in getting information HSP-name of person and telephone numer of Human Resource Development (HRD) HRD-information	During weekly visits, Kay and HSP will make a list of questions about HRD Program and GED. Kay will call person at telephone number to get information about the program and decide if she wants to enroll.	10-10-90 01-16-90	6 7
10-01-90 / 8	Matthew will take at least 4oz. of milk during feeding to be sure he is getting enough to eat.	Kay-ability to feed and care for Matthew Health Department Nurse-feeding suggestions and monitoring HSP-encouragement	Nurse will give suggestions on feeding and monitoring how much milk Matthew takes. Kay will keep a record of the amounts Matthew takes. HSP will offer encouragement to Kay during weekly contacts and consult with the nurse, as needed.	10-10-90 10-16-90	3 3

Fig. 6-3. Example of a Portion of a Completed IFSP (Example B).

feed herself has not yet been accomplished.

4.... The family reports their child is beginning to use a spoon to get food to her mouth, but her use of it is still inconsistent.

5.... The family indicates that grandparents have been willing to provide babysitting which has met the parents' need to have time to go out occasionally, but the grandparents have not been willing to keep to the feeding schedule requested by the parents.

6.... Parents report that a child is using signs to communicate during certain routines in the day, but they are still aiming for consistent use of signs during all daily routines.

7.... Family indicates that their need for more information on the side effects of seizure medication has been satisfactorily met through reading printed material and a decision with the child's neurologist.

SAMPLE IFSPs

Figures 6-2 and 6-3 show portions of actual IFSPs for two families with which we have worked. The first shows family needs identified by a mother "Natasha" and her son "Willie," and the process the family and the human services practitioner working with the mother used to achieve the family's desired outcomes (Example A). The second example is from an IFSP of a teenage mother "Kay" and her infant son "Matthew" who are involved in a family support project for teen parents (Example B). This example illustrates some of the work the human services practitioner and Kay focused on as part of accessing resources that assisted Kay in meeting her and Matthew's needs. The two examples include only single pages from actual "sets" of IFSPs that were completed in work with these families. Actual IFSPs would include multiple pages of forms that reflected ongoing attention to changing and evolving needs.

SUMMARY AND CONCLUSION

The model described in this chapter is intended to provide a framework for (a) identifying family needs, (b) locating the informal and formal resources and supports for meeting needs, and (c) assisting families to use existing skills as well as learn new competencies to mobilize resources to meet their needs. The model was described from a family-centered perspective that emphasized a family strengths and positive, proactive approach to supporting and strengthening family functioning. The model has evolved and is continually revised as part of our efforts to learn about the best ways to intervene with families. To the extent that intervention practices can be kept simple, functioning, responsive, and individualized, the goal of supporting and strengthening family functioning should be realized in ways that have empowering consequences.

IV

FAMILY NEEDS, STRENGTHS, AND RESOURCES

The chapters in this section include material that elaborates upon the family-centered model briefly described in Chapter 1. More specifically, the chapters include descriptions of key features and characteristics of needs-based, strengths-based, and resource-based family-centered assessment and intervention practices. Collectively, the chapters provide a framework for understanding the relationships among the family needs, strengths, and resources components of the family-centered model, as well as include empirical evidence supporting the adoption of family-centered practices.

In addition to providing a framework and accompanying evidence for the three components of the model described in this section (Section V includes chapters pertaining to the help-giving component of the model), Chapters 7, 9, and 11 provide lists of misconceptions about the particular family-centered model presented in this book. These misconceptions emerged primarily in response to material originally described in <u>Enabling and Empowering Families</u>, and we address these misunderstandings as a way of clarifying our original intent.

The particular chapters (8, 10, and 12) presenting empirical evidence were selected to be representative of the kinds of research that have led us to the propositions and principles set forth in Section I. Additional empirical evidence supporting the family-centered model is presented in Volume 2 of this book.

CHAPTER 7

Needs-Based Family-Centered Intervention Practices

Carl J. Dunst & Angela G. Deal

THE FAMILY-CENTERED ASSESSMENT and intervention model described by Dunst, Trivette, and Deal (1988) in *Enabling and Empowering Families* gives primacy to the family as the "major player" deciding the focus of intervention activities. Such a focus presumes that a family is provided the necessary information to make informed, intelligent choices, and opportunities to use existing capabilities as well as to learn new competencies necessary to exercise these choices.

Family-centered practices that are "consumer-driven" are based upon the contention that a discrepancy between what a family's situation is like and what the family desires their situation to be are conditions that define *needs*. Needs-based family-centered intervention practices diverge considerably from the ways in which human services have traditionally been rendered to families.

The purpose of this chapter is to describe the needs-based component of the Dunst, Trivette, and Deal (1988) family-centered model. The strengths-based and resource-based components of the model are described in Chapters 9 and 11 respectively. The contents of this chapter include information necessary to more fully understand the meaning of family needs, as well as describe strategies helpful for identifying needs as the target of intervention practices.

MEANING AND PARAMETERS OF FAMILY NEEDS

TYPES OF NEEDS

According to Weissbourd (1987a), *all* families, regardless of socioeconomic status or other family characteristics, have needs that can be met by family support programs and personal social network members. A family's specific *need* for resources and supports, however, will differ depending upon many family circumstances. Nonetheless, it is still possible to think of needs as being determined or influenced by two different broad sets of conditions:

1. Needs that are ongoing and change very little on a day-in and day-out basis.
2. Needs that vary as a function of changes in a family's situation, whether anticipated or unanticipated.

The need for *financial resources* to pay for food and shelter is an example of the first type of need. The need for *information about school placements* and the need for *emotional support* in response to the sudden death of a family member are examples of anticipated and unanticipated needs that occur as a function of changes in a family's life situation. Needs-based assessment and intervention practices that are family-centered attempt to be responsive to both the *ongoing* and *changing* needs of families. Such practices fully recognize and address family concerns in both areas of needs.

NEEDS CATEGORIES

The ability to adequately identify a family's needs and resources for meeting needs requires that one first have an idea about what *all* families are likely to require for stable functioning, individual and family growth, and day-to-day coping and well-being. It is useful to organize needs into broad categories for guiding both assessment and intervention practices. The reader is referred to Dunst, Trivette, and Deal (1988), Hartman and Laird (1983), and Trivette, Deal and Dunst (1986) for useful lists of needs categories. The list provided by Dunst, Trivette, and Deal (1988) includes the following 12 groups of needs:

- Economic Needs
- Physical and Environmental Needs
- Food and Clothing Needs
- Medical and Dental Care Needs
- Employment and Vocational Needs
- Transportation and Communication Needs
- Adult Education and Enrichment Needs
- Child Education and Intervention Needs
- Child Care Needs
- Recreational Needs
- Emotional Needs
- Cultural and Social Needs

Table 7-1 gives examples of resources that are often required by families in each of these needs categories. This table provides a framework for structuring efforts to both assess needs and identify resources to meet needs (see Chapter 11).

NEEDS DETERMINANTS

Many different situations, factors, conditions, and so on influence what families define as their needs. Recognition of these *needs determinants* are extremely important as part of the needs identification process, and an understanding of these conditions can aid the practitioner as part of both assessment and intervention practices. There are at least four conditions or circumstances that influence which family needs take precedence at any particular point in time, and steer the family in a direction toward mobilization of resources to meet those needs.

1. *Normative and Non-Normative Life Cycle Changes.* Family needs change as a function of both normative life changes (such as marriage, the birth of a child, entry into school) and non-normative life changes (such as the birth of a child with a disability, a catastrophic accident, and loss of a job). These as well as other family life cycle changes must be taken into consideration as part of needs-based family-centered assessment and intervention practices.

2. *Family Structure and Organization.* Lower birth rates, longer life expectancies, the changing roles of women, increased number of the women in the workforce, and divorce and remarriage rates, among other factors, have produced dramatic changes in the definitions, functions, and needs of families. As Carter and McGoldrick (1988) stated: "It is time for professionals to give up attachments to the old ideals and to put a more positive conceptual frame around what *is* two paycheck marriages; permanent 'single-parent' households; unmarried couples and remarried couples; single-parent adoptions; and women of all ages alone" (p. 13). The nature of the

Table 7-1. Taxonomy of Needs

Need Category	Resources
Economic	Money for necessities Money for emergencies Money for special needs/project Money for the future Stable income level
Physical	Clean environment Adequate housing (space, safety, furnishings) Safe neighborhood (protection) Adequate heat, water and plumbing Housing accessible to other resources Resources for home repairs and maintenance
Food/Clothing	Adequate food for two meals a day Enough clothes for each season Reliable means for laundering clothes
Medical/Dental	Trustworthy medical/dental professionals Available general/emergency health care Means of acquiring medical/dental care
Vocational	Opportunity to work Satisfaction with work (in or out of home) Job security Available/accessible work
Transportation/Communication	Means for getting family members where they need to go Means for contacting relatives, friends and other sources of support
Adult Education	Available appropriate adult educational opportunities Accessible educational opportunities
Child Education	Accessible child educational opportunities Opportunities/activities to help teach/play with children Appropriate toys and other educational materials
Child Care	Help in routine daily care Emergency child care Available day care/babysitting for employment purposes Respite child care
Recreational	Opportunities for recreational activities for individual family members, couples, total family Available recreational facilities for individual members, couples, total family
Emotional	Positive intrafamily relationships Positive relationships outside the family Companionship Sense of belonging to family or group Opportunities to spend time with significant people
Cultural/Social	Opportunities to share ethnic or value-related experiences with others Opportunities to be involved with community/cultural affairs Accessible community/cultural affairs

family system, and how it is structured and organized, needs to be taken into consideration as part of identifying family needs since family structure will almost certainly determine the need for different kinds of resources (e.g., childcare for working mothers).

3. *Cultural, Ethnic and Religious Beliefs and Values.* Needs-based assessment and intervention strategies and practices must consider the influences of cultural, ethnic, and religious backgrounds on family functioning and the need for resources. Additionally, any definition of "family," as well as the importance of different family routines and rituals, will vary depending on a family's cultural, ethnic and religious beliefs. Culture, ethnicity, and religion play a major role in "determining what we eat, how we work, how we relate, how we celebrate holidays and rituals, and how we feel about life, death, and illness" (McGoldrick, 1988 p. 69). In striving to provide and mobilize resources that meet the unique needs of families, one must take into account the range of values and cultures represented in our country as part of both assessment and intervention practices.

4. *Community Context.* Where the family lives, as well as specific characteristics of the communities in which families reside, will influence the need or desire for different types of resources. These factors include, but are not limited to, community pride, housing arrangements, neighborhood safety, home–school relationships, etc. An understanding of the communities of families often times will be of tremendous benefit in understanding a family's concerns and needs.

Life cycle changes, family structure, family beliefs and values, and community context are several, but certainly not all, the systemic factors that influence a family's indicated need for certain resources. The implementation of assessment and intervention practices which are family-centered acknowledge and take into consideration these as well as other *determinants* as part of identifying family needs and resources to meet needs.

DEFINITION OF NEED

Needs-based family-centered assessment and intervention practices promote the flow of resources and supports to families in *response* to the desires, wishes, and aspirations of individual family members and the family unit. Thus far we have used the term *need* without any explicit definition of the meaning of the term. However, needs-based intervention practices necessitates that one first understand the meaning of, and the difference between, *concerns* and *needs*, and their implication for practice.

FAMILY CONCERNS

Areas of interest and importance to individual family members and the family unit are what generally bring people to the attention of professionals. These matters are often manifested as concerns. *Concerns* are operationally defined as the perception or indication of a discrepancy between *what is and what ought to be* (e.g., Parental worries about their 18-month-old child not yet walking). That is, there must be an awareness on the part of a family and its members that their situation is sufficiently different from what they want it to be so as to seek assistance from others or take action in response to what others may recommend. Terms such as *worry, problem, difficulty,* and *uneasiness* are often used interchangeably with the word *concern.* All these terms reflect a discrepancy between what is and what ought to be.

FAMILY NEEDS

A *need* is a judgment or indication that a resource (information, advice, assistance, etc.) is required or desired in order to achieve a goal or attain a particular end (e.g., "I need to know more about what I can do to help my child to walk. Where can I get information and advice about teaching my child to walk?"). Terms such as *desire, goal, aspiration, priority, want*, and *aim* often are used to mean the same thing as the word need as we have defined it here. All of these terms reflect efforts to procure resources and supports necessary to address concerns in ways that reduce or eliminate the discrepancy between what is and what ought to be.

RELATIONSHIP BETWEEN NEEDS AND CONCERNS

The relationship between *concerns* and *needs* is an important one, and is very useful as part of assessment practices. *Concerns* are the conditions that lead to the perception of discrepancies, whereas *need recognition* involves the identification of resources required to reduce the discrepancy between what is and what ought to be. The difference and relationship between concerns and needs may be described as follows:

1a. Concerns are conditions that lead to a recognition that the difference between what is and what ought to be is sufficiently disparate to warrant attention.
1b. Needs are conditions that lead to a recognition that something (i.e., a resource) will reduce the discrepancy between what is and what ought to be.
2. Concerns produce discrepancies, whereas need recognition and resource procurement (solution identification) reduce discrepancies.

In most cases, families do not explicitly specify what their needs are but rather share their concerns (interests, worries, etc.). Practitioners must remain cognizant of the difference between concerns and needs throughout the needs identification process, and help the family "translate" concerns into needs statements. One of the major objectives of needs identification is listening to family concerns as they are shared with you, and assisting the family in clarifying these concerns in ways that identify resources needed to reduce discrepancies between what is and what ought to be.

At least four *conditions* must be present before an individual or family perceives or indicates a need for certain resources (see especially McKillip, 1987; Reid, 1985). The conditions are as follows:

1. *Psychological Awareness*: There must be some concern, problem or perception that something is not as it ought to be. This is referred to as *psychological awareness*. An awareness of the difference (discrepancy) between what is and what ought to be must be present if a person is to consider his or her condition different enough to warrant action to alleviate or reduce the discrepancy.
2. *Value Influence*: The role that personal values and phenomenological beliefs play in determining a need must not only be taken into consideration, but must be explicitly recognized as one set of conditions that defines concerns or problems. This is referred to as *value influence*. The mere recognition of a discrepancy between what is and what ought to be is not sufficient to define a condition as problematic or worrisome unless the person makes a personal judgment that the discrepancy currently or will potentially influence his or her behavior in an expected way.

3. *Need Recognition*: There must be some evaluation or awareness that there is a resource potentially available that will reduce the discrepancy between what is and what ought to be. The desire for the resource is referred to as *need recognition*. Need recognition occurs whenever something (e.g., a resource) is identified as a form of aid or assistance that will reduce the perceived discrepancy.

4. *Solution Identification*: There must be a recognition that there is a way of procuring a resource to meet the need before a discrepancy is perceived as amendable to help. This is referred to as *solution identification*. In many cases people do not perceive themselves as having needs if they see no way in which resources can be procured to meet them regardless of the existence of the resources.

Both concerns and needs are to a large degree influenced by a personal awareness of the difference between what is and what ought to be; an assessment of whether the discrepancy is personally important; recognition that a resource exists to meet the need; and a belief that a solution exist to procure the resource to meet the need. The presence of all four conditions are necessary, though not sufficient, for concerns to be translated into needs statements. The absence of any one factor will likely interfere with the recognition of needs. As already noted, there are likely to be many factors or conditions which contribute to the family's assessment of their need for resources. A family's ability to share concerns as well as their recognition of the need for certain resources represent particular family strengths (see Dunst & Deal, 1990; Dunst, Trivette, & Mott, 1990). Quite often, however, a family may not have considered or may not be aware of all the options that are available for meeting needs. One valuable resource practitioners can provide to families is knowledge or information about various perspectives or options that the family may not have considered. However, sharing possible perspectives is appropriate after the family has indicated a general concern or desired outcome. The practitioner should follow the lead of the family while providing additional information that might be of benefit as indicated and in response to the family's situation.

This type of *information sharing* is illustrated in the following segment of an interview between a parent and professional.

Parent: One of our biggest worries right now is Timmy getting up during the night. His wandering through the house is dangerous and his being up keeps others from being able to sleep. We've tried everything we can think of, but the situation is not getting better.

Professional: I can certainly see how the possibility of Timmy getting hurt and the nighttime disruptions makes this situation a priority for your family. What are some of the things you have tried in dealing with his getting up in the night?

Parent: Well, we first tried putting him back to bed. But he is usually wide awake and ready to play, so trying to keep him in his bed or room is futile. We've tried putting him in our room to sleep, but he just keeps us awake. We've thought about fixing a special door for his room so we can hear him, but he cannot get out to other parts of the house. I'm not sure what would be involved in doing that.

Professional: Making his room a confined safe place to play is certainly one option for dealing with the possibility of his getting hurt. And we could look at what it would take to fix the door. Have you noticed any other changes in Timmy's or your family's routines that might be affecting his waking up in the night?

Parent: Now that you mention it, I've noticed since he has been attending day care that he gets tired much earlier in the evening and is ready for bed around 7:30. That has certainly allowed me to have more time available in the evenings to get household chores done, but by 3 a.m. Timmy's ready to get up for the day.

Professional: I think you may have just discovered the reason for his waking up in the night! And there may be some ways to gradually adjust his routine at day care or in the early evening to also deal with the night-time behavior. Let's continue to look at several of these options and what you might need in order to take action on some of these.

MISCONCEPTIONS OF NEEDS-BASED INTERVENTION PRACTICES

Needs-based assessment and intervention practices represent a significant departure from the ways in which resources and services have typically been rendered to families. The adoption of new or alternative intervention practices almost always carries with it some risk of misinterpretation. The following considerations clarify some, but certainly not all, misconceptions that surround needs-based family-centered assessment and intervention practices. The misconceptions and their clarification come from our own experiences implementing needs-based family-centered practices and training others to use the model, methods, and strategies described in this book and elsewhere (see Dunst, 1989; Dunst & Deal, 1990; Dunst, Trivette, & Deal, 1988).

Misconception: Needs-based family-centered intervention practices are deficit oriented because the only things addressed are things that are wrong.

Response: If I as a professional identify what a family needs, that can be construed as a deficit approach. However, if a family identifies its needs, desires, and aspirations, and interventions are responsive to a family's concerns and goals, this is a strengths oriented approach. This is the case because the ability to recognize needs, and take actions to meet needs, represents an important subset of intrafamily resources.

Misconception: Needs-based family-centered intervention practices do not take into consideration what professionals consider needed interventions.

Response: Strengths oriented needs-based intervention practices are responsive to and base interventions on what families consider important. Practitioners, however, have a professional and ethical obligation to raise concerns and sensitively bring to the family's attention areas they deem important. Withholding information from parents that they need to make informed decisions is perhaps the greatest dis-service one can show toward families.

Misconception: Needs-based family-centered intervention practices fail to adequately respond to child-level needs.

Response: First and foremost it must be recognized that children are members of families, and family-centered intervention practices, if done properly, will be highly responsive to any and all child-level needs. Secondly, the large majority of needs identified by parents concern their children's well-being, growth, and optimal development. Properly conducted family-centered intervention practices will insure a healthy balance between the needs of all family members.

Misconception: Some families don't know what their needs are and can't tell you what they want; that's why professionals have to tell parents what to do.

Response: Our experience tells us that the reason people sometimes are not able to articulate their needs is because they have rarely been asked what they want, think, or feel is best for themselves from their own perspective. It takes time and practice to be able to "self-identify" what one thinks is important, but all families can do it if adequately supported and encouraged. Additionally, many people, including a lot of practitioners we suspect, are taken back by the questions "What do you need?" Few people specifically say what they need, but most people are able to easily articulate their concerns and desires. "Effective" needs-based intervention practices elicit descriptions of concerns and desires, and help families translate these into need and outcome statements that guide efforts to meet needs.

Misconception: Needs-based family-centered intervention practices place practitioners in a position to "act against" their professional judgment and ethical standards.

Response: Needs-based intervention practices require that practitioners listen to and help families articulate their concerns and desires. If family needs and goals run counter to what professionals consider "best professional opinion," families need this sensitively explained to them. At the same time, however, whatever the family decides, albeit legal and lawful and short of abuse and neglect should constitute the focus of intervention practices. Effective help-givers are supportive even though they might not agree with a parent's decisions.

Misconception: Needs-based family-centered assessment scales and intervention procedures are intrusive and ask things that are "none of a professional's business."

Response: We have been using needs-based assessment procedures for almost a decade, and less than 2% of the families we have worked with have indicated that the procedures are intrusive. There are at least two reasons why this is the case. First, the reason the procedures are being used are fully explained and disclosed to the families. There is no hidden agenda. Most people who are reactive to needs-based assessment procedures so respond because they are not told why they are being asked the questions. Second, the families we work with understand that the "answers" belong to them and if they don't want someone to know something they don't have to respond to a question. "Effective" needs-based assessment procedures do not analyze and "dig" for things that are not relevant to what is important to families. Rather, they are focused and "stick to" what parents have to say about their families.

Misconception: Needs-based family-centered intervention practices mean being "everything to everybody."

Response: Needs-based intervention practices mean being responsive to all family needs, but they do not mean doing everything or providing every service or resource to meet those needs. "Effective" needs-based intervention practices help link families with appropriate resources and services. Sometimes that means resources from your own program, and sometimes it means families procuring resources from other sources.

Misconception: All family-identified needs should be met by human services program staff.

Response: This misconception stems from the assumption that practitioners and their programs constitute the only or primary support system available to children and families participating in family support programs. Resources that human services programs offer are certainly important, but they are not the only source of support that can be used to meet family needs. An important role that practitioners can play as part of family centered intervention practices is linking families with, and informing families about, other sources of support and resources.

With the above material as a background,

we now describe a number of different methods and strategies for identifying family needs.

METHODS AND STRATEGIES FOR NEEDS IDENTIFICATION

The process of identifying and defining family needs may be conducted through the use of three general methods: *interviews*, *observations*, and *self-report needs-based assessment scales*. All three provide a basis for gathering information about the family's concerns from its own unique perspective. The combined use of the strategies insures that the family's indication of their concerns and priorities is adequately explored. Each method is designed to have family members identify and clarify *their* concerns and desires from their own perspective rather than have *others* determine what ought to be priorities for the family.

The major *goal* of the needs identification process is to promote the family's identification and prioritization of their needs, goals, and aspirations. It is important that practitioners not allow their personal agendas to predetermine the outcome of the needs identification process. This requires a willingness to

invest time and energy in listening to family members to develop an understanding of their perspectives and viewpoints on their situation. Stoneman (1985) captured this point when she said: "To be effective, service providers must want to hear what parents have to say and must be truly interested in understanding the family's concerns and needs" (p. 463). Table 7-2 includes a list of questions that can serve as a framework for guiding the process for identifying family needs. These questions should be answered by the practitioner as part of the needs identification process.

INTERVIEW STRATEGIES

An interview is a face-to-face interaction between a professional and one or more family members for the purpose of gathering information about the family's needs, goals, priorities, and aspirations. "Seasoned" practitioners can become quite proficient in using interview procedures for identifying family needs. These methods solicit descriptions about concerns and aspirations from the family as well as help families clarify and define their needs. A number of key sources (e.g., Carkhoff & Anthony, 1979; Garrett, 1982a; Gordon, 1987) provide excellent descriptions of interview techniques for conducting needs assessments.

Table 7-2. Examples of Questions Practitioners May Pose to Themselves for Identifying Family Needs

-What are the family's concerns and interests?
-What characteristics, factors or conditions contribute to the family's concerns and interests?
-What are the needs and aspirations that derive from these concerns and interests?
-In which ways does the family define its needs (aspirations, goals, etc.)?
-Is there consensus or disagreement about family needs? How might any disagreement be resolved?
-Are there other concerns or interests expressed by individual family members?
-If there are individualized needs, in what ways are other family members supportive and in agreement with the person's appraisal of his or her own needs and aspirations?
-Are there apparent reasons why other needs are not currently defined as important by the family? If so, what are the reasons? If not, are there ways of helping the family see its situation differently so needs become more readily apparent?
-Does the family have the time and energy for meeting needs? If not, why? What can be done to change their situation?
-Does the family see the benefits of devoting time and energy to meet needs? If not, are there ways of sharing a different perspective of their situation?

There are a number of considerations that should be taken into account when interviewing a family for the purpose of understanding their concerns and identifying needs. The following are some but certainly not all the issues, techniques, etc. that should be considered when using interview procedures:

1. *The purpose of the interview should be made clear and the family's consent obtained.* Unclear agendas or unannounced visits do not set the occasion for a productive interaction with family members. Clearly stating the purpose of the interview, what topics will be covered, and how information will be used should be openly discussed with the family. It is helpful to explain to the family that all information shared during the interview "belongs" to the family, and no information will be shared with others without the family's explicit permission.

2. *The location where the interview will occur should be decided upon in collaboration with the family.* Talking with the family in their home can provide a more comfortable and less formal environment than an office setting, but there are more opportunities for interruptions. Ask the family where they would feel most comfortable talking about their family's situation. If the family chooses their own home, and if interruptions are likely, discuss this with the family and try to decide what might be done to minimize any disruptions. If the interview is conducted in a place other than the family's home (e.g., an office), the setting should be comfortable and the atmosphere conducive for the family to share their concerns.

3. *Before beginning the interview, take time to establish rapport with the family.* Taking the time to place the family at ease before beginning the interview cannot be overemphasized. Acknowledge all the people who are present and thank them for taking the time to meet with you. Briefly share background information about yourself and your program as a way to establish initial rapport. Remember, however, that the focus of the interview should be the family's agenda, and any and all opportunities to build rapport and place the family at ease should be used to make the family feel as comfortable as possible.

4. *Talk with as many family members as possible in order to gain as complete an understanding about the family's situation, needs, and concerns.* This may include the parents, children in the family, and extended family members (grandparents, aunts, cousins, etc.) as well as others who are important sources of support to the family. Obtaining the family's input in deciding who will participate in the interview insures that the "key players" are included. It is especially important to include those individuals who generally have "final say" in what the family may decide to do to meet its needs.

5. *Take the necessary time to get a perspective of "the big picture" of the family's concerns and need for certain resources.* This generally involves the family "telling their story" about what has led to their current situation, as well as a discussion of factors that have contributed to their present concerns. As the family's situation is "uncovered," the interviewer should make mental or written notes on key points to explore in further depth at a later time.

6. *Use open-ended questions, leading statements, and requests for clarification to promote the exchange of information for clarifying concerns and identifying needs.* Avoid asking "yes" or "no" questions when you are trying to get the family to share their concerns. Table

7-3 gives examples of the types of questions and statements that can be useful in helping a family clarify concerns and identify needs. Be especially sensitive to the relationship between different concerns, and ask questions about how different concerns influence the family's ability to recognize the important aspects of their situation. For example, the need for a resource (e.g., childcare) may be the result of any number of conditions (need to work, time to attend to other family members, etc.). Knowing something about these related factors, and assisting the family to see how they are related, will influence the types of assistance and resources that are explored as options for meeting the need. The appropriate match of resources-to-needs is a critical component of providing support to families, and having as complete an understanding as possible of the family's situation increases the likelihood of making informed recommendations.

7. *Be sensitive and responsive to the verbal as well as nonverbal messages (body posture, tone of voice, etc.) conveyed by family members throughout the interview.* Information and attitudes are communicated through both words and actions. Acknowledging and encouraging discussion of the more subtle, nonverbal messages can help insure that important issues are not overlooked (e.g., "I noticed some doubt in your voice as we were talking about the possibility of surgery for your child. What are your concerns about this?").

8. *Promote the family's prioritization of their needs.* Interviews often generate a tremendous amount of information about a family's concerns and needs. In those cases where multiple needs are identified, it is generally helpful if they are prioritized with respect to the order in which they will be addressed. An important step in the interview process is having the family describe which needs will be addressed first, second, and so on until all needs have been prioritized.

Hartman and Laird (1983) offer the following observations about family-centered interview techniques:

> No matter how experienced a person is in interviewing individuals, the leap to interviewing families requires new and different perspectives and skills. Frequently, in beginning family interviews even seasoned workers feel inundated by the enormous amount of information and confusing communication among family members, and they resort to doing what amounts to individual interviewing with a family mem-

Table 7-3. Questions and Statements for Identifying Family Needs
Fill me in on the background of................................
Tell me more about ....
How does the situation look to you?.......................
What was your reaction to ....?
How is .... affecting you (your family)?
What information do you have about.....................?
What would you like to do about.............................?
How does this fit with what you expected?.............
What do you (your family) think is best? ....
What have you figured out thus far?.......................
Who have you talked with about...............................?
How do you think things stand right now? ....
Where do you think this will lead?...........................
What is your ultimate goal? ....
In what ways do you think the situation could be better? ....
If you had your choice, what would you do? ....
What would it take to do that?.................................
How do you suppose that could work? ....
How would you go about doing it? ....
Are there any other angles you can think of? ....

ber while the rest of the group observes. Occasionally this may be done as a planned strategy, but it is not the usual approach to family interviewing. (p. 142)

They emphasize, however, that: "The initial focus in the family interview, following the establishment of rapport, should be on the *concerns which have mobilized the family to seek help*" (p. 148, emphasis added). This should always be the focus of needs-based assessment practices.

OBSERVATION STRATEGIES

Observation strategies are another method that can be used to identify family needs. The use of observation strategies for needs assessment purposes can focus on individual family members (e.g., family observation of a child eating), interactions among family members (e.g., observation of a family discussion), or observation of the physical and social environments of the family (e.g., housing arrangements). The opportunity to observe a family in their home environment (or other familiar situations) can yield a wealth of information useful for understanding a family's concerns and needs.

A major consideration and *caution* must be mentioned and made explicitly clear as part of the use of observation strategies for needs identification purposes. The fact that a practitioner "perceives" a potential need based upon what (s)he observes should not be taken as evidence that a need exists. Observations that raise concerns should be used to ask questions or make requests for additional information (e.g., I've noticed that Jimmy has been sick for the past several weeks. Has this worried you?). The family's response to any queries, together with any information provided by the practitioner (e.g., If you think it

would be helpful, we could think about what you might want to do to figure out why Jimmy's not been feeling well), would then be used to engage the family in discussion about whether they are sufficiently concerned with the situation and whether or not they feel they want to pursue procurement of resources to meet needs. Extreme sensitivity must be used in sharing with the family observations that are made by the practitioner. Remember that it must be the family's decision whether or not their situation is of concern to them and whether or not they want to pursue options for meeting needs if they identify their concerns as deserving attention.

Several need categories that might be considered as part of an observational assessment include the following:

1. *The need for basic resources (shelter, furnishings, clothing, food, etc.) can often be assessed through observation of the family's physical environment.* For instance, if it is noted that the children are not adequately dressed, and one is aware that the family is concerned about the children going back to school, this could be used as a basis for engaging the family in discussion about their concern or need for school clothing.

2. *The need for medical care can be determined by observation of the general health status of individual family members.* If, for example, a particular family member is repeatedly sick, a comment might be made like "I've noticed that Nellie has been sick for several weeks now. Has she gone to the doctor to find out what's wrong?" The response to this question would then provide a basis for further discussion about whether the illness is of concern to the family or whether the family has the necessary financial resources to pay for medical treatment.

3. *The need for different types of community resources can be assessed through observation of the family's neighborhood and community.* This requires knowledge and familiarity with the communities in which families reside. If, for example, a parent is concerned about social opportunities for their children, knowledge of play groups, swim clubs, etc. provide a basis for sharing information with the family so a decision might be made about whether to "look into" these socialization opportunities.

4. *The need for assistance or advice with child rearing matters or intervention techniques for promoting child development may be apparent from observation of parents or other caregivers and their children during daily routines in the home.* If, for example, an observation of a child's meal times indicates ongoing frustration on the part of the parents to get the child to eat, this would provide an opportunity to raise concerns or offer suggestions that the family may want to consider.

5. *The need for transportation may be observed by assessing whether or not family members are able to "get to" resources required to meet needs.* Generally, the need for transportation is easily determined by knowing that a family desires certain resources, but because of a disabled car or lack of money to ride a bus or take a cab, the family is unable to get to the resources. Observations of this sort easily provide a basis for engaging the family in a discussion about what might be done to access the resources.

Many different concerns, needs, desires, and aspirations can be ascertained using observation procedures. The above are just a few examples of areas in which observation strategies are useful as part of the needs identification process. Observation procedures can be very effective if the *caution* raised above is always taken into consideration. The practitioner must be sensitive to the family's situation and not assume that there is a need until the family indicates a need for a resource. This must be a guiding principle as part of the use of observational assessment techniques.

More than 60 years ago, Stern (1930, p. 35) carefully and thoughtfully developed guidelines for inexperienced practitioners who might use observation procedures for assessment purposes. His guidelines, actually written for the observation of children's behavior, can be restated in terms of family-centered assessment techniques.

1. *Make a clear distinction between what is actually seen or heard and conclusions drawn from it.* In everyday life, people have a tendency to explain, excuse, embroider, and expound on what they see and hear. An observer must clearly separate observed fact from interpretation.

2. *Try to interpret what you observe from the family's viewpoint rather than imposing your own perceptions on the material.* The ability to get into a family's head is a rare one. Some adults seem to have a talent for putting themselves in a family's place. But most adults need to be wary when interpreting a family's actions; too often the interpretation is a better reflection of how observers reason and react than it is of a family's response.

3. *Draw no conclusions which cannot be positively justified by the actual observation.* This touches on a common weakness in us all. We are all apt to go a bit beyond the actual evidence if we have a hunch that something might be true.

SELF-REPORT SCALES

Self-report, needs-based assessment scales provide another means for helping families share their concerns and identify their needs. A number of needs-based, family-centered assessment scales have been developed specifically for this purpose (see Dunst & Trivette, 1985). Among these are the following:

- Family Needs Survey (Bailey & Simeonsson, 1985)
- How Can We Help? Scale (Child Development Resources, 1988)
- Parent Needs Survey (Darling, 1988)
- Family Needs Scale (Dunst, Cooper, Weeldreyer, Snyder, & Chase, 1988)
- Family Resource Scale (Dunst & Leet, 1987)
- Parent Needs Inventory (Fewell, Meyer, & Schell, 1981)

Any one of these, as well as other scales, might be used in conjunction with a family interview or use of observation techniques for gathering information from the family about concerns and needs. For practitioners who have not been trained in use of clinical interviewing techniques, or who initially find interview or observation techniques particularly difficult, the use of a self-report instrument can provide the context for allowing the family to make initial indications of what they may need. In selecting an appropriate instrument, one should be certain to match the actual content of the instrument with the type of information that is needed. For example, choosing a scale which measures informational needs pertaining to child development would not be appropriate where information about the family's basic needs is desired. Additionally, one would not use a measure of marital satisfaction, when one is attempting to identify family needs related to adequacy of medical or dental care.

The use of self-report scales for identifying family needs must be done in a way that insures that the assessment data are gathered in a helpful, proactive manner rather than being reactive and intrusive. Several steps and considerations should be taken into account when self-report scales are used to assess needs:

1. First, explicitly state why you are asking the family to complete the scale (e.g., "Could you please take the time to fill out this scale about what you might need so that I can be of optimal assistance to you and your family?").
2. Second, be very clear about how the results will be used (e.g., "After you complete the scale, I'd like us to go over your responses to get a better idea about your concerns and needs.").
3. Third, use the responses to help the family clarify and define what they perceive to be concerns or needs (e.g., "You indicated that child care is a need. Can you tell me more about what types of child care you feel would be most beneficial?").
4. Fourth, restate the needs as they are clarified to be sure the family sees your perceptions as accurate (e.g., "If I understand you correctly, you are saying because you will be going back to work, you will need to find day care that is open hours that fit with your work schedule.").

Following these four simple steps can significantly help promote the identification of family needs using self-report instruments in a non-intrusive manner.

SUMMARY AND CONCLUSION

The *purpose* of this chapter was to describe both a framework and set of assessment strategies for identifying family needs as a basis for mobilizing resources to meet needs. A number of considerations were addressed as part of describing a particular framework for conceptualizing the needs identification process. Three different but complementary assessment strategies were described for identifying family needs. Taken together, the material presented in this chapter provides the necessary information for practitioners to identify family needs from a family-centered assessment and intervention perspective.

Methods and strategies for *mobilizing resources* to meet needs are described in detail in Deal et al. (1989); Dunst (1989); Dunst and Deal (1990); and Dunst, Trivette, and Deal (1988), as well as in Chapter 11. These involve basically *matching* resources-to-needs by mapping a family's support and resource network against each need identified as part of the use of the kinds of assessment strategies described in this chapter. That is, once needs have been specified, the next step is to identify sources of support and resources for meeting needs. *Personal social network mapping* is used to accomplish the goal of identifying sources of support and resources for meeting needs. The persons and institutions with which a family and its members come in contact–either directly or indirectly–are referred to as the family's *personal social network*, and it is this network that is the primary source

of support to families and individual family members (Cohen & Syme, 1985b). For each family need, the range of options for meeting needs are identified and their viability as sources of support and resources determined. A simple rule-of-thumb is followed in network mapping: *Potential sources of support are mapped for each need separately so as to focus the resource and support identification and mobilization process.* By doing so, the practitioner gathers information specifically and only in relationship to family-identified needs. Table 7-1 can be used as a guide for this part of the assessment and intervention process.

Needs-based family-centered assessment and intervention practices emphasize the active participation of both the family and practitioner in identifying the family's concerns and needs from their own, unique perspective. The methods and strategies described in this chapter provide a framework for families and practitioners to collaborate in identifying needs and mobilizing resources to meet needs. To the extent that needs identification and resource mobilization occur in ways that build upon family strenghts and capabilities, the family ought to be strengthened and empowered in ways consistent with the aims of family support programs.

CHAPTER 8

Measuring the Adequacy of Resources in Households with Young Children

Carl J. Dunst & Hope E. Leet

Aₛ NOTED IN CHAPTER 7, a number of needs-based self-report scales are available for assessing family concerns and priorities. Properly used, these instruments can assist practitioners in identifying family needs. One instrument, the Family Resource Scale, developed as a result of our own work, has proven especially useful for this purpose. The Family Resource Scale (FRS, see Appendix) is easily administered and yields a potentially rich amount of information for gleaning a better understanding of a family's situation.

The purpose of this chapter is to describe the procedures used to establish the reliability and validity of the FRS. The FRS is an objective measure for assessing the adequacy of both resources and needs in households with young children. The scale is designed to assess the types of resources which have been identified as major components of both intrafamily and extrafamily support (Bronfenbrenner, 1979; House & Kahn, 1985; Wills, 1985). The scale includes 30 items that measure the adequacy of both physical and human resources, including food, shelter, financial resources, transportation, time to be with family and friends, health care, etc. The individual FRS items are roughly ordered in a hierarchy from the most to the least basic. Each item is rated on a five-point scale ranging from Not-At-All-Adequate to Almost-Always-Adequate.

The development of the scale was guided by several lines of research, including human ecology (Bronfenbrenner, 1979; Garbarino, 1982), the social support literature (Cohen & Syme, 1985b), family systems theory (Hartman & Laird, 1983), and the help-seeking literature (DePaulo, Nadler, & Fisher, 1983). Human ecology emphasizes the interdependencies among ecological settings (home, work, church, etc.), and how events in these different settings reverberate and affect human behavior in settings in which a person is not even present. Bronfenbrenner (1979), for example, noted that resources like adequacy of child care arrangements and the quality of health care affect parents' capacity to function effectively in their child-rearing roles. The social support literature defines support as "resources provided by other persons...potentially useful information or things" that affect health and well-being (Cohen & Syme, 1985a, p. 4). Since resources constitute one component of the social support construct, one would expect to find that adequacy of resources would affect personal and familial well-being. A fundamental proposition of family systems theory is that needs are one set of forces that influence behavior, and because needs can be arranged in a hierarchy from the most to least basic, emphasis is likely to be placed on meeting unmet needs that are high in the hierarchy (i.e., those that are most basic). For instance, Hartman and Laird (1983) have argued that inadequate resources affect a family's patterns of stability, growth, and

This chapter appeared in *Child: Care, Health and Development*, 1987, *13*, 11-125. Reprinted by permission of the publisher.

competence, and Minuchin (1985) reviewed available evidence to support the contention that disruptions in the family system can negatively affect parent as well as child functioning (see also Cochran & Brassard, 1979). The help-seeking literature suggests that the extent to which professionally-prescribed regimens are followed depends upon whether the client views these needs and prescriptions as relevant for action (Zola, 1966). Thus, whenever there is a "mismatch" between what a family and professional sees as child, parent, and/or family needs, the probability of a family adhering to professional prescriptions would be diminished.

The notion of "environmental press" permeates each of the above frameworks, and helps explain the interdependencies between person and setting events. Garbarino (1983) defined environmental press as:

the combined influence of forces working in an environment to shape the behavior and development of individuals in that setting. It arises from the circumstances confronting and surrounding an individual that generate (needs and) psychosocial momentum, which tend to guide that individual in a particular direction. (p. 8)

When expanded to include needs and needs hierarchies, environmental press takes on added meaning, especially in terms of understanding the conditions that take precedence and steer behavior in certain directions. Moreover, a needs hierarchy perspective of environmental press helps explain why certain families, especially those labeled as noncompliant, resistive, and those with multiple problems, fail to adhere to professionally-prescribed regimens. It is our contention that the behavior of families with inadequate personal and family resources

(i.e., those with minimal support) is steered toward getting needs met, and that inadequate resources negatively affects well-being and health, and lowers the probability that families will adhere to professionally prescribed regimens that do not address unmet needs. The development of both the FRS and needs hierarchy perspective of environmental press has evolved from our work with families of preschool-aged children enrolled in early intervention programs. The scale was specifically designed as an assessment tool that could be used by practitioners for measuring adequacy of resources and provide a concrete basis for deciding upon intervention targets and appropriate intervention strategies for addressing unmet needs (see Chapter 7). The two studies described next were implemented in order to establish both the reliability and validity of the FRS, and test the adequacy of the conceptual framework used as a basis for development of the scale.

STUDY 1

The purposes of Study 1 were (a) to establish the scalability (hierarchical ordering) of the 30 FRS items and (b) to determine the test-retest reliability of the rank orderings.

METHOD

Subjects

The subjects were 28 professionals with extensive experience working with preschoolers with disabilities and their families. The sample included social workers, psychologists, special educators, speech therapists, and nurses. All of the subjects had either a bachelors or masters degree.

Procedure

The scale items were randomly ordered

and each subject was asked to rank-order the items from most-to-least basic. The instructions asked the subjects to give the most basic resource a score of one, the second most basic resource a score of two, and so on until all 30 items were rank-ordered.

RESULTS

Scalability

Correlational analyses were performed between the rank-ordering for the 28 professionals against the order shown on the scale. The mean correlation was .81 (SD= .09, p < .0001). The mean correlation among the rank-orderings for the 28 individual subjects was .75 (SD = .11, p < .0001).

Test-Retest Reliability

Twenty-three of the subjects rank-ordered the items on two occasions, two months apart to establish the test-retest reliability of the hierarchical ordering. The mean correlation for the test-retest rankings was .70 (SD = .17, p < .0001).

DISCUSSION

The findings from Study 1 showed that the FRS items are roughly ordered from most-to-least basic, and that the sequence represents a hierarchy of resources that can be reliably established by professionals with extensive experience working with young children and their families. The results provide support for a needs hierarchy perspective of human behavior (e.g., Hull, 1943; Murray, 1938), and especially Maslow's (1954) perspective of human growth which places needs on a hierarchy ranging from those that are basically physiological and intrapersonal to those that are interpersonal and growth oriented. The particular hierarchy depicted on the scale generally conforms to the sequence of needs and resource proposed by

Hartman and Laird (1983). This hierarchy ranges from nutritional needs (e.g., adequate and varied food) to generativity (planning for and contributing to the future). The extent to which the adequacy of resources as well as unmet needs affected parental functioning was examined as part of Study 2.

STUDY 2

The purposes of Study 2 were to establish both the reliability (internal consistency, split-half, and test-retest) and validity (construct, content and criterion) of the scale.

METHOD

Subjects

The subjects were 45 mothers of preschool-aged children participating in an early intervention program. The mothers' mean age and average years of school completed were, respectively, 28.64 (SD= 5.7) and 12.49 (SD = 2.56). The subjects' mean SES score on the Hollingshead (1975) four factor index of socioeconomic status was 30.04 (SD = 14.51), indicating that the mothers, on the average, fell into the low to middle SES range. Their mean gross monthly income was $1285 (SD = $784).

Procedure

The mothers completed three self-report measures as part of their participation in the study: Family Resource Scale (FRS), Health and Well-Being Index (HWI; Dunst, 1986d), and Personal Allocation Scale (PAS; Dunst, 1986d). The HWI scale is a five-item rating scale which measures the respondent's physical health, psychological well-being, coping mechanisms, and stress management skills. The sum of the ratings of the five items provides a global index of health and well-being. The PAS is a three-item rating scale that measures the extent to which respondents have the time, physical and emotional energy, and personal belief and investment to carry-out child-level interventions prescribed by professionals. The sum of the ratings of the three items provides an overall index of the *degree of commitment* to child-level interventions. (Both the reliability and validity of the HWI and PAS are described in the individual reports of the scales.)

RESULTS

Table 8-1 shows the means, standard deviations, and ranges for the 30 FRS items and total FRS score. The rating scale for the FRS is such that a score of 4 or 5 is considered optimal with respect to the adequacy of personal and family resources. As can be seen from inspection of Table 8-1, the majority of items had average ratings between Sometimes Adequate (3) and Usually Adequate (4). The range of scores for nearly all the items (80%) varied from 1 to 5, indicating that the scale was sensitive in detecting differences in adequacy of resources among individual subjects. Two items (time for family and time for children) had a range from 2 to 5, and three items (house/apartment, heat, and toys for child) had a range from 3 to 5. Only one item (indoor plumbing and water) showed minimal variability in the range of scores.

Reliability

Internal consistency. Coefficient alpha computed from the average correlation among the 30 items was 0.92. Coefficient alpha computed from the average correlation of the 30 items with the total FRS score was 0.97. The split-half (even vs. odd numbered item) reliability was 0.95 corrected for length using the Spearman-Brown formula.

Test-retest reliability. The short term stability of the FRS was determined for all 45 subjects administered the scale on two occasions, two to three months apart. The stability coefficient for the total scale scores was $r = 0.52$ ($p < .001$).

Validity

Factor structure. A principal components analysis using varimax rotation was used to discern both the construct and content validity of the FRS. The correlation matrix was factored with unities in the diagonal, and factors with eigenvalues exceeding 1.0 were retained for rotation. A factor loading of .40 or greater was taken as evidence of factor membership. The analysis yielded eight orthogonal factors which, together, accounted for 75% of the variance (see Table 8-2). The multiple factor solution indicates that the FRS is measuring independent dimensions of personal and family needs and resources.

Factor I includes items that measure both *Growth and Support* including availability of time for personal growth, interpersonal relationships, and money for different kinds of resources. Factor II includes items that assess both *Health and Necessities*, including money for food, shelter, utilities, and debts; source of income; and health and dental care. Factor III includes primarily *Physical Necessities* items, including adequacy of food, clothing, and transportation. Factor IV includes the *Physical Shelter* items, including an adequate house or apartment, heat, and indoor water and plumbing. Factor V is an *Intrafamily Support* factor that includes time to be with both child(ren) and family. Factor VI includes items that measure *Communication and Employment*, including availability of a telephone, dependable transportation, and source of income. Factor VII is a *Childcare* factor that includes availability of both childcare arrangements

Table 8-1. Means, Standard Deviations and Ranges of Scores for the Family Resource Scale Items

Scale Items	Mean	Standard Deviation	Range
1. Food for 2 meals a day	4.73	0.69	1-5
2. House or apartment	4.84	0.43	3-5
3. Money to buy necessities	3.91	1.06	1-5
4. Enough clothes for your family	4.27	1.03	1-5
5. Heat for your house or apartment	4.60	0.58	3-5
6. Indoor plumbing/water	4.87	0.34	4-5
7. Money to pay monthly bills	3.99	1.11	1-5
8. Good job for yourself or spouse	4.24	1.28	1-5
9. Medical care for your family	4.18	1.71	1-5
10. Public assistance	4.56	0.92	1-5
11. Dependable transportation	4.47	0.97	1-5
12. Time to get enough sleep/rest	3.49	1.25	1-5
13. Furniture for your home or apartment	4.42	1.01	1-5
14. Time to be by yourself	3.07	1.21	1-5
15. Time for family to be together	4.00	0.93	2-5
16. Time to be with child(ren)	4.27	0.75	2-5
17. Time to be with spouse or close friend	3.25	1.07	1-5
18. Telephone or access to a phone	4.27	1.25	1-5
19. Babysitting for your child(ren)	3.62	1.17	1-5
20. Child care/day care for your child(dren)	4.38	1.07	1-5
21. Money to buy special equipment/supplies for children	3.44	1.32	1-5
22. Dental care for your family	3.64	1.35	1-5
23. Someone to talk to	3.80	1.14	1-5
24. Time to socialize	3.13	1.24	1-5
25. Time to stay in shape and looking nice	3.31	1.45	1-5
26. Toys for your child(ren)	4.38	0.72	3-5
27. Money to buy things for yourself	3.16	1.36	1-5
28. Money for family entertainment	3.16	1.36	1-5
29. Money to save	2.45	1.41	1-5
30. Time and money to travel/vacation	2.65	1.46	1-5
Total Scale Score	116.54	17.76	75-150

Note. Four items (8,10,20,21) did not apply to a number of subjects because they were not relevant for one or more reasons. In such instances, the subject was given a score of 5 since this implied that the resource was almost always adequate.

Table 8-2. Factor Analysis Solutions for the Family Resource Scale

	Factor Solutions							
	I	II	III	IV	V	VI	VII	VIII
Scale items	Growth/ Support	Health/ Necessities	Physical Necessities	Physical Shelter	Intrafamily Support	Communication Employment	Childcare	Personal Resources
Time to socialize	.87							
Someone to talk to	.79							
Time to keep in shape	.78							
Time to be with spouse	.59		-.49					
Time to be with self	.54		-.59					
Time/money to travel	.81							
Money to save	.69	.47						
Money for entertainment	.69	.55						
Money for self	.60	.57						
Money for necessities	.46	.68						
Toys for child(ren)	.41	.53						
Dental care		.89						
Medical care		.76						
Enough clothing for family		.67	.46					
Money to buy special child equipment		.55					.42	
Money to pay bills		.54						
Furniture		.46	.63					
Public assistance		.44				.44		
Good job for self/spouse		.43				.43		.56
Heat for house or apartment		.40		.47				
Babysitting for child		.40				-.63		
Food for two meals a day			.54					
Dependable transportation			.42			.57		
House or apartment				.90				
Indoor water and plumbing				.76				
Time to be with children					.82			
Time to be with family					.74			
Telephone/access to a phone						.67		
Childcare							.74	
Time to rest/sleep								.78
Variance explained	*33%*	*12%*	*8%*	*5%*	*5%*	*4%*	*4%*	*4%*
Cumulative variance	*33%*	*45%*	*53%*	*58%*	*63%*	*67%*	*71%*	*75%*

and special equipment for the child. Factor VIII is a *Personal Resources* factor.

Criterion validity. The criterion validity of the FRS was determined through partial correlation analysis predicting HWI and PAS scores from the total FRS scores and subscale scores derived from seven logically formed subcategories of needs, partialling-out the effects of mothers' age, education, SES, and income. The FRS subscale categories were: food and shelter, financial resources, time for family, extrafamily support, childcare, specialized child resources, and luxuries. The results are shown in Table 8-3. Both the well-being and commitment measures were significantly related to the total FRS scores. Four of the seven FRS subscale scores were significantly related to well-being, and all seven subscale scores predicted parental commitment to child-level interventions.

DISCUSSION

The findings from Study 2 provide support for both the reliability and validity of the Family Resource Scale. The internal consistency, split-half, and test-retest reliability coefficients were of moderate to substantial magnitude, and psychometrically acceptable. Both the internal consistency and split-half reliability findings indicated that the FRS is measuring a relatively homogeneous construct which we labeled "needs and resources." The test-retest results showed that adequacy of resources was found to be generally stable over a two to three month period of time.

The factor analysis of the FRS showed that the scale is measuring independent dimensions of resources and needs. The particular set of solutions parallel the categories of resources and needs which Hartman and Laird (1983) described as essential for optimal family functioning. On the one hand, the factor analysis findings provide evidence regarding the content validity of the scale since the

individual FRS items appear to be representative of the types of resources and needs that are important to family functioning as well as are cast in a form that permits an assessment of the adequacy of different types of resources and needs (Nunnally, 1967). On the other hand, the findings provide support for the construct validity of the scale since the particular sets of solutions tend to measure relatively homogeneous types of resources and needs.

The importance of a good job as a resource for meeting personal and family needs was highlighted in Study 2 by the fact that the employment item was the only resource that loaded substantially on 3 of the 8 solutions. According to Hartman and Laird (1983), although there are a number of major categories of family resources, "the need for money to purchase needed resources, whether food, shelter, and material goods, or opportunities for enrichment, is assumed basic to the entire list" (p. 164). The present results provide support for this contention.

The criterion validity of the FRS was established with respect to the relationship between adequacy of resources and both personal well-being and maternal commitment to carrying-out professionally prescribed, child-level regimens. The pattern of significant correlations between resources and well-being adds to a burgeoning body of evidence documenting the fact that social support has positive influences on health and well-being (Cohen & Syme, 1985b). The fact that all eight measures of resources were significantly related to the maternal commitment measure indicates that the influence of adequacy of resources extends beyond well-being to personal belief systems (Sigel, 1985). The pattern of results is consistent with evidence from the help-seeking literature which indicates that the extent to which professional prescriptions are seen as relevant for action depends upon the match between per-

Table 8-3. Partial Correlation Coefficients Between the Predictor and Criterion Measures

Predictor measures	Criterion measures	
	Personal well-being	Commitment to intervention
Total FRS scores	.52***	.63***
Food and shelter	.22	.49***
Financial resources	.23	.37**
Time for family	.68***	.54***
Extrafamily support	.75***	.54***
Childcare	.23	.53***
Specialized child resources	.30*	.37**
Luxuries	.48***	.53***

Note. Correlations with mothers' age, education level, income, and SES partialled.
*p<.025, **p<.01, ***p<.001.

sonal and professional priorities (DePaulo et al., 1983; Merton, 1976; Zola, 1966).

GENERAL DISCUSSION

Taken together, the results from both studies provide support for a needs hierarchy perspective of environmental press (Garbarino, 1982, 1983). Personal and family needs were found to form a hierarchy and constitute a set of forces shaping behavior, and that unmet needs took precedence in terms of influencing and directing behavior. That is, mothers who reported inadequacies in family resources were less likely to see child-level educational and therapeutic needs as *immediately* important, and consequently were not likely to invest the time and energy to work on professionally prescribed treatments. Presumably, the mothers were more concerned about getting other more basic family needs met, and were investing time and energy towards this end.

The findings also provide support for the conceptual framework upon which the scale was developed. Resources were found to be a form of support (Cohen & Syme, 1985b) that affected human behavior and family functioning (Bronfenbrenner, 1979; Garbarino, 1982; Hartman & Laird, 1983; Minuchin, 1985), including health and well-being (Cohen & Syme, 1985b) and adherence to professionally prescribed regimens (DePaulo et al., 1983; Zola, 1966). This particular social systems perspective of the relationships among person and setting variables provides support for the ecological validity of the needs hierarchy perspective of human behavior presented in this chapter. Specifically, the model helps explain the manner in which inadequacies in needs influence and steer behavior in certain directions (Garbarino, 1982, 1983).

IMPLICATIONS FOR PRACTICE

The FRS has direct application for assess-

ment and intervention purposes. As an assessment tool, the FRS can help discern the
adequacy of family's resources. On the one
hand, the findings can help decide the probability of parents having the time and energy
to carry-out child-level interventions. To the
extent that basic needs are unmet, the likelihood of parents making a commitment to
child-level interventions is diminished. On
the other hand, the results can provide a basis
for understanding how professional demands
placed upon a family can produce negative
effects. To the extent that a family is expend-
ing time and energy meeting basic needs,
added demands are likely to increase stress
and negatively affect health and well-being.

As an intervention tool, the FRS can help
identify parent and family needs, and provide a
basis for deciding upon the appropriate targets
for intervention. Those items rated as Not-At-
All-Adequate or Seldom-Adequate, especially

those high in the hierarchy, may be taken as
evidence that basic needs are not being met, and
suggest that efforts be made to mediate provisions of support in order to provide the types of
resources necessary for normative family functioning. Inasmuch as targets would be selected
by the family, the probability of the intervention efforts being successful should be enhanced (see especially Chapter 7).

We are currently witnessing a shift away
from child-focused to family-centered approaches in human services practices. This
shift necessitates the use of broader-based,
social-systems perspectives of family functioning, especially conceptual frameworks that
attempt to understand the interdependencies
among person and setting events. The FRS
was specifically developed from this type of
broader-based, social-system perspective, and
should prove useful to practitioners as both
an assessment and intervention tool.

APPENDIX

Family Resource Scale

Hope E. Leet & Carl J. Dunst

INSTRUCTIONS: This scale is designed to assess whether or not you or your family have adequate resources (time, money, energy, and so on) to meet the needs of the family as a whole as well as the needs of individual family members. For each of item, please circle the response that best describes how well the needs are met on a consistent basis in this family (that is, month-in and month-out).

To what extent are the following resources adequate for this family:	Does Not Apply	Not at All Adequate	Seldom Adequate	Sometimes Adequate	Usually Adequate	Almost Always Adequate
1. Food for 2 meals a day	NA	1	2	3	4	5
2. House or apartment	NA	1	2	3	4	5
3. Money to buy necessities	NA	1	2	3	4	5
4. Enough clothes for your family	NA	1	2	3	4	5
5. Heat for your house or apartment	NA	1	2	3	4	5
6. Indoor plumbing/water	NA	1	2	3	4	5
7. Money to pay monthly bills	NA	1	2	3	4	5
8. Good job for yourself or spouse/partner	NA	1	2	3	4	5
9. Medical care for your family	NA	1	2	3	4	5
10. Public assistance (SSI, AFDC, Medicaid, etc.)	NA	1	2	3	4	5
11. Dependable transportation (own car or provided by others)	NA	1	2	3	4	5
12. Time to get enough sleep/rest	NA	1	2	3	4	5
13. Furniture for your home or apartment	NA	1	2	3	4	5
14. Time to be by yourself	NA	1	2	3	4	5
15. Time for family to be together	NA	1	2	3	4	5
16. Time to be with your child(ren)	NA	1	2	3	4	5
17. Time to be with spouse/partner or close friend	NA	1	2	3	4	5
18. Telephone or access to a phone	NA	1	2	3	4	5
19. Babysitting for your child(ren)	NA	1	2	3	4	5
20. Child care/day care for your child(ren)	NA	1	2	3	4	5
21. Money to buy special equipment/supplies for child(ren)	NA	1	2	3	4	5
22. Dental care for your family	NA	1	2	3	4	5
23. Someone to talk to	NA	1	2	3	4	5
24. Time to socialize	NA	1	2	3	4	5
25. Time to keep in shape and looking nice	NA	1	2	3	4	5
26. Toys for your child(ren)	NA	1	2	3	4	5
27. Money to buy things for self	NA	1	2	3	4	5
28. Money to buy things for yourself	NA	1	2	3	4	5
29. Money to save	NA	1	2	3	4	5
30. Travel/vacation	NA	1	2	3	4	5

(May be duplicated without permission with proper acknowledgment and citation.)

CHAPTER 9

Strengths-Based Family-Centered Intervention Practices

Carl J. Dunst, Carol M. Trivette & Donald W. Mott

THE CURRENT INTEREST in the assessment of family strengths, as well as efforts to support and strengthen family functioning, has a short but rich history. The pioneering work of Otto (1962, 1963, 1975) forms the foundation of current work in the family strengths arena. In the early 1980s, Bowman (1983) aggregated and summarized much of what was currently believed to be the major indicators of family strengths. Curran (1983) and Karpel (1986a) as well provided extensive descriptions of the traits and personal resources of healthy, well-adjusted families.

The most ambitious work on identifying family strengths has been conducted by Stinnett and his colleagues (Lingren et al., 1987; Rowe et al., 1984; Stinnett, 1979,1985; Stinnett, Chesser, & DeFrain, 1979a; Stinnett, Chesser, DeFrain, & Knaub, 1979b; Stinnett & DeFrain, 1985a; Stinnett, DeFrain, King, Knaub, & Rowe, 1981; Stinnett et al., 1982; Stinnett, Lynn, Kimmons, Fuenning, & DeFrain, 1984; Stinnett, Knorr, DeFrain, & Rowe, 1981; Van Zandt et al., 1986; Williams, Lingren, Rowe, Van Zandt, & Stinnett, 1985). Collectively, the information included in these reports and documents, as well as material in other sources (e.g., Beavers & Hampson, 1990; Hill, 1971; Lewis, Beavers, Gossett, & Phillips, 1976; Satir, 1972; Walsh, 1982), provide the necessary framework for defining and assessing family strengths, and conducting interventions in ways that support and strengthen family functioning. This chapter is devoted to a number of considerations related to strengths-based family-centered assessment and intervention practices. The material is intended to serve as a framework for practitioners to use for identifying and building upon family strengths as the principle way of supporting and strengthening family functioning.

DEFINITION OF FAMILY STRENGTHS

A number of definitions of family strengths can be found in the published literature. Each provides a basis for understanding both the meaning and components of family strengths. Otto (1975) defined family strengths as:

> those forces and dynamic factors... which encourage the development of the personal resources and potentials of members of the family and which make family life deeply satisfying and fulfilling to family members. (p. 16)

Similarly, Williams et al. (1985) defined family strengths as:

> those relationship patterns, interpersonal skills and competencies, and social and psychosocial characteristics

which create a sense of positive family identity, promote satisfying and fulfilling interaction among family members, encourage the development of the potential of the family group and individual family members, and contribute to the family's ability to deal effectively with stress and crisis (Preface).

These as well as other definitions of family strengths (see Bowman, 1983) share three common features and characteristics. First, these definitions indicate that family strengths are primarily *interpersonal* and *intrafamily* in nature. Second, these definitions indicate that family strengths are comprised of a complex array of *cognitive, attitudinal, and behavioral characteristics.* Third, and perhaps most importantly, these definitions make it explicit that family strengths are one set of factors that *enhance* and *promote* other important aspects of family functioning (e.g., health and well-being).

Strengths-based assessment and intervention practices represent a significant departure from the ways in which human services practitioners have typically viewed and intervened with families. A family strengths approach to working with families aims to support and strengthen family functioning. This, however, will likely become a reality if and only if a major shift occurs in the ways in which professionals view families and family functioning, and family-centered assessment and intervention practices. This paradigmatic shift has not yet occurred on a broad scale, but the transformation has been put into motion (Dunst, 1985; Weiss, 1989; Weiss & Jacobs, 1988a; Weissbourd & Kagan, 1989; Zigler & Black, 1989). At least five considerations need to be taken into account as part of making family-centered assessment and intervention practices strengths-oriented.

1. First, it must be recognized that all families have strengths and that these strengths are unique and depend upon the family's beliefs, cultural background, ethnicity, socioeconomic background, and so forth. As noted by Stoneman (1985), "every family has strengths, and if the emphasis is on supporting strengths rather than rectifying weaknesses, chances for making a difference in the lives of children and families are vastly increased" (p. 462).

2. Second, the failure of a family or individual family member to display competence must *not* be viewed as a deficit within the family system or family member, but rather the failure of social systems and institutions (e.g., human services programs) to create opportunities for competencies to be displayed or learned. This is the cornerstone of an empowerment philosophy that aims to strengthen functioning by enhancing competencies and a sense of control over important aspects of one's life (Rappaport, 1981, 1987).

3. Third, work with families must be approached in ways that focus and build on the positive aspects of functioning, rather than seeing families as being "broken" and "needing to be fixed." This requires not only the acceptance but the valuing of individual differences (Dokecki, 1983; Dokecki & Heflinger, 1989; Hobbs et al., 1984). According to Zigler and Berman (1983), this orientation "encourages a more productive approach to intervention in which we do not try to change children (and their families) but instead try to build on strengths" (p. 895).

4. Fourth, a shift must be made away from the use of either treatment or prevention models toward the adoption of promotion and enhancement models which are more consistent with the aim of strengthening family

functioning (Dunst, Trivette, & Thompson, 1990; Edelman & Mandle, 1986; Stanley & Maddux, 1986; Zautra & Sandler, 1983). The enhancement of human development is a preferable goal to prevention or treatment of pathology, because development is measured in terms of self-efficacy, self-reliance, positive mental health, competence, and mastery (Zautra & Sandler, 1983) outcomes that reflect the strengthening of family functioning.

5. Fifth, the goal of intervention must *not* be seen as "doing for people" but rather the strengthening of functioning in ways that make families less and not more dependent upon professionals for help (Dunst, 1987; Maple, 1977; Skinner, 1978). This will require a shift away from the "pervasive belief that experts should solve all of (a family's) problems" (Rappaport, 1981, p. 17), and toward one whereby the family is enabled and empowered to become capable of mastering important aspects of their lives.

Collectively, these five considerations suggest an alternative to the deficit, reactive approach that has dominated the ways in which both child- and family-level assessments and interventions have traditionally been conducted in most human services fields. A family strengths approach does not merely suggest but demands a positive, proactive approach toward the family and the purposes and goals of assessment and intervention practices.

MISCONCEPTIONS OF STRENGTHS-BASED INTERVENTION PRACTICES

The adoption of new or alternative intervention practices carries with it certain risks of misunderstanding or misinterpretation. This is especially true with regard to family strengths-based intervention practices. In our own work with families, as well as in work training others, we have noted a number of misconceptions that repeatedly surface as part of making the above paradigmatic shift toward strengths-based, family-centered intervention practices.

We share several of these misconceptions before proceeding with a more complete discussion of the characteristics of family strengths to place the remainder of the material in this chapter in proper perspective.

Misconception: Not all families have strengths.

Response: Let's get right to the nitty-gritty of a family strengths-based approach to intervention. The belief that certain families do not have strengths is blatantly wrong. *All families have strenghts*, and if professionals take the time to recognize and build upon strengths, families will become more capable and competent in adequately dealing with the demands and desires they experience in daily living. The misconception that some families do not have strengths is derived, in part, from the deficit, pathologically-based training most of us received as part of our formal education. Therefore, professionals tend to pay attention to what is not working rather than what is working well. The failure to believe in and recognize the capabilities of families has at least one major implication for intervention practices. If you believe that families have no strengths and capabilities, you will treat them as incompetent, likely "do for them" rather than promote their ability to do for themselves, and deprive the families of opportunities to become stronger and capable.

Misconception: The failure of a family to display strengths is a "sure sign" that a family has weaknesses.

Response: This misconception again derives from the fact that one is taking a deficit perspective of the family. A family strengths orientation does not view the failure to display competencies as deficits or weaknesses in the family, but rather due to the failure of social systems or institutions to create opportunities for competencies to be displayed or learned. Therefore, one does not attempt to "fix" families but rather enables families to use their existing strengths to mobilize resources to meet needs, solve problems, and achieve aspirations, as well as learn new competencies to reach other desired outcomes.

Misconception: The correction of family weaknesses will strengthen family functioning.

Response: Perhaps, but it's not very likely. Dunst, Trivette, and Thompson (1990; Chapter 4) recently reviewed existing studies and found that the absence of problems (correction of weaknesses) was not at all related to presence of positive functioning (enhancement of family strengths). A family strengths and enhancement orientation to intervention is necessary if a family is to be supported and strengthened. Correcting weaknesses or preventing poor functioning will not likely accomplish this aim.

Misconception: Adopting a family strengths approach to intervention is a denial of a family's problems.

Response: A family strengths approach to intervention does not ignore or deny the fact that a family may have problems. As Stinnett and DeFrain (1985b) noted, "strong families have lots of problems just like everybody else" (p. 7). However, strong or healthy families deal differently and more effectively with their problems because they have at their disposal a richer repertoire of knowledge, skills, and capabilities. The latter is why promoting and building on family strengths is a better approach to family-centered intervention practices.

Misconception: Strong families are characterized by the presence of the same qualities.

Response: A review of the literature finds that there are a host of nonmutually-exclusive family strengths (see below). No one family, however, would ever be expected to be characterized by the presence of all indicators of strengths, and the absence of any particular indicators is in no way an indication of weaknesses or deficits. The unique combination of qualities for a particular family is what defines that family's unique functioning style. It is this style that one attempts to understand so as to be able to support and strengthen family functioning.

With these misconceptions as a backdrop, we now examine the major characteristics and components of family strengths. A model for viewing family strengths as three sets of interrelated factors is proposed as one way of conceptualizing a family's unique functioning style.

MAJOR COMPONENTS AND INDICATORS OF FAMILY STRENGTHS

COMPONENTS OF FAMILY STRENGTHS

A review and synthesis of the family strengths literature (see especially Bowman, 1983; Karpel, 1986b) indicates that family strengths are comprised of three, nonmutually exclusive sets of cognitive, attitudinal, and behavioral components:

- Family Values
- Family Competencies
- Family Interactional Patterns

Family values refer to the interrelated and interacting influences of attitudes and beliefs that contribute to a family's unique functioning style. These values include a variety of *affirmations* and *expectations* that uniquely characterize a family's "life style." *Family competencies* refer to the knowledge, skills, capabilities, capacities and abilities that individual family members and the family unit have at their disposal in order to mobilize internal and external resources. Concretely, family competencies are those behaviors that reflect the *performances* of a family as they go about mobilizing intrafamily and extrafamily resources. *Interactional patterns* refer to those characteristics of interpersonal family relationships that promote the flow of information and resources among family members in ways that are mutually supportive. These patterns are behavioral in nature and are manifested in either or both the verbal and nonverbal domains. Collectively, the *values, competencies,* and *interactional patterns* of a family are the types of family capabilities that can be built upon to support and strengthen family functioning.

Figure 9-1 shows a particular way of con-

ceptualizing how family values, competencies, and interactional patterns "make up" *family strengths*, and how the unique combination of strengths defines a *family's functioning style.* The term family functioning style is the preferred way of characterizing a family's strengths because it implies unique ways of dealing with life events and promoting growth and development. There are no right or wrong family functioning styles, but rather differentially effective styles that are likely to be employed in response to different life events and situations. Additionally, functioning styles can be expected to change as families move through different stages of development. Families have various kinds of values, competencies, and interactional patterns that collectively define their unique *family functioning style,* and these styles reflect the ways in which families cope and grow. Indeed, the presence and combination of different psychological and behavioral characteristics constitute the defining fea-

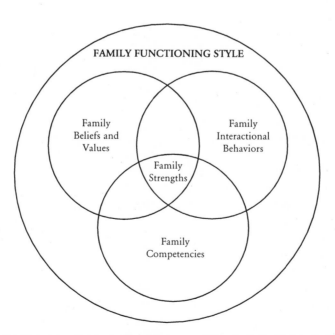

Fig 9-1. A Model for Conceptualizing the Key Elements of Family Functioning Style.

tures of unique family functioning styles (Lewis et al., 1976; Pearlin & Schooler, 1978).

INDICATORS OF FAMILY STRENGTHS

An examination of the family strengths literature (see Dunst, Trivette, & Deal, 1988; Trivette et al., 1990) suggests that there are a number of nonmutually exclusive characteristics that are indicators of family strengths. Before listing these characteristics, however, it must be made explicitly clear that *no family is characterized by the presence of all of these values, competencies, and interactional patterns.* A combination of characteristics make a family uniquely strong, with certain combinations contributing to unique family functioning styles. As Lewis and his colleagues (1976) have demonstrated, "optimally functioning or competent families appear to be (the result of) the presence and interrelationship of a number of variables" (p. 205). Similarly, Otto (1962) noted that "strengths are not isolated variables, but form clusters and constellations which are dynamic, fluid, interrelated, and interacting" (p. 80). Therefore, one must always remain cognizant of the fact that no single family unit would ever display all the characteristics. With this caveat noted, the indicators of family strengths include the following:

Family Values. The following are the kinds of family values that have been identified as particular types of strengths:

1. A belief in and sense of commitment toward promoting the well-being and growth of individual family members as well as that of the family unit.
2. A clear set of family rules, values, and beliefs that establishes expectations about acceptable and desired behavior.
3. A sense of purpose that permeates the reasons and basis for "going on" in both bad and good times.
4. A sense of shared responsibility.

5. Respect for the privacy of others.
6. A strong sense of family rituals and traditions.
7. A belief in the importance of being active and learning new things.
8. The belief that things will work out for the better if the family works together.
9. A concern for family unity and loyalty.

Family Competencies. The knowledge and skills that constitute family strengths include the following:

1. A varied repertoire of coping strategies that encourage positive functioning in dealing with both normative and nonnormative life events.
2. Flexibility and adaptability in the roles necessary to procure resources to meet needs.
3. A balance between the use of internal and external family resources for coping and adapting to life events and planning for the future.
4. Knowledge and skills used to recognize concerns, identify needs, and specify desired outcomes.
5. Knowledge and skills used to identify sources of support and resources for meeting needs.
6. Knowledge and skills used to take action to mobilize needed resources and supports.
7. Ability to be positive and see the positive in almost all aspects of their lives, including the ability to see crises and problems as an opportunity to learn and grow.
8. Ability to mobilize family members to acquire needed resources.
9. Ability to initiate and maintain growth-producing relationships within and outside of the family.
10. Ability to plan ahead to make things happen that are important to the family.

11. Ability to use humor in dealing with the events of their lives.

Interactional Patterns. The types of intrafamily interactions that constitute these kinds of family strengths are as follows:

1. Congruence among family members regarding the value and importance of assigning time and energy to what the family considers its goals, needs, projects, and functions.
2. The expression of appreciation for the small and large things that individual family members do well, and encouragement to do better.
3. Concentrated effort to spend time and do things together, no matter how formal or informal the activity or event.
4. Communication with one another that emphasizes positive interactions among family members.
5. Engaging in collective problem-solving activities designed to evaluate options for meeting needs and procuring resources.
6. Listening to one anothers problems, desires, hurts, aspirations, fears, and hopes in a supportive manner.
7. Expressions of affirmation and support of individual family members.

VALIDITY OF THE FRAMEWORK

Whether the three-dimensional model of family strengths was substantiated empirically was tested in our own research as part of a study using the Family Functioning Style Scale (Trivette, Dunst, Deal, Hamer, & Propst, 1990; Chapter 10) as a measure of family strengths. The parents of preschool age children were asked to complete this 26 item instrument. Their responses were subjected to a series of exploratory factor analyses to discern the structure of the relationship between

the items. The initial analysis produced a five factor solution. Items loading .60 or greater were retained as part of a second analysis which yielded a three factor solution, with the items included in each factor separately measuring the three aspects of family strengths.

The four items that factored together and were indicators of *family values* included the following:

1. Pride in the accomplishments of individual family members.
2. Commitment to sticking together in difficult times.
3. The belief that family relationships will outlast material possessions.
4. Personal sacrifices should be made in order to help the whole family.

The four items that factored together and were indicators of *family competencies* were as follows:

1. Finding the "bright side" of a bad situation.
2. Keeping busy in order to not dwell on situations beyond the family's control.
3. Asking for help from others when needed.
4. Finding informal supports to help in a crisis.

The six items that factored together and were indicators of *family interactional patterns* were as follows:

1. Talking about different ways of dealing with problems.
2. Finding time to be together.
3. Listening to all points of view in a discussion.
4. Willingness to help each other out.
5. Making time to get things done that are important to us.

6. Sharing concerns and feelings in constructive ways.

The findings from this exploratory study provide tentative evidence regarding the three dimensional model of family strengths depicted in Figure 9-1 above.

RECOGNIZING AND UTILIZING FAMILY STRENGTHS

The primary value of recognizing and utilizing family strengths in working with families is implicit in the definitions previously given. Families represent a tremendous resource both to themselves and to society as a whole. The notion that every family has a unique combination of strengths as determined by each family's particular values, cultural beliefs, and lifestyle has direct implications for understanding and working with families.

1. First, work with families will be most productive if the family itself is viewed as a major resource for meeting its own needs. As Karpel (1986b) has stated, "every successful intervention (with) a family...rests as much on the resources of the family as on those of the (interventionist)" (p. xiii).
2. Second, work with families will be most productive if families are viewed as being able to participate actively in the process of identifying their needs and developing and implementing methods to meet their needs.
3. Third, it must be recognized that all families have strengths and capabilities, and if we take the time to identify these characteristics and build on them rather than focus on correcting deficits or weaknesses, families are not only more likely to respond favorably to interventions but

the chances of making a significant positive impact on the family unit are enhanced considerably. A major consideration of strengthening families is promoting their ability to use existing strengths for meeting needs in a way that produces changes in family functioning.

METHODS AND STRATEGIES FOR IDENTIFYING FAMILY STRENGTHS

The major purpose of a family strengths assessment is to gather information about the values, competencies, and interactional patterns of families *from their own perspectives*. Knowledge of family strengths and family functioning style provides the necessary basis for promoting the acquisition of new competencies, as well as building upon existing capabilities. This is particularly the case when assessment information is used as part of procedures designed to have families use their competencies to mobilize resources and supports to meet their needs (Deal, Dunst, & Trivette, 1989; Dunst, Trivette, & Deal, 1988).

The process of identifying and building upon family strengths begins with an assessment of a family's functioning style. A family strengths assessment can be done using interviews, observations, or self-report family strengths scale, or a combination of the three strategies (see Dunst, Trivette, & Deal, 1988). The use of these approaches for assessing family functioning style is described next.

INTERVIEW AND OBSERVATIONAL PROCEDURES

The identification of family strengths using interview and observation procedures requires one to pay particular attention to both individual family member's behavior and interactions among family members. The following are several considerations and strategies that we have found helpful as part of identifying family strengths.

1. The major sources of material for identifying family functioning style are the descriptions, behaviors, and interactional patterns displayed by the family. People rarely explicitly name their strengths and capabilities. Rather, they generally *demonstrate* and *describe* strengths and capabilities by "way of example" (e.g., "When my wife has to be at the hospital with Johnny, we all pitch-in to do whatever needs to get done around the house."). The intervenor should make note of the various behaviors that a family displays, and determine to what extent these behaviors reflect appreciation for one another, involvement and commitment to "family project," a shared sense of purpose, and other family capabilities.

2. As part of getting a family to "tell their story" to you during an assessment process, pay particular attention to the various anecdotes which include numerous examples of behaviors that reflect strengths and capabilities as well as the ways the family employs intrafamily resources for meeting needs.

3. Another way to identify family strengths is to observe and take notice of the family's physical environment, and use the things the family "takes for granted" as a way of identifying their capabilities. Are the children safely occupied (e.g., "You always have interesting toys and activities for the children"), are there homemade crafts located throughout the house ("You have a real skill in needlework, and your framed pieces around the house really add a nice touch"); is there a vegetable or flower garden ("I'm sure you must enjoy the fresh vegetables you get from your garden and the savings you have on your grocery bill"); is there the smell of home cooked meals ("Your homemade breads and desserts must make your family feel really special"); etc.. These are the types of things that provide a concrete basis for an intervenor to comment on the family's strengths and capabilities, and such occurrences can be used for obtaining information about intrafamily resources.

4. One of the best ways to get a family to make known their functioning style is to ask them to describe the types of daily activities and routines that they engage in, and to describe the things they do to "get through the day" (e.g., "Can you tell me more about mealtimes? Who generally prepares the meals? Do other family members help out by watching the younger children? Do you find that dinner time is an enjoyable event?"). Pay particular attention to the ways in which the family deals and copes with both enjoyable as well as difficult tasks. These "ways of coping" are one set of intrafamily resources, and constitute the ways a family uses their resources for meeting daily needs.

5. In addition to the strategies described above, one can ask specific questions designed to elicit descriptions of family strengths and capabilities ("What are your favorite things to do together?" "Do you have any hobbies or interests that you enjoy or find relaxing?" "What things do you and your child(ren) do that you find the most fun?"). Questions like these set the occasion for a family to talk about the things that reflect strengths and capabilities.

6. Many families who describe concerns and dilemmas focus on the negative aspects of family functioning (e.g., "We never seem to be able to get ahead financially.").

Remember that there is always an alternative way of viewing things, and by restating and reframing a problem or concern in a more positive way, it may help the family see the ways in which things are working well (e.g., "It's really nice the way you are willing to help out with some of your mother's expenses. You must feel good that you are able to be of help to her."). Rephrasing, restating, and reframing what family members say can emphasize the healthy and positive aspects of family functioning style.

7. Many families, particularly those that seem to be characterized as having long histories of problems and failures, are rarely asked about the "good things" that characterize their families. Remember that all families have strengths, and that by pointing out and commenting upon what the family does do well, one can begin to help the family recognize their capabilities (e..g, "Although you have many demands on you right now, your willingness to do things together seems to have provided you with some 'good' times in the midst of your difficulties.").

The ability to discern family functioning style can be a major asset as part of helping families mobilize resources for meeting needs. Awareness of both the presence of family strengths and the ways in which they are collectively used to cope with life events as well as promote growth and development provides a basis for building upon and strengthening the things the family already does well.

FAMILY STRENGTHS SCALES

As was true with respect to the use of needs-based assessment tools, the responses on self-report, family strength measures should not be taken as the goal, but rather used as a basis for further discussion with the family about the meaning of their responses. For example, a family member might indicate that the ability to communicate is a strength in his or her household. This response should be used as a basis of pinpointing how the family communicates, the ways in which communication occurs, etc. as the means for discerning the specific behaviors that make this strength an intrafamily resource.

Additionally, it must be continually remembered that not all families will display all the qualities that represent family strengths, and that it is the unique combination of qualities that defines family functioning style. As noted by Otto (1962), "strengths are not isolated variables, but form clusters and constellations which are *dynamic, fluid, interrelated, and interacting*" (p. 80, emphasis added.) The use of family strengths scales should focus primarily on the interrelatedness of different qualities and how qualities are employed in daily living as intrafamily resources and as a way of procuring extrafamily resources. The latter should be the major emphasis of using family strengths scales.

A review of the family strengths literature identified four instruments that measure all or a subset of the qualities of strong families listed above. The use of self-report family strengths scales as part of family-centered assessment and intervention practices is described in the next section. The four scales that measure family strengths are described next.

1. *Family Strengths Inventory* (Stinnett & DeFrain, 1985a). This scale includes 13 items that measure six major qualities of strong families and a number of aspects of the interpersonal relationships among family members. The six qualities include commitment of family members in pro-

moting each other's welfare and happiness, appreciation for each other on a frequent basis, communication skills used by family members, spending time together and doing things important to the family, a sense of spiritual wellness that gives the family strength and purpose, and the ability to cope with stress and crisis in a way that provides the family an opportunity to grow. Other scale items assess the degree of closeness, happiness, confidence, and worthiness in the relationships among family members. Each item is rated on a five-point rating scale, based on the degree to which the quality or characteristic is present in the respondent's family. The scale yields a total score that provides a basis for determining the overall presence of family strengths. However, it is the individual responses to the 13 scale items that are most useful for determining family functioning style.

2. *Family Strengths Scale* (Olson, Larsen, & McCubbin, 1983). This scale includes 12 items that assess two dimensions of family functioning: family pride (loyalty, optimism, trust in the family) and family accord (ability to accomplish tasks, deal with problems, get along together). For each item, the respondent indicates the extent to which the quality is present in his or her family. The scale items measure many of the qualities described above, and provide a basis for establishing which qualities are characteristic of the respondent's family.

3. *Family Hardiness Index* (McCubbin, McCubbin, & Thompson, 1987). This scale includes 20 items that assess the internal strengths of families, and how those strengths are used to both control life events and produce positive growth in the family unit. Each item is rated on a

four-point scale in terms of the degree to which each statement is true for the family. The items are organized into four subscales: coordinated commitment (internal strengths, dependability, and ability to work together); confidence (family's sense of being able to plan ahead and of being appreciated for individual efforts, and the ability to endure hardships); challenge (efforts to be innovative, be active, and to experience new learning opportunities); and control (being able to control important aspects of life).

4. *Family Functioning Style Scale* (Deal, Trivette, & Dunst, 1988). This scale includes 26 items designed to assess all 12 qualities of strong families listed above (see Chapter 10). The instrument was developed as part of a family-centered assessment and intervention model (Dunst, Trivette, & Deal, 1988) that evolved from efforts to intervene in ways that support and strengthen family functioning. The scale assesses the extent to which a family, either as individuals or a group, believes that their family is characterized by different strengths and capabilities. Each item is rated on a five-point scale by noting the degree to which the 26 statements are "Not-At-All-Like-My-Family" to "Almost-Always-Like-My-Family."

Assessment Considerations. Several considerations should be taken into account when family strengths scales are used for assessment purposes.

1. First, it is extremely important to state explicitly why the family is being asked to complete the scale (e.g., "Could you please take the time to fill out this scale about your family's strengths? Your responses will help me get a better idea of what you

consider your family's special capabilities.").

2. Second, be very clear about how the results will be used (e.g., "After you complete the scale, I'd like to talk to you about some of the reasons you consider these qualities the strengths of your family. This will help me focus on what you feel are the positive things about your child[ren] and family").

3. Third, use the family's responses to clarify and specify the concrete ways these qualities are manifested (e.g., "You indicated that family members are willing to pitch in and help each other. In what ways do you do this?").

4. Fourth, emphasize the positive aspects of functioning as part of responding to the family's descriptions of its strengths (e.g., "The fact that you communicate so well in your family must really help in dealing with the concerns we talked about earlier.").

5. Fifth, prompt descriptions and make suggestions about how the family can use its strengths to mobilize resources to meet needs (e.g., "Since you have already looked at possible ways to help your child to learn to talk, which procedures do you feel most comfortable using at home?").

6. Sixth, build upon the competencies of the family and individual family members by using these skills and capabilities as part of the necessary actions for mobilizing resources to meet needs (e.g., Now that we have identified five things that need to be done to get Johnny enrolled in school, how do you feel about getting information from the teacher and therapist?").

These considerations should be used as a basis for both identifying family strengths and building on strengths as part of assessment and intervention practices (see Deal et al., 1989). Although described in a sequential manner, it is best to consider strengths assessment as a dynamic, fluid process that takes shape through ongoing interactions between family members and the interventionist (see Dunst, Trivette, Davis, & Weeldreyer, 1988; Dunst, Trivette, & Deal, 1988). The families we have worked with in our program, as well as our own staff have indicated that family strengths assessments can be beneficial and not intrusive if done in the proactive manner described above.

FROM ASSESSMENT TO PRACTICE

The case studies presented next were selected to illustrate family strengths and their use in two different families having quite different family situations. Both case studies illuminate (a) the range of existing family capabilities and strengths and those that were enhanced and promoted as part of participation in a family-centered early intervention program and (b) the advantages of building upon strengths rather than correcting weaknesses. The short vignettes are but a small amount of rich case study material that could have been used to describe and illustrate the meaning and components of family strengths as presented in this chapter.

KYLE FAMILY

The "Kyle" family includes "Martha," her children, "Steve," "Bill" and "Marcy," and Martha's nephew, "Daryl." Daryl experienced an intracranial hemorrhage at birth, which resulted in severe aplastic quadriplegia and profound mental retardation. Daryl's parents died in an automobile accident shortly after his birth, and Martha became Daryl's legal guardian.

Martha had married as a teenager, though

her husband was not in the home often. The Kyle family lived in a two-bedroom mobile home which they owned, but they usually had no income except from public support (Social Security, SSI, AFDC, and Medicaid for Daryl). At the time this report was written, the family was involved with a number of social services agencies in their community, and were described by the staff of these agencies as "users" and "abusers" of the human services system because of their continued reliance on public assistance.

Martha's extended family lived nearby, but only an aunt provided considerable emotional support and some assistance with child care for Daryl and her other children. Several other extended family members also lived nearby, but generally had minimal involvement with the family. The family became involved in a family-centered early intervention program at the time Daryl was approximately six-months old until he was enrolled in a center-based preschool classroom at four years of age.

Although the number and intensity of both child and family needs of the Kyle family were great, the family had many strengths which were utilized to meet needs during their involvement in the family-centered early intervention program. Many of these strengths were present at the time the family became involved in the program, whereas others were enhanced during the family's participation in the program.

The Kyle family's beliefs and values included a strong sense of family unity and commitment to one another; a high degree of intrafamily support, which included emotional, social and instrumental assistance; a commitment to "do what you can" to survive each day and help others in the family function adequately; a commitment to keeping the entire family together, including Daryl; a

commitment to assuring the highest possible quality-of-life for Daryl; a commitment to furthering the education of all family members, including Martha obtaining a GED; a belief that the family was "entitled" to help from the system; and a desire to help others in the community who were also in need of help. The idea of entitlement was particularly important in light of the fact that some agencies saw the family as "users" of the system. Martha was aware of this perception, resented it, and expressed the desire to be as self-sufficient as possible.

The family's positive interaction patterns included good communication among all family members; frequent expressions of commitment and caring about one another; the ability to "pull together" during difficult times to solve problems or provide support to one another; and sharing household and child care responsibilities.

The ability to manage Daryl's medical needs; the ability to fix or repair things around the house and motor vehicles; the ability to identify and utilize a variety of informal and formal support network resources to meet needs; the ability to advocate for Daryl's needs; and excellent child care skills in areas related to meeting Daryl's special needs were some of the family's competencies.

The Kyles' existing family strengths proved important as part of meeting the family's, as well as Daryl's needs. For example, their commitment to working together as a family unit, their ability to communicate among themselves, and their ability to provide each other emotional support were essential for effectively coping on a daily basis. The family, and especially Martha, used their knowledge of the human service systems in their community to manage Daryl's medical needs very effectively. Additionally, Steve and Bill frequently used their mechanical abilities to repair the family's automobile, as well as to build a ramp for Daryl when he became too heavy to carry.

A number of family strengths were used and enhanced during the family's involvement in the family-centered early intervention program. These strengths led to changes in the lifestyle of the family that had endured more than eight years. The most significant of these were Martha's development of skills related to Daryl's care. For example, she became quite competent in areas related to feeding and positioning, and promoting his motor and cognitive development. Martha also developed an appreciation of the uniqueness of each child in her family, and the need for the children to learn at their own pace and in their own way. She also became interested in working with other children in addition to Daryl, and volunteered to work in a community preschool program. Martha later worked as a staff member in this program, and also became a specialized foster parent for several children with developmental disabilities. As Martha gradually became able to financially support herself and her family as a result of earning money providing foster care, she began working toward her GED which she eventually received. At the same time, the staff member working with her helped Martha develop her advocacy skills regarding the most constructive strategies to use to gain access to needed services and resources. The family was eventually able to move into a larger home, and to purchase a variety of pieces of adaptive equipment to meet Daryl's needs.

Throughout involvement with the Kyle family, the staff member working with the family expressed respect for the family's values and assisted the family in clarifying and prioritizing goals that were consistent with their values. At many times these goals were related to meeting basic needs for food, shelter and safety, and day-to-day issues related to Martha's children. The family faced many challenges during the four years they were involved in the family-centered early intervention program, including Martha's health problems, the pregnancy of Marcy (a teenage daughter), and ongoing financial struggles. At times the family felt they might have to give up caring for Daryl, but they were able to use their own strengths, particularly their commitment to family unity and their willingness to share responsibilities related to Daryl, to surmount these difficult times. They also used respite care frequently (as much as one week per month) during two particularly difficult years. Since that time, the family's use of respite has decreased steadily, and they have gradually relied more and more on relatives and friends in their informal network to provide needed child care for Daryl.

CARTER FAMILY

The "Carter" family includes "Steve" and "Kristine," both in their 30's, and their preschool-aged children, "Tricia" and "Daniel." Daniel was born at 32 weeks gestation and developed a visual impairment, seizures, and hydrocephalus. The family participated in a family-centered early intervention program from the time Daniel was 9-months-old until he entered kindergarten.

At the time Daniel was born, the family lived in a small two bedroom home which they owned. Steve worked as a salesman at a furniture-supply wholesaler. The family had two dependable vehicles and adequate income for food, clothing, and other necessities but strug-gled to pay their co-payments for Daniel's medical bills. Both Steve and Kristine's parents lived within a few miles of their home, and both provided emotional support; however, they provided little or no financial assistance or other types of aid or assistance in response to family identified needs. None of the grandparents provided child care either, and the family received minimal support from members of their informal support network.

The Carter family's values and beliefs included a strong commitment to the education and general development and well-being of both their children; a belief in working hard to accomplish goals; a commitment to a lifestyle which allowed Kristine to be free to manage the home and care for the children during the day until both Tricia and Daniel entered kindergarten; a strong spiritual belief which they expressed openly with others; a strong commitment to their marriage and family unity; and an optimistic and hopeful outlook on life.

The family's interaction patterns included good communication skills, both between Steve and Kristine and between themselves and their children; cooperation regarding the division of labor and the roles that each parent played in rearing the children and managing the household; spending time together each day in different family activities (meals, going to the park, watching TV, etc.); spending individual time each day with the children; spending time together each day as a couple; spending time socializing with others in the community; and participating in community activities such as PTA, church and civic groups.

The family's competencies included good household and financial management skills; the ability to identify and describe their needs; knowledge of child development, behavior management, and managing Daniel's health needs; the ability to advocate effectively for both Daniel and Tricia; and the willingness and ability to "pay back" to their social network members by helping other families and particular human service agencies.

The family's strengths were an essential part of their ability to meet their family needs,

including the needs of Tricia and Daniel. Their family values were especially important during the first three years of Daniel's life, when they had many medical bills and his development was substantially delayed. For example, they frequently described their belief in God and the strength that they gained from their faith as a major source of support. Steve and Kristine also described the strength that they gained from each other, particularly in terms of their commitment and ability to share workloads and responsibilities equitably. Another important strength was their commitment to spending time together as a family, and in various one-to-one activities with each other and the children. Even during the most difficult times, they indicated that they were able to engage in activities in order to have fun together and simply enjoy each other.

Another strength that was utilized during their involvement in the family-centered early intervention program was their commitment to spending time together as a couple. This was manifested through their involvement in a parent support group, which expanded their social network, and gave them confidence to leave Daniel in the care of other individuals. Involvement in this group also provided the family with the opportunity to reciprocate with others by "giving back" their time and energy in a number of ways, including transporting other families, providing food to several families, participating in a "phone-tree," and eventually by serving as chairpersons of the parent support group.

A number of the Carter's family strengths were also enhanced during the family's participation in the family-centered early intervention program. Although the family had a considerable number of abilities prior to involvement in the program, different family strengths were specifically developed during contacts between the family and the staff member of the program.

For example, as Daniel made progress developmentally and medically, the family gained skills in areas such as communication and advocacy which were helpful to themselves and their children at the time, and which continued to be beneficial to them for many years.

The family also became more comfortable and proficient in their ability to identify their needs. Although Steve and Kristine had good communication skills, they were initially quite reluctant to question professionals' opinions or continue to seek answers if they were not satisfied with professional advice. Similarly, they were somewhat apologetic when asking for assistance or when describing their own concerns or needs. When they did attempt to share concerns, their needs were often expressed in general terms. This was especially true in areas not related directly to Daniel's medical status or development (such as the family's desire to become more involved in social activities, and particularly in the church). During their involvement in the family-centered early intervention program, Steve and Kristine gained increased confidence in their ability to express themselves to professionals, and perhaps more important, gained the ability to do so clearly and persistently without being apologetic.

The Carters also gained skills as advocates for their children, and used these skills effectively in negotiating positive and constructive courses-of-action plans to meet their children's needs in school. Issues that were addressed included mainstreaming Daniel into kindergarten, obtaining an increased amount of therapy for Daniel, and managing his occasional behavior problems in school in the least restrictive manner possible. They also used their advocacy skills to resolve a conflict which arose between Tricia (who is academically gifted) and one of her teachers.

The Carters used virtually all of their family strengths to meet their family needs and to promote the development of both Daniel and Tricia. The fact that some of their family strengths were enhanced through this process is a reflection of the enabling and empowering process used by the staff member which focused not just on the needs and strengths of the child but on those of the entire family.

The experiences of the Carter and Kyle families demonstrate several important aspects of a strengths-based approach to working with families. The approach recognizes and utilizes existing strengths as well as develops new abilities in family members. Consequently, the roles staff members play often involve working with families to identify and enhance strengths and capabilities. A strengths-based approach also utilizes a diversity of family strengths and recognizes that every family has unique strengths that can be used to meet needs. The Kyle and Carter families exemplify the importance of utilizing family strengths in combination with other resources available to the family in order to meet differing family needs. For example, access to financial support, equipment and respite services, though crucial to the ability of the Kyle family to continue to keep Daryl in their family, would not have been possible without the family's strong value system and ability to work together to mobilize these resources. Similarly, the Carter family relied heavily on their own strengths to meet many of their family needs, as well as the needs of the children, even though they also had many external resources available to them.

The Kyle and Carter families demonstrate how families often utilize their strengths to "give back" and support and assist other families. The Carters reciprocated by supporting many other families through a parent support group and by contributing to a family-centered program through their involvement in panel discussions and committees. The Kyles reciprocated through contacts with other families of children with disabilities, and through Martha's volunteer and foster care work. The two case studies illustrate that a strengths-based approach is useful with a variety of families, including those with obvious resources, such as the Carter's, as well as families with more limited resources, such as the Kyle's. The examples also illustrate the usefulness of a strengths-based approach with families having unique family situations.

SUMMARY AND CONCLUSION

Recognizing and building upon family strengths is paramount in promoting positive family functioning. While substantial progress has been made in terms of family-strengths intervention practices, many advances are still needed, including a greater awareness on the part of society in general and help-givers, in particular, of the tremendous strengths of families. Additionally, families need access to a broader range of resources to call upon when their own intrafamily strengths and informal supports are not adequate to meet their needs. As Hobbs and his colleagues (1984) point out:

Families are the critical element in the rearing of healthy, competent, and caring children. We suggest, however, that families–all families–cannot perform this function as well as they might unless they are supported by a caring and strong community, for it is community (support) that provides the informal and formal supplements to families' own resources. Just as a child needs nurturance, stimulation, and the resources that caring adults bring to his or her life, so, too, do parents –as individuals and as adults filling socially valued roles... need the resources made possible by a caring community if they are to fulfill their roles well. (p. 46)

CHAPTER 10

Assessing Family Strengths and Capabilities

Carol M. Trivette, Carl J. Dunst, Angela G. Deal, Deborah W. Hamby & David Sexton

As NOTED IN CHAPTER 9, a number of strengths-based, self-report scales are available for assessing families' strengths. One such instrument, the Family Functioning Style Scale (FFSS; see Appendix), developed as part of our work, is an easily administrated scale which yields important information from the family's perceptions of their strengths and capabilities. The purpose of this chapter is to describe the procedures used to establish the reliability and validity of the FFSS (Deal, Trivette, & Dunst, 1988).

Although family strengths are generally recognized as one set of resources for promoting and enhancing family functioning, it is surprising how little is known about identifying and assessing family functioning style, let alone how to build upon existing or develop new family strengths and capabilities. As Otto (1963) noted 30 years ago:

> Although the professional literature is replete with criteria for identifying "problem families" and criteria useful in the diagnosis of family problems or family disorganization, little is known about how we might identify a "strong family". (p. 329)

The current interest in the assessment of family strengths comes from the pioneering work in the 1960s of Otto (1962, 1963, 1975). This foundation was built upon by Bowman (1983), Curran (1983), and Karpel (1986a) who identified major indicators of strengths as well as provided extensive descriptions of the traits and personal resources of healthy, well-adjusted families. Stinnett and his colleagues have conducted the most ambitious work in this area: (Lingren et al. 1987; Rowe et al., 1984; Stinnett, 1979; Stinnett, Chesser, & DeFrain, 1979a; Stinnett, Chesser, DeFrain, & Knaub, 1979b; Stinnett & DeFrain, 1985b; Stinnett, DeFrain, King, Knaub, & Rowe, 1981; Stinnett et. al., 1982; Stinnett, Lynn, Kimmons, Fuenning, & DeFrain, 1984; Van Zandt et. al., 1986; Williams, Lingren, Rowe, Van Zandt, & Stinnett, 1985). Collectively, Stinnett's work as well as that found in other sources (e.g., Beavers & Hampson, 1990; Hill, 1971; Lewis, Beavers, Gorsett, & Phillips, 1976; Satir, 1972) provides the necessary framework for assessing family strengths in ways that support and strengthen family functioning. As described in Chapter 9, this framework requires a major shift in how families and family functioning are viewed, and how the purposes and functions of assessment are conceptualized and implemented.

This paradigmatic shift was a central force in the development of the FFSS. The framework includes the contention that all families have strengths; that these strengths are *unique* depending upon the beliefs, cultural backgrounds, ethnicity, and socioeconomic backgrounds of the family; and that work with families should build upon the positive aspects of family functioning, is reflected in the scale items. The scale also reflects the belief that the enhancement of human development is a preferable goal to prevention or treatment of pathology (Dunst, Trivette, & Deal, 1988).

The FFSS includes 26 items designed to assess various kinds of family strengths and capabilities. The instrument was developed as part of a family-centered assessment and intervention model (Dunst, Trivette, & Deal, 1988) that has evolved from efforts to intervene in ways that support and strengthen family functioning. The scale assesses the extent to which an individual family member, or two or more family members completing the scale together, believe their family is characterized by different strengths and capabilities. Ratings are made on a five-point Likert scale ranging from Not-At-All-Like-My-Family to Almost-Always-Like-My-Family. The scale was specifically developed so that it tapped positive aspects of family functioning consistent with the themes described in Chapter 9. Evidence regarding the reliability and validity of the scale is described next.

METHOD

SUBJECTS

The participants were 241 parents of preschool-aged children. The sample included 162 parents of children at risk for poor outcomes and 79 parents of children with developmental disabilities or delays participating in different early intervention programs. Ninety-seven percent of the families include at least one child six years of age or younger. Of the total sample of parents, 206 were mothers and 35 were fathers. The mean age and education level of the mothers was 30.30 (SD = 6.64) and 12.70 (SD = 2.40), respectively. The mean age and education

level of the fathers was 33.51 (SD = 7.11) and 13.15 (SD = 3.16), respectively. Almost half (46.3%) of the sample fell into the lowest two socioeconomic groups using the Hollingshead classification system (1975).

PROCEDURE

Participants completed four self-report measures as part of their participation in the study: Family Functioning Style Scale (FFSS), the Family Hardiness Index (FHI; McCubbin, McCubbin, & Thompson, 1987), Psychological Well-Being Index (PWI; Bradburn, 1969; Bradburn & Caplovitz, 1965) and the Mastery and Health subscale of the Family Inventory of Resources and Management (FIRM; McCubbin, Comeau, & Harkins, 1981). The FHI scale is a 20-item rating scale which measures different kinds of family strengths. This scale has four subscales which contain five items each: commitment, confidence, challenge, and control. The PWI scale is a 14-item rating scale which measures the respondent's psychological well-being. Two dimensions of psychological well-being (positive and negative affect) as well as a total scale score are derived from this scale. The Mastery and Health subscale of the FIRM includes a 20-item subscale which yields an overall measure of family well-being by summing the scores on the individual items.

RESULTS

Table 10-1 shows the means, standard deviations, and ranges for the 26 FFSS items. The scoring system is such that a score of 4 or 5 is considered optimal with respect to the items representing the functioning style of the family. As can be seen from inspection of Table 10-1, the majority of the items had average ratings between Sometimes-Like-My-Family (3)

Table 10-1. Means, Standard Deviations, and Ranges of Scores for the Family Functioning Style Scale

Scale Items	Mean	Standard Deviation	Range
1. Make personal sacrifices if it benefits the family	4.08	0.99	1-5
2. We agree about how family members should behave	3.91	1.07	1-5
3. Believe there is good in the worst situations	3.69	1.10	1-5
4. Take pride in family accomplishments	4.49	0.81	1-5
5. Family members share concerns and feelings	3.73	1.08	1-5
6. Family sticks together no matter the difficulties	4.53	0.84	1-5
7. Ask for help outside the family when needed	2.92	1.28	1-5
8. Agree about important matters	4.21	0.83	1-5
9. "Pitch in" and help each other	4.07	0.98	1-5
10. Try not to worry about uncontrollable events	3.40	1.02	1-5
11. Try to look at the "bright side of things"	3.98	0.89	1-5
12. Spend time together	3.93	1.00	1-5
13. Family has "rules" about acceptable behavior	3.78	1.03	1-5
14. Informal network will help when needed	3.95	1.22	1-5
15. Family makes decisions about solving problems	4.19	0.90	1-5
16. Enjoy spending time together	4.04	1.03	1-5
17. Try to forget overwhelming problems	3.53	1.06	1-5
18. Family members listen to "both sides of the story"	3.63	1.05	1-5
19. Make time for important things	4.04	0.96	1-5
20. Can depend upon each other in difficult times	4.49	0.84	1-5
21. Talk about different ways of dealing with problems	3.71	1.14	1-5
22. Believe family relationships will outlast material possessions	4.57	0.86	1-5
23. Decision making done to benefit entire family	4.20	1.17	1-5
24. Family members can depend upon each other	4.42	0.83	1-5
25. Don't take each other for granted	4.04	0.94	1-5
26. Solve own problems before asking others for help	4.56	0.76	1-5

and Usually-Like-My-Family (4). The range of scores for all the items varied from 1 to 5, indicating that the scale was sensitive in detecting differences in family functioning style among individual subjects.

RELIABILITY

Internal consistency. The split-half (even vs. odd numbered items) reliability coefficient was .85 corrected for length using the Spearman-Brown formula. Coefficient alpha computed from the average correlation among the 26 items for the total was .92. Collectively, these data indicate that the FFSS is an internally consistent instrument.

VALIDITY

Factor structure. A principal components factor analysis using an oblique rotation was used to discern the factor structure of the scale. Oblique rather than an orthogonal rotation was used because it was expected, as others have suggested, that the different strengths of families would be interrelated (Lewis et al.,1976; Otto, 1962). A factor loading of .40 or greater was taken as evidence of factor membership. The analysis produced five interpretable factor solutions accounting for 55% of the variance. The results are displayed in Table 10-2.

The first factor includes items that measure the *Interactional Patterns* of the family; for example, not taking each other for granted, spending time together, listening to all points of view, and sharing concerns and feelings. The second factor includes items that assess *Family Values*, including taking pride in accomplishments of family members, making personal sacrifices for the benefit of the family, and believing that family relationships are more important than material possessions. The third factor includes items that reflect intrafamily *Coping Strategies*, including looking for the bright side of things, not worrying

about uncontrollable events, trying to forget overwhelming problems, and believing there is good even in the worst situations. The fourth factor, *Family Commitment*, includes items such as making decisions that benefit the whole family, depending on other family members, and trying to solve problems within the family first before asking for outside help. The fifth factor, *Resource Mobilization*, includes two items that tap extrafamily support utilization. Taken together, the factor analysis results indicate that the types of family strengths and capabilities measured by the FFSS are multidimensional in nature.

Interdimensional relationships. The correlations between the factor scores on the five family strengths dimensions are shown in Table 10-3. The magnitude of the correlations between the different dimensions are moderate and all but two are statistically significant. This set of findings demonstrates that the different dimensions of family strengths are somewhat interrelated although not substantially so, providing support for the contention that each dimension represents a unique set of family strengths.

Criterion validity. The criterion validity of the scale was assessed using the Family Hardiness Index (FHI; McCubbin et al., 1987) as the criterion measure. The correlations between the FFSS total scale score, the five FFSS factor scores, and the FHI total scale score are also shown in Table 10-3. All 30 pairwise comparisons were statistically significant. A canonical correlation analysis between the five FFSS factor scores and the four FHI subscale scores was $R = .67$, $p < .0001$, indicating that both scales are measuring to a large degree similar qualities of family functioning.

Predictive validity. The importance of family strengths is partly dependent upon whether or not the qualities and intrafamily resources of families are related to other behavior out-

Table 10-2. Oblique Rotated Solutions for the Family Functioning Style Scale

Scale Items	Factor Solutions				
	I	II	III	IV	V
	Interactional Patterns	Family Values	Coping Strategies	Family Commitment	Resource Mobilization
Don't take each other for granted	.77				
Talk about different ways of dealing with problems	.75				
Spend time together	.67				
"Pitch in" and help each other	.64				
Family members listen to "both sides of the story"	.62				
Make time for important things	.60				
Family members share concerns and feelings	.58				
Enjoy spending time together	.50				
Agree about important family matters	.43				
Family has "rules" about acceptable behavior	.42				
Take pride in family accomplishments		.76			
Believe family relationships will outlast material possessions		.69			
Family sticks together no matter the difficulties		.68			
Make personal sacrifices if it benefits the family		.65			
Family members can depend upon each other		.50			
Try to look at the "bright side of things"			.84		
Try not to worry about uncontrollable events			.67		
Believe there is good in the worst situations			.60		
Try to forget overwhelming problems			.41		
Decision making done to benefit entire family				.73	
Family members can depend upon each other				.61	
Solve own problems before asking for help				.42	
Ask for help outside family when needed					.77
Informal network will help when needed					.69
Variance explained	*33%*	*7%*	*6%*	*5%*	*4%*
Cumulative variance	*33%*	*40%*	*46%*	*51%*	*55%*

comes. The predictive validity of the FFSS was examined in terms of its relationship to the personal and familial well-being of the respondents in the study. The Psychological Well-Being Index (PWI; Bradburn, 1969; Bradburn & Caplovitz, 1965) was used as the outcome measure of personal well-being. The Mastery and Health subscale of the Family Inventory of Resources and Management (FIRM; McCubbin, Comeau, & Harkins, 1981) was used as the outcome measure of family well-being. The correlations between the FFSS and the outcome measures are shown in Table 10-3. In all cases, elevated FFSS scores (total and factor scores) were related to fewer family-related health problems (FIRM), fewer indications of negative affect (PWI), and a better overall sense of personal well-being (PWI). A

Table 10-3. Correlations Between the Family Functioning Style Scale Scores and Both the Criterion and the Outcome Variables

| Family Functioning Style Scale | Family Functioning Style Scale | | | | | Criterion Measure | | | | | Outcome Measure | | | |
| | | | | | | Family Hardiness Index [a] | | | | | FIRM [b] | Psychological Well-Being Index [c] | | |
	IP	FV	CS	FC	RM	TS	CC	CF	OH	CT	MH	TS	PA	NA
Total Scale Score	83***	68***	64***	43***	44***	62***	52***	48***	46***	30***	-51***	38***	31***	-36***
Interactional Pattern (IP)	-	37***	38***	26***	21**	48***	41***	31***	43***	21**	-43***	31***	26***	-26***
Family Values (FV)	-	-	31***	21**	21**	41***	38***	40***	20**	21**	-27***	17*	15*	-17*
Coping Strategies (CS)	-	-	-	11	19**	46***	43***	27***	36***	25***	-32***	29***	30***	-24***
Family Commitment (FC)	-	-	-	-	07	35***	19**	39***	22**	22**	-38***	28***	08	-36***
Resource Mobilization (RM)	-	-	-	-	-	27***	21***	24***	18**	12*	-25***	20**	13*	-22**

Note. Decimal points omitted.

[a] Family Hardiness Index: TS=Total Scale Score; CC=Coordinated Commitment; CF=Confidence; CH=Challenge; and CT=Control

[b] FIRM (Family Inventory for Resources and Management): MH=Mastery and Health. Higher scale scores reflect depressed health and well-being.

[c] Psychological Well-Being Index: TS=Total Scale Score; PA=Positive Affect; and NA=Negative Affect.

*p<.05, **p<.01, ***p<.001.

canonical correlation analysis between the five FFSS subscale scores and both the PWI positive and negative affect measures and FIRM mastery and health scores was $R = .59$, $p < .0001$, indicating that family strengths are an important determinant of the well-being and health of the family unit and individual family members.

DISCUSSION

Taken together, the data presented in this chapter provide strong evidence regarding the reliability and validity of the Family Functioning Style Scale among families of pre-school-aged children. The scale has excellent internal consistency characteristics, measures clearly discernible dimensions of family strengths and capabilities, and is related to both criterion and outcome measures in an expected manner.

The findings provide support for the conceptual framework upon which the scale was developed. Family strengths were found to include a number of definable dimensions (Williams et al., 1985) that were only somewhat interrelated, supporting the contention that the different dimensions represent a number of unique sets of family strengths (Lewis et al., 1976). The relationship between family competencies and personal and family well-being was also confirmed by the analysis reported in this chapter (Folkman, Lazarus, Dunkel-Schetter, DeLorgis, & Gruen, 1986; Stinnett, Tucker, & Shell, 1985). Taken together, the results support a proactive, promotional perspective of functioning and development, and seem to add validity to the approach to working with families described in the previous chapter of the book.

IMPLICATIONS FOR PRACTICE

The FFSS would seem to have application in clinical work for both assessment and intervention purposes. As an assessment tool, the FFSS can help discern the unique functioning styles of a family. Not only can the results help identify strengths from a family's perspective, they can also provide a basis for asking respondents specific questions about how the family uses strengths as a way of meeting needs.

As an intervention tool, the FFSS can help identify those family strengths that are already being employed by family members so that interventions are built on the things a particular family already does well, thus increasing the likelihood of success. By building on a family's strengths and capabilities, the probability that the family unit will become even stronger and more capable of supporting the development of individual family members and the family unit should be realized. To the extent that the use of family strengths scales like the FFSS promotes the family's ability to identify and access their own family resources, and to mobilize extrafamily supports, families should become even stronger when they face future demands and challenges.

APPENDIX

Family Functioning Style Scale

Angela G. Deal, Carol M. Trivette & Carl J. Dunst

INSTRUCTIONS: Every family has strengths and capabilities, although different families have different ways of using their abilities. This questionnaire asks you to indicate whether or not your family is characterized by 26 different qualities. Please read each statement, then circle the response which is most true for your family (people living in your home). Please give your honest opinions and feelings. Remember that your family will not be like all the statements.

How is your family like the following statements:	Not At All Like My Family	A Little Like My Family	Sometimes Like My Family	Usually Like My Family	Almost Always Like My Family
1. We make personal sacrifices if they help our family	1	2	3	4	5
2. We usually agree about how family members should behave	1	2	3	4	5
3. We believe that something good always comes out of even the worst situations	1	2	3	4	5
4. We take pride in even the smallest accomplishments of family members	1	2	3	4	5
5. We share our concerns and feelings in useful ways	1	2	3	4	5
6. Our family sticks together no matter how difficult things get	1	2	3	4	5
7. We usually ask for help from persons outside our family if we cannot do things ourselves	1	2	3	4	5
8. We usually agree about the things that are important to our family	1	2	3	4	5
9. We are always willing to "pitch in" and help each other	1	2	3	4	5
10. We find things to do that keep our minds off our worries when something upsetting is beyond our control	1	2	3	4	5
11. We try to look "at the bright side of things" no matter what happens in our family	1	2	3	4	5
12. We find time to be together even with our busy schedules	1	2	3	4	5
13. Everyone in our family understands the "rules" about acceptable ways to act	1	2	3	4	5
14. Friends and relatives are always willing to help whenever we have a problem or crisis	1	2	3	4	5
15. Our family is able to make decisions about what to do when we have problems or concerns	1	2	3	4	5
16. We enjoy time together even if it is doing household chores	1	2	3	4	5
17. We try to forget our problems or concerns for a while when they seem overwhelming	1	2	3	4	5
18. Family members listen to "both sides of the story" during a disagreement	1	2	3	4	5
19. We make time to get things done that we all agree are important	1	2	3	4	5
20. We can depend on the support of each other whenever something goes wrong	1	2	3	4	5
21. We usually talk about the different ways we deal with problems and concerns	1	2	3	4	5
22. Our family's relationships will outlast our material possessions	1	2	3	4	5
23. We make decisions like moving or changing jobs for the good of all family members	1	2	3	4	5
24. We can depend upon each other to help out when something unexpected happens	1	2	3	4	5
25. We try not to take each other for granted	1	2	3	4	5
26. We try to solve our problems first before asking others to help	1	2	3	4	5

(May be duplicated without permission with proper acknowledgment and citation.)

CHAPTER 11

Resource-Based Family-Centered Intervention Practices

Carl J. Dunst, Carol M. Trivette & Angela G. Deal

THE PURPOSE OF THIS CHAPTER is to describe a unique approach for identifying and mobilizing community resources and services that can be used to meet child and family needs. This approach is one component of a model (see Dunst, Trivette, & Deal, 1988; Chapter 1) which defines the goals of family-centered assessment and intervention as: (1) identifying *family needs*, (2) locating the *formal and informal supports and resources* for meeting the needs, and (3) helping families identify and use their *strengths and capabilities* to procure resources in ways that strengthen family functioning (Dokecki & Heflinger, 1989; Dunst, Trivette, & Deal, 1988; Hobbs et al., 1984). The needs-identification component of this model is described in Chapter 7 and the strengths-based component is described in Chapter 9. A particular approach for conceptualizing and defining the full range of resources, supports, and services for meeting child and family needs is the focus of this chapter.

Nearly a decade ago in an article entitled *Rethinking Early Intervention*, Dunst (1985) proposed an expanded definition of early intervention specifically, and human services practices more generally, as the "provision of support (and resources) to families of young children from members of informal and formal social support networks that impact both *directly* and *indirectly* upon parent, family, and child functioning" (p. 179). Such a definition

recognizes the fact that families of young children experience events in addition to those provided by human services programs that can and do influence family functioning and child development.

Since the *Rethinking* paper was written, we have continued the study of the relationship between social support and its effects on children and families (Dunst & Trivette, 1986, 1987b, 1988a, 1988b, 1988c, 1990; Trivette & Dunst, 1987, 1992). This work as well as that of others has led to additional insights and considerations about the best ways to conceptualize human services practices so as to maximize the benefits associated with such practices. As will be described in a moment, the emphasis of the approach advocated for in this chapter is based upon a conceptual and procedural distinction between *resource-based* and *service-based* intervention practices.

An expanded perspective of human services practices that moves beyond single sources of professional services for meeting child and family needs has been voiced by a number of authorities. For example, Sarason and his colleagues (Sarason, Carroll, Maton, Cohen, & Lorentz, 1977) made the following observations about the restrictive orientation of thinking about human services solutions solely in terms of services:

> We have never known of a human service agency of any kind that asserted

that it had the resources to accomplish its goals. That is to say, the demand for the agency's services always exceeds what the agency feels it can and should supply. The solution, far more often than not, is put in terms of obtaining more money to hire more staff. Occasionally, it is put not in terms of obtaining more money but of being unable to locate and attract personnel who are in known short supply. However it is put, it always reflects a concept of "the market," in which it is competing for limited resources. Put in another way, the agency defines resources as those it can purchase and, therefore, control and distribute, consistent with its definition of its task. The agency usually knows where the additional resources are located, but unless it has the funds to purchase them (in whole or in part), the resources do not, so to speak, exist. (pp. 19-20)

As is evident from this quote, defining human services practices in terms of service-based solutions is problematic for a host of reasons. For example, there will likely never be enough public funds to provide all the services children and families need when solutions to meeting needs are defined solely or primarily in terms of professional supports. In order to meet the largest number of needs among the greatest number of families, programs will most likely have the greatest positive impact if resource-based, as opposed to service-based approaches to intervention, are used to meet family needs and address their concerns. As we shall see next, this alternative way of thinking about resources does not "box oneself into a corner" in terms of limiting how to best meet the needs of children and families.

DIFFERENCES BETWEEN RESOURCE-BASED AND SERVICE-BASED INTERVENTION PRACTICES

Contemporary human services practices to a large degree are conceptualized primarily in terms of *service-based* solutions to meeting child and family needs. That is, programs that work with children and families generally define the relationships with their "clients" in terms of the particular services the program offers, and sometimes the services that other human services programs provide (hence interagency coordination). This way of conceptualizing human services practices is both limited and limiting. In contrast, a resource-based approach to meeting child and family needs is both expansive and expanding because it focuses on mobilization of a broad range of community supports to meet child and family needs.

Distinguishing between a *service* and *resource* is a first step in understanding the benefits of resource-based over service-based approaches to human service practices. Operationally, a *service* is defined as a specific or particular activity employed by a professional or professional agency for rendering help or assistance to an individual or group. Generally, but not always, services are the "unit of intervention" used by human service programs to provide assistance to "clients" served by an agency or program. *Resources* on the other hand are operationally defined as the full range of possible types of community help or assistance that might be mobilized and used to meet the needs of an individual or group. Additionally, and perhaps more importantly, a resource-based approach to intervention does not rely on a single type of (professional) help or assistance, but rather promotes the mobilization and utilization of multiple sources of informal and formal community supports for meeting needs.

Table 11-1 details three major characteristics that operationally distinguish between resource-based and service-based human services practices. These characteristics to a large degree are based on the work of Katz (1984), McKnight (1987, 1989), McKnight and Ketzmann (1984), and Sarason, Carroll, Maton, Cohen, and Lorentz (1977), as well as our own work with children and families (Dunst, Trivette, & Deal, 1988; Dunst, Trivette, Starnes, Hamby, & Gordon, 1993).

First, service-based approaches to meeting needs tend to be limited and constricted because they are defined primarily in terms of what professionals do (hence professionally-centered). Services they provide are made available to only certain people under certain conditions dictated by the professionals. In contrast, resource-based approaches to meeting needs view a wide array of community people and organizations as sources of support. Resources are viewed as unlimited and broadly available; that is, they exist in abundance and lie ready to be used at almost any time.

Second, service-based approaches to intervention are underscored by the adoption of a "scarcity paradigm" in which help and assistance is assumed to be scarce and therefore distributed or given to only those determined in need of the help by professionals (Katz, 1984). In contrast, resource-based approaches to intervention are derived from a "synergy paradigm" in which help and assistance is assumed to be expandable and renewable.

Third, service-based intervention practices are typically described in terms of what professionals and professionally-oriented organizations offer as help and assistance. This is generally referred to as *formal support*. In contrast, resource-based intervention practices are defined in terms of both what *informal and formal support* network members can provide to persons needing help or assistance.

Who are the community people and groups that might be viewed as sources of support to children and families? They include, but are not limited to, family members, relatives, friends, neighbors, day care centers, neighborhood and community organizations, churches and synagogues, recreation centers and YMCAs, hospitals and community health centers, pub-

Table 11-1. Major Characteristics of Service-Based and Resource-Based Approaches to Meeting Child and Family Needs

Service-Based Practices	Resource-Based Practices
Professionally-Based (Defines solutions primarily in terms of centralized professional expertise)	Community-Based (Defines solutions in terms of the resources and supports available from a wide array of community people and organizations)
Scarcity Paradigm (Professional services are seen as scarce and thus made available to people using means-tested eligibility criteria)	Synergistic Paradigm (Community resources are seen as varied, rich, expandable, and renewable)
Emphasis on Formal Supports (Solutions to meeting child and family needs are seen as residing in what professionals and professional agencies "do best")	Emphasis on Formal and Informal Supports (Solutions to meeting needs are defined in terms of mobilization of the formal and informal community social network members of children and families)

Note. See especially Dunst, Trivette, Starnes, Hamby and Gordon (1993), Chapter 24 , for an expanded description of these contrasting approaches to human services practices.

lic health and social services departments, and early intervention and human services programs, to mention just a few. In resource-based approaches to human service delivery, any and all potential sources of community support are seen as viable options for meeting child and family needs. Many of the potential sources of support for meeting needs are listed below.

EXAMPLES OF RESOURCE-BASED PRACTICES

The difference that we are attempting to make between service-based and resource-based human services practices perhaps is best illustrated by way of example. The examples we have chosen are real and not hypothetical. They come from our own experiences working with children and their families in a human service program.

Families of children with disabilities often indicate a need for a "break" from day-to-day child rearing demands (actually, most parents need this!). A person attempting a service-based solution might think of meeting this need in terms of a professional or formal respite care program. In contrast, a resource-based approach would look to babysitters, mothers-day-out programs, babysitting co-ops, day care programs, etc. as ways of meeting this need. The latter approach will most likely prove more successful because the family will be building and mobilizing a resource network rather than depending on a single source of support for meeting the need (see especially Dunst, Trivette, Gordon, & Pletcher, 1989).

Children with disabilities participating in human services programs are often seen as needing particular kinds of interventions provided by particular kinds of professionals (speech pathologists, teachers, physical therapists, etc.). This is a service-based approach for meeting child needs. In contrast, resource-based approaches define needs not in terms of what professionals do, but rather in terms of the full range of experiences that children require to develop competence. For instance, for a child who has motor development needs, a resource-based approach would not define meeting these needs in terms of physical therapy, but would include the broad-based kinds of experiences (community play groups, YMCA exercise programs, early intervention programs, etc.) that can be used to enhance this aspect of child behavior. We would even go so far as to say that there are very few children with disabilities whose needs can only be met by professionals in human services programs. The needs of the largest majority of children with disabilities can be adequately addressed by a range of experiences provided by a host of community members.

Does it make a difference as to whether one employs service-based vs. resource-based solutions to meeting needs? Available evidence indicates that it does. For example, in a study we recently completed with families of persons with disabilities, positive outcomes associated with human services practices were found to be greatest in those cases where human services practitioners used resource-based as opposed to service-based intervention practices for meeting needs (see Dunst, Trivette, Starnes, Hamby, & Gordon, 1993).

Resource-based human services practices constitute at least one alternative way of conceptualizing and implementing child and family interventions. Additionally, building support systems that include a broad range of sources of support for meeting child and family needs is indicated if the benefits to human services program participants is to be maximized (see especially Chapter 17).

MISCONCEPTIONS OF RESOURCE-BASED INTERVENTION PRACTICES

Resource-based intervention practices represent an expanded perspective for viewing the range and types of supports that might be mobilized to meet family needs. The adoption of new or alternative intervention practices carries certain risks of misinterpretation. The following attempts to clarify some but certainly not all the misconceptions that surround resource-based family-centered assessment and intervention practices. These misconceptions and their clarifications come from our own experiences employing the model, methods, and strategies described throughout this book and elsewhere (see Dunst, 1989; Dunst, Trivette, & Deal, 1988).

Misconception: Professional help-givers are the primary sources of support to families of children at-risk for poor outcomes.

Response: This misconception is based on the assumption that the family's needs can only be met by professionals "trained" to deal with the "special" problems faced by families of children who are at risk. This stance, if adopted, tends to result in the overprofessionalization of supports, and the lessening of use of natural sources of support and resources for meeting needs. Many families who have described this set of conditions to us have said they were "lulled" into believing that only professionals can provide necessary resources to meet needs. The fact is, natural sources of support meet the majority of needs identified by families. Professionals who even unintentionally disrupt the use of natural sources of support to families of children may be doing a tremendous disservice to families.

Misconception: Suggesting that families use natural sources of support to meet their needs will "burn out" relatives, friends and other informal social support network members.

Response: This statement is true if, and only if, the family does all the taking and their personal social network members do all the giving. A necessary condition for informal social support networks to be viable sources of support is *reciprocity* between the family and personal social network members. Mobilization and use of natural support systems must involve give-and-take between the family and others (e.g., a friend babysitting in exchange for the family preparing a meal for their friend's children) as part of resource exchanges. Think about your own relationship with friends and other personal network members. The mutual sharing between ourselves and others is what makes our relationships rewarding and satisfying. Reciprocity and mutuality must be part of social exchanges if natural sources of support are used to meet the needs of families of special needs children.

Misconception: Many families do not have natural support systems that can be used to meet needs.

Response: The research that we have been conducting shows that nearly all families have potential sources of support available to them, but some families require assistance in identifying and mobilizing personal social support networks. While some families indeed have very few informal sources of support, our research has shown that it is possible to help these families build and mobilize natural support systems (Dunst, Trivette, Gordon, & Pletcher, 1989). Our experience has been that with a little thought and some initial effort, the benefits of building informal support systems far outweigh the development of new professional services for meeting many unmet family needs to the extent that this is appropriate.

Misconception: Human services programs must uniformly have a wide range of professional services available to meet the needs of children and their families.

Response: Certainly there are particular child and family needs that can best be met, and in some cases can only be met, by professionals (e.g., heart surgery). But it is a misconception to think that any single human service program can or ought to have every possible service that might be required to meet child and family needs. Believing this potentially sets ourselves up for failure. This occurs when one conceptualizes intervention as a *set of services* provided by specialized professionals (teachers, physical therapists, nutritionists, etc.). We believe we need to stop thinking about intervention as predetermined sets of *services* that must be mobilized to meet needs, but rather as the range of possible resources to meet needs. Then there will almost certainly be more than enough sources of support to meet the majority of child and family needs.

A resource-based approach to meeting child and family needs is described next in terms of a framework for defining resources and sources of support having these resources.

A FRAMEWORK FOR IMPLEMENTING RESOURCE-BASED INTERVENTIONS

The ability to adequately identify the full range of community resources for meeting needs necessitates that one first have an idea about what *all* families are likely to require for stable functioning, individual and family growth, and day-to-day coping and well-being. It is useful to organize family resources into broad categories for guiding both assessment and intervention practices. The reader is referred to Dunst, Trivette, and Deal (1988), Hartman and Laird (1983), and Trivette et al. (1986) for useful lists of resource categories.

The list provided by Dunst, Trivette, and Deal (1988) includes the following 12 groups of resources:

- Economic Resources
- Physical and Environmental Resources
- Food and Clothing Resources
- Medical and Dental Care Resources
- Employment and Vocational Resources
- Transportation and Communication Resources
- Adult Education and Enrichment Resources
- Child Education and Intervention Resources
- Child Care Resources
- Recreational Resources
- Emotional Resources
- Cultural and Social Resources

Table 11-2 gives examples of resources that are often required by families to meet their needs. This table provides a framework for structuring efforts for both assessing needs (see Chapter 7) and identifying the full range of possible resources and supports to meet these needs.

MAJOR SOURCES OF SUPPORT AND RESOURCES

A resource-based approach to human services practices "look toward" a broad range of community people, organizations, groups, programs, etc. as sources of support for meeting child and family needs. The following represents some, but certainly not all, people and associational groups (McKnight, 1989) that one might mobilize as sources of support.

Personal Social Network Members. There are many individuals to whom families can and often do turn when seeking advice, assistance,

Table 11-2. Taxonomy of Resources for Meeting Family Needs	
Resource Category	**Examples**
Economic	Money for necessities Money for emergencies Money for special needs/project Money for the future Stable income level
Physical	Clean environment Adequate housing (space, safety, furnishings) Safe neighborhood (protection) Adequate heat, water, plumbing Housing accessible to other resources Resources for home repairs and maintenance
Food/Clothing	Adequate food for two meals a day Enough clothes for each season Reliable means for laundering clothes
Medical/Dental	Trustworthy medical/dental professionals Available general/emergency health care Accessible medical/dental care Means of acquiring medical/dental care
Vocational	Opportunity to work Satisfaction with work (in or out of home) Job security Available/accessible work
Transportation/Communication	Means of getting family members where they need to go Means for contacting relatives, friends, and other sources of support
Adult Education	Available appropriate adult education opportunities Accessible educational opportunities
Child Education	Accessible child educational opportunities Opportunities/activities to help/teach/play with children Appropriate toys and other educational materials
Child Care	Help in routine daily care Emergency child care Available daycare/babysitting for employment purpose Respite child care
Recreational	Opportunities for recreational activities for individual family members, couples, total family Available recreational facilities for individual members, couples, total family
Emotional	Positive intrafamily relationships Positive relationships outside the family Companionship Sense of belonging to family or group Opportunities to spend time with significant people
Cultural/Social	Opportunities to share ethnic or value-related experiences with others Opportunities to be involved with community/cultural affairs Accessible community/cultural affairs

nurturing, etc. Among these are the following:

- Spouse or Partner
- Own Children
- Blood Relatives
- Spouse or Partner's Relatives
- Friends
- Neighbors
- Co-Workers
- Clerics
- Church or Synagogue Members
- Babysitters
- Day Care Personnel
- . Teachers
- Car Pool Partners

Associational Groups. McKnight (1989, p. 8) lists the following kinds of associational groups as potential sources of support for meeting people's needs:

- Artistic Organizations
- Business Organizations
- Charitable Groups and Drives
- Church Groups
- Civic Events
- Collector's Groups
- Community Support Groups
- Elderly Groups
- Ethnic Associations
- Health and Fitness Groups
- Interest Clubs
- Men's Groups
- Mutual Support (Self-Help) Groups
- Neighborhood and Block Clubs
- Outdoor Groups
- Political Organizations
- School Groups
- Service Clubs
- Social Cause Groups
- Sports Leagues
- Study Groups

- Veteran Groups
- Women's Groups
- Youth Groups

Community Programs and Professionals. Almost every community in the United States has at least some of the following kinds of people, programs, and agencies that provide services and supports to members of their communities:

- Public and Private Schools
- Family Resource Programs
- Day Care Centers
- Senior Citizen Programs
- Financial Planning Programs
- Community Colleges
- Institutions of Higher Education
- Recreational Programs and Camps
- Libraries
- Community Health Care Centers
- Family Planning Clinics
- Police and Fire Departments
- Hospitals
- Family Physicians/Nurses
- Social Workers/Counselors
- Community Officials
- Employment Agencies
- Legal Assistance Agencies
- Social Service Agencies and Programs
- Housing Programs (Habitat for Humanity, public housing, etc.)

Specialized Professional Services. Many child and family needs can be met by particular professionals and professional programs and agencies. These include:

- Public Health Clinics
- Home Health Agencies
- Mental Health Programs/Agencies
- Early Intervention Programs

- Special Education Programs
- Vocational Rehabilitation Programs
- Child Welfare Agencies
- Family Preservation Programs
- Special Health Care Clinics
- Adult Basic Education Programs
- Resource and Referral Programs
- Parent Education Programs
- Child Development Specialists (physicians, special education teachers, psychologists, developmental specialists, physical and occupational therapists, speech therapists, etc.)
- Substance Abuse Programs
- Specialized Transportation Services
- Emergency, Crisis, and Disaster Relief Services
- Hospice Care
- Respite Care
- Case Management/Care Coordination Programs

The above four lists of people, programs, organizations, and agencies include more than 75 potential sources of support and resources for meeting child and family needs. What is the ultimate goal of building and mobilizing these kinds of informal and formal supports and resources? According to McKnight (1989),

> The goal is not to create independence-except from (professionalized) systems. Rather, we are recognizing that every life in community is, by definition, one that is *interdependent*. It is filled with *trusting* relationships. It is *empowered* by the collective wisdom of citizens in discourse. (p. 20)

We are often told that communities are limited in resources needed by children and families for strengthening functioning and pro-moting competence. This is perhaps true if one adopts a service-based approach for guiding human services practices. It is not true if one employs a resource-based approach for meeting needs.

ASSESSMENT CONSIDERATIONS

Potential sources of support and resources may be identified using observational, self-report, or interview procedures (see Dunst & Trivette, 1990; Dunst, Trivette, & Deal, 1988). The use of one or more of these procedures to identify sources of support for meeting family-identified needs provides a basis for exploring existing and potential options within the family's social network. In addition, it can provide a basis for exploring the characteristics of family and professional help-giver exchanges that promote or impede mobilization of those resources (see especially Dunst, Trivette, & Deal, 1988).

MAPPING RESOURCES TO MEET CHILD AND FAMILY NEEDS

The *processes* used to identify needs and translate these into outcome statements provide a framework for initiating mobilization of resources and supports. This was described in Chapters 5 and 6 with respect to the development of Individualized Family Support Plans (IFSPs). Once needs have been identified and translated into outcome statements, the next step is to identify sources of support and resources for meeting needs. *Personal social network mapping* is used to accomplish the goal of identifying appropriate sources of support and resources for meeting needs. The persons and institutions with which a family and its members come in contact-either directly or indirectly-are referred to as the family's *personal social network*, and it is this network that is the primary source of support to families and individual family members (Cohen & Syme, 1985b). For each need/outcome statement identified as part of the IFSP process described in Chapters 5 and 6, the range of options for meeting needs are identified and their viability as sources of support and resources determined. A simple rule of thumb is followed in network mapping: *Potential sources of support are mapped for each need/outcome statement separately so as to focus the resource and support identification and mobilization process.* By doing so, the practitioner gathers information specifically and only in relationship to family-identified needs. This insures that the identification of resources and supports does not become intrusive.

In mapping sources of support and resources, it should be remembered that the assessment and mobilization of social support and resources should be done within the context of the family system and the family's indicated need for support (see Dunst & Trivette, 1990). This stance toward working with families was stated in the following way by Pilisuk and Parks (1986) in terms of the relationship between a family and interventionist as part of social support interventions:

> The (family) defines the need for service. *(A) need for assistance is not assumed until the (family) has set forth such a need.* This request for assistance might originate with one individual or with the...(family) system.... (T)he social support facilitator helps the (family) crystallize the (concern). (pp. 162-163, emphasis added)

Thus, a determination of an indicated need for aid and assistance is the first and fundamentally most important part of social support interventions, and *all* intervention efforts must be based on these family identified needs if they are to be successful in affecting parent, family, and child functioning.

Another consideration involving the assessment and mobilization of supports and resources has to do with the range of personal social network members available to a family. It should be remembered that *informal* support network members (spouse/partner, relatives, friends, neighbors, other parents, self-help groups, etc.) as well as *formal* support network members (e.g., early intervention practitioners) constitute sources of support and resources for meeting needs. To the extent possible and appropriate, major emphasis should be placed upon identification and use of informal personal network members as sources of support and resources for meeting family needs. So often we overprofessionalize all types of interventions in human services programs, which only interferes with and precludes opportunities to build and strengthen more natural family and community support (Hobbs et al., 1984).

The process of identifying and evaluating the usefulness of different sources of support for meeting needs, although simple and efficient, requires that one be sensitive to the verbal and nonverbal behavior of the family when matching resources to needs. This is especially true in terms of the willingness of the family to seek out and ask for help and the willingness of different network members to provide aid and assistance. Therefore, one should be sensitive to how the family responds to different options for meeting needs, and use their responses as a basis for prompting clarifications (e.g., "You indicated that your aunt might be able to provide transportation to take your child to therapy, but I sense that you are hesitant about asking her. Is there some reason why you feel this way?"). This type of follow-up question provides a way of helping family members clarify their reasons for not wanting to ask for assistance, and provides a basis for exploring ways of making a particular source of support a viable option or for exploring alternative options. One should not assume that because a network member has a resource a family could use to meet a need that it automatically means this is an appropriate source of support to the family. One must be careful to take into consideration qualitative aspects of social exchanges as a basis for making suggestions about viable sources of support.

The combined processes for identifying needs and resources and mobilizing sources of support for meeting needs does require some shift and expansion in the roles human services employ in interactions with families and their personal social network members (see especially Dunst, Trivette, & Deal, 1988; Trivette et al., 1986). However, with practice, interventionists can become proficient in assessing and mobilizing support by employing expanded roles in interactions with families and community members.

SUMMARY AND CONCLUSION

Resource-based human services programs define interventions not in terms of only specific kinds of professional services (e.g., respite care) but rather the full range of community supports and resources (respite care, day care, sitter or companion services, etc.) that can be mobilized for meeting specific child and family needs (e.g., child care assistance). Resource-based approaches view sources of support as renewable and expandable, whereas service-based approaches view program specific services as generally scarce and limited (Katz, 1984). Evidence from our own research contrasting resource-based and service-based human services practices found the former associated with better outcomes compared to the latter (Dunst, Trivette, Starnes, Hamby, & Gordon, 1993).

Based upon both research evidence and clinical experience, we have increasingly come to the conclusion that human services practices will more likely be successful if meeting child and family needs are defined in terms of the broad-based resources and supports required for normal community life and stable family functioning. As noted in this chapter, this includes, but is not limited to, economic; physical and environmental; life necessities; medical and health; employment and vocation; transportation and communication; child and adult education; child care; recreational; emotional; and cultural and social resources (see Deal & Dunst, 1990; Dunst, Trivette, & Deal, 1988; Hartman & Laird, 1983; Trivette et al., 1986; Turnbull, Summers, & Brotherson, 1986). It should be noted, however, that defining the targets of intervention in terms of these various resource categories does not mean being "everything to everybody," as some have interpreted resource-based family-centered intervention practices. It does mean being responsive to all family needs, and in some cases providing resources and supports to families, and in other cases linking families with appropriate resources and services. Building and strengthening community support systems for meeting child and family needs is more likely to be beneficial in the long run. This is the case because community supports tend to be more stable than professional support systems.

How can we make a shift from a service-based to a resource-based approach to meeting child and family needs? First, we must broaden the manner in which we define solutions for meeting these needs. This necessitates that we not limit ourselves to specific kinds of professional services for achieving intended outcomes, but rather define solutions in terms of a number of kinds of experiences that create opportunities for children and families to learn skills and acquire behaviors to strengthen functioning. Second, we must try to avoid thinking about resources as limited and scarce. One way of thinking more broadly is to engage in the exercise of community-mapping. Community-mapping literally involves the identification of specific kinds of community resources (childcare, recreation opportunities, counseling, etc.) and the pinpointing of the location of these resources on a large map of the catchment and surrounding areas of the human services program wanting to employ resource-based practices. The yellow pages of a phone directory, knowledge of one's community, county and city resource guides, etc. are often good starting points for beginning the network mapping process. Third, it is often beneficial to seek out and engage in discussions with those community people who deal with human resources concerns of the community at large and not just special population segments of the community. Their unique perspectives can have synergistic effects on broadening one's own view of the meaning of community and its riches (i.e., resources). Making the shift to a resource-based approach to meeting child and family needs is possible when we can cease thinking about communities as having limited resources and begin to think of them as having limitless opportunities.

CHAPTER 12

Measuring Social Support in Families with Young Children with Disabilities

Carl J. Dunst, Carol M. Trivette & Deborah W. Hamby

Dunst and Trivette (1990) recently reviewed a number of social support scales that can be used to identify potential sources of resources for meeting child and family needs in the manner described in Chapter 11. Social support scales, when properly used (see Dunst, Trivette, & Deal, 1988), can be extremely useful as part of promoting adoption of resource-based family-centered assessment and intervention practices. The term social support is defined in this chapter as the resources provided by other persons and groups to children and families. More specifically, social support refers to the emotional, psychological, physical, informational, instrumental, and material aid and assistance provided by others that directly or indirectly influences the behavior of the recipient of these various kinds of resources.

A sizeable body of literature exists to indicate that social networks and the social support they provide lessens stress, promotes well-being, and enhances use of coping strategies (Affleck, Tennen, & Rowe, 1991; Bott, 1971; Crnic, Greenberg, Ragozin, Robinson, & Basham, 1983; Crockenberg, 1985; Dean & Lin, 1977; McCubbin, Joy, Cauble, Comeau, Patterson, & Needle, 1980; Mitchell & Trickett, 1980). Social networks serve the functions of providing assistance, advice, help, services, guidance, etc. (Barrera, 1986; Caplan, 1974; Tolsdorf, 1976; Weiss, 1974). The influences social support have on human functioning

has become a focal point of research designed to explicate the relationships between different dimensions and types of support and physical and emotional well-being (Cohen & Syme, 1985b; Gore, 1978; Janis, 1975; LaRocco, House, & French, 1980); support and life satisfaction (Crnic et al., 1983); to mention just a few investigative areas.

This chapter describes the findings of recent analyses designed to further establish the reliability and validity of the Family Support Scale (Dunst, Jenkins, & Trivette, 1984; see Appendix). The Family Support Scale (FSS) is an 18 item self-report measure designed to assess the degree to which potential sources of support have been helpful to families rearing young children. Ratings are made on a five-point Likert scale ranging from Not-At-All-Helpful to Extremely-Helpful. The scale was originally developed as part of an investigation examining the mediating effects of social support on the personal and familial well-being and coping of parents rearing preschool children with disabilities or those at-risk for poor outcomes (Dunst, 1982; Dunst, Trivette, & Cross, 1988).

The FSS is based on a conceptual model developed by Bronfenbrenner (1979) and operationalized by Dunst (1982, 1985). The model describes how events in different ecological contexts and settings influence the development of children as members of different ecological niches. According to Bronfenbrenner, ecological units, or social networks, may be conceived topologically as a nested arrangement of concentric structures each embedded within one another. At the innermost level is the developing child and his or her family members (mother, father, & siblings). The family unit is embedded in broader ecological units consisting of blood and marriage relatives, friends, and other acquaintances. These kinship units are further embedded in larger social units, including neighborhoods, churches, social organizations, the parents' place of work, and professional helpers and agencies. Dunst's (1982, 1985) operationalization of Bronfenbrenner's ecological model delineates four levels of ecological units: nuclear (and extended) family, formal and informal kinship members, formal and informal social groups and organizations (church, neighborhood, etc.), and human service professionals and agencies.

According to Bronfenbrenner (1979), different ecological units do not operate in isolation, but impact upon one another both directly and indirectly (Cochran & Brassard, 1979; Holahan, 1977) so that provisions of support in one unit or subunit may reverberate and influence the behavior of persons in other social units. This set of conditions are viewed as the factors that influence well-being of persons receiving support, which in turn is likely to affect how parents interact and treat their children, which then in turn is likely to influence the child's behavior and development (Bronfenbrenner, 1979; Cochran & Brassard, 1979). The extent to which these relationships could be empirically established constituted, in part, the focus of the research described next.

METHOD

SUBJECTS

The subjects were 224 parents (174 mothers and 50 fathers) of children with developmental disabilities or children at-risk for poor developmental outcomes. Eighty-four percent of the sample were married, while the remaining 16% were single, widowed, separated, or divorced. The parents and their children were participating in an early intervention program (Dunst, 1982; Dunst & Trivette, 1988d) at the time data collection occurred. Selected characteristics of the families are shown in Table 12-1.

Table 12-1. Selected Characteristics of the Families Participating in the Study			
Characteristics	N	Mean	SD
Mother's Age (Years)	224	28.81	6.99
Father's Age (Years)	191	32.07	7.40
Mother's Education*	222	11.92	2.49
Father's Education*	188	11.78	2.77
Socioeconomic Status**	220	29.23	12.92
Gross Monthly Income (Dollars)	178	1229.58	764.43
Years of Marriage	136	7.69	5.06

Note. The data in this table includes information available on both mothers and fathers who did and did not participate in the study.
*Years of school completed.
**Hollingshead's (1975) four-factor index of socioeconomic status. The scores for the five-level model are distributed as follows: I-8-19 (Low SES), II-20-29 (Low Middle), III-30-39 (Middle), IV-40-54 (Upper Middle) and V-55-66 (Upper SES).

PROCEDURE

The respondents completed the FSS as part of their participation in a study examining the relationship between social support and parental well-being, family integrity, and child behavior and development. The "helpfulness" responses on the FSS were used to determine the internal consistency, split-half reliability, construct validity, and content validity of the scale. Twenty-five of the parents completed the FSS on two occasions, one month apart, to determine short-term test-retest reliability, whereas 60 parents completed the FSS on two occasions, 1 to 2 years apart, to establish long-term test-retest reliability.

The subjects also completed a number of subscales of the Questionnaire on Resources and Stress (QRS, Holroyd, 1987) as part of the study. The particular QRS subscales completed by the respondents were the poor health/mood, excess time demands, and family integrity measures. The criterion validity of the FSS was determined with regard to its ability to predict these aspects of personal and familial well-being.

RESULTS

Table 12-2 shows the means and standard deviations for both the 18 FSS items and the total scale scores. For the majority of items (78%), the mean scores tend to vary around the central point of the 5-point Likert scale, and the standard deviations are quite alike for most items. The range of scores for all 18 items varied from 1 to 5, indicating that the scale was sensitive in detecting differences in ratings of helpfulness among the subjects.

The correlations between the total FSS support scores and the demographic variables shown in Table 1 were as follows: mother's age (r = .12), father's age (r = -.01), mother's education (r = .19), father's education (r = .16), socioeconomic status (Hollingshead, 1975) (r = .19), gross monthly income (r = .10), and years of marriage (r = .23). All the measures except father's age was significantly correlated (p < .05) with the FSS total scale score, although the magnitude of the correlations were generally quite low, indicating that social support was minimally related to parent and family characteristics.

RELIABILITY

Internal consistency. Coefficient alpha computed from the average correlations among the 18 scale items was .79. The split-half (even vs. odd item) reliability was .77 corrected for length using the Spearman-Brown formula. The magnitude of both the internal consistency and split-half reliability coefficients indicate that the FSS has substantial internal consistency, thus yielding evidence to substantiate the contention that the scale is measuring a broad construct which we labelled social support.

Test-retest reliability. The short-term stability of the FSS was determined for 25 of the subjects who completed the scale on two occasions one-month apart. The analyses yielded an average r = .75 (SD = .17) for the 18 separate items and r = .91 for the total scale score. Only one scale item (social group/clubs) had a test-retest correlation (r = .26) that was not statistically significant. All the other test-retest coefficients were significant beyond the .005 level (one-tailed test). These test-retest findings show that social support is a relatively stable construct at least over short periods of time.

The stability of the FSS administered 1 to 2 years apart was assessed for 60 participants to ascertain test-retest reliability over a longer period of time. The analyses yielded an average r = .42 (SD = .15) for the 18 separate items and r = .50 for the total scale score. Only one scale item (professional helpers) had a test-retest correlation that was marginally statisti-

Table 12-2. Means, Standard Deviations, and Range of Scores for the Family Support Scale			
Scale Items	Mean	Standard Deviation	Range
1. Own Parents	3.35	1.43	1-5
2. Spouse's or Partner's Parents	2.80	1.51	1-5
3. Relatives/Kin	2.53	1.22	1-5
4. Spouse's or Partner's Relatives/Kin	2.30	1.26	1-5
5. Spouse or Partner	3.94	1.39	1-5
6. Friends	2.62	1.29	1-5
7. Spouse's or Partner's Friends	2.13	1.20	1-5
8. Own Children	2.55	1.52	1-5
9. Other Parents	1.99	1.16	1-5
10. Co-Workers	1.86	1.19	1-5
11. Parent Groups	1.75	1.24	1-5
12. Social Groups/Clubs	1.41	0.95	1-5
13. Church	2.78	1.51	1-5
14. Family/Child's Physician	3.52	1.17	1-5
15. Early Intervention Programs	4.07	1.26	1-5
16. School/Day Care	2.48	1.69	1-5
17. Professional Helpers	3.87	1.13	1-5
18. Professional Agencies	2.45	1.51	1-5
Total Scale Score	*48.42*	*10.73*	*24-77*

Note. N=224 for all items.

cally significant (p < .05). All the other stability coefficients were significant beyond the .001 level (one-tailed test). Taken together, these data indicate that the FSS is able to detect stability in social support relationships over extended periods of time.

VALIDITY

Factor structure. A principal components analysis using varimax rotation was used to discern the construct validity of the FSS. The correlation matrix was factored with unities in the diagonal, and factors with eigenvalues exceeding 1.0 were retained for rotation. The solutions obtained are shown in Table 12-3. The analysis yielded five orthogonal factors which, together, accounted for 55% of the variance. The multiple factor solution indicates that the FSS is measuring different, independently available sources of social support.

Content validity. The factor analysis results also provide evidence regarding the content validity of the scale. First, the fact that all 18 FSS items load substantially on the different factors indicates that all the scale items are indeed measuring specific aspects of support. Second, the factor solutions fit nicely to the conceptual model upon which the FSS is based. The pattern of solutions are consistent with a five-levels of support model which generally paralleled the types of embedded relationships described in the introduction. Table 12-3 includes the tentative labels for the factor solutions: I–Informal Kinship, II–Spousal/ Partner Support, III–Social Organizations, IV–Formal Kinship, and V–Professional Services.

Convergent and discriminant validity. The solutions obtained from the factor analysis provide evidence for both the convergent and discriminant validity of the FSS. Items loading heavily on the same factor indicate convergence whereas the orthogonality of the separate fac-

Table 12-3. Varimax-Rotated Factor Solutions for the Family Support Scale

Scale Items	Factor Solutions				
	I	II	III	IV	V
	Informal Kinship	Spouse/Partner Support	Social Organizations	Formal Kinship	Professional Services
Friends	.68				
Spouse's/Partner's Friends	.66				
Own Children	.64				
Other Parents	.62				
Church	.50				
Spouse/Partner		.79			
Spouse's/Partner's Parents		.75			
Spouse's/Partner's Relatives/Kin		.55			
Social Groups/Clubs			.69		
Parents Groups			.59		
School/Day Care Centers			.58		
Co-Workers			.56		
Own Relatives/Kin				.77	
Own Parents				.72	
Early Intervention Programs					.74
Professional Helpers					.72
Family/Child's Physician					.44
Professional Agencies					.44
Variance Explained	*23%*	*11%*	*8%*	*7%*	*6%*
Cumulative Variance	*23%*	*34%*	*42%*	*49%*	*55%*

tors shows that the different factors are measuring different dimensions of support. This dependence/independence relationship is shown in a different way in Table 12-4. The table shows the average correlations of both the items comprising the five factors (diagonal elements) and the across-factor averages. The average within-factor correlations are much higher than the across-factor correlations, thus indicating that the latter are measuring homogeneous aspects of support and the latter are measuring heterogeneous dimensions of support.

Criterion validity. The concurrent predictive validity of the FSS was determined in two ways: Correlations between the FSS total helpfulness scores and selected QRS personal and familial well-being scales, and through analysis of variance predicting QRS personal and familial well-being from FSS group membership.

The correlational analyses showed that the total support scores were significantly related to the Questionnaire on Resources and Stress (QRS) Poor Health/Mood (r = -.25, p < .025), Excessive Time Demands (r = -.22, p < .025), and Family Integrity (r = -.17, p < .025) subscales. The results were all in the predicted direction: Higher levels of support were associated with lower levels of personal and family problems.

A second type of analysis involved a tripartite split of social support scores into three groups of subjects having low, median, and high degrees of support. ANOVAs on the QRS scale scores, using orthogonal comparisons, showed that the high support group differed from the combined low and median support groups on the Poor Health/Mood, F(1, 218) = 11.82, p < .001, Excessive Time Demand, F(1, 183) = 6.28, p < .01, and Family Integrity, F(1, 183) = 6.47, p < .01 subscales. The low and median support groups differed from each other on the Poor Health/Mood, F(1, 218) = 5.31, p < .05, and the Excessive Time Demands, F(1, 183) = 10.19, p < .002, subscales. The results were all in the predicted directions. Higher levels of support were associated with less personal and family-related problems.

DISCUSSION

The results of this study establish both the reliability and validity of the Family Support Scale (FSS). The internal consistency, split-half, and test-retest reliability coefficients were all quite high, and psychometrically acceptable. Both the internal consistency and split-

Table 12-4. Average Within- and Between-Factor Scale Item Correlations

Factors	Factors				
	I	II	III	IV	V
I: Informal Kinship	.34	.17	.17	.23	.17
II: Spousal/Partner Support		.40	.09	.19	.10
III: Social Organizations			.22	.07	.13
IV: Formal Kinship				.39	.13
V: Professional Services					.24

half reliability findings indicated that the FSS is measuring a relatively homogeneous construct which we labelled "social support." The test-retest findings showed that social support is a relatively stable construct both over short and long periods of time.

The factor structure of the FSS showed that the scale is measuring different dimensions of support. The particular set of solutions obtained paralleled the predicted nested arrangement of social units (Bronfenbrenner, 1979; Dunst, 1982). The results, however, would appear to necessitate some refinement of the embedded social unit model inasmuch as a five rather than four level model was obtained. The informal and formal kinship unit appear to be comprised of two separate groups of persons: extrafamily acquaintances/friends (Factor I) and blood/marriage relatives and kin (Factor IV). The proposed embedded relationships may then be conceived topologically in the following order: spousal/partner support, informal kinship, formal kinship, social organizations, and professional services.

As expected, the FSS was significantly related to personal and familial well-being. Thus, the scale is a sensitive instrument for discriminating between individuals who manifest differing levels of stress and coping. This finding provides yet additional evidence in support of the contention that social support is related to physical and emotional well-being (Dean & Lin, 1977; McCubbin et al., 1980; Mitchell & Trickett, 1980).

Taken together, the results of our analyses indicate that the FSS is a highly reliable and valid instrument. The principal utility of the scale rests on its ability to discriminate between persons differing in levels and degrees of stress, coping, and family integrity. The strengths of the scale include its ease of administration, compactness, and comprehensiveness with re-

gard to the range of support networks rated. Its weaknesses include its failure to tap specific characteristics of support networks and the social support they provide (e.g., types of support provided, reciprocal relationships, etc.) (see Mitchell & Trickett, 1980).

The utility of the scale for research purposes has been established in a number of studies (Dunst, 1983; Dunst & Trivette, 1984, 1986, 1988a, 1988d; Dunst, Trivette, & Cross, 1986a, 1986b; Trivette & Dunst, 1992). The FSS has been found to be sensitive in discriminating between persons differing in degrees of social support on a number of important dimensions of well-being, including stress, coping, and family integrity. We have replicated these findings with both different populations of subjects and with different measures of physical and emotional well-being (see Trivette & Dunst, 1992). Besides predicting personal and familial well-being, our findings also indicate that FSS scores are related to styles of parent-child interactions, parental expectations for their children, and parental perceptions of child behavior problems (Dunst & Trivette, 1984, 1986, 1988a, 1988d; Dunst, Trivette, & Cross, 1986a, 1986b; Trivette & Dunst, 1992). Taken together, these sets of findings provide credence for the contention that social support is related both directly and indirectly to a host of parent, family, parent-child, and child behavior characteristics (Bronfenbrenner, 1979; Cochran & Brassard, 1979; Crnic et al., 1983; Dean & Lin, 1977; Dunst, 1983; Mitchell & Trickett, 1980; McCubbin et al., 1980).

IMPLICATIONS FOR PRACTICE

Besides its empirical utility, the FSS would appear to have clinical value as an assessment and intervention instrument. The scale could be used to assess both the number and quality of social support available to families, and provide a basis for querying respondents about specific aspects of both help and lack of help. The FSS might also be used to gauge the success of interventions designed to mediate provisions of support by plotting changes in the helpfulness scores over time.

Social support is an important mediating and explainer variable in the helping professions. Scales like the FSS can help explicate the relationships between social support and the ability to cope and manage different life crises.

APPENDIX

Family Support Scale

Carl J. Dunst, Vicki Jenkins & Carol M. Trivette

INSTRUCTIONS: Listed below are people and groups that oftentimes are helpful to members of a family raising a young child. This questionnaire asks you to indicate how helpful each source is to your family.

Please circle the response that best describes how helpful the sources have been to your family during the past 3 to 6 months. If a source of help has not been available to your family during this period of time, circle NA (Not Available) response.

How helpful has each of the following been to you in terms of raising your child(ren):	Not Available	Not at All Helpful	Sometimes Helpful	Generally Helpful	Very Helpful	Extremely Helpful
1. My parents	NA	1	2	3	4	5
2. My spouse or partner's parents	NA	1	2	3	4	5
3. My relatives/kin	NA	1	2	3	4	5
4. My spouse or partner's relatives/kin	NA	1	2	3	4	5
5. Spouse or partner	NA	1	2	3	4	5
6. My friends	NA	1	2	3	4	5
7. My spouse or partner's friends	NA	1	2	3	4	5
8. My own children	NA	1	2	3	4	5
9. Other parents	NA	1	2	3	4	5
10. Co-workers	NA	1	2	3	4	5
11. Parent groups	NA	1	2	3	4	5
12. Social groups/clubs	NA	1	2	3	4	5
13. Church members/minister	NA	1	2	3	4	5
14. My family or child's physician	NA	1	2	3	4	5
15. Early childhood intervention program	NA	1	2	3	4	5
16. School/day-care center	NA	1	2	3	4	5
17. Professional helpers (social workers, therapists, teachers, etc.)	NA	1	2	3	4	5
18. Professional agencies (public health, social services, mental health, etc.)	NA	1	2	3	4	5
19. _____	NA	1	2	3	4	5
20. _____	NA	1	2	3	4	5

(May be duplicated without permission with proper acknowledgment and citation.)

V

EFFECTIVE HELP-GIVING PRACTICES

The chapters in this section describe our evolving thoughts about the roles professionals ought to play as part of family-centered assessment and intervention practices. The major thesis of the contents, taken together, is that the manner in which resources and supports are made available to families as part of help-giver/help-seeker exchanges makes a difference in terms of whether the transactions have positive or negative consequences. Chapter 13 describes our initial thinking about the characteristics of effective and ineffective help-giving practices. A model that has guided both research and practice focusing on enabling and empowering help-giving beliefs, attitudes, and behaviors is described in Chapter 14. Chapter 15 illustrates the applicability of the help-giving model for case management practices, whereas Chapter 16 describes the overlap between effective help-giving practices and the key characteristics of parent-professional collaboration and partnerships. The findings from several lines of help-giving research are summarized in Chapter 17. The results from this work demonstrate that help-giving practices which are consistent with an empowerment philosophy are associated with parental self-efficacy appraisals indicating a greater sense of control over obtaining needed resources and supports. Collectively, the contents of the five chapters included in this section support the need for adoption of empowering help-giving practices if family control appraisals are to be maximized.

CHAPTER 13

What is Effective Helping?

Carl J. Dunst & Carol M. Trivette

THE PURPOSE OF THIS CHAPTER is to explore the meaning of the term *helping* and examine under what conditions helping acts may have either positive or negative consequences. It should be noted at the outset that the perspective of helping acts and helping relationships described in this chapter is based upon an empowerment philosophy about human behavior (Dunst & Trivette, 1987a; Dunst, Trivette, & Deal, 1988; Rappaport, 1981, 1987). An empowerment philosophy includes three main components. First, the philosophy assumes that *all* people have existing strengths and capabilities as well as the capacity to become more competent. Second, the philosophy states that the failure to display competence is *not* due to deficits within a person but rather the failure of social systems to create opportunities for competencies to be acquired or displayed. Third, the philosophy states that in those cases where a help-seeker (learner, client, etc.) needs to acquire competencies to solve a problem, meet a need, or achieve a goal, he or she must attribute observed changes from helping acts at least in part to his or her own behavior if help-giving is to have positive consequences. With these caveats laid out, an operational definition of effective helping can be offered.

DEFINITION OF EFFECTIVE HELPING

Based upon an aggregation of the help-giving literature (Dunst & Trivette, 1988c), effective helping may be defined as an

act of enabling individuals or groups (e.g., a family) to become better able to solve problems, meet needs, or achieve aspirations by promoting the acquisition of competencies that support and strengthen functioning in a way that permits a greater sense of individual or group control over its developmental course.

This definition includes five key terms and elements that deserve additional definition and consideration.

The first consideration pertains to the meaning of the term enablement. *Enabling individuals or groups* means the process of creating opportunities for competencies to be acquired or displayed as part of solving problems, meeting needs, or achieving aspirations. Such opportunities are called *enabling experiences* (Dunst, Trivette, & Deal, 1988).

The second consideration pertains to the meaning of the terms *problems, needs, and aspirations*, and the influence these conditions have on human behavior. These terms are collectively defined as a discrepancy between actual states or conditions and what is considered normative, desired, or valued from a help-seeker's and not a help-giver's perspective (see especially Chapter 7). Unless there is a perceived

---

This chapter is based on a presentation made at the Plenary Session "What is Helping?" held at the Fifth Biennial National Training Institute of the National Center for Clinical Infants Programs, Washington, DC, Dec. 1987.

discrepancy between *what is* and *what ought to be* on the part of a help-seeker, there is not likely to be a concern regardless of what a help-giver believes to be the case (McKillip, 1987). A corollary of this is the contention that perceived or indicated discrepancies constitute at least one major force that shapes the behavior of a person, and guides that person's behavior in a direction specifically designed to alleviate the discrepancies (Dunst, Leet, & Trivette, 1988; Garbarino, 1982).

The third consideration pertains to the meaning of the term *promotion*. Promotion means the enhancement of competencies that permit an individual or group to become better able to solve problems, meet needs, and achieve aspirations (see Chapter 3). In contrast to prevention efforts which deter or hinder the occurrence of negative outcomes, or treatment approaches that remediate or ameliorate disorders or their consequences, promotion efforts emphasize the acquisition of competencies that enhance an individual or group's ability to successfully negotiate its developmental course (Dunst & Trivette, 1987a). The distinction between promotion, prevention, and treatment is neither trivial nor semantic. Not only do people respond more favorably to helping efforts that enhance knowledge and skill acquisition, a promotion approach to helping relationships is more likely to strengthen functioning in ways that produce developmental growth (Dunst & Trivette, 1988c; Dunst, Trivette, & Thompson, 1990).

The fourth consideration pertains to the meaning of the terms *supporting and strengthening functioning*. Supporting and strengthening functioning means providing enabling experiences that promote an individual or group's ability to attain what it believes is in its best interest to the extent that the well-being of others is protected (Hobbs et al., 1984). Promoting a help-seeker's ability to nurture and promote its own development as well as that

of others in positive directions is the ultimate positive consequence of truly effective helping relationships.

The fifth consideration pertains to the meaning of a *greater sense of control*. The term control refers to at least two major aspects of self-efficacy: (1) an individual's ability to deploy competencies to meet needs, solve problems, or achieve aspirations and (2) the individual's beliefs about the role he or she played in reaching the goal (Bandura, 1977, 1982). A help-seeker must be both actively involved in the helping act and attribute observed changes resulting from helping acts, at least in part, to his or her own efforts if there are to be positive consequences of helping relationships.

Collectively, the five major features of the proposed definition of helping provide a perspective from which to structure efforts designed to enable and empower help-seekers (see Dunst, Trivette, & Deal, 1988). It is suspected that most readers would agree with the contentions set forth as part of the working definition of effective helping. Some would probably say that very little of what has been offered is new. Notwithstanding this possibility, one question nonetheless must be asked: "Do most helping acts have the competency promoting influences that are the key features of the definition of help-giving proposed above?" The answer to this question is pursued next.

INEFFECTIVE HELPING ACTS AND HELP-GIVING PRACTICES

For over a decade, we have been engaged in a line of research designed to assess the impact of different types of social support (Cohen & Syme, 1985b) on parent, family, and child functioning. This research has demonstrated that social support has both direct and indirect influences on various aspects of individual and family functioning (Dunst & Trivette, 1984, 1987b, 1988a, 1988b, 1988d; Trivette & Dunst, 1992). Examination of individual cases shows that for most persons, support has positive influences, while for a few, support has no apparent positive effects, and in some instances, it appears to have negative consequences. The latter cases led us to examine the differences between *what* was provided and *how* it was provided as a way of explaining these differential outcomes. We began with an extensive review of the help-giving literature, and somewhat to our surprise, found considerable evidence regarding the negative consequences of helping acts (Dunst, 1986a; Dunst & Trivette, 1987a, 1988c). The findings from our synthesis of the available evidence resulted in eight major conclusions regarding the negative effects of certain types of helping acts. Before listing the conclusions from our synthesis of the literature, however, it should be explicitly noted that no single help-seeker/help-giver exchange is likely to produce catastrophic negative effects. It would seem that it is repeated experiences with ineffective help-givers who violate basic principles of effective helping that set the occasion for ineffective interactions, and that this in turn constitutes the conditions that produce detrimental and debilitating consequences.

Based upon a review and integration of available evidence, it was found that help-giving increased the likelihood of negative consequences if it: (1) undermined a help-seeker's sense of competence and control over different aspects of his or her life in ways that produced learned helplessness (Coates, Renzaglia, & Embree, 1983), (2) fostered dependencies when help-givers, typically professionals as part of client-professional relationships, took relative and in some instances absolute control over the help-seeker's fate by exercising paternalistic authority (Merton, Merton,

& Barber, 1983), (3) attenuated the help-seeker's self-esteem either when the help-giver conveyed a sense that the help-seeker was inferior, incompetent or inadequate, or was patronizing to the help-seeker (Nadler & Mayseless, 1983), (4) fostered a sense of indebtedness in the help-seeker which directly threatened his or her self-esteem, created dependencies, and evoked other negative reactions (Greenberg & Westcott, 1983), (5) was unsolicited and only reinforced already negative feelings toward oneself, especially when advice or aid was offered by those whom the help-seeker did not know or did not wish to have advice from (e.g., a neighbor who gives unsolicited childrearing advice) (Fisher, Nadler, & Whitcher-Alagna, 1983b), (6) was incongruent with what was sought, and refusal of the help by the help-seeker was seen as ungrateful by the help-giver (Fisher, 1983), (7) was seen as needed by a help-giver but the individual perceived no problem and had no identified need (Fisher et al., 1983b), and (8) was provided noncontingently and did not require the help-seeker to learn new competencies or even reinforced maintenance of maladaptive behavior (Brickman et al., 1983). Noncontingent help-giving, more than any other aspect of helping relationships, was found to set the occasion for increased passivity and dependence because it directly undermined and interfered with the acquisition of needed competencies. Noncontingent helping most often occurs by well-intentioned helpers who *do for others* rather than teaching others to *do for themselves*.

NONCONTINGENT HELPING

Skinner (1978) called noncontingent help-giving unethical because it "postpones the acquisition of effective behavior and perpetuates the need for help" (p. 251). To the extent that "Help supplies a needed resource but leads the person to see the production of that resource as contingent on what the helpers do rather than on his or her own behavior"

(Brickman et al., 1983, p. 34), the helping relationship is likely to have harmful consequences. Indeed, meeting needs and solving problems is likely to have long-term positive effects only when help-seekers actively participate in solving problems, meeting needs, and achieving aspirations; "take pride in their accomplishments; (and) ascribe successes to their own abilities and efforts" (Bandura, 1978, p. 349). Noncontingent help-giving may seem expedient in terms of solving the problems and meeting the needs of help-seekers, but in the long run it deprives people of enabling experiences and opportunities that are important for future learning, acquisition of independent and problem-solving behavior, and enhancement of self-esteem.

Noncontingent helping is most characteristic of social agencies serving the poor (Pettigrew, 1983), and is perhaps best exemplified by social welfare programs (e.g., Aid to Families of Dependent Children). Many of the types of help offered noncontingently by social and human services agencies not only postpones and interferes with the acquisition of self-sustaining behaviors, but often implicitly (and sometimes explicitly) reinforce a help-seeker's sense of inadequacy and incompetence. This in turn reduces efforts to acquire effective coping and problem-solving behaviors. Consequently, one would more likely find a greater sense of helplessness, hopelessness, dependency, and negative feelings toward oneself and others resulting from noncontingent provisions of aid and assistance.

Although noncontingent helping can most often be found in helping relationships involving publicly-operated human services programs, one finds many examples of this type of help in less formal help-seeker/help-giver exchanges (Morse, 1983; Skinner, 1978). Noncontingent helping by friends, neighbors, relatives, the church, and so on may do more harm than good, at least under certain conditions. Two concrete examples of noncontingent helping are briefly described next to illustrate the context, conditions, and consequences of this particular type of help-giving act.

EXAMPLES OF NONCONTINGENT HELPING

An increasing number of human services programs and community agencies and organizations "operate" food pantries, clothes closets, soup kitchens, toy lending libraries, etc. for "less fortunate" individuals and families. One must wonder what influences this non-contingent helping has on the self-esteem and sense of competence of these persons? Don't misunderstand us. We are not suggesting that we should not feed the hungry, clothe the poor, or shelter the homeless. We wonder, however, why help-givers do not seize the opportunity when interacting with these people to promote the acquisition of competencies that would allow these persons to become better able to meet their needs, become more capable, and foster a sense of self-worth that has growth producing influences (see especially Dunst, Trivette, Gordon, & Pletcher, 1989). *If help does not require a recipient to acquire effective behavior, and thus renders the person helpless or dependent, the immediate needs of the person may be met, but the opportunity to teach and foster effective behavior is diminished.*

The second example comes from our experience working with families of infants and toddlers participating in early intervention programs for children with disabilities. The unique developmental needs of these youngsters generally require educational and therapeutic interventions to influence and promote optimal growth. In many programs, teachers and therapists assume primary responsibility for implementing such interventions. Parents often watch professionals teach their infants and toddlers things that the parents have been unable to teach their own children. This can be disconcerting to some parents because in our society parents are expected to be the "first and primary" caregivers of their children, and any violation of this expectancy can be potentially damaging. What are the consequences of a parent seeing his or her child become more competent as the result of efforts of professional help-givers? Many parents have shared the following with us: Seeing others get their children to do what they themselves have been unable to accomplish can directly threaten their sense of competence as a parent, and in some cases results in parents questioning their own child-rearing capabilities. It would seem that some parents feel this way because certain professionally-implemented educational and therapeutic interventions are a form of noncontingent helping in cases where parents play little or no active role in understanding and influencing their own children's behavior. This in turn leads the parents to attribute observed changes in child behavior to the efforts of others, and produces negative effects in other aspects of functioning (e.g., parent self-esteem). *To the extent that professionally implemented interventions with infants and toddlers cause parents to question their child rearing capabilities, which in turn attenuates their efforts to promote and enhance their children's development, the negative effects the interventions have on the parent's belief systems will likely have detrimental consequences for the children* (Sigel, 1985; Sigel, McGillicuddy-DeLisi, & Goodnow, 1992). Therefore, it would seem necessary that we begin to systematically examine the effects of different types of help-giving behavior to be sure that positive influences in one aspect of functioning (e.g., child performance) do not have negative conse-

quences in other areas of functioning (e.g., parental sense of competence).

EFFECTIVE HELPING ACTS AND HELP-GIVING PRACTICES

Not all helping acts are ineffective in the manner described above. A review, synthesis, and aggregation of the literature on effective help-giving practices has led us to propose a help-giving model and associated "principles" that have been found to produce a variety of positive consequences. The helping model described next de-emphasizes help-seeker responsibility for causing their problems and emphasizes help-seeker responsibility for acquisition of competencies necessary to solve problems, meet needs, realize personal aspirations, or otherwise attain goals or goal states. We label the helping perspective an *enablement model* to stress the stance that we believe is necessary in order to increase the likelihood that a person will become empowered. The term enablement reflects the underlying rationale of the model, namely that help-givers *create opportunities for competencies to be acquired or displayed by help-seekers. All* help-seekers are assumed to be competent or capable of being competent, and when provided opportunities to do so, will be able to deal effectively with problems, demands, and aspirations.

The model, to the extent possible, focuses on promotion of growth producing behaviors rather than treatment of problems or prevention of negative outcomes. Emphasis is placed on promoting and strengthening individual and family functioning by fostering the acquisition of prosocial, self-sustaining, self-efficacious, and other adaptive behaviors. Help-seekers are encouraged to play a major role in deciding what is important to them, what options they will choose to achieve intentions, and what actions they will take in carrying-out intervention plans. The help-seeker is viewed as the essential agent of change; whereas, the help-giver's roles are to support, encourage, and create opportunities for the help-seeker to become competent. The help-giver does not mobilize resources on behalf of the help-seeker, but rather creates opportunities (modeling, teaching, etc.) for the help-seeker to acquire competencies that permit him or her to mobilize their own sources of resources and support necessary to cope, adapt, and grow in response to life's many challenges. Help-givers are expected to be positive, see the strengths of help-seekers, and assist help-seekers to see their potential and capabilities. This is all done in a co-operative, partnership approach that emphasizes joint responsibility between the help-seeker and help-giver. The goal of this model is to make help-seekers better able to deal effectively with future problems, needs, and aspirations, not to make them problem or trouble free.

PRINCIPLES OF EFFECTIVE HELP-GIVING

The enablement model suggests a number of help-giving behaviors that are likely to increase the probability that a person will become empowered as part of help-seeker and help-giving exchanges. The proposed principles are nonmutually exclusive, and taken together, represent a *helping style* that creates opportunities for a person to become empowered. Based upon an extensive review and integration of the literature, it was found that *help is most likely to be empowering if help-giver:*

1. *Is both positive and proactive* (Fisher, 1983). Help-givers who display a sincere sense of caring, warmth, and encouragement when offering or responding to requests for help are more likely to have health promoting and competency producing influ-

ences on help-seekers. "When positive donor motives are attributed (e.g., the donor is perceived to act out of kindness or generosity), aid is more supportive and results in more favorable reactions" (Fisher et al., 1983a, p. 73).

2. *Offers rather than waits for help to be requested* (Fisher et al., 1983a). Help-seeking may be implicit or explicit, and the help-giver's sensitivity to verbal, nonverbal, and paraverbal messages displayed by a help-seeker is a key to being able to read a person's behavior and respond appropriately. Help-givers are viewed as more positive by help-seekers when they offer help in response to help-seeker identified needs (Gross, Wallston, & Piliavin, 1979).

3. *Engages in help-giving acts in which locus of decision making clearly rests with the help-seeker, including decisions about the need or goal, the options for carrying out the intentions, and whether or not to accept or reject help that is offered* (Fisher et al., 1983a). To be maximally effective, the ability to refuse help must be explicitly recognized by the help-giver, the decision sanctioned, and the opportunity for future exchanges left open as an option for the help-seeker to use. Aid that implies no or few lost freedoms is most likely to have positive effects in response to help-giving.

4. *Offers aid and assistance that is normative in terms of the help-seeker's own culture* (Fisher et al., 1983a). Nonnormative help is often times demeaning and conveys a sense that the help-seeker has an inferior status or is incompetent (Hobbs et al., 1984). Help is maximally effective if it does not infer deviance or undue variation with respect to how other members of the help-seeker's culture or social network would deal with the same problem or need (Gross & McMullen, 1983).

5. *Offers aid and assistance that is congruent with the help-seeker's appraisal of his or her problem or need* (Fisher, 1983). Positive reactions to help-giving are more likely to occur when aid and assistance is appropriate, and matches the help-seeker's appraisal of his or her problems or needs.

6. *Offers aid and assistance in which the response costs of seeking and acceptance of help do not outweigh the benefits* (Gross & McMullen, 1983). Help-giving that reduces threats to self-esteem, moderates psychological obligations to repay, protects behavior freedoms (decision making), and promotes competence and a sense of adequacy, are more likely to be seen as personally cost-effective.

7. *Offers help that can be reciprocated and sanctions the possibility of "repaying" the help-giver* (Fisher et al., 1983a). "Reciprocity is (most) likely to be the preferred mode of reducing indebtedness to the extent that recipients are made aware of this option and they perceive that the opportunity to reciprocate exists" (Greenberg & Westcott, 1983, p. 95). A help-giver who provides aid and assistance and accepts advice and assistance makes the exchanges fair and equitable, which in turn bolsters a help-seeker's sense that he or she has as much to give as to take.

8. *Bolsters the self-esteem of the recipient, and helps the individual experience immediate success in solving a problem or meeting a need* (Nadler & Mayseless, 1983). Bolstering self-esteem is accomplished by using a person's existing strengths as a basis for helping the person solve small problems and experience immediate success before tackling more difficult problems and needs. "If help is given after efforts toward self-esteem enhancement have been successful, it is more likely to precipitate adaptive

behaviors (e.g., self-help efforts and subsequent improved performance) than if given before such efforts are attempted" (Nadler & Mayseless, 1983, p. 178).

9. *Promotes the help-seeker's use of natural support networks and neither replaces nor supplants them with professional services* (Hobbs, 1975; Hobbs et al., 1984). According to Hobbs (1975), help-giving efforts are empowering if they strengthen normal socializing agents (relatives, neighbors, friends, etc.), and enhance a sense of community that emphasizes the promotion of the competence and well-being of all members in the help-seeker's social network.

10. *Conveys a sense of cooperation and joint responsibility (partnership) for meeting needs and solving problems* (Hobbs et al., 1984). Help-giving exchanges that promote participatory decision-making and shared responsibility between a help-seeker and help-giver set the occasion for the help-seeker to feel valued, important, and an "equal."

11. *Promotes the acquisition of effective behavior that decreases the need for help, thus making the person more capable and competent* (Skinner, 1978). This type of help "enables the recipient to become more self-sustaining and less in need of future help" (Brickman et al., 1983, p. 19), thus promoting competence and independence (Fisher et al., 1983a) and problem-solving capabilities (DePaulo, Nadler, & Fisher, 1983).

12. *Helps the recipient to see that not only have problems been solved or needs met, but that the help-seeker functioned as an active, responsible agent who played a significant role in improving his or her own life* (Bandura, 1977). It is the "recipient's own belief in (himself or herself) as a causal agent that determines whether the gains made will last or disap-

pear" (Brickman et al., 1983, p. 32). Recipients must therefore perceive improvement, see themselves as no longer in need of help, and see themselves as both responsible for producing the observed changes and maintenance of these changes, if help-seeking/help-giving exchanges are to be effective (Bandura, 1977). This sense of intra-and inter-personal control is most likely to be acquired as a function of learning effective, instrumental behavior.

Collectively, these 12 principles constitute a *helping style* that is consistent with the enablement model described in Chapter 2. Our helping model and 12 help-giving principles have evolved from extensive research and clinical experience working with families of young children (see especially Dunst & Trivette, 1988d), although we believe that the model and principles have general utility for creating opportunities for persons to become more capable and competent in any kind of human services setting.

IMPLICATIONS FOR PRACTICE

The material described in this chapter forms the basis for one of the four components of the family-centered assessment and intervention model described in Chapter 1. Each component is guided by a substantive principle, assessment/intervention goal, and set of intervention operatives (Dunst, Trivette, & Deal, 1988). The use of this model and its guiding principles have significantly improved our efforts to work effectively with families, especially with respect to our ability to both enable and empower families in the manner described in this book.

The enablement model of helping has been operationalized and field tested as part of our efforts to better understand the key characteristics of *effective helping practices*. The

various projects and services which have employed our enabling model and help-giving principles are described in Dunst and Trivette (1988c). For example, Project SHaRE (Sources of Help Received and Exchanged) was one of the most successful projects we have ever operated because it put into practice nearly all the above help-giving principles as part of service-delivery efforts (Dunst, Trivette, Gordon, & Pletcher, 1989). The project consisted of a SHaRE Network of individuals ranging from teenagers to the elderly, lower to upper SES background families, single and married persons, parents and nonparents, etc. The common thread that held the group together was their individual needs and strengths. SHaRE members engaged in exchanges of services and products in order to get needs met (e.g., providing babysitting in exchange for canned or cooked food). The project was based on the premise that each and every individual had capabilities and strengths that could be of benefit to others, and that by creating opportunities for persons to utilize their strengths, the person became empowered par excellence (Rappaport, 1981).

Besides its utility for work with adults, our enabling model is useful in work with children as well, and may be illustrated with reference to school children who show difficulty in mastering academic material. In contrast to a treatment program that might focus on supplemental assistance (e.g., a resource room) designed directly to improve academic performance, an enabling approach would assume an already existing level and set of competencies, and find ways to build upon existing strengths. In a number of investigations that have taken this approach, children having learning difficulties were asked to teach younger children in the subject areas in which they were having difficulty (see Allen, 1976). The results showed that academic performance significantly improved as a function of serving in the tutor (helper) role (Allen & Feldman, 1974; Erickson & Cromack, 1972). This strategy for enhancing academic performance reflects what we would describe as enablement and empowerment.

The ability to work effectively with help-seekers in general, and children and their parents specifically, in ways that have empowering consequences requires a shift in how we think about helping relationships and the ways in which we engage in help-giving exchanges. To the extent that a help-giver takes pride in and derives rewards from seeing others become more competent and self-sustaining, the use of our enabling model and empowering principles seem to be at least one way to obtain this type of success.

CONCLUSIONS

Two major conclusions can be drawn from the material briefly examined in this chapter regarding effective helping.

1. *It is not just an issue of whether problems are solved or needs are met, but rather the manner in which mobilization of resources occurs that is a major determinant of the empowerment of individuals or groups.*

For helping relationships to be both empowering and supportive in a way that promotes an individual or group's capabilities and competencies, help-seekers on the one hand must be actively involved in the helping process, and on the other hand must attribute behavior change at least in part to their own actions resulting from the helping relationship.

2. *To be truly successful in helping relationships, professionals must take pride in and derive intrinsic personal rewards in seeing others become more competent and self-sustaining.*

Deriving pleasure and gratification in seeing others become competent and capable is a fundamental attribute of a helping professional who is a proponent of an empowerment philosophy. To the extent that we do not recognize and explicitly consider the empowerment of help-seekers as the goal of helping relationships, we are more likely to fool ourselves into believing that we have done a good job when in fact we have lost an opportunity to enable and empower individuals or groups, and perhaps have even created dependencies by engaging in noncontingent helping. These contentions cannot be stated any better than Frank Maple (1977) described them in his book *Shared Decision Making*. He noted that when help-givers see themselves as principally (or solely) responsible for rescuing individuals from their troubles,

> ...the rescuer becomes a star. It is my view that your goal as helpers is not to learn how to become a star, but rather to help (others) become the "star" in some aspects of their lives. (p. 7)

To help others become stars and shine brightly is what is meant when individuals or groups become empowered. Producing capable and competent individuals and groups must be the major goal of helping relationships if helping efforts are to be considered truly successful. Consequently, helping may be considered effective only to the extent that help-seekers become more capable, competent, and empowered as a result of help-giving acts.

CHAPTER 14

Characteristics of Effective Help-Giving Practices

Carl J. Dunst, Carol M. Trivette, Michelle Davis & Janet C. Cornwell

PROFESSIONALS WHO PROVIDE help to help-seekers do so with the intent that it will have positive consequences. There is evidence, however, that certain types of help, and the manner in which it is provided, can and often does have debilitating effects (DePaulo, Nadler, & Fisher, 1983; Fisher, Nadler, & DePaulo, 1983a; Nadler, Fisher, & DePaulo, 1983). For example, help-giving is likely to create dependencies when professionals take relative and, in some cases, absolute control over their help-seekers' fates, and occurs most often in response to help-seeking involving acute medical or psychological problems. Because the "professional consulted when the help-seeker needs help may never (have) seen the help-seeker in a state of general well-being, (the help-giver) can therefore have only an indirect sense of the help-seeker's capabilities and strengths. This limited perspective reinforces the already ingrained tendency for the professional to exercise paternalistic authority" (Merton, Merton, & Barber, 1983, p. 21).

Surrender or usurpation of active control and autonomy to "powerful others" is one of the major determinants of dependency (Brickman, Rabinowitz, Karuza, Coates, Cohn, & Kidder, 1982; Merton, Merton, & Barber, 1983). Dependency, in turn, is likely to result in a sense of helplessness, hopelessness, depression, or alienation on the part of a help-seeker (Reid, 1984). Research on patterns of help-giving has consistently produced findings which demonstrate that dependency and its consequences are often induced by certain types of professional practices (e.g., Taylor, 1979). Interventions with families of children with developmental disabilities or those at-risk for poor outcomes oftentimes result in child and parental dependency upon professional help-givers (Brickman et al., 1982; Kohrman & Diamond, 1986; Rappaport, 1981, 1987; Swift, 1984), despite the fact that the literature abounds with references to the need for active involvement of both children (van Eys, 1984) and their families (Affleck, Tennen, & Rowe, 1991; Anderson, 1985; Chesler, 1985; Dunst, 1991; Zimmerman, 1990b) as part of human services program interventions.

The plea for more active involvement of family members in human services programs has been voiced on a number of fronts (Association for the Care of Children's Health, 1985; Kohrman & Diamond, 1986; National Center for Clinical Infant Programs, 1985; Shelton, Jeppson, & Johnson, 1987; van Eys, 1984, 1985). Despite recent advances (e.g., Association for the Care of Children's Health, 1985), why have families of children involved in human services programs not been more frequently given the rightful role to be involved in discussions about and decisions regarding what is in the best interest of their offspring? The answer, in part, comes from the failure of proponents of increased family involvement to recognize a dilemma of helping that must be acknowledged

The material in this chapter is based on an article appearing in *Children's Health Care*, 1988, *17*(2), 71-81. Reprinted with permission from the publisher.

and addressed if family-centered assessment and intervention is to become remotely possible, let alone a reality.

The dilemma that must be resolved is the disparity between the model of helping typically employed by professionals and the beliefs, attitudes, and behaviors necessary to promote greater participatory involvement on the part of the family. According to Merton *et al.* (1983), most professionals have been socialized to believe that they must have all the right answers, and to suggest that others might be capable of managing events that professionals have been trained to deal with as experts becomes a direct threat to their sense of competence. Thus, despite calls for more involvement, many professionals would rather have help-seekers succumb to their decisions concerning the course of care.

> Assuming an attitude of need, dependency, and trust can be a powerful means of influencing others' behavior....When joined with the legitimized role expectations that the professional is going to improve the client's lot, it takes on added force. It makes the professional feel important, responsible, and–at least by comparison with the client–capable. A client who fails to play the complementary role of dependent in some sense deprives the professional of a tool of the trade....Thus *the prospect of clients' taking a more active and responsible role in their own care is unnerving* in part because it seems that the less helpless the client, the less helpful the professional can be. (Merton et al., 1983, pp. 21-22, emphasis added.)

To the extent that this position and stance is embraced by a professional helper, it is in direct conflict with the conditions necessary

for more active family involvement in interventions with their children (Chesler, 1985; Shelton et al., 1987).

How are we to resolve the dilemma between these apparently contradictory alternatives? We believe the predicament can be resolved by employing a conceptual framework of helping relationships that on the one hand permits greater understanding of the types of helping styles that have health and competency promoting influences, and on the other hand expands the legitimized roles of help-givers. In this chapter we describe at least one way of doing this that has proven beneficial as a way of enabling and empowering families to become more actively involved in interventions with the parents and their children (Dunst & Trivette, 1987a, 1988a). By *actively involved* we mean a family's increased understanding of the needs of the child, the ability to deploy competencies to meet those needs, and self-attributions about the role family members played in meeting needs. Collectively, the three conditions– understanding, deployment, and self-efficacy–define several major components of an *empowerment* philosophy (see Chapter 2). Before we proceed, it should be noted that our model and its corollaries are based upon a philosophy of human behavior that explicitly aims to support and strengthen family functioning (Hobbs et al., 1984) as a way of promoting the ability of the family (Rappaport, 1981, 1987) to negotiate its developmental course in response to both normative and non-normative life events. This philosophical position sets the tone for all that follows.

The chapter is divided into three sections. First, we describe the major features of an empowerment philosophy and propose a definition of effective helping that operationalizes the philosophical stance toward help-seekers and helping relationships. Second, we describe a model of helping and helping relationships that attempts to specify the types of professional help-giver attitudes, beliefs, and behaviors that are likely to promote increased involvement and a sense of empowerment. Third, we summarize the results from a study designed to test the validity of the assumptions and assertions central to the empowerment model of helping.

A SYSTEMS PERSPECTIVE OF EMPOWERMENT

A number of definitions of empowerment can be found in the literature (e.g., Brickman et al., 1982; Dunst, 1985; Hobbs et al., 1984; Solomon, 1985). Three characteristics of these definitions have guided the ways in which most investigators have typically defined and attempted to operationalize this construct. These include the help-seeker's: (a) access and control over needed resources, (b) decision-making and problem-solving abilities, and (c) acquisition of instrumental behavior needed to interact effectively with others in order to procure needed resources. Although this may have proven a useful approach for defining empowerment, it has nonetheless constrained our understanding of what it means to be empowered and *how we can go about enabling and empowering families*. Indeed, we would go so far as to say that the problem-solving/decision-making approach to conceptualizing empowerment, which focuses almost entirely on the help-seeker's behavior without consideration of the help-giver's role in helping relationships, has restricted our understanding of empowerment because it fails to explicitly consider a number of broader-based issues as part of help-seeker (client) and help-giver (professional) exchanges.

A more complete understanding of empowerment requires that we take a broader-based perspective of the conditions that influence the behavior of people during help-seeker and help-giver exchanges. A social systems perspective seems to offer this type of framework, and is perhaps best reflected in Rappaport's (1981) contention that

Empowerment implies that many competencies are already present or at least possible.... Empowerment implies that what you see as poor functioning is a result of social structure and lack of resources which make it impossible for the existing competencies to operate. It implies that in those cases where new competencies need to be learned, they are best learned in a context of living life rather than in artificial programs where everyone, including the person learning, knows that it is really the expert who is in charge. (p. 16)

This set of assertions includes three conditions that we believe reflect the way in which we need to think about helping relationships and empowerment. First, it states that people are already competent and that they have the capacity to become competent. This is what we refer to as a *proactive* stance toward help-seekers. Second, it states that the failure to display competence is not due to deficits within the help-seeker but rather the failure of social systems to create opportunities for competencies to be displayed. Creating opportunities for competence to be displayed is what we refer to as *enabling experiences*. Third, it implicitly states that the person who is the learner, help-seeker, etc. must be able to deploy competencies to obtain resources to meet needs, and attribute behavior change at least in part to his or her own actions, if one is to acquire a sense of control over life events. This is what we mean when we say a person is *empowered*. Taken together, these three assertions provide a basis for viewing empowerment from a broader-based systems perspective that suggests the importance of the help-giver's behavior as part of both enabling and empowering families. Additionally, this philosophical stance toward help-seekers suggests a new and expanded definition of effective helping. Based upon the major features of the above perspective of empowerment, Dunst (1987) defined effective helping as the

> act of enabling individuals or groups (e.g., family) to become better able to solve problems, meet needs, or achieve aspirations by promoting acquisition of competencies that support and strengthen functioning in a way that permits a greater sense of individual or group control over its developmental course. (p. 1)

These particular perspectives of empowerment and effective helping have guided our attempts to better understand how helping acts and helping relationships influence help-seeker behavior. Our interest in helping relationships and empowerment derives from efforts to develop, test, and validate a social systems model of family functioning for effectively working with families of young children (Dunst & Trivette, 1988a). On the one hand, we have developed a conceptual model of development that permits greater understanding of family functioning, and thus can be used as a framework for generating and testing hypotheses about factors that are likely to influence behavior and development (Dunst & Trivette, 1988a, 1988b). On the other hand, we have developed an intervention model that includes guidelines and

principles that structure efforts to promote positive changes in child, parent, and family functioning (Dunst, Trivette, & Deal, 1988; Trivette, Deal, & Dunst, 1986). The underpinnings of the help-giving components of this model are described next.

EMPOWERMENT AND EFFECTIVE HELPING

In a project involving an extensive review and synthesis of the help-giving literature, we uncovered the types of helping behaviors that were likely to backfire and produce negative consequences, as well as discovered the types of help-giving behaviors that were likely to be enabling and have positive consequences (Dunst, 1986c; Dunst & Trivette, 1987a, 1988c). This project was carried out with the explicit intent of unraveling the complexities of helping relationships as a way of identifying the particular helping behaviors and styles that were likely to have either empowering or usurping influences. The major conclusion we drew from our review of the literature was that helping acts are likely to be effective and empowering, in part, as a function of the manner in which aid and assistance is offered and provided by help-givers.

There appear to be three clusters of variables that both contribute to effective helping and promote a sense of family empowerment: (1) Prehelping attitudes and beliefs, (2) help-giving behaviors, and (3) posthelping responses and consequences. Prehelping attitudes and beliefs refer to the help-giver's posture and stance toward help-seekers and helping relationships. Help-giving behavior refers to the interactional styles employed by help-givers during helping acts. Posthelping responses and consequences refer to ensuing influences of the help-giver's behavior on the help-seeker.

Figure 14-1 shows the temporal relationship among the three sets of variables, and the influences these variables potentially have on help-seeker behavior. According to this model, prehelping attitudes and beliefs influence help-giver behavior, and help-giver attitudes, beliefs, and behaviors influence posthelping responses and consequences. (The feedback loops from posthelping responses and consequences to the other two process phases reflects the fact that help-giving experiences are likely to influence the subsequent attitudes, beliefs and behaviors of help-givers toward help-seekers.) Collectively, prehelping, helping, and post-helping characteristics define the help-giver's contributions to helping relationships. Together, these three clusters of variables are seen as determinants of a help-seeker's sense of control and efficacy resulting from help-seeker/help-giver exchanges which, in turn, are seen as exerting positive influences on the physical and psychological health outcomes of the person receiving help (e.g., well-being).

Table 14-1 shows the particular help-giver attitudes, beliefs, behaviors, and responses that are most consistent with the positive, competency-producing influences defined above. Both direct and corroborative theoretical and empirical evidence show that individual help-giving characteristics within and across clusters tend to occur simultaneously and exclude the use of characteristics incongruent with competency producing attitudes, beliefs, and behaviors (e.g., Brickman et al., 1982, 1983; DePaulo et al., 1983; Fisher et al., 1983a; Fisher, Nadler, & Whitcher-Alagna, 1983b; Hobbs et al., 1984; Nadler et al., 1983; Rappaport, 1981, 1987). We now briefly examine these characteristics to illustrate those aspects of effective helping that increase the likelihood that helping acts will have empowering influences. The reader is referred to Dunst (1986a) and Dunst and Trivette (1987a, 1988c) for detailed descriptions of the negative consequences of different types and forms of helping.

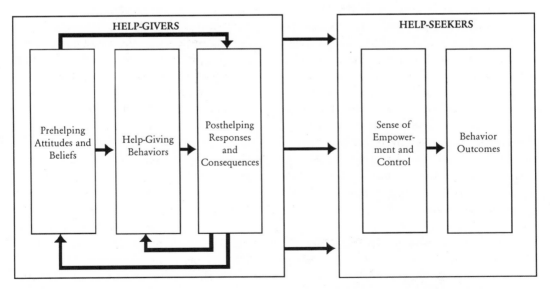

Fig. 14-1. A Model for Depicting the Influences of Prehelping, Helping, and Posthelping Behavior on Help-Seeker Outcomes.

Table 14-1. Help-Giving Attitudes, Beliefs, and Behaviors Associated with Empowering and Competency Producing Influences

Prehelping Attitudes and Beliefs	Help-Giving Behaviors	Posthelping Responses and Consequences
Positive attributions toward help-seeker and helping relationships.	Employs active and reflective listening skills.	Accepts and supports help-seeker decisions.
Emphasis on help-seeker responsibility for meeting needs and solving problems.	Helps clients clarify concerns and needs.	Minimizes the help-seeker's sense of indebtedness.
High expectations regarding the capacity of help-seekers to become competent.	Pro-offers help in response to help-seeker needs.	Permits reciprocity as part of help-giver/help-seeker exchanges.
Emphasis upon building on help-seeker strengths.	Offers help that is normative.	Minimizes the psychological response costs of accepting help.
Proactive stance toward helping relationships.	Offers help that is congruent and matches the help-seeker's appraisal of needs.	Enhances a sense of self-efficacy regarding active involvement in meeting needs.
Promotion emphasis as the focus of help-giving.	Promotes acquisition of competencies to meet needs, solve problems, and achieve aspirations. Employs partnerships and parent-professional collaboration as the mechanism for meeting needs. Allows locus of decision-making to rest with the help-seeker.	Maintains confidentiality at all times; shares information only with help-seeker permission.

PREHELPING ATTITUDES AND BELIEFS

The attitudes and beliefs that help-givers hold toward help-seekers and helping relationships set the occasion for whether or not helping acts are likely to have empowering or usurping consequences. The predispositional posture most consistent with an empowerment stance toward help-seekers and helping relationships is characterized by the attitudes and beliefs in Table 14-1. Collectively, help is most likely to be effective and empowering if a help-giver assumes all or most of the following attitudes and beliefs.

1. *Help-giving will be more effective if help-givers assume a positive stance toward help-seekers and helping relationships.* Help-givers approach helping relationships with a sincere sense of caring, warmth, honesty,

and empathy are more likely to engage in help-giver/help-seeker exchanges that have health promoting and competency producing influences (Fisher, 1983). "When positive donor motives are attributed (e.g., the donor is perceived to act out of kindness or generosity), aid is more supportive and results in more favorable reactions" (Fisher et al., 1983b, p. 73).

2. *Help-giving will be more effective if help-givers employ helping models that de-emphasize the help-seeker's responsibility for their problems or needs and emphasize the help-seeker's responsibility for acquisition of competencies to solve problems or meet needs.* Brickman et al. (1982) labeled this a compensatory model to emphasize the fact that needed information, resources, and skills are not due to inherent deficiencies, but result from

external forces and events that cause problems or concerns. Aid and assistance provided from this perspective are "designed to empower (help-seekers) to deal more effectively with their environment. An interventionist who approaches a (help-seeker) in the spirit of the compensatory model says to the (help-seeker), in effect, 'I am your servant. How can I help you?' rather than 'Do what I say'" (Brickman et al., 1982, p. 372).

3. *Help-giving will be more effective if help-givers assume that help-seekers have the capacity to understand, learn, and manage events in their lives.* Anything less will result in help-givers treating help-seekers as less than capable, and will likely deprive them of experiences that permit help-seekers to become better able to mobilize resources to meet their needs and control important aspects of their lives (Rappaport, 1981, 1987).

4. *Help-giving will be more effective if the help-giver believes that building upon help-seeker's strengths rather than correcting deficits is the most efficacious way to enhance acquisition of needed competencies* (Hobbs et al., 1984). As noted by Stoneman (1985), "Every family has strengths, and if the emphasis is (placed upon) supporting strengths rather than rectifying weaknesses, chances for making a difference in the lives of children and families are vastly increased" (p. 462).

5. *Help-giving will be more effective if help-givers approach helping relationships with a proactive rather than reactive stance toward provision of aid and assistance* (Borman, 1982; Cowen, 1985). Proactive approaches are anticipatory and focus on acquisition of knowledge and enhancement of skills that are necessary to strengthen adaptive functioning. In contrast, reactive approaches focus on decreasing the consequences of

noxious events by buffering help-seekers from these occurrences.

6. *Help-giving will be more effective if help-givers employ promotion as opposed to either prevention or treatment models* (Conyne, 1987; Hoke, 1968). In contrast to prevention efforts which deter or hinder the occurrence of negative outcomes, or treatment approaches that remediate or ameliorate disorders or their consequences, promotion efforts emphasize the acquisition of competencies that enhance an individual or group's ability to successfully negotiate its developmental course (Dunst & Trivette, 1987a; Dunst, Trivette, & Thompson, 1990). Not only do people respond more favorably to helping efforts that enhance skill acquisition, a promotion approach to helping relationships is more likely to strengthen functioning in a way that produces developmental growth (Dunst & Trivette, 1988a).

Collectively, these six different but highly related attitudes and beliefs constitute the elements of what we have come to call an enabling model of helping (Dunst & Trivette, 1987a). The term enablement reflects the underlying rationale of the model, namely that help-givers create opportunities for competencies to be acquired by help-seekers by assuming a stance that is positive, proactive, and competency producing. The particular help-giving behaviors that are likely to accomplish this are described next.

HELP-GIVING BEHAVIOR

In addition to the preconceived notions that help-givers bring to helping relationships, the ways in which attitudes and beliefs are translated into help-giving behaviors can either promote or impede acquisition of a sense of help-seeker understanding and control over managing life events. Table 14-1 shows the cluster of interactional behaviors that are most consistent with the competency producing influences central to our definition of effective helping, and include the following characteristics.

1. *Help-giving is most effective if help-givers employ active and reflective listening skills as a basis for understanding help-seeker concerns and needs.* As an active listener, one demonstrates interest and concern about what is important to a family and how different members feel or perceive family circumstances. As a reflective listener, one rephrases what a family says in order to help clarify exactly what is being said. Functioning as a close, trusted source of support and a proactive, empathetic listener are roles that are extremely important if help-giver/help-seeker exchanges are to be effective.

2. *Help-giving is most effective if it assists the help-seeker to identify, clarify, and prioritize aspirations as well as needs* (McKillip, 1987; Zautra & Sandler, 1983). Focusing only on problem identification and resolution becomes reactive, whereas explicit efforts to identify developmental needs and personal aspirations forms the basis for competency producing interventions.

3. *Help-giving is most effective if the help-giver offers rather than waits for help to be requested* (Fisher et al., 1983b). Help-seeking may be implicit or explicit, and the help-giver's sensitivity to verbal and nonverbal messages displayed by the help-seeker is a key to being able to read a person's behavior and respond appropriately. Help-givers are viewed as more positive by help-seekers when they offer help *in response* to help-seeker identified needs (Gross, Wallston, & Piliavin, 1979).

4. *Help-giving is most effective if the help-giver offers aid and assistance that is normative in terms of the family's own culture* (Fisher et al., 1983a). Nonnormative help is often times demeaning and conveys a sense that a help-seeker is inferior or incompetent (Hobbs et al., 1984). Help is maximally effective if it does not infer deviance or undue variation with respect to how other members of the family's culture or social network would deal with the same problem or need (Gross & McMullen, 1983).

5. *Help-giving is most effective if the help-giver offers aid and assistance that is congruent with the help-seeker's appraisal of his or her problem or need* (Fisher, 1983). Perceptions of problems and indications of needs constitute forces that steer and propel behavior in certain directions (Garbarino, 1982). Positive reactions to help-giving are more likely to occur when aid and assistance match a help-seeker's appraisal of problems or needs.

6. *Help-giving is most effective if the help-giver promotes the help-seeker's acquisition of effective behavior that decreases the need for help, thus making the person more capable and competent* (Skinner, 1978). This type of help "enables the recipient to become more self-sustaining and less in need of future help" (Brickman et al., 1983, p. 19). Promotion of behaviors that result in the acquisition of competencies that permit greater independence, perhaps more than any other aspect of helping relationships, is the cornerstone of effective help-giving (Dunst, 1987).

7. *Help-giving is most effective if the help-giver conveys a sense of cooperation and joint responsibility (partnership) for meeting needs and solving problems* (Hobbs et al., 1984). Help exchanges that promote participatory decision-making and shared responsibility

among the help-seeker and help-giver set the occasion for the help-seeker to feel valued, important, and an "equal" (National Center for Clinical Infant Programs, 1985). Partnerships represent the most productive condition for enabling and empowering people with the knowledge, skills, and resources to feel competent and in control of their lives.

8. *Help-giving is most effective if the help-giver engages in help-giving acts in which locus of decision making clearly rests with the help-seeker, including decisions about the need or goal, the options for carrying-out interventions, and whether or not to accept or reject help that is offered* (Fisher et al., 1983b). To be maximally effective, the ability to refuse help must be explicitly recognized by the help-giver, the decision sanctioned, and the opportunity for future exchanges left open as an option for the help-seeker to use. Aid that results in no or few lost freedoms is most likely to have positive help-giving effects.

The help-giving style embodied by these eight behavior characteristics seems necessary if helping acts are to be both effective and empowering. This helping style places major emphasis upon truly understanding the needs and concerns of help-seekers, being responsive to what is important to help-seekers, and promoting acquisition of competencies that permit help-seekers to become better able to manage life events and negotiate their developmental course. Unfortunately, best intentions can be marred depending upon what happens following help-giving.

POSTHELPING RESPONSES AND CONSEQUENCES

One aspect of helping and helping relationships often overlooked as part of assessing the extent to which helping acts have either positive or negative influences is the posthelping responses and consequences of the help-giver and help-giving, respectively. The competency producing attitudes, beliefs, and behaviors of help-givers can be undone by what happens as a result of, and following, help-giver/help-seeker exchanges. Table 14-1 shows the cluster of responses and consequences that are most consistent with our definition of effective helping. These include the following characteristics.

1. *Help-giving will more likely result in positive influences if the help-giver accepts and supports the decisions of help-seekers* (Fisher et al., 1983b). It is not sufficient simply to encourage help-givers to make decisions during help-giver help-seeker exchanges. The enabling and empowering professional must accept what the help-seeker believes is in his or her best interest and be supportive of those decisions. It must be noted, however, that acceptance does not imply approval or agreement. "Accepting a person's (decisions) means neither approving nor disapproving of what (s)he says or feels. It means simply acknowledging him (or her) as a person with the right to feel or think differently" (Brammer & Shostrom, 1968, p. 177).

2. *Help-giving will more likely result in positive influences if it minimizes the sense of indebtedness felt by the help–seeker toward the help-giver* (Gouldner, 1960). Indebtedness refers to a psychological state of obligation to repay a help-giver. The greater the sense of indebtedness, the greater the negative reactions to aid and assistance (Greenberg & Westcott, 1983). A sense of indebtedness can be minimized by the help-giver promoting the help-seeker's competence and belief (see 5 below) regarding the role he or

she played in mastering the skills necessary to solve problems, meet needs, or achieve aspirations.

3. *Help-giving will more likely result in positive influences if the help-giver sanctions and approves reciprocity but does not expect it* (Fisher et al., 1983b). "Reciprocity is (most) likely to be the preferred mode of reducing indebtedness to the extent that recipients (help-seekers) are made aware of this option and they perceive that the opportunity to reciprocate exists" (Greenberg & Westcott, 1983, p. 95). Generally, individuals feel less indebted when help is offered to them rather than requested in response to an indicated problem or need (Broll, Gross, & Piliavin, 1974). This suggests that offers of help may alleviate or prevent negative consequences.

4. *Help-giving will more likely result in positive influences if the psychological response costs of accepting help do not outweigh the benefits* (Gross & McMullen, 1983). Help-giving that reduces threats to self-esteem, moderates obligations to pay, protects behavioral freedoms (e.g., decision-making), and promotes competence and a sense of adequacy, is more likely to be seen as personally cost-effective. This in turn will likely enhance the probability that aid and assistance will produce positive effects.

5. *Help-giving will more likely have positive influences if the aid and assistance promotes and enhances the help-seeker's sense of active involvement in improving his or her own life* (Bandura, 1977). It is the "recipient's own belief in (him or herself) as a causal agent that determines whether the gains will last or disappear" (Brickman et al., 1983, p. 32). Help-seekers must, as a result of help-giver/help-seeker exchanges, perceive improvement, see themselves as no longer in need of help, and see themselves as both responsible for producing the observed changes and for maintaining these changes, if helping is to be effective (Bandura, 1977).

6. *Help-giving will more likely be effective if the help-giver maintains and preserves confidentiality at all times.* The help-giver must communicate to the help-seeker that what is shared during interactions will be held in strictest confidence. If the information is to be shared or discussed with others, this must be made explicitly clear to the help-seeker, and that no information will be shared with others without the help-seeker's permission. Any violation of this trust will likely undo any good that has occurred.

Reactions to help-giving are major determinants of whether or not aid and assistance will have positive or negative influences. Help-givers must be cognizant about how their responses to help-seeker decisions, and the ways in which help is offered, may influence help-seeker reactions. Awareness of help-giving responses and consequences provides a basis for insuring that help-givers and helping acts have empowering rather than usurping effects.

FAMILY DESCRIPTIONS OF HELP-GIVERS AND HELP-GIVING PRACTICES

As a first step in validating our enablement and empowerment model of helping, we conducted a case study with two families of children with special health care needs. The purpose of the study was to discern whether or not help-seeker/help-giver exchanges in which families perceived they had control were associated with descriptions of help-giving consistent with the three clusters of (a) attitudes and beliefs, (b) behaviors, and (c) reactions and consequences shown in Table 14-1. We used a case study methodology (Yin, 1984) in which we sought to elicit descriptions from the families that permitted inferences to be drawn regarding the manner in which help-givers approached and interacted with them. We expected (hypothesized) that descriptions of situations in which families perceived control would be associated with the characteristics described above, whereas the opposite would be true for situations in which the families felt little or no control.

PARTICIPANTS

The participants were two families of children with special health care needs. The "Andrews" family includes mother ("Jane") and father ("Rob"), both in their late 20s, and their 4-year-old daughter "Jill." Jill was diagnosed at one year of age as having an autosomal recessive disorder that has degenerative consequences. She is currently on a heart monitor and respirator due to her life threatening disability. The family has been involved with a large number of human services agencies and professionals during the past three years, and Jill is currently receiving 24-hour-a-day home health care services.

The "Matthews" family includes the mother ("Mary"), 29 years of age, and her 3 1/2-year-old daughter "Sue." The mother is divorced, and both she and Sue live with her parents. Sue was diagnosed as profoundly retarded and microcephalic with spastic quadriplegia at four months of age. She also has a severe seizure disorder that continually poses health problems. Sue is currently tube fed and must be routinely suctioned to prevent asphyxiation. The family has been involved with many agencies and professionals since Sue was born, and the child currently receives

nursing care during the mother's working hours.

METHOD AND PROCEDURE

Both families were interviewed regarding their experiences and interactions with professional help-givers. It was explained to each family that the purpose of the interview was to obtain information about the things professionals did that were helpful or not helpful and created a sense of control or lack of control, respectively, over their involvement in the care of their children. It was expected that the families, because of their extensive experiences with professional help-givers, could provide important insights about help-giving situations and conditions that were either empowering or usurping.

The study was conducted using a case study research methodology (Yin, 1984). This investigative strategy was used because we were specifically interested in whether or not case material (data) matched (was correlated with) the hypothesized patterns depicted in Table 1. As noted by Yin (1984), "case studies are the preferred (research) strategy when 'how' and 'why' questions are being posed, when the investigator has little control over events, and when the focus is on a contemporary phenomenon within some real-life context" (p. 13).

A Three-Helping Phase (prehelping vs. helping vs. posthelping) x Assessment of Family Control (high vs. low) x Outcome (positive vs. negative) matrix framework was used to structure data collection and facilitate data summary and interpretation. The interviewers specifically sought to elicit descriptions from the families that permitted classification of responses in the appropriate cells of the matrix. In coding the data, the families' sense of control over different situations were classified as either high or low (with only one or two exceptions, all situations could be so classified), and the descriptions of attitudes, behaviors, responses, and outcomes associated with high and low control entered into the appropriate cells of the matrix. This approach thus allowed an assessment of the extent to which the clusters of behaviors shown in Table 14-1 were correlated with effective helping and a sense of self-efficacy, while at the same time discerning whether or not incompatible behaviors were correlated with helping deemed ineffective by the informants.

Each family was interviewed by a different interviewer. Both interviews used the same set of instructions for explaining and conducting the interviews. The interviews were tape recorded. A third coder scored the tapes for reliability purposes. The percentages of agreement between the interviewers and coder were 90% for prehelping, 95% for helping, 92% for posthelping, and 92% for behavior outcomes for the data from the responses of both families combined.

RESULTS

The overall pattern of results provided considerable support for the contention that highly specific descriptions of help-giver attitudes, behaviors, and posthelping responses would be associated with the families' sense of control over life events, and that degree of control (high vs. low) would be correlated with different behavior outcomes. As expected, the behavior characteristics shown in Table 14-1 were correlated with the families' sense of control over the care of their children, which in turn were correlated with positive attributions regarding the outcomes the families experienced as a result of help-giver/help-seeker exchanges. Although each family described their unique situations and experiences in different ways, the case studies replicated one another with respect to the hypothesized relationships. Indeed, the aggregate of the case study material finds considerable similarity in the patterns of occurrences despite the different health care needs and conditions of the children.

Prehelping attitudes and beliefs. In situations in which the families indicated they felt a sense of control, both used descriptors consistent with the attitudes and beliefs shown in Table 14-1. Mary Matthews used terms like "friendly," "easy to get along with," and "made me feel like I belonged" to describe helpful professionals. Similarly, the Andrews described helpful professionals as "honest," "sincere," "loving," and "respectful." In contrast, the Andrews described professionals who were not helpful as "dishonest," "unethical," "making excuses," and "lacking sincere interest" in Jill's well-being and that of the family. Mary described nonhelpful professionals in much the same way. Her descriptors included "lazy," "not being honest," and "did not care about Sue."

There were a number of instances in which other types of attributions were made by the families that were indicative of different help-giver attitudes and beliefs. The Andrews, for example, described one help-giver as treating them as if they were capable of both understanding and learning to manage Jill's medical condition. This stance by the help-giver was correlated with the family's sense of control over Jill's health care. In contrast, feeling a lack of control was correlated with a description of a situation in which a help-giver placed direct blame on the family when she conveyed to the parents that "we (the agency) have some problems with you" in response to the family asking questions about the health care being provided to Jill.

Both families described situations that reflected positive, proactive, and promotion attitudes of help-givers. Mary Matthews described an employer who, with full knowledge of Sue's health care needs and the necessity for the mother to be able to leave work at a moment's notice, not only hired the mother but was extremely supportive of her in terms of attending to Sue's care. Not surprisingly, this positive, proactive stance was correlated with a high degree of family control. The Andrews, as well, described help-giver attitudes that set the occasion for enabling and empowering influences. In one situation, for example, a help-giver began her interactions with the family by clearly communicating that she was there to serve them, and that the family was in control of the health care of Jill. This positive stance became the cornerstone of a very effective helping relationship.

The above are but a few examples of the attitudes and beliefs professional help-givers often have toward help-seekers, and the ways in which different postures promoted or impeded a sense of control in these particular families. Many of these attitudes and beliefs were translated into intervention practices which either strengthened or weakened the families' ability to adequately attend to their children's needs.

Help-giving behaviors. The descriptions of the helping behaviors that were correlated with either a high or low sense of control were both clear cut and revealing. A high sense of control was associated with help-giver behavior that was responsive, competency producing, participatory, and accepting. In contrast, usurpation of control was associated with an unresponsive posture, paternalism, and the failure to recognize or accept family decisions.

Both families described empowering help-givers as listening to what they had to say and truly wanting to understand their concerns and needs. In contrast, help-givers judged nonhelpful were described as "not wanting to hear" the families and their concerns. Effective helping, for example, occurred when a help-giver assisted the Andrews in clarifying their concerns and identifying their needs by clearly communicating that she was there to assist the family ("How can I help you?"), and spent two hours listening to and talking with the family before offering advice and assistance. In contrast, the Andrews described another help-giver as being aloof and "treating us as if we didn't know anything about our child."

Two particular helping styles and behaviors were consistently mentioned by both families as having either empowering or usurping influences. One concerned partnerships and parent–professional collaboration, and other concerned locus of decision making. Descriptions of help-giver/help-seeker exchanges that occurred within the context of joint efforts were consistently correlated with high degrees of control. The Andrews described one help-giver as "willing to work with us" to get needed resources. Similarly, Mary Matthews described one situation where she and the help-giver "started getting into rhythm with one another and everything." In contrast, paternalistic tendencies were correlated with the families' lack of sense of control. One help-giver, for example, told the Andrews that "we (the professionals) are in charge here" and told the family how they wanted Jill to be cared for. Likewise, Mary Matthews described a situation in which a help-giver "wanted to take over completely" and leave her out of all health care decisions involving Sue.

Allowing decision making to rest with the families was perhaps the one aspect of help-giving most highly associated with a sense of control. Mary Matthews described one situation where a help-giver offered advice but said "it is your decision about whether to do it or not." Mary interpreted the opportunity to have final decision-making as the help-giver not only respecting her opinion, but seeing her as capable of deciding what was in the best interest of her family. In contrast, numerous descriptions were elicited from Mary that were indicative of usurpation of decision making. In one situation, a therapist proceeded with ordering a piece of adapted equipment for Sue despite the fact that Mary explicitly stated she did not want that particular apparatus.

Similar differences in locus of decision making was noted by the Andrews. A high degree of control was correlated with help-giver comments like "you have the right to do whatever you want," whereas a low sense of control was associated with comments like "I want you (Jane) to quit work and spend more time with Jill." Professional help-givers who told the Andrews what to do, and therefore restricted their choices and decision making, were clearly seen as direct threats to autonomy.

The messages that we give families as a result of the ways in which we engage in helping acts cannot be better stated than was described by Rob Andrews who works for a beverage company and used business etiquette as an analogy for explaining ineffective help-giving practices. As part of a description of a situation in which a health care professional was asked to procure a piece of equipment that would help prolong his daughter's life, the help-giver actually said "it was too much trouble" to go through the necessary steps to obtain the resource! Rob responded to this situation in the following manner:

> If a customer came into the store and asked for a case of beer, the attendant would never think of telling the customer that getting the beer was too much trouble. Yet we have been told by professionals that it was too much trouble to get something that would save my child's life. It is sad to think that a beer company is more ethical than a health service agency.

Surely this is not a message that we as help-givers want to give to families, and such an incident only reinforces our contention that use of enabling and empowering help-giving behaviors are necessary if help is to have positive and not negative consequences.

Posthelping responses and consequences. As hypothesized, certain posthelping responses and consequences were correlated with enhancement of a sense of control, whereas other posthelping occurrences attenuated self efficacy, and in some instances, undid the positive effects of helping acts. Accepting and supporting family decisions was highly correlated with enhancement of control and self-efficacy. Mary Matthews, for example, described one situation where a help-giver didn't agree with a decision she made, but nonetheless accepted and supported her decision regarding the methods of treatment for Sue. Similarly, the Andrews described empowering professionals as "accepting what we have to say and decide without question" and "don't argue with anything we say, and they do what we ask" when a decision is made. The failure to accept and support family decisions was one posthelping response that clearly interfered with both families' sense of control. Mary Matthews described the failure of help-givers to accept her decisions as "you would think I'd committed the worse sin possible," and "they act like I don't know what I'm talking about." Similarly, nonhelpful professionals were described by the Andrews as "not believing us" and "never giving us credit" for what the family had accomplished. Attenuation of self-efficacy was also apparent from descriptions that reflected help-givers refusal to listen, let alone accept, what the family had to say.

Breach of confidentiality was one posthelping response that often elicited strong emotional reactions in both families. Mary

Matthews, in describing her interactions with help-givers from one human services agency, said, "I can tell the agency people things that are supposed to be confidential, and Sue's daddy and his parents will know what I have said even before I get home." An interesting version of violation of confidentiality was described by the Andrews whenever help-givers didn't believe or accept what the family said or decided to do. The help-givers, without the parents' permission, would call other professionals who were involved with the family and discuss matters shared in confidence with the help-giver. This raises difficult ethical questions, especially in light of increased call for interagency collaboration (e.g., Elder & Magrab, 1980). Do different professionals involved with the same family have a right to share information among one another without parent consent? Both the Andrews and Matthews families thought not, and we would agree. Sharing information is only sanctioned with the families' approval.

Behavior outcomes. We expected to find positive outcomes correlated with the help-giving characteristics included in Table 14-1, whereas the opposite was expected for help-giving characteristics that were usurping rather than empowering. The pattern of results confirmed our expectations. Descriptors like "peace of mind," "sense of pride," and "feeling happy, pleased, or satisfied" were correlated with the helping behaviors of enabling professionals. In contrast, descriptions including "mad," "angry," "disillusioned," and "feeling guilty, isolated, and scared" were most often associated with help-giving behavior that was usurping and nonhelpful. Help-giving behavior that was empowering tended to produce positive reactions, whereas help-giving behavior that was usurping in nature had negative consequences.

DISCUSSION

The above descriptions are but a small portion of a rich and enlightening source of material about different types of help-giving behaviors and their consequences. The data provide considerable support for the hypothesized relationships derived from our enabling and empowering model of helping. Methodologically, the case study approach we used yielded insightful descriptions from the families about help-giver/help-seeker exchanges that were seen as either empowering or usurping. Practically, the findings clearly point to the fact that unless professional helpers employ help-giving styles that are both enabling and empowering, the chances of making positive impacts upon families will be diminished considerably. The findings from this study have now been replicated in a number of other investigations of help-giving practices (Dunst, Trivette, Gordon, & Starnes, 1993; Dunst, Trivette, Starnes, Hamby, & Gordon, 1993).

CONCLUSION

All of what we have attempted to communicate about effective helping can be summed up in the following way: Many professional help-givers have a tendency to rush in and "fix" children and families without any explicit recognition or understanding of the consequences of their help-giving behavior. Taking control and filling in missing resources may seem expedient in terms of meeting the needs of children and their families, but in the long run it deprives families of enabling experiences and opportunities that will make them more competent and better able to understand and meet their children's needs as well as their own. What we have argued for in this chapter is an expansion in the legitimized roles of professional help-givers; namely, the empowerment of families to become more actively involved and in control of identifying and meeting their needs and the needs of their children. We strongly believe, with the exception of immediately life-threatening conditions, that use of the competency-producing helping style suggested by our enablement model of helping will increase the likelihood that family-centered intervention practices can become a reality and not just a "call to arms."

IMPLICATIONS FOR PRACTICE

In addition to shifting the focus in how one thinks about help-giving and helping relationships, the model described in this chapter has direct implications for improving the help-giving behavior of front-line human services practitioners. The three sets of characteristics listed in Table 14-1 can be used as a basis for self-evaluating what one already does well in interactions with families as well as for selecting particular characteristics that one wants to improve upon in help-giving exchanges with families. Practitioners can use Table 14-1, for example, as a checklist for determining the characteristics that one feels comfortable with and capable of using, and for selecting the particular characteristics that "need improvement." To the extent possible, those characteristics already performed in an enabling and empowering manner should be used to improve performance in the areas targeted for improvement. For example, one may be quite good at helping families clarify their concerns and needs, but not require that the families assume a major role in learning how to go about meeting their needs. In this case, the practitioner would ask him- or herself how needs can be met by offering help that promotes acquisition of knowledge and skills that makes the person better able to deal effectively with demands and challenges. Our experiences tell us that this type of self-evaluation enhances the use of helping behaviors and styles that are proactive, supportive, and competency producing.

In adopting and practicing the application of new attitudes and behaviors, it is often helpful to engage in ongoing discussions with colleagues as a basis for promoting fuller understanding of the best ways to go about assuming new roles. With practice and persistence, practitioners can become much more comfortable in use of the enabling and empowering principles and behaviors. The reward is seeing families become more active and capable in ways that improve parent, child, and family functioning (Dunst & Trivette, 1988a).

CHAPTER 15

Empowering Case Management Practices:
A Family-Centered Perspective

Carl J. Dunst & Carol M. Trivette

SOME YEARS AGO, as part of their reassessment of parental involvement practices in early intervention programs, Foster, Berger, and McLean (1981) noted that "good ideas should be commended, and if they work, they should be adopted. Even exceptional ideas, however, should be reviewed periodically to see whether the premises under which they were adopted still hold and their influence is still positive" (p. 55). Some ideas should be closely examined before they are implemented. After analysis and evaluation in terms of their consequences, only those approaches with the greatest probability for producing desired outcomes should be adopted. The extent to which case management can be made a "good idea" is the focus of this chapter.

The ways in which professionals "help" families gain access to resources necessary to meet their needs will to a large degree determine whether or not they are better off or worse following the helping acts. This is true with respect to case management practices in general and those relating to help-giving practices used with families in particular. The purpose of this chapter is to describe help-giver (case management) characteristics that are proactive and enabling, and are designed to empower families with the knowledge and skills necessary to meet their needs and those of their children as part of participation in human services programs.

To what extent case management practices support and strengthen rather than weaken the family depends upon how such practices are conceptualized, operationalized, and implemented. Figure 15-1 shows one way in which case management can be conceptualized. According to this model, case management is seen as a particular set of functions for *linking* what is needed with what resources are provided. The first part of the chapter concerns itself with how these functions are operationalized and implemented. We begin with an overview of the historical and contemporary approaches to case management practices to place our proposed model in proper perspective. The second section of the chapter describes a help-giving model that is the cornerstone of the case management model we advocate as most appropriate for human services practices. This section contains a description of the beliefs, attitudes, and behaviors that are essential if case management is to be of benefit to families. The contents constitute a specific translation of the material described in Chapter 14 for effectively employing case management practices in work with families.

HISTORICAL BACKGROUND

The historical roots of case management can be traced to the casework practices of social workers in the 1920s and 1930s (Richmond, 1922, 1930; Robinson, 1930). The current interest in case management can be di-

This is an extended version of a keynote presentation made at the Professional Association on Retardation Conference "Families, Children and Professionals: Shaping the Future Together," Columbus, Ohio, June 1988.

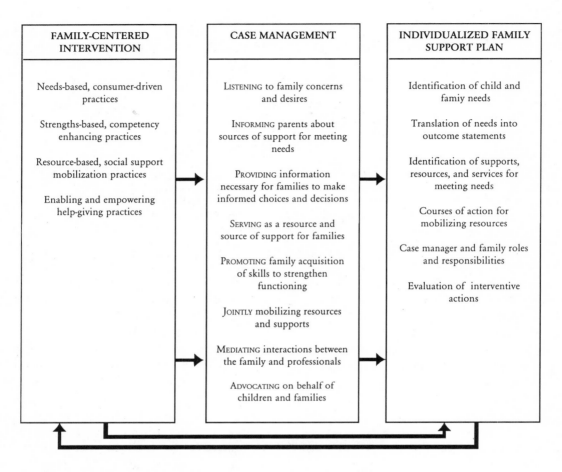

Fig. 15-1. A Framework for Conceptualizing Case Management as a Linkage Function.

rectly linked to the deinstitutionalization movements in both the mental health and mental retardation fields during the 1960s and 1970s (Bassak & Gerson, 1978; Lamb & Goertzel, 1977; Segal & Aviram, 1978) and in the human services integration initiatives of the 1970s and 1980s (Baker & Northman, 1981, Chapter 7; Dewitt, 1977; Gans & Horton, 1975). The most recent formulations of case management practices can be found in the family support and family-centered care initiatives of the 1980s (Freedman, Reiss, & Pierce, 1988).

Case management has been used widely with different persons and groups, including chronically mentally disabled adolescents and adults (Berzon & Lowenstein, 1984; Sanborn, 1983), developmentally disabled adolescents and adults (Berzon & Lowenstein, 1984; Pelletier, 1983), the elderly (Steinberg & Carter, 1983), abused children (Cohn & DeGraaf, 1982), health-impaired children (Gittler & Colton, 1987a, 1987b), retarded and disabled children (Freedman et al., 1988; Garland, Buck, & Woodruff, 1988; MacQueen, 1987), and most recently the parent and families of these individuals (Allen & Hudd, 1987; Caires & Weil, 1985). The primary focus of all of these efforts, regardless of the target population, has been the mobilization of resources and services required to meet the needs of these persons and groups (Erikson, 1981).

An historical review of case management practices during the 21st Century shows an interesting and somewhat ironic twist of events (see especially Hartman & Laird, 1983, pp. 11-22; Weil & Karls, 1985). The foundations for current case management practices were originally laid by Richmond (1901, 1917) who emphasized the need for a family-systems approach to casework practices. The importance of the family and not the individual as the *unit of intervention* was made clear in Richmond's (1917) contention that any positive influences of "individual treatment would crumble away" if not carried out within the context of the family system (p. 134). This family-systems approach was undone, however, early in the casework practices movement by Southard (1918) who attacked Richmond by saying that he wished to "demolish what seems to be an erroneous pet view of social workers. That is to say, I want to replace the family as a unit of social inquiry with the individual as the unit of social inquiry" (p. 337). Much of the *individual as unit of intervention* orientation of case management practices in the 1960s, 1970s, and early 1980s can be traced to Southard's influences.

The rediscovery of the family as the unit of intervention as part of case management practices received renewed impetus from the family support initiatives of the mid and late 1980s (Caires & Weil, 1985; Vohs 1987). The current emphasis on the family as the unit of intervention in the human services field is a welcome change, and no doubt will result in broader-based positive influences on all family members if properly conceptualized and implemented (Dunst, 1985; Dunst & Trivette, 1988a; Hobbs et al., 1984). As we shall see in

a moment, there is danger in using the individual-focused models of case management practices developed in the 1960s and 1970s in work with families, because such practices are based upon assumptions that are likely to have harmful rather than positive influences.

DEFINITIONS AND CHARACTERISTICS

Contemporary case management practices emerged in response to the rapid but fragmented and uncoordinated development of human services programs begun in the 1960s and 1970s and expanded in the 1980s (Baker & Weiss, 1984; Intagliata, 1982; Schwartz, Goldman, & Churgin, 1982). Case management in the most general sense refers to the use of a *number of functions for mobilizing resources to meet client needs* (Austin, 1983; Weil & Karls, 1985).

Although all definitions of case management share common features, it is nonetheless possible to categorize case management practices into one of three approaches (role focused, resource procurement, and client empowerment) based upon the clarity, distinction, and relative importance given to case manager *functions, procedural goals, and client outcomes*. An examination of the case management literature shows that the manner in which functions, goals, and outcomes are defined, to a large degree, depend upon the premises and assumptions upon which the different approaches are based. As a result, each approach has quite different implications, which in turn are likely to have differential effects on the individuals participating in case management programs. Table 15-1 shows both the definitional features and differential characteristics of the three approaches to case management.

Role Focused Approaches. The first category of case management practices defines case management primarily in terms of: (a) the

Table 15-1. Definitional Features and Characteristics of Three Different Approaches to Case Management

Type of Case Management	Clarity of Definitional Features			Assumptions Regarding Clients			Client Outcome
	Case Manager Functions	Procedural Goals	Client Outcomes	Capacity to Be Competent	Decision-Making Responsibilities	Participatory Expectancies	
I. Role Focused Approaches (Places major emphasis on the roles case managers play in coordinating and integrating services on behalf of clients).	High	Low	Low	Low	Low	Passive	Dependency and Learned Helplessness
II. Resources Procurement Approaches (Places major emphasis on identifying client needs and mobilizing resources to meet needs on behalf of clients).	High	High	Low	Low	High	Passive	Dependency
III. Help-seeker Empowerment Approaches (Places major emphasis on enhancing and promoting the capacity of clients to identify their needs and procure resources in a manner that is competency producing).	High	High	High	High	High	Active	Self-efficacy

functions (roles) of case managers and (b) case manager accountability, efficiency, and effectiveness as the goals of case management practices (Freedman et al., 1988; Rubin, 1987; Schwartz et al., 1982), although functions and goals often are confounded and not easily differentiated. For example, it is not unusual to find case management practices based upon this approach described and evaluated in terms of what is attempted by case managers and whether it is accomplished, but with no explicit attention to either procedural goals or help-seeker outcomes (Boone, Coulton, & Keller, 1981; Davies, Ferlie, & Challis, 1984).

Role focused approaches to case management focus almost entirely on case manager integration and coordination of services *for* the help-seeker (e.g., Johnson & Rubin, 1983; Kurtz, Bagarozzi, & Pollane, 1984; Rubin, 1987; Schwartz et al., 1982) and emphasize primarily the case manager's functions and responsibilities with respect to the "extent of the manager's *control over services and resources*" (Schwartz et al., 1982, p. 1006, emphasis added).

Case management practices based upon this approach only superficially addresses the relationship between case manager functions and procedural goals (e.g., identifying help-seeker needs) and almost entirely ignore the implications and consequences (outcomes) of the ways in which case management is implemented to meet needs.

Case managers who employ role focused approaches generally usurp client decision-making by assuming responsibility for and taking control of service provision on behalf of their clients. This appears to be a direct consequence of how case managers either implicitly or explicitly view their clients. Case management practices that place major emphasis on the "control" functions of case management practices appear to do so because they consider help-seekers as generally incompetent, unable to make informed decisions, and, therefore, only passive recipients of services (Johnson & Rubin, 1983; Rubin, 1987). As a result, case managers do for others rather than having clients learn to do for themselves.

When case managers do all the planning, development, and procurement of resources and services for clients, and clients themselves play no active role in either identifying their needs or obtaining needed resources, case managers engage in *noncontingent helping* (Dunst, 1987, 1988). Skinner (1978) called noncon-tingent help-giving unethical because it "postpones the acquisition of effective behavior and perpetuates the need for help" (p. 251). To the extent that "Help supplies a needed resource but leads the person to see the production of that resource as contingent on what the helpers do rather than on his or her own behavior" (Brickman et al., 1983, p. 34), the helping act is likely to have harmful consequences. Indeed, meeting needs is likely to have long-term positive effects only when clients actively participate in accessing re-

quired resources; "take pride in their accomplishments; (and) ascribe successes to their own abilities and efforts" (Bandura, 1978, p. 349). Noncontingent help-giving may seem expedient in terms of meeting the needs of clients, but in the long run it deprives them of experiences that are important for future learning, acquisition of independent and problem-solving behavior, and enhancement of self-esteem.

Resource Procurement Approaches. The second category of case management practices defines case management in terms of the relationship between case manager functions and procedural goals, but explicitly fails to acknowledge or address either the positive or negative outcomes of the ways in which resource mobilization occurs. That is, the relationship between client needs and case manager functions are explicitly recognized (i.e., the goal of case management practices is to mobilize resources to meet needs), but the methods and strategies used to do so are neither well articulated nor are the consequences of case manager actions clearly addressed. It is therefore not surprising to find this approach to case management practices typically characterized by both coordination and integration of services and case manager provision or mobilization of services and supports intended to meet the needs of the clients (e.g., Austin, 1983; Baker & Weiss, 1984; Compher, 1984; Freedman et al., 1988; Intagliata, 1982; Lamb, 1980). And although this approach generally recognizes the client's role in deciding his or her needs, it assumes, like role focused approaches, that help-seekers are generally unable and incapable of assuming primary responsibility for procuring required resources (Lamb, 1980; Stein & Test, 1980). Clients therefore become primarily passive recipients of services in the same way that they do in role focused approaches.

While resource procurement approaches to case management explicitly recognizes and acknowledges client needs and accessing resources to meet needs as the goal of case management practices, they nonetheless fail to address the relationship between the manner in which needs are met and how this influences client behavior. Thus, although a case manager may be highly responsive to the needs of clients, a client may be no better off or even worse after a needed resource is supplied because the client was not actively involved in accessing the resources. If help does not require a client to acquire effective behavior, and thus renders the person more helpless and dependent, the immediate needs of the person may be met, but the ability to teach and promote self-sufficient and independent behavior is diminished (Dunst, 1987, 1988; Dunst & Trivette, 1987a, 1988c). Proponents of resource procurement approaches to case management who fill in missing resources for help-seekers, despite being well intentioned, can fool themselves into believing they have successfully "helped" their clients when in fact they have lost the opportunity to enhance acquisition of client competencies that promote self-sufficiency with respect to needs identification and resource procurement.

*Help-Seeker Empowerment Approaches.*The third category of case management practices not only defines and clearly specifies the relationship between case manager functions, procedural goals, and client outcomes, but explicitly emphasizes enhancement of the client's capabilities as a way of improving their capacity to negotiate service systems to obtain resources to meet their needs (Levine & Fleming, 1984; Rapp & Chamberlain, 1985; Vohs, 1987; Weil & Karls, 1985). Case management practices in this category emphasize: (a) integration and coordination of services, (b) identification of needs and provision of sup-

ports in response to client needs and (c) do so in ways that are empowering to clients and therefore enhance their abilities to become as capable and self-sustaining as possible (Weil & Karls, 1985). This perspective of case management is reflected in the following set of principles proposed by Levine and Fleming (1984):

1. The needs of individual clients are unique and wide ranging and vary over time; therefore, the system must be flexible.
2. Clients can function in the community when provided with varying degrees of support and should be *encouraged to function as independently as possible.*
3. Clients should be *encouraged to assume an active, rather than passive role* in the case management process.
4. Case management is not a time-limited service, but rather is ongoing and provides clients with what they need, when they need it, and when they want it for as long as necessary (p. 8, emphases added).

Proponents of client empowerment approaches to case management assume clients have existing strengths as well as the capacity to become more competent, give clients decision making power in terms of defining their needs and deciding upon the particular resources and sources of support that they wish to obtain, and expect help-seekers to be actively involved in procuring needed resources (Levine & Fleming, 1984; Rapp & Chamberlain, 1985; Rappaport, 1981; Vohs, 1987). Consequently, case managers function primarily in an enabling capacity that creates opportunities to enhance and promote client capabilities (Dunst & Trivette, 1987a).

SUMMARY AND CONCLUSION

The above distinctions between the three different approaches to case management illustrate how they are conceptually, logically, and procedurally distinct. The brief descriptions of each approach show that the manner in which functions, goals, and outcomes are operationalized depends, in part, upon the assumptions regarding client capabilities, decision making responsibilities, and expectancies regarding needs identification and resource procurement. To what extent case management practices employed by professionals in human services programs strengthen rather than weaken a family's capacity to mobilize resources to meet needs in ways that have positive consequences depends upon the particular assumptions that underlie implementation.

The ways that misapplied assumptions can potentially influence client functioning have been noted by a number of writers. Bailey (1989), in his discussion of the assumptions of case management within the context of early intervention programs, noted that adopting the belief that clients are incapable of managing their own affairs "would undermine both the intent and the effects of P.L. 99-457." Lehr (1987), in a recent article on support services to families of children with disabilities noted that

professionals have assumed the role of telling parents not only what they need but what they can have...Family support services have tended to be determined by the agency of professionals rather than by the family itself. If family support is to be just that, it must be determined and directed by the family, with the assistance of the professionals, not the other way around. (p. 4)

Similarly, Halpern and Parker-Crawford (1982) found that parental "sense of loss and control over their lives...was heightened by the dependence on professionals to meet their needs" (p. 59) as part of their efforts to obtain resources and services on behalf of their children and families. Dunst, Trivette, Davis, and Weeldreyer (1988) found considerable variations in parents' positive and negative responses to help-giving behavior based upon the attitudes, beliefs, and behaviors of professional help-givers. Such accounts demonstrate that well-intentioned professionals can make things worse by the way they interact with families. It is therefore necessary to be very careful about how case management practices are conceptualized and implemented. One way of doing so that will likely have positive influences is described next.

FAMILY-CENTERED CASE MANAGEMENT PRACTICES

The model for structuring case management practices described in this section has evolved from efforts designed to identify the best ways to support and strengthen family functioning (Dunst & Trivette, 1987a, 1988a, 1988c; Dunst, Trivette, & Deal, 1988), and is based upon corroborative evidence regarding the characteristics of effective and ineffective help-giving by professionals as well as others (Dunst, 1985; Dunst & Trivette, 1987a, 1988c; Dunst, Trivette, Deal, 1988; Trivette, Deal, & Dunst, 1986). The model is based upon a definition of effective help-giving (Dunst, 1987) that describes: (a) the types of help-giver (case manager) characteristics that are likely to create opportunities for families to become competent, (b) case manager functions (roles) that promote acquisition of competencies necessary for families to become actively involved in (c) identifying their needs and mobilizing resources (procedural goals), and (d) family empowerment as the major outcome of case management practices. Figure 15-2 shows the relationship among the components of the model.

EFFECTIVE HELP-GIVING AND
EMPOWERMENT

The model shown in Figure 15-2 considers family empowerment as the outcome *par excellence* of effective helping. Effective helping is defined as:

> The act of enabling individuals or groups (e.g., family) to become better able to solve problems, meet needs, or achieve aspirations by promoting acquisition of competencies that support and strengthen functioning in a way that permits a greater sense of individual or group involvement and control over its developmental course. (Dunst, 1987, p. 1)

All of the major functions of the case management proposed model are embedded in this definition (see especially Dunst, 1987, 1988), and are intended to specify the conditions that are most likely to have empowering consequences. Empowerment is operationally defined as creating opportunities for a family to deploy competencies to obtain resources to meet needs in ways that increase self-attributions about the role family members played in accessing resources and meeting needs. This definition is based upon Rappaport's (1981) contention that

> Empowerment implies that many competencies are already present or at least possible.... Empowerment implies that what you see as poor functioning is a result of social structure and lack of resources which make it impossible for the existing competencies to operate. It implies that in those cases where new competencies need to be learned, they are best learned in a context of living life rather than in artificial programs where everyone, including the person learning, knows that it is really the expert who is in charge. (p. 16)

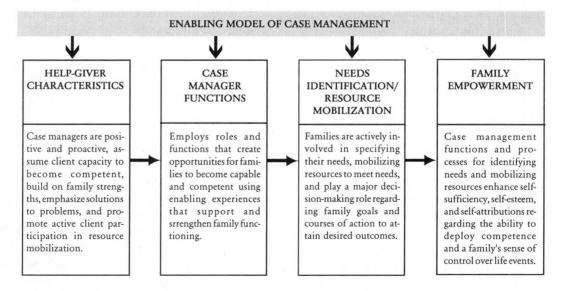

Fig.15-2. The Major Features of the Enabling Model of Case Management, Depicted as an Effective Helping Process.

This set of conditions in turn suggests the types of help-giver characteristics that are likely to be enabling and result in family empowerment.

EMPOWERING CASE MANAGER PRACTICES

The cornerstone of the proposed approach to help-giving (case management) is *enabling experiences*; that is, opportunities created by case managers for promoting and enhancing the use and acquisition of competencies that permit families to identify their needs and mobilize resources in ways that have empowering consequences. (The reader is referred to Bandura, 1977, 1982; Brickman et al., 1982, 1983; Dunst & Trivette, 1987a, 1988c; Hobbs et al., 1984; Chapter 13; for detailed discussions of the theoretical and empirical bases of the model.)

Help-givers are more likely to employ enabling experiences that have empowering consequences if they assume certain beliefs and behaviors in their actions with families. Help-giving will be most effective (as defined above) if help-givers: (a) assume a positive and pro-active stance toward families; (b) emphasize the families' responsibility for solving problems and meeting needs; (c) assume that all families have the capacity to understand, learn, and manage events in their lives; (d) build upon family strengths rather than correct deficits; (e) proactively work with families in an anticipatory fashion rather than wait for things to go wrong before intervening; and (f) promote acquisition of competencies that permit families to become better able to negotiate their developmental course. Additionally, enabling and empowering professionals: (a) place major emphasis upon helping families identify and prioritize their needs from their own and not a professional's point of view; (b) encourage active family participa-tion as part of mobilizing resources to meet needs; (c) use partnerships and parent-professional collaboration as the foundation for creating opportunities for families to become more capable and competent; (d) provide families with the necessary information to make informed decisions about their needs and courses of action to meet needs; and (e) accept and support decisions made by families. Collectively, these characteristics are the underpinnings of an enablement model of help-giving (see Chapters 13 & 14). To the extent that case management practices embody all or most of these characteristics, not only will help-giving efforts have competency-producing influences, but families will more likely come away from help-giving exchanges with a greater sense of being able to manage life events effectively (Bandura, 1977, 1982).

CASE MANAGER FUNCTIONS, FAMILY NEEDS, AND RESOURCE MOBILIZATION

The help-giver characteristics that form the basis for the enablement model of case management suggest expanded professional roles and functions, and also a shift in the ways in which roles are performed (Dunst, Trivette, & Deal, 1988; Trivette et al., 1986). Although traditional case manager functions (mobilizer, advocate, broker, etc.) can be subsumed under the enablement model, the ways in which they are enacted differ considerably. For example, case managers would not integrate or coordinate services on behalf of families, but rather would create opportunities for service providers to become more responsive to the needs of families. Similarly, case managers would not decide what families needed, but would enable families to clarify their concerns and identify their own needs. Still further, case managers would not mobilize resources on behalf of families, but rather would promote acquisition of effective behavior necessary for families to be actively involved in accessing needed resources. These differences are neither semantic nor trivial. Doing for others, despite being well intentioned, would likely create passivity and dependence, whereas promoting and enhancing the competence of families would likely have positive consequences.

IMPLICATIONS FOR PRACTICE

The material presented in the chapter has both definitional and procedural implications for case management practices, particularly as part of developing and implementing IFSPs as described in Chapters 5 and 6. Definitionally, the family-centered case management model suggests that a case manager ought to function in a number of capacities intended to empower families with the knowledge and skills necessary to mobilize resources to meet needs rather than be responsible for implementing the IFSP to the extent that the latter usurps rather than empowers families.

Procedurally, the material suggests several pitfalls that should be avoided as well as practices that should be embraced. One trap that should be avoided has to do with how success is measured with respect to the IFSP. If the provision that case managers are responsible for implementation of IFSP is interpreted literally, a role focused approach to case management will likely be adopted, success defined in terms of case manager functions, and the likelihood of families becom-

ing the passive recipients rather than the active participants in the service system increased considerably.

A second trap that should be avoided has to do with how needs are identified and resources are mobilized. If professionals rather than families determine what children and their parents need and what services they can have, conflicted encounters between the professionals and families will almost certainly ensue, and the likelihood of parents making any commitment to prescribed regimens decreased considerably (Dunst, Leet, & Trivette, 1988).

One overriding consideration should guide how one conceptualizes and implements case management practices. Enabling experiences ought to be used for assisting families to identify their needs and mobilize resources, and family empowerment ought to be the explicit outcome for case management practices. According to Hobbs et al. (1984), policies and practices that operate according to enabling and empowering principles are by far the preferred strategies for strengthening family functioning. Accordingly, "Parents become able to develop and to become effective decision makers when they are treated as capable adults and are helped by service organizations and professionals to become even more capable" (Hobbs et al., 1984, p. 51). Therefore, case management may be considered effective only to the extent that families become more capable, competent, and empowered as a result of the help-giving practices of case managers.

CHAPTER 16

Parent–Professional Collaboration and Partnerships

Carl J. Dunst, Carol M. Trivette & Charlie Johanson

THE ADAGE that "two heads are better than one" fundamentally explains the benefits of cooperative arrangements. Cooperative endeavors are underscored by the joint efforts of a number of people that are mutually beneficial to all involved parties. The benefits which accrue from such endeavors are assumed to be greater than if efforts are carried out by one party or person alone.

It has long been believed that coordination and cooperation between parents and professionals are mutually beneficial and advantageous not only to both parties but to the children who are reared and educated by parents and professionals, respectively (see Kagan, 1987; Lombana, 1983). For example, home–school communication has been advanced as a fundamental ingredient for educational efforts to have maximum positive impact on child achievement (Smith, 1968). Similarly, Mittler, Mittler, and McConachie (1987) noted that collaboration between parents and professionals contributes to improved educational programs and social services for families and their children. According to Bronfenbrenner (1979), such parent-professional linkages form the basis for interconnecting home and school settings in ways that promote exchange of ideas, information, and skills, which in turn build positive attitudes toward "educating" children by both parents and professionals.

The terms *collaboration* and *partnership* are now used most frequently to describe parent-professional relationships that aim to promote cooperation between parents and professionals (e.g., Buswell & Martz, 1988; Dunst & Paget, 1991; Jones, 1989; Lipsky, 1989; Lombana, 1983; National Center for Clinical Infant Programs, 1985; Powell, 1990; Schulz, 1987; Shelton, Jeppson, & Johnson, 1987; Weissbourd, 1987b). Both terms have implicit meaning and presumed characteristics that make these types of relationships different than other cooperative endeavors. The purpose of this chapter is to examine the major characteristics of parent-professional partnerships and draw implications from the material for both policy and practice. The contents illustrate that effective collaboration and partnerships share key features with effective helping as described in Chapter 14.

DEFINITION OF PARTNERSHIPS

Dunst and Paget (1991) recently reviewed and integrated the literature on parent-professional relationships and found no *operational* definition of either collaboration or partnership. An operational definition of a construct like a partnership is a necessary (though not sufficient) condition for being able to recognize a partnership when one observes its manifestation. Additionally, knowledge of the characteristics of partnerships is necessary for

This chapter is based upon presentations made at the symposium "Working Collaboratively With Parents of Handicapped Children" held at the annual meeting of the American Psychological Association, Atlanta, Georgia, August 1988 and the Sixth Annual International Conference on Children with Special Needs, Division for Early Childhood, Council for Exceptional Children, Albuquerque, NM, October 1990.

informing practitioners about the behaviors that need to be adopted if one chooses to use partnerships as a *collaborative helping style.*

Borrowing from the business literature (Clifford & Warner, 1987; Phillips & Rasberry, 1981; Uniform Partnership Act, 1941), Dunst and Paget (1991) defined a parent-professional partnership as:

> An association between a family and one or more professionals who function collaboratively using agreed upon roles in pursuit of a joint interest or common goal. (p. 29)

This definition provides a starting point from which to begin disentangling the characteristics that uniquely make a relationship between people a *partnership*.

Also borrowing from the business literature, Dunst and Paget (1991) proposed that partnership relationships are characterized by at least the following features: (a) mutual contributions and agreed upon roles, (b) desire to work together in pursuit of agreed upon goals, (c) shared responsibility in taking actions to achieve such goals, (d) loyalty, trust and honesty in all "dealings" involving the partnership, (e) full disclosure of pertinent information between partners and (f) parental locus of decision-making in exercising their rightful role to decide what is in the best interest of their family and its members, particularly a developing child. Although not as exacting as the "rules" of business partnerships, this list of characteristics nonetheless provides guideposts for both knowing when relationships are partnerships as opposed to other types of collaborative arrangements, and structuring how one can behave in a way that shows a *presumption toward* adoption of partnership characteristics as a helping style.

Since Dunst and Paget (1991) reviewed

and integrated information from the partnership literature, a number of recent articles provide additional insights about the major characteristics of parent-professional partnerships (e.g., Collins & Collins, 1990; Jones, 1989; Lipsky, 1989; Powell, 1990; Thornton, 1990; Vosler-Hunter, 1988). Vosler-Hunter (1988), for example, proposed that parent-professional collaboration is characterized by the following elements: (a) mutual respect for skills and knowledge, (b) honesty and clear communication, (c) understanding and empathy, (d) mutually agreed upon goals, (e) shared planning and decision making, (f) open and two-way sharing of information, (g) accessibility and responsiveness, (h) joint evaluation of progress, and (i) absence of labeling and blame. These elements are used by Vosler-Hunter and his colleagues as part of parent and professional collaborative training efforts aimed at improving cooperative relationships between the respective partners. The emphasis and benefits of this training were stated in the following way:

> If, as parents and professionals, we strive for open and honest communication, mutual respect for our skills and knowledge, and shared planning and decision making, (any) conflicts will not necessarily go away, but a working relationship will be established that can only serve to *improve services for our children.* (Vosler-Hunter, 1988, pp. 2-3, emphasis added)

Both the Dunst and Paget (1991) and Vosler-Hunter (1988) descriptions of parent-professional partnerships, as well as complementary perspectives offered by others (e.g., Buswell & Martz, 1988; Lipsky, 1989; Lombana, 1983; Miller, Lynch, & Campbell, 1990; Schulz, 1987; Walker, 1989), provide a preliminary framework for (a) defining the meaning of partnerships and (b) operationally establishing the characteristics which make partnerships unique forms of cooperative relationships. The extent to which the proposed characteristics of partnerships could be empirically established was the major focus of the work reported in this chapter. However, whether or not partnerships can be recommended as a "best practice" depends upon the relative efficacy of partnerships as a *helping style* compared to other, more traditional ways of influencing behavior change in parents or children, or both. The relationship between partnerships and both effective helping and empowerment is briefly discussed next in order to place the material presented in the following and subsequent sections in proper perspective.

PARTNERSHIPS, EFFECTIVE HELPING, AND EMPOWERMENT

A number of investigators have noted the relationship between partnerships and both effective helping (Dunst, 1987; Maple, 1977) and empowerment (Collins & Collins, 1990; Whaley & Swadener, 1990). Others have also noted the relative advantage of partnerships over more traditional client-professional relationships as a way of influencing the behavior of help-seekers (Dunst & Paget, 1991; Rappaport, 1981, 1987; Weissbourd, 1987b). Maple (1977), for example, argued that participatory and equal involvement of help-seekers in the helping process promotes the capabilities of help-seekers in ways that allow them to "take control" over important parts of their lives so as to achieve desired outcomes. Participatory involvement, as used by Maple, is very much like partnerships as defined above.

Collins and Collins (1990), as well as others (e.g., Whaley & Swadener, 1990; Rappaport, 1981), specifically noted the relationship between partnerships and empowerment. Empowerment is an interactive process that builds upon and enhances people's acquisition of knowledge and competencies as part of partnership arrangements (see Chapter 2). Partnerships are at least one mechanism for promoting the types of give-and-take between partners that make the "whole greater than the sum of the parts" with respect to competency enhancing influences. According to Dunst and Paget (1991), partnerships: (a) create opportunities for persons to work together in pursuit of a goal or interest and (b) build upon and promote each partner's capabilities and capacities. Thus, professionals who attempt to work together with parents as partners are more likely to employ helping behaviors that have competency enhancing effects. Partnerships, by definition, *enable people by creating opportunities to become competent in areas of life that partners deem important.* Partnerships would therefore be expected to strengthen the functioning of partners as a result of collaborative experiences. Thus, to the extent that partnerships create opportunities (i.e., are enabling) for partners to collaboratively pursue agreed upon goals in ways that achieve desired intentions, the efforts should have empowering consequences.

There is now a corroborative body of evidence which indicates that a helping style that embodies the major characteristics of partnerships, particularly one that emphasizes active involvement of help-seekers that is competency enhancing, has greater positive impact compared to other types of helping acts in which help-seekers passively respond to help-giver advice (see Brickman, Kidder, Coates, Rabinowitz, Cohn, & Karuza, 1983; Brickman, Rabinowitz, Karuza, Coates, Cohn,

& Kidder, 1982; Coates, Renzaglia, & Embree, 1983; Dunst & Trivette, 1988c; Dunst, Trivette, & Deal, 1988; Karuza, Zevon, Rabinowitz, & Brickman, 1982; O'Leary, 1985). Abstracting from available conceptual and empirical evidence, the case can be made that partnerships are an effective helping style that creates opportunities which are competency enhancing and in turn have empowering consequences.

AN EMPOWERMENT PHILOSOPHY

The idea of empowerment has come of age in the human services field (Rappaport, Swift, & Hess, 1984). Much of the current interest in empowerment can be traced to Rappaport's (1981) seminal paper on the topic. He proposed empowerment as an alternative to the paternalism that has for so long dominated the ways in which help is provided to help-seekers. According to Rappaport (1984), empowerment is viewed both as a process and an outcome, and can be understood as either an internalized psychological state or as an observable set of behavior. "Empowerment is easy to define in its absence; powerlessness, real or imagined; learned helplessness; alienation; loss of a sense of control over one's own life. It is more difficult to define positively only because it takes on a different form in different people and contexts" (p. 3). Inasmuch as business and parent–professional partnerships are formed for different purposes, one would expect that empowerment would take on different forms within the context of these collaborative arrangements.

The ways in which Rappaport (1981, 1984, 1987) has conceptualized empowerment suggest the need to consider the broader-based systems and social contexts that affect human behavior, and the bidirectional and transactional influences that people have on each others' behavior (Bronfenbrenner, 1979). Any

complete definition of empowerment should recognize these conditions and take them into consideration when operationalizing the concept in practice.

A number of definitions of empowerment can be found in the literature (e.g., Brickman et al., 1982; Dunst, 1985; Hobbs et al., 1984; Solomon, 1985), although few reflect these social systems considerations. Three characteristics of these definitions have guided the ways in which most investigators have typically defined and attempted to operationalize the empowerment construct. These characteristics include the help-seeker's (a) access and control over needed resources, (b) decision-making and problem-solving abilities, and (c) acquisition of instrumental behavior needed to interact effectively with others in order to procure needed resources. Although this approach to defining empowerment has stimulated interest in the concept, it has nonetheless constrained our understanding of what it means to be empowered and *how we can go about enabling and empowering people.* Indeed, we would go so far as to say that the problem-solving/decision-making approach to conceptualizing empowerment, which focuses almost entirely on the help-seeker's behavior without consideration of the help-giver's role in helping relationships, has restricted our understanding of empowerment because it fails to explicitly consider a number of broader-based issues as part of help-seeker (client) and help-giver (professional) exchanges. More specifically, it fails to consider how people become empowered through social transactions (e.g., partnerships) designed to achieve mutually agreed upon goals or interests.

A more complete understanding of empowerment requires that we take a broader-based perspective of the conditions that influence the behavior of people during help-seeker and help-giver exchanges. A social systems perspective offers this type of framework, and is perhaps best reflected in Rappaport's (1981) contention that

> Empowerment implies that many competencies are already present or at least possible.... Empowerment implies that what you see as poor functioning is a result of social structure and lack of resources which make it impossible for the existing competencies to operate. It implies that in those cases where new competencies need to be learned, they are best learned in a context of living life rather than in artificial programs where everyone, including the person learning, knows that it is really the expert who is in charge. (p. 16)

This set of assertions includes three characteristics that we believe reflect the way in which we need to think about partnerships and empowerment.

1. *Proactive stance toward help-seekers.* This characteristic of an empowerment philosophy assumes that people are already competent and have the capacity to become competent. Partnerships are built upon this assumption by the voluntary pooling of resources in pursuit of an agreed upon goal or interest. The belief that families have existing capabilities and strengths as well as the capacity to become more competent must be held by professionals before help-givers are likely to enter into partnership arrangements with families. As noted by Clifford and Warner (1987), "the most important attribute of any shared business is the competence of the co-owners and the trust they have in one another" (p. 10). Recognition of the mutual strengths (compe-

tence) and loyalty (trust) of partners in a partnership is essential if the venture is to get started in the right direction and eventually succeed.

2. *Enabling experiences are the cornerstone for promoting competence.* This characteristic explicitly states that the failure to display competence is not due to deficits within the help-seeker but rather the failure of social systems to create opportunities for competencies to be displayed. It concerns the potential and unrealized capabilities that all people have if afforded the necessary opportunities to learn and grow. A partnership is precisely the type of collaborative experience that creates opportunities for persons to work in concert in pursuit of a goal or interest, and which promotes each partner's capabilities and capacities. The planning, decision making, joining of interests, actions, etc. that are the fundamental ingredients of partnerships are the types of enabling experiences that support and strengthen individual and group functioning.

3. *Empowerment is the sense of control and meaningful contributions resulting from enabling experiences.* This characteristic of empowerment states that the person who is the learner, client, etc. must be able to deploy competencies to obtain resources to meet needs, and attribute behavior change, at least in part, to his or her own actions, if one is to acquire a sense of both control over important aspects of one's life and meaningful contributions to family and community (Hobbs et al., 1984). The active participation expected and required by partners is highly likely to enhance a sense of control and self-efficacy (Bandura, 1977), as well as promote a sense of meaningful contributions to the operation of the partnership to the extent that the "business"

succeeds in achieving its aims and goals. Parent-professional partnerships provide the context for help-seeker and help-giver alike to learn and grow from one another in ways that are mutually beneficial.

Taken together, these three characteristics provide a basis for viewing partnerships and empowerment from a broader-based social systems perspective. They also suggest the importance of the help-giver's behavior in empowering families and the role partnerships can play as enabling experiences in achieving this outcome. Additionally, this philosophical stance toward helping relationships suggests a new and expanded definition of effective helping which explicitly considers the conditions necessary for help-giver/help-seeker exchanges to have positive results. Based upon the major features of the above perspective of empowerment, Dunst (1987) defined effective helping as the

> act of enabling individuals or groups (e.g., family) to become better able to solve problems, meet needs, or achieve aspirations by promoting acquisition of competencies that support and strengthen functioning in a way that permits a greater sense of individual or group control over its developmental course. (p. 1)

This definition has been used to propose an enabling model of helping (see Chapter 13) that specifies the particular types of help-giving behaviors that are likely to have empowering consequences. The majority of the help-giver characteristics subsumed under the model are precisely the behaviors that define partnerships, and are expected by partners that are in "business" together. The model makes concrete what professionals can do to create collaborative interactions with families that promote the pooling and sharing of resources in ways that have strengthening and growth producing influences central to an empowering philosophy (Dunst, Trivette, and Deal, 1988; Hobbs et al., 1984; Rappaport, 1981, 1987). The model, in a nutshell, attempts to specify the professional roles and help-giving behaviors which reverses

> The pervasive belief that experts should solve all of (the help-seeker's) problems in living...which (only) extends the sense of alienation and loss of ability to control (one's) life....This is the path that the social as well as the physical health experts have been on, and we need to reverse this trend. (Rappaport, 1981, p. 17)

CHARACTERISTICS OF PARTNERSHIPS

The purpose of this section is to describe the findings from a parent-professional survey designed to obtain information about the specific characteristics that make parent-professional relationships partnerships. The investigation was undertaken in order to obtain information necessary to either validate or invalidate the contentions reported above regarding: (a) the key characteristics of partnerships and (b) the overlap between partnerships and effective help-giving practices. The data and results were expected to shed light and advance our knowledge about the specific meaning and impact of parent-professional partnerships.

SUBJECTS

The survey was conducted with 69 parents and 102 professionals in two states (Alaska &

North Carolina). The sample of parents included families of children with disabilities or children at-risk for poor developmental outcomes. The average age of the children was 4.1 years (SD = 3.97). The sample of professionals were all human services practitioners or administrators. The respondents were simply asked to list the behavioral and attitudinal characteristics that they believed were important for parent-professional relationships to be partnerships. The results were expected to yield information about the major elements and characteristics of parent-professional partnerships.

METHOD

Data summary and synthesis were carried out in several major steps. First, the various characteristics listed by the individual respondents were tabulated. A total of 94 separate descriptors were elicited. Second, the 94 descriptors were reduced to 26 characteristics by combining terms that had the same or very similar meaning. For example, the terms *reliable, consistent,* and *dependable* were combined and collectively labeled "dependability." Third, the 26 characteristics were rank ordered for the combined sample, and the parents and professionals separately, by computing the percentage of respondents that listed each element as a defining characteristic of partnerships. Fourth, chi-square analyses were used to discern whether the percentage of parents and professionals who listed each characteristic differed significantly between the two groups of respondents. Differences were tested at the .01 level in order to avoid spurious results given the fact that 26 separate analyses were performed on the data. Fifth, a Spearman rank-order correlation was computed between the rankings of the parents and professionals to establish whether there was agreement between the subsamples regarding the *relative importance* of the different characteristics. Sixth,

the 26 characteristics were organized in four, nonmutually exclusive categories using an *a priori* categorization scheme that divided the 26 descriptions into two groups of behavioral *states* (beliefs & attitudes) and *traits* (communication style & behavioral actions). Operational definitions of beliefs, attitudes, communication style, and behavioral actions were used to assign individual characteristics to the categories (see Table 16-1). Seventh, summary scores were computed for each respondent in each state and trait category and correlations computed between these scores and several other descriptive indices (e.g., parent vs. professional) to establish the relationship among the measures.

RESULTS

Table 16-2 shows the percentages of the combined sample and parents and professionals who indicated that certain characteristics were essential elements of partnerships. Trust, mutual respect, open communication, honesty, active listening, openness and flexibility, caring and understanding, shared responsibility, full disclosure of information, and information sharing, as well as a number of other characteristics, were listed as the major elements of parent-professional partnerships. A comparison of the characteristics listed in Table 16-2 with those described above (Dunst & Paget, 1991; Vosler-Hunter, 1988) finds considerable overlap between what has been proposed as the key elements of partnerships with the actual characteristics listed by both parents and professionals. There is, however, some difference in the relative importance attributed to different characteristics. For example, whereas Vosler-Hunter (1988) listed "mutually agreed upon goals" as an essential element of parent-professional collaboration, our findings indicated that this was a less important feature compared to other characteristics (e.g., shared responsibility & full disclosure of information).

Table 16-1. Operational Definitions of Four Behavioral States and Traits

Category	Definition
Beliefs	Cognitive attributions about how one should act or ought to behave toward other people. Beliefs are cognitive constructions or representations about objects (e.g., people) that reflect "truth" in how such objects ought to be treated.
Attitudes	Particular (emotional) feelings about a person, situation, or relationship. Attitudes refer to affective dispositions toward objects (e.g., people) that reflect favorable-unfavorable, desirable-undersirable, etc. evaluations of such objects.
Communicative Style	Methods and approaches for information sharing between partners. Communicative style refers to how information is given and received during interactions between people.
Behavioral Actions	Behaviors that reflect translation of attitudes and beliefs into actions. Behavioral actions include any implicit or explicit ways of acting toward others that are reciprocal in manifestation.

The series of 26 chi-square analyses yielded significant differences between groups for six of the characteristics. A larger percentage of professionals (compared to the parents) indicated that mutual respect, flexibility, mutual support, empathy, reciprocity, and humor were major elements of partnerships. These results reflect the fact that certain partnership characteristics were deemed more important by the professional respondents.

A Spearman correlation computed between the rank ordering of characteristics for the parents and professional yielded a $r_s = .69$, p<.00l. This finding showed that the ordering of the characteristics considered the most important, second most important, and so on by the parents and professionals was quite similar. This may be taken as evidence that both parents and professionals were in general agreement regarding the *relative* importance of the characteristics that define partnerships.

Further examination of the 26 characteristics listed most frequently as elements of parent-professional partnerships indicated that they could be organized into a number of sets of behavioral *states* and *traits*. Closer inspec-

tion suggested that the state characteristics could be subgrouped into beliefs and attitudes, and that the trait characteristics could be subgrouped into two behavioral sets (communication style & behavioral actions). An independent classification of the 26 individual characteristics into one or more state or trait categories were undertaken by four raters. Using *a priori* operational definitions of the four state and trait categories (see Table 16-1 above), the four raters agreed at least 85% of the time (Range = 85 to 89%) as to which behaviors belonged to which state and trait categories.

Table 16-3 shows the results of the categorization. The majority (N = 20) of the 26 characteristics (77%) were assigned to a single category. Six of the characteristics were assigned to two categories: mutual respect, humor, active listening, openness, and understanding. The latter indicated that the raters believed that these particular elements represented either states or traits depending upon how, and in which manner, the characteristic might be manifested in interactions between parents and professionals.

Table 16-2. Percentage of Parents and Professionals Listing Each Characteristic of Partnership

Characteristics	Both Groups Combined (N=171)	Parents (N=69)	Professionals (N=102)
Trust	51	45	55
Mutual Respect	51	39	59
Open Communication	46	44	47
Honesty	40	30	47
Active Listening	39	38	39
Openness	30	28	31
Flexibility	27	12	37
Caring	26	23	28
Understanding	25	20	28
Shared Responsibility	24	23	25
Full Disclosure Information	23	29	20
Information Sharing	23	28	21
Acceptance	22	17	26
Mutual Support	21	10	28
Commitment to the Relationship	20	15	24
Reciprocity Between Partners	19	09	27
Mutually Agreed Upon Goals	18	10	23
Empathy	17	06	25
Dependability of Partner	15	15	15
Equality	15	12	17
Nonjudgmental	15	09	19
Positive Stance Toward Partner	14	10	16
Presumed Parental Capabilities	14	07	18
Humor	12	04	17
Confidence	09	09	10
Mutual Problem Solving	07	07	07

Table 16-4 shows the correlations between the four partnership measures as well as the correlations between the partnership and descriptive measures. All six correlations between the partnership measures were statistically significant, indicating that the different dimensions of partnerships are interrelated rather than mutually exclusive. This was as

Table 16-3. A Categorization Scheme for Organizing the Major Characteristics of Parent-Professional Partnerships

Category	Definition	Characteristics
Beliefs	Cognitive attributions about how one should act or ought to behave toward other people	Trust, mutual respect, honesty, acceptance, mutually supportive, nonjudgmental, presumed capabilities
Attitudes	Particular (emotional) feelings about a person, situation or relationship	Caring, understanding, commitment, empathy, positive stance, humor, confidence
Communicative Style	Methods and approaches for information sharing between partners	Open communication, active listening, openness, understanding, full disclosure of information, information sharing
Behavioral Actions	Behaviors that reflect translation of attitudes and beliefs into actions	Mutual respect, openness, flexibility, understanding, shared responsibility, mutual support, reciprocity, mutual agreement about goals, dependability, equality, humor, problem-solving

expected, and may be taken as an indication of the related nature of the four behavioral dimensions of partnerships. The magnitudes of the correlations, however, were not so high as to reflect substantial overlap among the four measures. This was somewhat unexpected, and may be taken as evidence for the *multidimensional* nature of partnerships, at least as represented by our state and trait framework.

The set of three significant correlations between the partnership measures and professional status measure simply reflects, as already noted, the fact that professionals (compared to parents) listed more characteristics as being essential elements of partnerships. Child chronological age was also significantly correlated with 3 of the 4 partnership measures. This presumably reflects the fact that the parents of older children had more experience with parent-professional relationships, and were better able to articulate those characteristics that made such relationships partnerships. None of the other descriptive measures were significantly related to any of the partnership measures.

DISCUSSION

Collectively, the data from the parent and professional survey add to our knowledge about the meaning and characteristics of partnership relationships. On the one hand, the results provide empirical evidence to support the contentions made by others regarding the essential elements of partnerships (e.g., Dunst & Paget, 1991; Jones, 1989; Lipsky, 1989; Vosler-Hunter, 1988; Walker, 1989). On the other hand, the findings extend our knowledge about the defining characteristics of partnerships, particularly those that are deemed most important by both parents and professionals. What the survey results do not establish is the particular characteristics that *uniquely* define partnerships and differentiate partnerships from other types of relationships. For example, a comparison of the characteristics listed in Table 16-2 shows that many overlap with those considered essential elements of both effective interpersonal communication (e.g., DeVito, 1989) and various counselling techniques (e.g., Brammer & Shostrom, 1968;

Ehly, Conrley, & Rosenthal, 1985). DeVito (1989) noted, for instance, that active listening, acceptance, trust, understanding, and respect, as well as other behaviors, are characteristics of individuals who communicate effectively with others. Similarly, Brammer and Shostrom (1968) noted that honesty, acceptance, flexibility, understanding, and caring are defining characteristics of effective counselors. What appears to *operationally differentiate* these various characteristics in partner-

ships compared to other relationships is the operative "mutual." Mutual trust, respect, honesty, flexibility, etc. denote the *complementary, joint,* and *reciprocal* efforts of partners as compared to the single-sided manifestation of these characteristics by, say, counselors. In partnerships, both parties simultaneously display the defining characteristics, whereas in other types of relationships this may not necessarily be the case.

Other characteristics that uniquely define

Measures	Partnership Measures				Descriptive Measures				
	BL	AT	CS	BA	LO	PS	PD	CA	DX
Partnership Measures:									
Beliefs (BL)	--	.32***	.19**	.47***	.13	.46***	.11	.41***	.09
Attitudes (AT)		--	.38***	.58***	-.05	.25**	-.05	.10	.01
Communicative Style (CS)			--	.45***	-.08	.03	-.01	.22*	.03
Behavioral Actions (BA)				--	-.01	.37***	.01	.21*	.01
Descriptive Measures:									
Location (LO)[a]					--	.49***	.08	.52***	-.05
Professional Status (PS)[b]						--	.00	-e	-e
Professional Discipline (PD)[c]							--	-e	-e
Child Age (CA)								--	-.01
Child Diagnosis (DX)[d]									--

Table 16-4. Correlations Between the Partnership and Descriptive Measures

Note. Sample size is (N=171) except for Professional Discipline (N=95), and Child Age and Child Diagnosis (N=68).
[a]Alaska=1 vs. North Carolina=2.
[b]Parent=1 vs. Professional=2.
[c]Educational Background=1 vs. Other=2 (Therapy, Psychology, Social Work).
[d]At-Risk=1 vs. Handicapped=2.
[e]Not computed.
*p<.05, **p<.01, ***p<.001.

partnerships are also listed in Table 16-2. These include open (two-way) communication, shared responsibility, full disclosure of information, mutual support, reciprocity between partners, (mutual) dependability of partners, and equality in the relationship. These particular behaviors, more than any others, reflect differing forms of *reciprocity* between partners. These behavioral characteristics, together with the *mutual* display of the other states and traits described above, may at least tentatively be considered a "working" list of empirically and operationally defined elements that make partnerships different from other types of "helping" relationships.

IMPLICATIONS FOR PRACTICE

The concepts and material presented in this chapter can be found as part of numerous efforts to improve communication and working relationships between professionals and families. Lombana (1983) has devoted an entire volume on home–school partnerships, with particular attention to the methods and strategies that can be used to promote a variety of collaborative and participatory parent–professional relationships. She describes a model for conceptualizing different types of home-school partnerships, and then proceeds to detail how opportunities can be created to enhance increased collaborative arrangements.

Both Schulz (1987) and Farkas (1981) address the ways in which professionals can employ enabling experiences to promote participatory involvement on the part of parents of children with special needs. Schulz's treatment of parent–professional relationships is taken from the perspective of the special education teacher, whereas Farkas focuses on what school principals can do to increase the involvement of families in their children's education. The Farkas' (1981) "guide" includes a number of useful checklists for deter-

mining whether school policy, and the ensuing behavior of school personnel, are consistent with the belief that families can and should function as informed decision makers in their children's education.

One of the most useful documents available for encouraging professionals to include families as partners in the care of their children is *Family-Centered Care for Children with Special Health Care Needs* published by the Association for the Care of Children's Health (Shelton, Jeppson, & Johnson, 1987). Shelton and her colleagues describe eight elements of family-centered care, one of which is parent-professional collaboration. The essentials of collaboration are detailed at the help-giver/ help-seeker, service-delivery, and policy levels. The document includes a number of useful checklists for assessing whether family-centered care practices are consistent with a participatory philosophy regarding meaningful family involvement in the care of their children. Among the checklists included in the Shelton et al. book, one specifically addresses the characteristics of collaborative parent-professional relationships, and another considers the ingredients of collaboration and family-centered care from the perspective of state-level policy and program developers. The Shelton et al. (1987) book is essential reading for anyone committed to parent–professional partnerships as a mechanism for empowering families and strengthening family functioning.

Buswell and Martz (1988), as part of their discussion of the meaning of partnership within the context of P.L. 99-457 (Education of the Handicapped Act of 1986) and multidisciplinary team functioning, describe four key ingredients necessary for parent- professional partnerships to become a reality.

First, everyone on the team must accept

the fact that the roles of the various team members are different, and as such, there undoubtedly will be differences of opinion as to what the child's needs are.... In this kind of situation, however, the "conflicts" can be the catalyst for all the "experts"...to create the kind of individualized program that the child really needs.

Second, people must be honest and share what they are thinking directly to each other. Parents must tell professionals their thoughts...(and) professionals have an obligation to be honest with parents as well.

Third...everyone needs to listen carefully (to everyone else).... It is important to ask questions to try to clarify issues rather than replay it over and over and not participate actively.

Fourth...partners need to be effective collaborators in their ability to negotiate and compromise.... Give and take in compromise is an essential part of the (empowering) process. (Buswell & Martz, 1988, p. 6)

On the one hand, these key ingredients mirror the attributes and characteristics of both partnerships and effective helping as described above, and on the other hand provide a concrete set of recommendations regarding how to put the principles into practice.

We have employed (Deal, Dunst & Trivette, 1989; Dunst, 1985, 1987; Dunst & Trivette, 1988a; Dunst, Trivette, & Deal, 1988) the material presented in this chapter as a foundation for: (a) delineating an empowerment philosophy regarding human services intervention and family support practices, (b) implementing a family-centered approach to working with families, (c) specifying the nec-

essary roles and functions for an enabling approach to case management, and (d) operationalizing partnerships within the context of developing and implementing individualized family support plans. These various applications were formulated at the Family, Infant and Preschool Program (FIPP; Dunst, 1985; Dunst & Trivette, 1988a), and specifically aim to support and strengthen family functioning vis-a-vis enabling and empowering experiences.

The methods and approaches used at FIPP for supporting families are guided by a philosophy called *Proactive Empowerment through Partnerships* (PEP). The PEP philosophy places major emphasis on (a) recognizing and strengthening child and family capabilities using a proactive rather than a deficit approach, (b) enabling and empowering parents with the necessary knowledge, skills, and resources needed to perform family and parenting functions in a competent manner, by (c) using partnerships between parents and professionals as the means to strengthen, enable, and empower families. FIPP is proactive in the sense that the program takes a positive stance toward children and their families. A proactive approach focuses on the child's and family's strengths and not their weaknesses, and promotes positive functioning by supporting families. FIPP enables and empowers families by creating opportunities that permit greater understanding and control over resources and decision making. This is done within the context of partnerships between families and professionals that avoids the paternalism characteristic of most client-professional relationships. As noted by Rappaport (1981), enabling and empowering families "requires a breakdown of the typical role relationship between professionals and community people" (p. 19). Partnerships are used at FIPP for accomplishing this breakdown and building collaborative arrangements between staff and families.

The family-centered assessment and intervention model used at FIPP to operationalize this philosophy includes a set of four principles that guide practices designed to enable and empower families (Dunst, Trivette, & Deal, 1988). The model is implemented in the following way: (1) Identify family needs to determine the things the family considers important enough to devote time and energy, (2) build upon family strengths and capabilities as a basis for promoting the family's ability to mobilize resources to meet needs, (3) strengthen the family's personal social network and mobilize potential but untapped sources of aid and assistance necessary to meet needs, and (4) function in a number of different roles to enable and empower the family to become more competent in mobilizing resources to attain stated outcomes and achieve desired goals.

The particular roles, or case management practices, that are used at FIPP to enable and empower families include expanded functions and responsibilities that help-givers employ as part of helping relationships and parent–professional partnerships (Dunst & Trivette, 1988c; Dunst, Trivette, & Deal, 1988). As noted by Hobbs et al. (1984), policies and practices that operate according to enabling and empowering principles are by far the preferred strategies for strengthening family functioning. Accordingly, "Parents become able to develop and to become effective decision makers when they are treated as capable adults and are helped by service organizations and professionals to become even more capable" (Hobbs et al., 1984, p. 51). Therefore, case management may be considered effective only to the extent that families become more capable, competent, and empowered as a result of the help-giving acts of case managers (see Chapter 15).

Lastly, all of the above is put into practice and operationalized at the direct service level by the ways in which Individualized Family Support Plans (IFSPs) are developed and implemented (see Chapters 5 & 6). The IFSP used at FIPP is a "working" document which guides needs specification and resource mobilization. It includes: (1) A list of family identified needs, aspirations, projects, etc. in order of priority, (2) a series of statements regarding the sources of support and resources that will be mobilized to meet needs, (3) a series of statements regarding the actions that will be taken by the family and early intervention practitioner to mobilize resources, and (4) procedures for evaluating the extent to which needs are met. The "steps" that are taken to mobilize resources to meet needs are listed for both the family and early intervention practitioner, and are stated in terms of what will be done by each "partner" to actualize the plan. Doing so emphasizes shared responsibility (partnership) between the family and early intervention practitioner.

Collectively, the family-centered philosophy, assessment and intervention model, case management practices, and IFSP procedures and practices used at FIPP represent a "system" that places major emphasis upon *partnerships* and *empowerment* as the mechanisms for supporting and strengthening family functioning. This integrated system has proven useful as a framework for operationalizing the concepts and notions described in this chapter (Deal et al., 1989; Dunst, 1987; Dunst & Trivette, 1987a; Dunst, Trivette, & Deal, 1988).

CONCLUSION

We conclude our discussion of partnerships with a brief description of the implications of the material presented in our chapter for both policy and practice. The implications for policy are both radical and far reaching (see especially Maple, 1977; Rappaport, 1981, 1984, 1987; Weissbourd, 1987b). Striving to employ partnerships between parents and professionals as a way of influencing parenting competencies and affecting positive changes in children's behavior and development necessitates a major change in the typical role relationships between professionals and parents (Rappaport, 1984). Such a shift requires abdication of paternalistic approaches to helping relationships and adoption of empowerment, participatory involvement, and competency enhancement approaches to help-giving (e.g., Hobbs et al., 1984; Maple, 1977; Rappaport, 1981). This is no small task. It will require major policy changes in how social programs view, interact, and treat families.

The implications for practice are somewhat more straightforward. Dunst and Paget (1991) reviewed and summarized much of what is known about working with practi-tioners who choose to employ partnerships as a helping style (see also Vosler-Hunter, 1988). Additionally, the findings reported in this chapter have several other implications for practice. First, the list of characteristics found to be the major elements of partnerships may be used as a "checklist" for assessing whether or not professionals assume certain attitudes and beliefs and manifest particular behaviors as part of interactions with parents. Second, the same list may be used to ask parents whether or not they believe the states and traits are behaviors particular professionals display in interactions with themselves. This information would be of particular value as a "validity check" for practitioners since it would provide a "second perspective" on the nature of their relationships between themselves and the parents with whom they work.

In summary, the material presented in this chapter hopefully extends and expands our knowledge about parent-professional partnerships. We highlighted major concerns and considerations as an attempt to more fully explicate the meaning and characteristics of partnership relationships. We hope that our perspective on partnerships contributes to the understanding of partnerships as an effective helping process.

CHAPTER 17

Help-Giving Practices and the Self-Efficacy Appraisals of Parents

Carl J. Dunst, Carol M. Trivette, Kimberly Boyd & Jeffri Brookfield

THE PURPOSE OF THIS CHAPTER is to summarize the results from three studies that examined the relationships between human service program models and help-giving practices, and between help-giving practices and parent self-efficacy appraisals. The latter involved an assessment of the extent to which parents indicated they had control in procuring supports and resources from a target help-giver and his or her program or agency. The studies specifically examined whether the contentions set forth in Chapter 2 concerning empowerment, and the hypothesized relationships between help-giving practices and control appraisals described in Chapter 14, could be supported empirically.

The investigations were guided by two separate but complementary frameworks that distinguish between different models of help-giving (Brickman et al., 1982; Michlitsch & Frankel, 1989) and the particular characteristics of help-giving practices that are expected to be related to empowering outcomes and consequences (Rappaport, 1981, 1987; Dunst, Johanson, Rounds, Trivette, Hamby, 1992; Trivette, Dunst, LaPointe, & Hamby, 1993). According to Brickman et al. (1982) and Michlitsch and Frankel (1989), human services programs differ either implicitly or explicitly based upon the help-giving models used to structure and guide intervention practices. Similarly, Rappaport (1987) and Swift (1984) have differentiated between human

services program models varying on a continuum from those that are predominately paternalistic to those that are primarily empowerment oriented.

An aggregation of both the empowerment and help-giving literatures (see Chapters 2 and 14, respectively), as well as a synthesis of both the human services intervention practices (Dunst, Trivette, & Thompson, 1990) and family-oriented intervention (Dunst, Trivette, LaPointe, & Hamby, 1993) literatures, suggest a continuum of models varying from those that are expertise-based (professionally-centered, paternalistic, medical model, etc.) to those that view clients as agents-of-professionals (direct guidance, parent training models, etc.) to those that are empowerment-based. Expertise-based models, which are often described as professionally-centered, assume that people are generally incapable of solving their own problems; and therefore need the assistance of professionals in order to adequately meet their needs and mobilize resources and supports. Clients as agents-of-professional models, described in this chapter as direct guidance models, enlist the involvement of clients in carrying out interventions professionals deem important for the well-being of those seeking help. Empowerment models involve practices which encourage and promote active client involvement in acquiring knowledge, learning new skills, exercising choices, etc. that strengthen client functioning and enhance the competencies necessary to solve problems and meet needs.

The above framework was found useful for categorizing the diverse types of programs included in the studies described next. We hypothesized that help-giving practices used by staff in empowerment-oriented programs would be rated as more competency-enhancing compared to the other two types of programs, and that the help-giving practices in the direct guidance (clients as agents-of-professional) programs would be assessed as more empowering compared to those in expertise-based programs. We also tested the hypothesis that control appraisals would be directly related to the degree to which help-giving practices were deemed consistent with an empowerment philosophy.

METHOD

SUBJECTS

The participants in all three studies were parents of preschool aged children. The families where involved in a number of different kinds of human services programs at the time data collection occurred. The "type of program" families were involved in was used as a blocking variable in each study to ascertain whether help-giving practices differed as function of program affiliation.

Study 1. The participants were 107 mothers of preschool aged children involved in three different types of programs. The first type of program (family support and early intervention programs) was guided by an empowerment philosophy (Rappaport, 1981) that placed families in pivotal decision-making roles in all aspects of the selection and provision of supports and resources. The second type of program (public health departments) was guided by a direct guidance phi-

losophy where participants were viewed as needing services deemed important by professionals who used their "authority" to ensure that prescribed interventions were carried-out by the participants (Brickman et al., 1982). A third type of program (public social services agencies) was guided primarily by a paternalistic and professional-as-expert philosophy (Swift, 1984) that gave families little say in how resources and services were rendered. Comparatively, the three types of programs showed very little overlap in terms of the help-giving models used to guide work with children and their families.

Study 1 was conducted with families from rural western North Carolina, all of which were from low SES (socioeconomic) backgrounds (Hollingshead, 1975). The mothers were, on the average, 25.22 (SD=6.23) years of age, and completed an average of 11.45 (SD=1.98) years of school. The average SES score of the sample was 25.45 (SD=7.77), whereas the families' average monthly income was 1000 (SD=456) dollars. A series of one-way between group ANOVAs using type of program as a blocking variable found no significant differences between groups on mothers' education, or family's SES and income. The mothers in the early intervention/family support program were, however, on the average, 5 years older than the mothers in the other two groups.

Study 2. The participants included 141 parents (mostly mothers) of preschool aged children involved in three different types of human services programs located in western Pennsylvania. The first were early intervention programs that showed a presumption toward being empowerment oriented although they also were characterized by certain features of a direct guidance model. The largest majority of these programs employed educational rather than therapeutically-based intervention practices for guiding work with children and their families. The second were early intervention programs that used predominately direct guidance models, although there was evidence indicating that these programs were undergirded at least to a certain degree by features of an expertise model. The largest majority of these programs employed therapeutic (speech therapy, occupational therapy, and physical therapy) rather than educationally-oriented intervention practices for working with children and their families. The third were public school, special education, and health-care programs that were predominately guided by an expertise model of helping. Comparatively, the two types of early intervention programs were similar in several respects, and both differed dramatically from the programs characterized as employing expertise-based models.

The families participating in Study 2 were specifically recruited so that they were quite diverse with respect to their background characteristics. The parents were, on the average, 33.73 (SD=7.34) years of age, and completed a mean of 14.10 (SD=2.47) years of school. The average SES score (Hollingshead, 1975) of the sample was 37.99 (SD=14.36), and the families' average monthly income was 1976 (SD=1000) dollars. A series of one-way between group ANOVAs with program type as a blocking variable indicated that there were no significant differences between groups on any of the parent and family background measures.

Study 3. The participants were 1110 parents of preschool aged children enrolled in 104 early intervention programs located throughout the state of Pennsylvania. All the programs served children with disabilities or developmental delays. The programs, in principle, were all guided by the same family-focused philosophy although the differences noted below were apparent upon close inspection of program practices. In contrast to Studies 1 and 2, "program type" in Study 3 was determined by the chronological age of the children: Birth to 24 months (early intervention programs), 24 to 36 months (transition between early intervention and preschool programs), and 36 to 60 months (preschool programs). This was done because it was determined, based upon available information about the programs, that the early intervention programs employed primarily direct guidance models, although there was some indication that the programs showed a presumption toward adopting elements of an empowerment model. The preschool programs to a large degree were characterized by the key elements of an expertise model, although there were features indicating a presumption toward inclusion of direct guidance components into program practices. The children and families in the "transition phase" were experiencing help-giving practices from both the early intervention and preschool programs, and therefore were expected to "fall between" the other two program types with respect to families' assessments of the help-giving practices of the staff.

The Study 3 participants, like those in Study 2, were quite diverse in terms of their demographic characteristics. The participants were, on the average 32.85 (SD=6.04) years of age, and had completed an average of 13.85 (SD=2.49) years of school. The mean SES score of the sample was 39.44 (SD=14.65). (Information regarding family income was not available for this sample.) A series of one-way between group ANOVAs yielded no significant differences between groups on any of the family background measures.

PROCEDURE

The participants in each study completed either a long-form or short-form version of the Professional Helpers Characteristics Scale (HCS) (Trivette & Dunst, 1990) and a self-efficacy appraisal scale. These measures have been used as part of an ongoing line of research about the meaning of empowerment, and how help-giving attitudes, beliefs, and practices either consistent or inconsistent with an empowerment philosophy, are related to a person's sense of control and mastery over different life events and experiences (Dunst, 1986a, 1987, 1991; Dunst & Trivette, 1987a, 1988c; Dunst, Trivette, Davis, & Weeldreyer, 1988; Dunst, Trivette, & Deal, 1988; Dunst, Trivette, Gordon, & Pletcher, 1989; Dunst, Trivette, Gordon, & Starnes, 1993; Dunst, Trivette, & LaPointe, 1992; Dunst, Trivette, Starnes, Hamby, & Gordon, 1993; Dunst, Trivette, & Thompson, 1990).

Help-Giving Measure. The long-form HCS includes 26 items (α = .92), whereas the short-form HCS includes 5 items (α = .86). Both measure a number of help-giving attitudes, beliefs, and behaviors that have been extensively studied by researchers interested in the characteristics and consequences of different help-giving styles (Fisher, Nadler, & DePaulo, 1983a; Nadler, Fisher, & Depaulo, 1983). The scale items were developed as indicators of help-giving beliefs and practices based upon previous research which found that the particular help-giving characteristics measured by the scale are empirically related to a variety of positive help-seeker outcomes, including perceived control (see Dunst, Trivette, Davis, & Weeldreyer, 1988; Dunst, Trivette, & Deal, 1988; Chapter 15; for reviews of the empirical bases of the scale).

A person completing the scale is asked to indicate, for each item, whether a target help-giver displayed one of five behaviors during interactions with the respondent. The five responses from which a respondent selects are different for each item, and are designed to measure a continuum of help-giving behavior. The parents completed the scale for purposes of the studies described in this chapter on a staff member who worked with the family

on a regular basis as part of their participation in the target programs. The sum of the ratings for the HCS items administered was used to compute a total help-giving scale score.

Perceived Control Measure. The participants in the studies also rated the extent to which they were able to procure needed supports and resources from the target program and help-giver. Perceived control was rated on a 10-point scale varying from very little control (1) to a great deal of control (10). This particular kind of control appraisal has been used extensively by Affleck and his colleagues (see e.g., Affleck, Tennen, and Rowe, 1991), and measures what Bandura (1977, 1986) calls efficacy expectations. The latter refers to a person's personal "conviction that one can successfully execute the behavior required to produce a (desired) outcome" (Bandura, 1977, p. 193).

METHODS OF ANALYSIS

Chi-square analyses were used to analyze the data and included tests of linear trends to test specifically whether there were (a) increases in the proportion of families who rated staff as effective help-givers as a function of program type and (b) increases in self-efficacy appraisals consistent with the predictions about the differences between paternalistic and empowering help-giving practices. This is equivalent to testing whether the slopes in a regressions analysis increase (or decrease) as a function of changes on an ordered independent variable.

The relationship between program type and help-giving practices was determined by computing the percentage of respondents who assessed the human services programs staff as effective helpers (operationally defined as a help-giving score above the median for the total sample in each study) using program type as an ordered blocking variable. The relationship between help-giving practices and control appraisals was determined by computing the percentage of respondents who indicated they had a high degree of control in obtaining resources and supports (operationally defined as a self-efficacy score of 8 or higher) using help-giving scores as an ordered blocking variable. HCS scores were divided into quartiles for purposes of establishing four "levels" of help-giving varying on a continuum from highly ineffective to highly effective.

RESULTS

STUDY 1

Figure 17-1 shows the percentage of program staff rated as effective help-givers in the three types of programs included in Study 1. Both the chi-square and linear trend analyses were highly significant. As predicted, a greater percentage of staff were assessed effective help-

givers from the empowerment-oriented programs compared to the other two types of programs, and a greater percentage of staff were assessed as effective helpers in the direct guidance (client as agent-of-professional) compared to the expertise model programs.

The percentage of parents indicating they had a high degree of control in obtaining program services and resources from the staff with which they worked is shown in Figure 17-2. The pattern of findings was as predicted, and confirmed the expectation that help-giving practices deemed most empowering (i.e. highly effective) would indeed be related to higher control appraisals.

STUDY 2

The relationship between the different types of programs included in Study 2 and the percentage of parents rating program staff as effective helpgivers is shown in Figure 17-3.

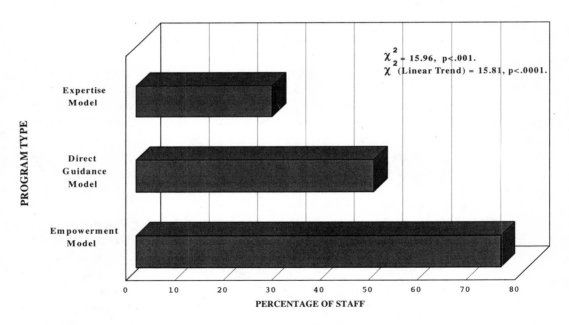

$\chi^2_2 = 15.96$, p<.001.
χ^2 (Linear Trend) = 15.81, p<.0001.

Fig. 17-1. Percentage of Staff Rated by Families as Effective Helpers (Study 1).

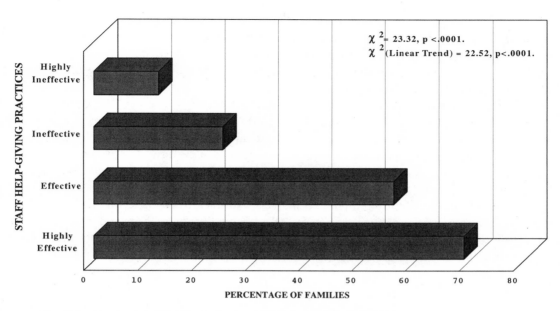

Fig. 17-2.   Percentage of Families Indicating a High Degree of Control (Study 1).

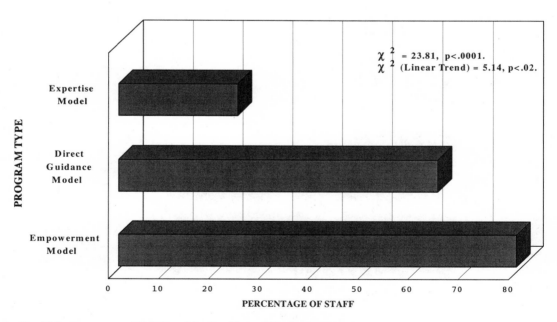

Fig. 17-3.   Percentage of Staff Rated by Families as Effective Helpers (Study 3).

The results are very similar to those found in Study 1, and again confirm the expectation that the help-giving models implicitly guiding program practices would be differentially related to the percentage of human services practitioners rated as effective helpers.

Figure 17-4 shows the relationship between help-giving practices and the percentage of parents indicating they had a high degree of control in obtaining needed resources and supports from the target help-giver and program. As was found in Study 1, there was a stair-step increase in the percentage of parents reporting high self-efficacy appraisals as one moves from highly ineffective to highly effective help-giving practices.

STUDY 3

Inasmuch as the program types in Study 3 were more similar than different compared to the contrasting kinds of programs included in Studies 1 and 2, it was not surprising that the pattern of the relationship between program type and the percentage of staff rated as effective helpers was not as strong (see Figure 17-5). Nonetheless, the predicted pattern is evident from the linear trend in the data, and indicates that even subtle differences in program philosophies and help-giving models can be detected by parental assessments of staff attitudes, beliefs, and practices.

Figure 17-6 shows the relationship between help-giving practices and the parents' self-efficacy appraisals. The results again confirm the prediction that control appraisals would be differentially related to the kinds of help-giving practices used by the human services staff in the early intervention and preschool programs.

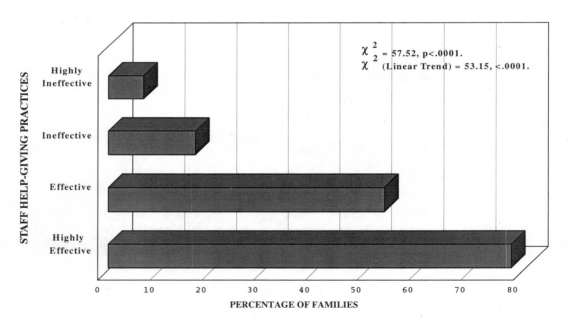

Fig. 17-4. Percentage of Families Indicating a High Degree of Control (Study 2).

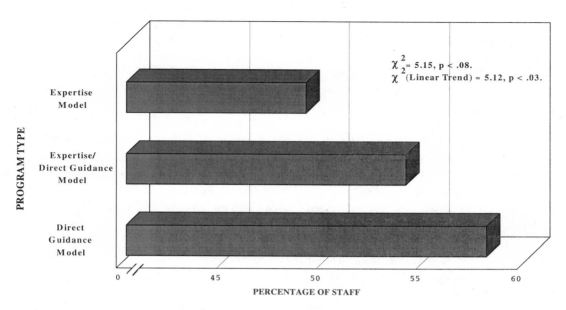

Fig. 17-5. Percentage of Staff Rated by Families as Effective Helpers (Study 3).

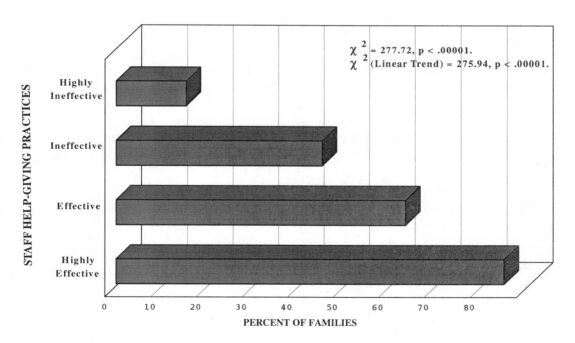

Fig. 17-6. Percentage of Families Indicating a High Degree of Control (Study 3).

DISCUSSION

The results reported in this chapter demonstrate a highly predictable and discernable relationship between the implicit and explicit help-giving models used by different types of human services programs and the extent to which parents rated staff as effective helpers. In every case, the adoption of empowerment-oriented models, or models showing a presumption toward an empowerment perspective, were associated with a greater percentage of parents rating program staff as effective helpers. In contrast, programs deemed expertise-based (i.e., professionally-centered) were found to be related to a considerably smaller percentage of parents rating staff as effective helpers. Inasmuch as the data from the three studies were gathered on help-givers from various kinds of programs in two different states, with the programs located in both rural and urban areas, the results are particularly robust.

Even more robust are the findings pertaining to the relationship between help-giving practices and parental self-efficacy appraisals. The results from all three studies, both separately and taken together, demonstrate a remarkably powerful association between the kinds of practices used by human services program staff and the degree to which parents indicated they could procure needed supports and resources from the help-givers and their programs. In each study, the greatest percentage of families who reported a high degree of control worked with staff who were rated as highly effective help-givers.

Collectively, the studies reported in this chapter yielded convincing evidence demonstrating a relationship between program types or models and help-giving practices, and between help-giving practices and self-efficacy appraisals of families participating in human services programs serving children birth to six years of age. On the one hand, the results add credence to the postulations set forth in Chapter 2 regarding the adoption of an empowerment philosophy and its consequences, and the contentions set forth in the four preceding chapters on effective help-giving practices and their differential benefits. On the other hand, the findings add to a burgeoning body of evidence indicating that adoption of particular kinds of program models and practices can be expected to have quite different influences on the people served by human services programs (Brickman et al., 1982; Michlitsch & Frankel, 1989; Rappaport, 1981, 1987; Swift & Levin, 1987; Zimmerman, 1990b). Our findings are highly consistent with research showing that participatory experiences (e.g., help-giving behaviors) considered empowering are associated with enhanced feelings of self-efficacy and personal control (Affleck et al., 1991; Karuza, Zevon, Rabinowitz, & Brickman, 1982; Lord & Farlow, 1990; O'Leary, 1985; Ozer & Bandura, 1990; Prestby, Wandersman, Florin, Rich, & Chavis, 1990; Rabinowitz, Karuza, & Zevon, 1984; Wandersman & Florin, 1990; Zimmerman, 1990b; Zimmerman & Rappaport, 1988; Zimmerman, Israel, Schulz and Checkoway, 1992), thus demonstrating the benefits that are realized from empowerment-based intervention practices.

VI

GENERAL CONCLUSION

This closing section provides final comment about the family-centered model described in the various chapters in this book. We re-emphasize the major points made throughout by couching our contentions as a series of paradigm shifts that seem necessary if family-centered policy and practices are to become a reality. The shifts concern adoption of: (a) needs-based, consumer-driven intervention practices, (b) strengths-based and competency enhancing intervention practices, (c) resource-based approaches to meeting child and family needs, and (d) help-giving practices that aim to empower people participating in human services programs. Collectively, these four shifts would reorient policy and practice in ways consistent with the assertions about the key characteristics of family-centered interventions made throughout the book.

CHAPTER 18

Final Thoughts Concerning Adoption of Family-Centered Intervention Practices

Carl J. Dunst, Carol M. Trivette & Angela G. Deal

THIS BOOK CONTAINS a wealth of descriptive information and empirical evidence about a particular family-centered assessment and intervention model that has been developed, validated, and improved upon based on extensive work with children and families. It includes both previously published articles as well as papers specifically prepared for this book. The contents collectively represent our current thinking about the characteristics of effective family-centered human services practices and the kinds of broad-based benefits that accrue from such practices.

The book as a whole constitutes a blueprint for reorienting policy and practice aimed at supporting and strengthening family functioning. The blueprint, shown in graphic form in Figure 18-1, includes the major components of the family-centered model described in the different chapters of the book. (The reader is referred to Chapter 3 for a detailed description of each component.) The components of the model, as well as the relationships among components represent an overall design for developing and implementing interventions in ways that will have empowering consequences and other positive benefits for both children and families. Although the components were described separately for heuristic reasons, it is the gestalt that makes the whole greater than the sum of the parts.

The contents of the book are intentionally responsive to the increased call for ecologically oriented, family-centered, and promotion/empowerment approaches to working with children and families participating in human services programs (Bond, 1984; Brewer, McPherson, Magrab, & Hutchins, 1989; Dunst, Johanson, Trivette, & Hamby, 1991; Dunst, Trivette, & Thompson, 1990; Garbarino & Long, 1992; Kagan, Powell, Weissbourd, & Zigler, 1987; Rappaport, 1981, 1987; Shelton, Jeppson, & Johnson, 1987; Thurman, 1993; Weissbourd, 1990; Weissbourd & Kagan, 1989; Zautra & Sandler, 1983; Zigler & Berman, 1983; Zigler & Black, 1989; Zigler & Weiss, 1985). Ecologically-oriented practices recognize the fact that a child and family are embedded within the context of broader-based social systems and units, and that the people, agencies, organizations and programs that a family comes in contact with either directly or indirectly can influence child, parent and family functioning. Family-centered intervention practices are responsive to the needs of all family members as well as the family unit; are provided in an individualized, flexible, and culturally sensitive manner; and place families in pivotal roles as decision-makers concerning all aspects of the provision of services and mobilization of supports and resources. Promotion and empowerment approaches to working with families build upon existing child and family capabilities and enhance new competencies in ways that sup-

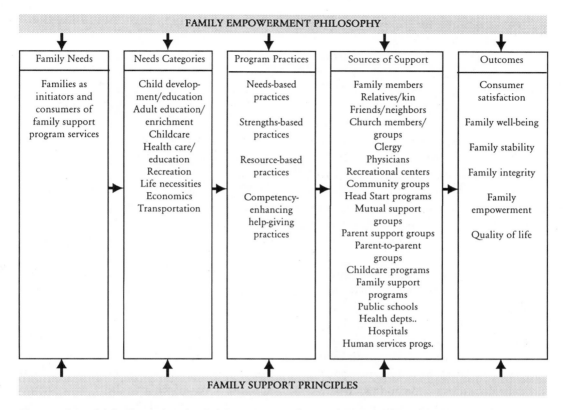

Fig.18-1. A Model for Depicting the Key Components of a Family-Centered Support Program.

port and strengthen functioning. These three aspects of human services interventions triangulate the material presented in this book. Taken together, the use of our family-centered model for structuring the development and implementation of human services programs and practices has proven useful for working with diverse kinds of families having equally diverse child and family needs.

The particular assessment and intervention model described in this book is best thought of as an evolving conceptualization of family-centered practices. While the contents of the chapters retain central and fundamental elements and features described in *Enabling and Empowering Families*, we have made significant modifications and additions

since that book was published. No doubt additional changes will be made as we acquire more knowledge and gain additional insights about effectively working with children and their families. Even as this book goes to press, several investigations have been completed and new intervention studies planned that will likely lead to further developments and refinements in our family-centered model. The kinds of evidence that have shaped our thinking, as well as the kinds of research findings that provide credence to the assertions made throughout this book, are described and elaborated upon in *Supporting and Strengthening Families (Volume 2): Research Findings and Intervention Outcomes* (Dunst, Trivette, & Hamby, in press).

The adoption of the family-centered model and practices described in this book is no simple task. Reflections on work with our own staff as well as work with others as part of a number of training projects repeatedly finds a "resistance to change." This resistance is often encountered even among staff who are committed to becoming family-centered, and often, but not always, it matters little that empirical evidence indicates a need to "do business a new way." Perhaps this set of conditions was best stated nearly 500 years ago by Machiavelli (1513) in *The Prince* when he said that:

> It must be remembered that there is nothing more difficult to plan, more doubtful of success, nor more dangerous to manage than the creation of a new system. For the initiator has the enmity of all who would profit by the preservation of the old institution and merely lukewarm defenders in those who would gain by the new ones.

This is as true today as it was when first written by this great Florentine statesman and writer.

The changes that are required to become family-centered in the ways described in this book requires not *a* paradigm shift but a number of paradigm shifts with regard to the ways one thinks about, conceptualizes, operationalizes, and implements human services practices. The four shifts that we believe are necessary in order to become family-centered are briefly described next as a way of reiterating the major points made in the various chapters in this book.

The first paradigm shift concerns a move away from intervention practices based solely on professionally-identified needs to interventions that are responsive to family concerns and desires, both for the family as a whole and for individual family members. These kinds of intervention practices assume that family members are truly listened to, are provided the necessary information and assistance to make informed, intelligent choices, and that intervention practices are responsive and tailored to individual family needs. This shift requires that professionals impart knowledge that can be used to promote decision making capabilities.

The second paradigm shift concerns a move away from intervention practices that focus primarily on correcting child and family deficits and weaknesses toward practices that build upon and strengthen child and family capabilities. Adoption of the belief that all people have existing strengths as well as the capacity to become more competent is fundamentally important if this shift is to occur. It is well worth remaining continuously cognizant of the fact that "the professional consulted when the client needs help may never have seen the client in a general state of well-being and therefore have only an indirect sense of the client's capabilities and strengths. This limited perspective reinforces... [an]...ingrained tendency for the professional to exercise paternalistic authority" (Merton, Merton, & Barber, 1983, p. 21). Both common sense and everyday experience (as well as research; see Dunst & Trivette, 1988) tell us that promoting competence and strengthening functioning is best accomplished by utilizing what one already does well as a basis for learning new skills needed to reach desired outcomes.

The third paradigm shift concerns a move away from defining solutions to child and family needs solely in terms of professional services, towards practices that utilize both informal and formal community resources and supports as ways of meeting needs. This shift requires that one recognize the fact that *all* communities have a wealth of supports, resources, and services for children and families (Katz, 1984), and that by actively seeking these out and making them viable options for meeting needs, a sense of community can be promoted and strengthened (Hobbs et al., 1984). Viewing solutions to meeting family needs primarily in terms of professional services is both limited and limiting, and can potentially deprive children and families of opportunities that promote the flow of community resources and supports in ways that support and strengthen family functioning.

The fourth paradigm shift concerns a change in the help-giving practices employed by professionals away from those that are paternalistic and dependency-forming towards practices that create opportunities for both children and families to learn skills and acquire competencies that have empowering consequences. This shift requires changes in the roles and responsibilities of help-giving practitioners predicated upon changes in the objectives and goals of interventions. These *new* roles and responsibilities are ones that help people become better able to meet their needs. The *new* goals are to promote help-seeker competencies in ways that truly result in people becoming competent.

Collectively, these four shifts bring us full circle to the contentions made about the key element of family-centered assessment and intervention practices described in Chapter 1. The ability to become family-centered requires a shift in the beliefs professionals have about families and the models which guide the translation of beliefs into practices that truly support and strengthen family functioning. This book describes at least one way to structure efforts to accomplish this goal.

REFERENCES

ADAMHA. (1981). *Alcohol, Drug Abuse, and Mental Health Administration prevention policy and programs: 1979-1982*. Rockville, MD: U.S. Department of Health and Human Services.

Affleck, G., Tennen, H., & Rowe, J. (1991). *Infants in crisis: How parents cope with newborn intensive care and its aftermath*. New York: Springer-Verlag.

Albert, V. (1988). *Welfare dependence and welfare policy*. New York: Greenwood Press.

Allen, D. A., & Hudd, S. S. (1987). Are we professionalizing parents? Weighing the benefits and pitfalls. *Mental Retardation, 25*, 133-139.

Allen, V. L. (1976). *Children as teachers: Theory and research on tutoring*. New York: Academic Press.

Allen, V. L., & Feldman, R.S. (1974). Learning through tutoring: Low-achieving children as tutors. *Journal of Experimental Education, 42*, 1-5.

Anderson, B. (1985). Parents of children with disabilities as collaborators in health care. *Coalition Quarterly, 4*, 15-18.

Anglin, J., & Glossop, R. (1987). Parent education and support: An emerging field for child care work. In C. Denholm, R. Ferguson, & A. Pence (Eds.), *Professional child and youth care: The Canadian perspective* (pp. 175-196). Vancouver: University of British Columbia Press.

Antonovsky, A. (1981). *Health, stress, and coping*. San Francisco: Jossey-Bass.

Austin, C. D. (1983). Case management in long-term care: Options and opportunities. *Health and Social Work, 8*, 16-30.

Bailey, D., Jr. (1989). Case management in early intervention. *Journal of Early Intervention, 13*(2), 120-134.

Bailey, D., & Simeonsson, R. (1985). *Family Needs Survey*. Chapel Hill, NC: Frank Porter Graham Child Development Center, University of North Carolina.

Baker, F., & Northman, J. E. (1981). *Helping: Human services for the 80s* (pp. 115-131). St. Louis: C. V. Mosby Company.

Baker, F., & Weiss, R. S. (1984). The nature of case manager support. *Hospital and Community Psychiatry, 35*, 925-928.

Bandura, A. (1977). Self-efficacy: Toward a unifying theory of behavioral change. *Psychological Review, 84*, 191-215.

Bandura, A. (1978). The self system in reciprocal determinism. *American Psychologist, 33*, 344-358.

Bandura, A. (1982). Self-efficacy mechanism in human agency. *American Psychologist, 37*, 122-147.

Bandura, A. (1986). *Social foundations of thought and action: A social cognitive theory*. Englewood Cliffs, NJ: Prentice-Hall, Inc.

Barrera, M. (1986). Distinctions between social concepts, measures, and models. *American Journal of Community Psychology, 14*, 413-445.

Bassak, E. L., & Gerson, S. (1978). Deinstitutionalization and mental health services. *Scientific American, 238*, 46-53.

Beavers, W. R., & Hampson, R. (1990). *Successful families*. New York: W.W. Norton and Co.

Beebe-Center, J. G. (1932). *The psychology of pleasantness and unpleasantness*. (Reprinted by Russell, 1965.) New York: New York Public Library.

Beiser, M. (1974). Components and correlates of mental well-being. *Journal of Health and Social Behavior, 15*, 320-327.

Belasco, J. A. (1990). *Teaching the elephant to dance: Empowering change in your organization.* New York: Crown Publishers.

Berger, P. L., & Neuhaus, R.J. (1977). *To empower people: The role of mediating structures in public policy.* Washington, DC: American Enterprise Institute for Public Policy Research.

Berzon, P., & Lowenstein, B. (1984). A flexible model of case management. In B. Pepper & H. Ryglewicz (Eds.), *Advances in treating the young adult chronic patient* (pp. 49-57). San Francisco: Jossey-Bass.

Biegel, D.E. (1984). Help seeking and receiving in urban ethnic neighborhoods: Strategies for empowerment. *Prevention in Human Services, 3,* 119-143.

Bond, L. (1982). From prevention to promotion: Optimizing infant development. In L. Bond & J. Joffe (Eds.), *Facilitating infant and early childhood development* (pp. 5-39). Hanover, NH: University Press of New England.

Boone, C. R., Coulton, C. J., & Keller, S. M. (1981). The impact of early and comprehensive social work services on length of stay. *Social Work in Health Care, 7*(3), 65-73.

Borman, L. D. (1982). Introduction. In L. D. Borman, L. E. Borck, R. E. Hess, & F. L. Pasquale (Eds.), *Helping people to help themselves: Self-help and prevention* (pp. 3-15). New York: Haworth Press.

Bott, E. (1971). *Family and social networks.* London: Tavistock Publication.

Bowman, T. W. (1983). Promoting family wellness: Implications and issues. In D. Mace (Ed.), *Prevention in family services: Approaches to family wellness* (pp. 39-48). Beverly Hills, CA: Sage.

Bradburn, N. M. (1969). *The structure of psychological well-being.* Chicago: Aldine.

Bradburn, N. M., & Caplovitz, D. (1965). *Reports on happiness: A pilot study of behavior related to mental health.* Chicago: Aldine.

Bradshaw, J. (1972). The concept of social need. *New Society, 30,* 640-643.

Brammer, L., & Shostrom, E. (1968). *Therapeutic psychology: Fundamentals of actualization counseling and psychotherapy* (2nd ed.). Englewood Cliffs, NJ: Prentice-Hall.

Brandtstadter, J. (1980). Relationships between life-span developmental theory, research, and intervention: A revision of some stereotypes. In R. R. Turner & H. W. Reese (Eds.), *Life-span developmental psychology: Intervention* (pp. 3-28). New York: Academic Press.

Brenner, B. (1975). Enjoyment as a preventive of depressive affect. *Journal of Community Psychology, 3,* 346-357.

Brewer, E., McPherson, M., Magrab, P., & Hutchins, V. (1989). Family-centered, community-based, coordinated care for children with special health care needs. *Pediatrics, 83,* 1055-1060.

Brickman, P., Kidder, L. H., Coates, D., Rabinowitz, V., Cohn, E., & Karuza, J. (1983). The dilemmas of helping: Making aid fair and effective. In J. D. Fisher, A. Nadler, & B. M. DePaulo (Eds.), *New directions in helping: Vol. 1. Recipient reactions to aid* (pp. 18-51). New York: Academic Press.

Brickman, P., Rabinowitz, V., Karuza, J., Coates, D., Cohn, E., & Kidder, L. (1982). Models of helping and coping. *American Psychologist, 37,* 368-384.

Broll, L., Gross, A. E., & Piliavin, I. (1974). Effects of offered and requested help on help-seeking and reactions to being helped. *Journal of Applied Social Psychology, 4,* 244-258.

Bronfenbrenner, U. (1975). Is early intervention effective? In B. Friedlander, G. Sterritt, & G. Kirk (Eds.), *Exceptional infant: Vol. 3. Assessment and intervention.* New York: Brunner/Mazel.

Bronfenbrenner, U. (1979). *The ecology of human development: Experiments by nature and design.* Cambridge: Harvard University Press.

Bronfenbrenner, U. (1986). Ecology of the family as a context for human development: Research perspectives. *Developmental Psychology, 22,* 723-742.

Buswell, B., & Martz, J. (1987). The meaning of partnerships: Parents' perspectives. *Mainstream.* Washington, DC: The Legal Center.

Buswell, B., & Martz, J. (1988). The meaning of partnerships: Parents' perspectives. *Early Childhood Facilitator, 4*(2), 6-7. (Newsletter of the Colorado Division for Early Childhood.)

Caires, K. B., & Weil, M. (1985). Developmentally disabled persons and their families. In M. Weil, J. M. Karls et al. (Eds.), *Case management in human service practice* (pp. 233-274). San Francisco: Jossey-Bass.

Caplan, G. (1974). *Support systems and community mental health.* New York: Behavioral Publications.

Carkhuff, R. R., & Anthony, W. A. (1979). *The skills of helping.* Amherst, MA: Human Resource Development Press.

Carter, B., & McGoldrick, M. (Eds.). (1988). *The changing family life cycle: A framework for family therapy.* New York: Gardner Press, Inc.

Center on Human Policy. (1986) *A statement in support of families and their children.* Syracuse: Division of Special Education and Rehabilitation, School of Education, Syracuse University.

Chesler, M. A. (1985). Active roles for parents in the care of chronically ill children. *Children's Health Care, 14,* 4-5.

Child Development Resources. (1988). *How Can We Help? Scale.* Lightfoot, VA: Child Development Resources.

Child Welfare League. (1989). *Standards for services to strengthen and preserve families with children.* Washington, DC: Child Welfare League of America.

Clark, P. G. (1989). The philosophical foundation of empowerment: Implications for geriatric health care programs and practice. *Journal of Aging and Health, 1(3),* 267-285.

Clifford, D., & Warner, R. (1987). *The partnership book* (3rd ed.). Berkeley, CA: Nolo Press.

Coates, D., Renzaglia, G. J., & Embree, M. C. (1983). When helping backfires: Help and helplessness. In J. D. Fisher, A. Nadler, & B. M. DePaulo (Eds.), *New directions in helping: Vol. 1. Recipient reactions to aid* (pp. 251-279). New York: Academic Press.

Cochran, M., & Brassard, J. (1979). Child development and personal social networks. *Child Development, 50,* 601-616.

Cochran, M., & Woolever, F. (1983). Beyond the deficit model: The empowerment of parents with information and informal supports. In I. Siegel & L. Laosa (Eds.), *Changing families* (pp. 225-246). New York: Plenum Publishing.

Cohen, S., Agosta, J., Cohen, J., & Warren, R. (1989). Supporting families of children with severe disabilities. *Journal of the Association for Persons with Severe Handicaps, 14,* 155-162.

Cohen, S., & Syme, S. L. (1985a). Issues in the study and application of social support. In S. Cohen & S. L. Syme (Eds.), *Social support and health* (pp. 3-22). New York: Academic Press.

Cohen, S., & Syme, S. L. (Eds.). (1985b). *Social support and health.* New York: Academic Press.

Cohn, A., & DeGraaf, B. (1982). Assessing case management in the child abuse field. *Journal of Social Service Research, 5,* 29-43.

Collins, B. & Collins, T. (1990). Parent-professional relationships in the treatment of seriously emotionally disturbed children and adolescents. *Social Work, 35,* 522-527.

Commission on Chronic Illness. (1957). *Chronic illness in the United States* (Vol. 1). Cambridge, MA: Harvard University Press.

Compher, J. V. (1984). The case conference revisited: A systems view. *Child Welfare, 63*(5), 411-418.

Conger, J. A., & Kanungo, R.N. (1988). The empowerment process: Integrating theory and practice. *Academy of Management Review, 13*(3), 471-482.

Conyne, R. K. (1987). *Primary preventive counseling: Empowering people and systems.* Muncie, IN: Accelerated Development.

Cornell Empowerment Group. (1989). Empowerment through family support. *Networking Bulletin: Empowerment and Family Support, 1*(1), 1-3.

Cornish, P. A., & Conway, J. B. (1991). *Defining empowerment: Towards the development of phenomenologically-based theory and research methods.* Unpublished study, University of Saskatchewan, Saskatoon, Canada.

Cowen, E.L. (1985). Person-centered approaches to primary prevention in mental health: Situation-focused and competence-enhancement. *American Journal of Community Psychology, 13,* 31-48.

Crnic, K.A., Greenberg, M.T., Ragozin, A., Robinson, N., & Basham, R. (1983). Effects of stress and social support on mothers of premature and full-term infants. *Child Development, 54*, 209-217.

Crockenberg, S. B. (1985). Professional support and care of infants by adolescent mothers in England and the United States. *Journal of Pediatric Psychology, 10*, 413-428.

Curran, D. (1983). *Traits of a healthy family*. Minneapolis, MN: Winston Press.

Damico, J. S., & Armstrong, M. B. (1990/91). Empowerment in the clinical context: The speech-language pathologist as advocate. *National Student Speech Language Hearing Association Journal, 18*, 34-43.

Danish, S. J., & D'Augelli, A. R. (1980). Promoting competence and enhancing development through life development intervention. In. L. A. Bond & J.C. Rosen (Eds.), *Primary prevention of psychopathology* (Vol. 4). Hanover, NH: University Press of New England.

Darling, R. (1988). Parent Needs Survey. In M. Seligman & R. Darling (Eds.), *Ordinary families, special children*. New York: Guilford Press.

Davies, B. P., Ferlie, E., & Challis, D. (1984). *A guide to efficiency-improving innovations in the social care of the frail elderly*. Canterbury, England:University of Kent, Personal Social Services Research Unit.

Deal, A. G., & Dunst, C. J. (1990). Needs-based family-centered intervention practices. *Family Systems Intervention Monograph, 2*, No. 2. Morganton, NC: Family, Infant and Preschool Program, Western Carolina Center.

Deal, A. G., Dunst, C. J., & Trivette, C. M. (1989). A flexible and functional approach to developing Individualized Family Support Plans. *Infants and Young Children, 1*(4), 32-43.

Deal, A. G., Trivette, C. M., & Dunst, C. J. (1988). Family Functioning Style Scale. In C. J. Dunst, C. M. Trivette, & A. G. Deal (Eds.), *Enabling and empowering families: Principles and guidelines for practice* (pp. 175-184). Cambridge, MA: Brookline Books.

Dean, A., & Lin, N. (1977). Stress-buffering role of social support. *Journal of Nervous and Mental Disease, 165*, 403-417.

De'Ath, E. (1988). Families and their differing needs. In E. Street & W. Dryden (Eds.), *Family therapy in Britain* (pp. 312-338). Milton Keynes: Open University Press.

De'Ath, E. (1989). The family center approach to supporting families. *Child Welfare, 68*(2), 197-207.

DePaulo, B., Nadler, A., & Fisher, J. (Eds.). (1983). *New directions in helping: Vol. 2. Help-seeking*. New York: Academic Press.

DeVito, J. (1989). *The interpersonal communication book* (5th ed.). New York: Harper and Row.

Dewitt, J. (1977). *Managing the human service "system": What have we learned from service integration?* Springfield, VA: National Technical Information Service (SHR0100401).

Diener, E. (1984). Subjective well-being. *Psychological Bulletin, 94*, 542-575.

Dokecki, P. (1983). The place of values in the world of psychology and public policy. *Peabody Journal of Education, 60* (3), 108-125.

Dokecki, P., & Heflinger, C. A. (1989). Strengthening families of young children with handicapping conditions. In J. Gallagher, P. Trohanis, & R. Clifford (Eds.), *Policy implementation and P.L. 99-457: Planning for young children with special needs* (pp. 59-84). Baltimore: Paul Brookes Publishing Co.

Dunst, C. J. (1982). *Early intervention, social support, and institutional avoidance*. Paper presented at the annual meeting of the Southeastern American Association on Mental Deficiency, Louisville, KY.

Dunst, C. J. (1983). Emerging trends and advances in early intervention programs. *New Jersey Journal of School Psychology, 2*, 26-40.

Dunst, C. J. (1985). Rethinking early intervention. *Analysis and Intervention in Developmental Disabilities, 5*, 165-201.

Dunst, C. J. (1986a, October). *Helping relationships and enabling and empowering families*. Paper presented at the 11th Annual Regional Intervention Program Expansion Conference, Cleveland, OH.

Dunst, C. J. (1986b). *Measuring parental commitment to professionally-prescribed, child-level interventions.* Unpublished paper, Family Infant and Preschool Program, Western Carolina Center, Morganton, NC.

Dunst, C. J. (1986c). Overview of the efficacy of early intervention programs. In L. Bickman & D. Weatherford (Eds.), *Evaluating early intervention programs for severely handicapped children and their families* (pp. 79-147). Austin, TX: PRO-ED.

Dunst, C. J. (1986d). *A short form scale for measuring parental health and well-being.* Unpublished paper, Center for Family Studies, Western Carolina Center, Morganton, NC.

Dunst, C. J. (1987, December). *What is effective helping?* Paper presented for the Plenary Session "What is Helping?" held at the Fifth Biennial National Training Institute of the National Center for Clinical Infant Programs, Washington, D.C.

Dunst, C.J. (1988, March). *Enabling and empowering families: Caveats, considerations and consequences.* Keynote presentation made at the Early Intervention: Innovations in Service Delivery Conference, Danbury, CT.

Dunst, C. J. (Ed.). (1989). Family-centered assessment and intervention practices. *Family Systems Intervention Monograph, 1,* No. 1. Morganton, NC: Family, Infant and Preschool Program, Western Carolina Center.

Dunst, C. J. (1990a). *Aims and principles of family resource programs.* Presentation made at the Sixth Annual Early Intervention Summer Institute, Williamsburg, VA.

Dunst, C. J. (1990b). Family support principles: Checklists for program builders and practitioners. *Family Systems Intervention Monograph, 2,* No. 5. Morganton, NC: Family, Infant and Preschool Program, Western Carolina Center.

Dunst, C. J. (1991, February). *Empowering families: Principles and outcomes.* Presentation made at the 4th Annual Research Conference, "A System of Care of Children's Mental Health: Expanding the Research Base," Tampa, FL.

Dunst, C. J., Cooper, C. S., Weeldreyer, J. C.,

Snyder, K. D., & Chase, J. H. (1988). *Family Needs Scale.* In C. J. Dunst, C. M. Trivette, & A. G. Deal (Eds.), *Enabling and empowering families: Principles and guidelines for practice* (pp. 149-151). Cambridge, MA: Brookline Books.

Dunst, C. J., & Deal, A. G. (1990). Individualized Family Support Plans: Model, methods and strategies. *Family Systems Intervention Monograph, 2,* No. 1. Morganton, NC: Family, Infant and Preschool Program, Western Carolina Center.

Dunst, C. J., Jenkins, V., & Trivette, C. (1984). Family Support Scale: Reliability and validity. *Journal of Individual, Family, and Community Wellness, 1*(4), 45-52.

Dunst, C.J., Johanson, C., Rounds, T., Trivette, C. M., & Hamby, D. (1992). Characteristics of parent-professional partnerships. In S. L. Christenson & J. C. Conoley (Eds.), *Home-school collaboration: Building a fundamental educational resource* (pp. 157-174). Washington, DC: National Association of School Psychologists.

Dunst, C. J., Johanson, C., Trivette, C.M., & Hamby, D. (1991). Family-oriented early intervention policies or practices: Family-centered or not? *Exceptional Children, 58,* 115-126.

Dunst, C. J., & Leet, H. E. (1987). Measuring the adequacy of resources in households with young children. *Child: Care, Health and Development, 13,* 111-125.

Dunst, C. J., Leet, H., & Trivette, C. M. (1988). Family resources, personal well-being, and early intervention. *Journal of Special Education, 22,* 108-116.

Dunst, C. J., & Paget, K. D. (1991). Parent-professional partnerships and family empowerment. In M. Fine (Ed.), *Collaborative involvement with parents of exceptional children* (pp. 25-44). Brandon, VT: Clinical Psychology Publishing Company, Inc.

Dunst, C. J., & Trivette, C. M. (1984, August). *Differential influences of social support on mentally retarded children and their families.* Paper presented at the annual meeting of the American Psychological Association, Toronto, Canada.

Dunst, C. J., & Trivette, C. M. (1985). A guide to measures of social support and family behavior. *Monograph of Technical Assistance Development System (No. 1).* Chapel Hill, NC: TADS.

Dunst, C. J., & Trivette, C. M. (1986). Looking beyond the parent-child dyad for the determinants of maternal styles of interaction. *Infant Mental Health Journal, 7,* 69-80.

Dunst, C. J., & Trivette, C. M. (1987a). Enabling and empowering families: Conceptual and intervention issues. *School Psychology Review, 16*(4), 443-456.

Dunst, C. J., & Trivette, C. M. (1987b, April). *Social support and positive functioning in families of developmentally at-risk preschoolers.* Presentation made at the symposium "Every Cloud Has a Silver Lining: Successful Adaptations to the Care of a Handicapped Child" held at the biennial meeting of the Society for Research in Child Development, Baltimore, MD.

Dunst, C. J., & Trivette, C. M. (1988a). A family systems model of early intervention with handicapped and developmentally at-risk children. In D. Powell (Ed.), *Parent education as early childhood intervention: Emerging directions in theory, research, and practice* (pp. 131-180). Norwood, NJ: Ablex Publishing Co.

Dunst, C. J., & Trivette, C. M. (1988b). Determinants of caregiver styles of interaction used with developmentally at-risk children. In K. Marfo (Ed.), *Parent-child interaction and developmental disabilities: Theory, research, and intervention* (pp. 3-31). New York: Praeger Publishers.

Dunst, C. J., & Trivette, C. M. (1988c). Helping, helplessness, and harm. In J. Witt, S. Elliott, & F. Gresham (Eds.), *Handbook of behavior therapy in education* (pp. 343-376). New York: Plenum Press.

Dunst, C. J., & Trivette, C. M. (1988d). Toward experimental evaluation of the Family, Infant and Preschool Program. In H. Weiss & F. Jacobs (Eds.), *Evaluating family programs* (pp. 315-346). New York: Aldine de Gruyter.

Dunst, C. J., & Trivette, C. M. (1989). An enablement and empowerment perspective of case man-

agement. *Topics in Early Childhood Special Education, 8*(4), 87-102.

Dunst, C. J., & Trivette, C. M. (1990). Assessment of social support in early intervention programs. In S. Meisels & J. Shonkoff (Eds.), *Handbook of early intervention* (pp. 326-349). New York: Cambridge University Press.

Dunst, C. J., Trivette, C. M., & Cross, A. H. (1986a). Mediating influences of social support: Personal, family, and child outcomes. *American Journal of Mental Deficiency, 90,* 403-417.

Dunst, C. J., Trivette, C. M., & Cross, A. H. (1986b). Roles and support networks of mothers of handicapped children. In R. Fewell & P. Vadasy (Eds.), *Families of handicapped children: Needs and support across the lifespan* (pp. 167-192). Austin, TX: PRO-ED.

Dunst, C. J., Trivette, C. M., & Cross, A. H. (1988). Social support networks of families with handicapped children. In S. E. Keefe (Ed.), *Appalachian mental health* (pp. 101-121). Lexington: University of Kentucky Press.

Dunst, C. J., Trivette, C. M., Davis, M., & Weeldreyer, J. (1988). Enabling and empowering families of children with health impairments. *Children's Health Care. 17*(2), 71-81.

Dunst, C. J., Trivette, C. M., & Deal, A. G. (1988). *Enabling and empowering families: Principles and guidelines for practice.* Cambridge, MA: Brookline Books.

Dunst, C. J., Trivette, C. M., Gordon, N. J., & Pletcher, L. L. (1989). Building and mobilizing informal family support networks. In G. S. Singer & L. K. Irvin (Eds.), *Support for caregiving families: Enabling positive adaptation to disability* (pp. 121-142). Baltimore: Paul H. Brookes.

Dunst, C. J., Trivette, C. M., Gordon, N. J., & Starnes, A. L. (1993). Family-centered case management practices: Characteristics and consequences. In G.H.S. Singer & L.E. Powers (Eds.), *Families, disability, and empowerment: Active coping skills and strategies for family interventions* (pp. 88-118). Baltimore, MD: Paul H. Brookes.

Dunst, C. J., Trivette, C. M., Jodry, W. L., Morrow,

J. B., & Hamer, A.W. (1988). *Personal Assessment of Coping Experiences Scale.* Unpublished scale, Center for Family Studies, Western Carolina Center, Morganton, NC.

Dunst, C. J., Trivette, C. M., & LaPointe, N. (1992). Toward clarification of the meaning and key elements of empowerment. *Family Science Review, 5*(1 & 2), 111-130.

Dunst, C. J., Trivette, C. M., & Mott, D. W. (1990). Strengths-based family-centered intervention practices. *Family Systems Intervention Monograph, 2,* No. 4. Morganton, NC: Family, Infant and Preschool Program, Western Carolina Center.

Dunst, C. J., Trivette, C. M., Starnes, A. L., Hamby, D.W., & Gordon, N. J. (1993). *Building and evaluating family support initiatives: A national study of programs for persons with developmental disabilities.* Baltimore, MD: Paul H. Brookes.

Dunst, C. J., Trivette, C. M., & Thompson, R. (1990). Supporting and strengthening family functioning: Toward a congruence between principles and practice. *Prevention in Human Services, 9*(1), 19-43.

Dunst, C. J., & Vance, S. D. (1989). *Accessing social supports and intervention services by teenage mothers.* Final report submitted to the U.S. Department of Health and Human Services, National Center for Prevention of Child Abuse (Grant No. 90CA1246).

Dunst, C. J., Vance, S. D., & Cooper, C. S. (1986). A social systems perspective of adolescent pregnancy: Determinants of parent and parent-child behavior. *Infant Mental Health Journal, 7,* 34-48.

Edelman, C., & Mandle, C. L. (Eds.). (1986). *Health promotion: Throughout the life span.* St. Louis, MO: C. V. Mosby.

Edgar, D. (1988). Positive family support needed, not patch-ups. *Family Matters, 21,* 2-5.

Edgar, D. (1989). Strengthening families in the 1990s. *Family Matters, 23,* 2-5.

Education of the Handicapped Amendments of (1986). *P.L. 99-457,* Sec. 677, 20 U.S.C. Sec. 1477.

Ehly, S., Conoley, J., & Rosenthal, D. (1985). *Working with parents of exceptional children.* St. Louis, MO: C. V. Mosby.

Elder, J., & Magrab, P. (Eds.). (1980). *Coordinating services to handicapped children: A handbook for interagency collaboration.* Baltimore: Paul Brookes Publishers.

Erickson, K. (1981). *Human services today* (2nd ed.). Reston, VA: Reston Publishing Company.

Erickson, M.R., & Cromack, T. (1972). Evaluating a tutoring program. *Journal of Experimental Education, 41,* 27-31.

Family Resource Coalition. (1987). *What are the assumptions of the Family Resource Movement?* Chicago: Family Resource Coalition.

Farkas, S. (1981). *Taking a family perspective. A principal's guide for working with families of handicapped children.* Washington, DC: Family Impact Seminar Center.

Federation of Families for Children's Mental Health. (1992). *Principles on family support.* Alexandria, VA: Federation of Families for Children's Mental Health.

Fewell, R. R., Meyer, D. J., & Schell, G. (1981). *Parent Needs Inventory.* Unpublished scale, University of Washington, Seattle, WA.

Fisher, J. D. (1983). Recipient reactions to aid: The parameters of the field. In J. D. Fisher, A. Nadler, & B. M. DePaulo (Eds.), *New directions in helping: Vol. 1. Recipient reactions to aid* (pp. 3-14). New York: Academic Press.

Fisher, J. D., Nadler, A., & DePaulo, B. M. (Eds.). (1983a). *New directions in helping: Vol. 1. Recipient reactions to aid.* New York: Academic Press.

Fisher, J. D., Nadler, A., & Whitcher-Alagna, S. (1983b). Four theoretical approaches for conceptualizing reactions to aid. In J. D. Fisher, A. Nadler, & B. M. DePaulo (Eds.), *New directions in helping: Vol. 1. Recipient reactions to aid* (pp. 51-84). New York: Academic Press.

Folkman, S., Lazarus, R. S., Dunkel-Shetter, C., DeLorgis, A., & Gruen, R. J. (1986). The dynamics of a stressful encounter: Cognitive appraisal, coping, and encounter outcomes. *Journal of Personality and Social Psychology, 50,* 992-1003.

Foster, M., Berger, M., & McLean, M. (1981).

Rethinking a good idea: A reassessment of parent involvement. *Topics in Early Childhood Special Education, 1*(3), 55-65.

Fox, M. R. (1989). More power to the families. *Hospital and Community Psychiatry, 10*(11), 1109.

Freedman, S. A., Reiss, J., & Pierce, P. M. (1988). *Focus and functions of family centered case management.* Gainsville, FL: Institute for Child Health Policy.

Gans, S. P., & Horton, G. T. (1975). *Integration of human services: The state and municipal levels.* New York: Praeger Publishers.

Garbarino, J. (1982). *Children and families in the social environment.* New York: Aldine Publishing.

Garbarino, J. (1983). Social support networks: RX for the helping professionals. In J. Whittaker & J. Garbarino (Eds.), *Social support networks: Informal helping in the human services* (pp. 3-28). New York: Aldine Publishing.

Garbarino, J. (1992). Developmental issues in human services. In J. Garbarino, *Children and families in the social environment* (2nd. ed., pp.231-270). New York: Aldine de Gruyter.

Garland, C., & Buck, D., & Woodruff, G. (1988). *Case management.* Division for Early Childhood, White Paper..

Garrett, A. (1982). *Interviewing: Its principles and methods.* New York: Family Service Association of America.

Gittler, J. (1988). *Community-based systems of comprehensive services for children with special health care needs and their families.* Iowa City: University of Iowa, National Maternal and Child Health Resource Center.

Gittler, J., & Colton, M. (Eds). (1987a). *Community-based case management programs for children with special health care needs.* Iowa City: IA: National Maternal and Child Health Resource Center.

Gittler, J., & Colton, M. (Eds). (1987b). *Proceedings of the National Conference of Future Directions of Case Management Services for Children with Special Health Care Needs.* Iowa City: IA: National Maternal and Child Health Resource Center.

Gordon, R. L. (1987). *Interviewing: Strategies, techniques and tactics.* Chicago: Dorsey Press.

Gore, S. (1978). The effect of social support in moderating the health consequences of unemployment. *Journal of Health and Social Behavior, 19,* 157-165.

Gottlieb, B. H. (1983). *Social support strategies: Guidelines for mental health practice.* Beverly Hills, CA: Sage.

Gouldner, A. W. (1960). The norm of reciprocity: A preliminary statement. *American Sociological Review, 25,* 161-178.

Greenberg, M. S., & Westcott, D. R. (1983). Indebtedness as a mediator of reactions to aid. In J. D. Fisher, A. Nadler, & B. M. DePaulo (Eds.), *New directions in helping: Vol. 1. Recipient reactions to aid* (pp. 85-112). New York: Academic Press.

Gross, A. E., & McMullen, P. A. (1983). Models of the help-seeking process. In B. DePaulo, A. Nadler, & J. Fisher (Eds.), *New directions in helping: Vol. 2. Help-seeking* (pp. 45-70). New York: Academic Press.

Gross, A. E., Wallston, B. S., & Piliavin, I. (1979). Reactance attribution, equity, and the help recipient. *Journal of Applied Social Psychology, 9,* 297-313.

Halpern, R., & Parker-Crawford, F. (1982). Young handicapped children and their families: Patterns of interaction with human service institutions. *Infant Mental Health Journal, 3,* 51-63.

Harding, S. D. (1982). Psychological well-being in Great Britain: An evaluation of the Bradburn Affect Balance Scale. *Personality and Individual Differences, 3,* 167-175.

Hartman, A., & Laird, J. (1983). *Family-centered social work practice.* New York: Free Press.

Hill, R. (1971). *The strengths of black families.* New York: Emerson Hall.

Hobbs, N. (1975). *The futures of children: Categories, labels, and their consequences.* San Francisco: Jossey-Bass.

Hobbs, N., Dokecki, P. R., Hoover-Dempsey, K. V., Moroney, R. M., Shayne, M. W., & Weeks, K. H. (1984). *Strengthening families.* San Francisco: Jossey Bass.

Hoke, B. (1968). Promotive medicine and the phenomenon of health. *Archives of Environmental Health, 16,* 269-278.

Holahan, C. J. (1977). Social ecology. In I. Iscap, B. Bloom, & C. Spielberger (Eds.), *Community psychology in transition.* New York: Wiley.

Hollingshead, A. B. (1975). *Four factor index of social status.* Unpublished paper, Yale University, Department of Sociology, New Haven, CT.

Holroyd, J. (1987). *Questionnaire on Resources and Stress: For families with chronically ill or handicapped members.* Brandon, VT: Clinical Psychology Publishing.

House, J. S., & Kahn, R. L. (1985). Measures and concepts of social support. In S. Cohen & S. L. Syme (Eds.), *Social support and health* (pp. 83-108). New York: Academic Press.

Hull, C. L. (1943). *Principles of behavior.* New York: Appleton-Century-Crofts.

Intagliata, J. (1982). Improving the quality of community care for the chronically mentally disabled: The role of case management. *Schizophrenia Bulletin, 8,* 655-674.

Janis, I. (1975). Effectiveness of social support for stressful decisions. In M. Deutach & H. Hornstein (Eds.), *Applying social psychology.* Hillsdale, NJ: Lawrence Erlbaum.

Jason, L., & Bogat, G. A. (1983). Preventive behavioral interventions. In R. Felner, L. Jason, J. Moritsugu, & S. Farber (Eds.), *Preventive psychology* (pp. 128-143). New York: Pergamon Press.

Johnson, B. (1990). The changing role of families in health care. *Children's Health Care, 19,* 234-241.

Johnson, B., McGonigel, M., & Kaufmann, R. (1989). *Guidelines and practices for the individualized family service plan.* Washington, DC: Association for the Care of Children's Health.

Johnson, P. J., & Rubin, A. (1983). Case management in mental health: A social work domain? *Social Work, 28,* 49-56.

Jones, B. (1989). Parents as partners. *New Ways, 16,* (Winter Issue).

Kagan, S. (1987). Home-school linkages: History's legacy and the family resource movement. In S. Kagan, D. Powell, B. Weissbourd, & E. Zigler (Eds.), *America's family support programs* (pp. 161-181). New Haven: Yale University Press.

Kagan, S.L., Powell, D., Weissbourd, B., & Zigler, E. (Eds.). (1987). *America's family support pro-grams: Perspectives and prospects.* New Haven, CT: Yale University Press.

Kagan, S. L., & Shelley, A. (1987). The promise and problems of family support programs. In S. L. Kagan, D. R. Powell, B. Weissbourd, & E. F. Zigler (Eds.), *America's family support programs* (pp. 3-18). New Haven, CT: Yale University Press.

Kammann, R., Christie, D., Irwin, R., & Dixon, G. (1979). Properties of an inventory to measure happiness (and psychological health). *New Zealand Psychologist, 8,* 1-9.

Kammann, R., & Fleet, R. (1983). Affectometer 2: A scale to measure current level of general happiness. *Australian Journal of Psychology, 35,* 257-265.

Kanner, A., Coyne, J., Schaefer, C., & Lazarus, R. S. (1981). Comparison of two modes of stress measure: Daily hassles and uplifts versus major life events. *Journal of Behavioral Medicine, 4,* 1-39.

Kanner, A., Feldman, S., Weinberger, D., & Ford, M. (1987). Uplifts, hassles, and adaptional outcomes in early adolescence. *Journal of Early Adolescence, 7,* 371-394.

Karpel, M. A. (Ed.). (1986a). *Family resources: The hidden partner in family therapy.* New York: Guilford Press.

Karpel, M. A. (1986b). Questions, obstacles, contributions. In M. A. Karpel (Ed.), *Family resources: The hidden partner in family therapy* (pp. 3-61). New York: Guilford Press.

Karuza, J., Jr., Zevon, M. A., Rabinowitz, V. C., & Brickman, P. (1982). Attribution of responsibility by helpers and recipients. In T. A. Wills (Ed.), *Basic processes in helping relationships* (pp. 107-129). New York: Academic Press.

Katz, R. (1984). Empowerment and synergy: Expanding the community's healing process. In J. Rappaport, C. Swift, & R. Hess (Eds.), *Studies in empowerment: Steps toward understanding and action* (pp. 201-226). New York: Haworth Press.

Klein, D. C., & Goldston, S. E. (Eds.). (1977). *Primary prevention: An idea whose time has come* (DHEW Publication No. ADM77-447). Rockville, MD: Alcohol, Drug Abuse, and Mental Health Administration.

Knoll, J., Covert, S., Osuch, R., O'Connor, S., Agosta, J., & Blaney, B. (1990). *Family support services in the United States: An end of decade status report.* Cambridge, MA: Human Services Research Institute.

Kohrman, A. F., & Diamond, L. (1986). Institutional and professional attitudes: Dilemmas for the chronically ill child. *Topics in Early Childhood Special Education, 5*(4), 82-91.

Kurtz, L. F., Bagarozzi, D. A., & Pollane, L. P. (1984). Case management in mental health. *Health and Social Work, 9,* 201-211.

L'Abate, L., & Young, L. (1988). *Casebook: Structured enrichment programs for couples and families.* New York: Brunner/Mazel.

Lamb, H. R. (1980). Therapist-case managers: More than brokers of services. *Hospital and Community Psychiatry, 31,* 762-764.

Lamb, H. R. & Goertzel, V. (1977). The long term patient in the era of community treatment. *Archives of General Psychiatry, 34,* 679-692.

Lamb, H.R., & Zusman, J. (1979). Primary prevention in perspective. *American Journal of Psychiatry, 136,* 12-17.

LaPointe, N., Trivette, C. M., & Dunst, C. J. (1990). *Parent Empowerment Survey.* Unpublished scale, Center for Family Studies, Western Carolina Center, Morganton, NC.

LaRocco, J., House, J., & French, J. (1980). Social support, occupational stress, and health. *Journal of Health and Social Behavior, 21,* 202-218.

Lehr, S. (1987, September). Family support...or is it? *The Center on Human Policy Bulletin,* 3-4.

Levine, I. S., & Fleming, M. (1984). *Human resource development: Issues in case management.* Baltimore, MD: Center of Rehabilitation and Manpower Services.

Lewis, J. M., Beavers, W. R., Gossett, J. T., & Phillips, V. A. (1976). *No single thread: Psychological health in family systems.* New York: Brunner/Mazel.

Lingren, H. G., Kimmons, L., Lee, P., Rowe, G., Rottmann, L., Schwab, L., & Williams, R. (Eds.). (1987). *Family strengths (Vol. 8-9): Pathways to well-being.* Lincoln: University of Nebraska Press.

Lipsky, D. K. (1989). The role of parents. In D. K. Lipsky & A. Gartner (Eds.), *Beyond separate education: Quality education for all* (pp. 159-179). Baltimore: Brookes Publishing Co.

Little, B. R. (1983). Personal projects: A rationale and method for investigation. *Environment and Behavior, 19,* 273-309.

Lombana, J. (1983). *Home-school partnerships.* New York: Grune & Stratton.

Lord, J., & Farlow, D. M. (1990). A study of personal empowerment: Implications for health promotion. *American Journal of Health Promotion, 5,* 2-8.

MacQueen, I. C. (1987). Community-based case management. In J. Gittler & M. Colton (Ed.), *Proceedings of the National Conference of the Future Directions of Case Management Services for Children with Special Health Care Needs* (pp. 15-38). Iowa City, IA: National Maternal and Child Health Resource Center.

Maple, F. F. (1977). *Shared decision making.* Beverly Hills: Sage.

Maslow, A. (1954). *Motivation and personality.* New York: Harper & Row.

McCubbin, H. I., Comeau, J. K., & Harkins, J. A. (1981). Family inventory of resources for management. In H. I. McCubbin & J. M. Patterson (Eds.), *Systematic assessment of family stress, resources and coping* (pp. 67-69). St. Paul, MN: Family Stress and Coping Project.

McCubbin, H. I., Joy, C. B., Cauble, A. E., Comeau, J. K., Patterson, J. M., & Needle, R. H. (1980). Family stress and coping: A decade of review. *Journal of Marriage and the Family, 42,* 855-871.

McCubbin, M. A., McCubbin, H. I., & Thompson, A. I. (1987). Family Hardiness Index. In H. I. McCubbin & A. I. Thompson (Eds.), *Family assessment inventories for research and practice* (pp. 125-130). Madison: University of Wisconsin.

McGoldrick, M. (1988). Ethnicity and the family life cycle. In B. Carter & M. McGoldrick (Ed.), *The changing family life cycle: A framework for family therapy* (pp. 69-90). New York: Gardner Press, Inc.

McGonigel, M. J. (1991). Philosophy and conceptual

framework. In M. J. McGonigel, R. K. Kaufmann, & B. H. Johnson (Eds.), *Guidelines and recommended practices for the Individualized Family Service Plan* (2nd ed., pp. 7-14) Bethesda, MD: Association for the Care of Children's Health.

McGonigel, M. J., & Garland, C.W. (1988). The individualized family service plan and the early intervention team: Team and family issues and recommended practices. *Infants and Young Children, 1*(1), 10-21.

McGrew, K. S., & Gilman, C. J. (1991). Measuring the perceived degree of parent empowerment in home-school relationships through a home-school survey. *Journal of Psychoeducational Assessment, 9*(4), 353-362.

McKillip, J. (1987). *Need analysis: Tools for the human services and education.* Beverly Hills, CA: Sage.

McKnight, J. (1987). Regenerating community. *Social Policy* (Winter Issue), 54-58.

McKnight, J. (1989, April). *Beyond community services.* Unpublished paper, Center for Urban Affairs and Policy Research, Northwestern University, Evanston, IL.

McKnight, J., & Ketzmann, J. (1984). Community organization in the 80s: Toward a post-Alinsky agenda. *Social Policy* (Winter Issue), 145-147.

Mecklem, C. (1989). Responses to empowerment through family support. *Networking Bulletin: Empowerment and Family Support, 1*(1), 15-16.

Merton, R. K. (1976). *Sociological ambivalence.* New York: Free Press.

Merton, V., Merton, R. K., & Barber, E. (1983). Client ambivalence in professional relationships: The problem of seeking help from strangers. In B. DePaulo, A. Nadler, & J. Fisher (Eds.), *New directions in helping: Vol. 2. Help-seeking* (pp. 13-44). New York: Academic Press.

Michlitsch, J., & Frankel, S. (1989). Helping orientations: Four dimensions. *Perceptual and Motor Skills, 69,* 1371-1378.

Miller, L., Lynch, E., & Campbell, J. (1990). Parents as partners: A new paradigm for collaboration. In W. Second (Ed.), *Best practices in school speech-language pathology (Vol. 1): Collaborative programs in the schools* (pp. 49-56). New York: Psychological Corporation.

Minuchin, P. (1985). Families and individual development: Provocations from the field of family therapy. *Child Development, 56,* 289-302.

Minuchin, S. (1974). *Families and family therapy.* Cambridge, MA: Harvard University Press.

Mitchell, R. E., & Trickett, E. J. (1980). Task Force Report: Social networks as mediators of social support: An analysis of the effects and determinants of social networks. *Community Mental Health Journal, 16,* 27-43.

Mittler, P., Mittler, H., & McConachie, H. (1987). Family supports in England. In D. Lipsky (Ed.), *Family supports for families with a disabled member* (pp. 15-36). New York: World Rehabilitation Fund.

Moroney, R. M . (1986). *Shared responsibility: Families and social policy.* New York: Aldine de Gruyter.

Moroney, R. M. (1987). Social support systems: Families and social policy. In S. L. Kagan, D. Powell, B. Weissbourd, & E. Zigler (Eds.), *America's family support programs* (pp. 21-37). New Haven, CT: Yale University Press.

Morse, S. J. (1983). The nature of the help-related interchange as a determinant of a person's attitude toward others. In J. D. Fisher, A Nadler, & B. M. DePaulo (Eds)., *New directions in helping: Vol. 1. Recipient reactions to aid* (pp. 305-332). New York: Academic Press.

Murray, H. (1938). *Explorations in personality.* New York: Oxford University Press.

Musick, J., & Weissbourd, B. (1988). *Guidelines for establishing family support programs.* Chicago: National Committee for Prevention of Child Abuse.

Nadler, A., Fisher, J. D., & DePaulo, B. M. (Eds.). (1983). *New directions in helping: Vol. 3. Applied perspectives on help-seeking and -receiving.* New York: Academic Press.

Nadler, A., & Mayseless, O. (1983). Recipient self-esteem and reactions to help. In J. D. Fisher, A. Nadler, & B. M. DePaulo (Eds.), *New directions in helping: Vol. 1. Recipient reactions to aid* (pp. 167-188). New York: Academic Press.

National Center for Clinical Infant Programs.

(1985). *Equals in this partnership: Parents of disabled and at-risk infants and toddlers speak to professionals.* Washington: National Center for Clinical Infant Programs.

Nelkin, V. (1987). *Family-centered health care for medically fragile children: Principles and practice.* Washington, DC: National Center for Networking Community Based Services.

Nunnally, J. C. (1967). *Psychometric theory.* New York: McGraw Hill.

O'Brien, W. (1988). Family support work: The Alys Kay family case model. *Australian Child and Family Welfare, 13* (2), 22-26.

O'Leary, A. (1985). Self-efficacy and health. *Behavior Research and Therapy, 23,* 437-451.

Olson, D. H., Larsen, A. S., & McCubbin, H. I. (1983). Family strengths. In D. H. Olson, H. I. McCubbin, H. L. Barnes, A. S. Larsen, M. L. Muxen, & M. A. Wilson (Eds.), *Families: What makes them work?* (pp. 261-262). Beverly Hills, CA: Sage.

Ooms, T., & Preister, S. (1988). *A strategy for strengthening families: Using family criteria in policymaking and program evaluations.* Washington, DC: AAMFT Research and Education Foundation.

Orden, S., & Bradburn, N. M. (1968). Dimensions of marriage happiness. *American Journal of Sociology, 73,* 715-731.

Oster, A. (1984). Keynote address. In *Equals in this partnership: Parents of disabled and at-risk infants and toddlers speak to professionals* (pp. 26-32). Washington, DC: National Center for Clinical Infant Programs.

Otto, H. A. (1962). What is a strong family? *Marriage and Family Living, 24,* 77-81.

Otto, H. A. (1963). Criteria for assessing family strengths. *Family Process, 2,* 329-334.

Otto, H. A. (1975). *The use of family strength concepts and methods in family life education: A handbook.* Beverly Hills, CA: The Holistic Press.

Ozer, E., & Bandura, A. (1990). Mechanisms governing empowerment effects: A self-efficacy analysis. *Journal of Personality and Social Psychology, 58,* 472-486.

Palys, T. S. (1980). Personal project systems and perceived life satisfaction. *Dissertation Abstracts International, 41,* 18948-18958.

Pearlin, L. I., & Schooler, C. (1978). The structure of coping. *Journal of Health and Social Behavior, 19,* 2-21.

Pelletier, S. (1983). Developmental disabilities program. In C. Sanborn (Ed.), *Case management in mental health services* (pp. 135-148). New York: Haworth Press.

Pettigrew, T. F. (1983). Seeking public assistance: A stigma analysis. In A. Nadler, J. D. Fisher, & B. M. DePaulo (Eds.), *New directions in helping: Vol. 3. Applied perspectives on help-seeking and receiving* (pp. 273-292). New York: Academic Press.

Phillips, M., & Rasberry, S. (1981). *Honest business.* New York: Random House.

Pilisuk, M., & Parks, S. H. (1986). *The healing web: Social networks and human survival.* Hanover, NH: University Press of New England.

Pooley, L. E., & Littell, J. H. (1986). *Family resource program builder: Blueprints for designing and operating programs for parents.* Chicago, IL: Family Resource Coalition.

Powell, D. (Ed.). (1988). *Parent education as early childhood intervention.* Norwood, NJ: Ablex.

Powell, D. (1990). Home visiting in the early years: Policy and program design decisions. *Young Children, 45*(6), 65-73.

Prestby, J., Wandersman, A., Florin, P., Rich, R., & Chavis, P. (1990). Benefits, costs, incentive management and participating in voluntary organizations: A means to understanding and promoting empowerment. *American Journal of Community Psychology, 18,* 117-119.

Rabinowitz, V. C., Karuza, J., Jr., & Zevon, M. A. (1984). Fairness and effectiveness in premeditated helping. In R. Folger (Ed.), *The sense of injustice* (pp. 63-92). New York: Plenum.

Rapp, C. A., & Chamberlain, R. (1985). Case management services for the chronically mentally ill. *Social Work, 30,* 417-422.

Rappaport, J. (1981). In praise of paradox: A social policy of empowerment over prevention. *American Journal of Community Psychology, 9,* 1-25.

Rappaport, J. (1984). Studies in empowerment: Introduction to the issues. In J. Rappaport, C.

Swift, & R. Hess (Eds.), *Studies in empowerment: Steps toward understanding and action* (pp. 1-7). New York: Haworth Press.

Rappaport, J. (1985). The power of empowerment language. *Social Policy, 16*, 15-21.

Rappaport, J. (1987). Terms of empowerment/ exemplars of prevention: Toward a theory for community psychology. *American Journal of Community Psychology, 15*(2), 121-128.

Rappaport, J. (1990). Research methods and the empowerment social agenda. In P. Tolan, C. Keys, F. Chertok, & L. Jason (Eds.), *Researching community psychology*. Washington, DC: American Psychological Association.

Rappaport, J., Swift, C., & Hess, R. (Eds.). (1984). *Studies in empowerment: Steps toward understanding and action*. New York: Haworth Press.

Reese, H., & Overton, W. (1980). Models of development and theories of development. In L. Goulet & P. Baltes (Eds.), *Life span developmental psychology: Research and commentary* (pp. 116-145). New York: Academic Press.

Reich, J., & Zautra, A. (1983). Demands and desires in daily life: Some influences on well-being. *American Journal of Community Psychology, 11*, 41-59.

Reid, D. W. (1984). Participatory control and the chronic-illness adjustment process. In H.M. Lefcourt (Ed.), *Research with the Locus of Control construct* (Vol. 3, pp. 361-389). Orlando, FL: Academic Press.

Reid, W. J. (1985). *Family problem solving*. New York: Columbia University Press.

Richmond, M. E. (1901). Charitable cooperation. In I. C. Barrows (Ed.), *Proceedings of the National Conference of Charities and Correction*. Boston: George Ellis.

Richmond, M. (1917). *Social diagnosis*. New York: Russell Sage Foundation.

Richmond, M. (1922). *What is social casework?* New York: Russell Sage Foundation.

Richmond, M. (1930). *The long view*. New York: Russell Sage Foundation.

Roberts, R. N. (1988). *Family support in the home*. Washington, DC: Association for the Care of Children's Health.

Robinson, V. A. (1930). *A changing psychology in social casework*. Chapel Hill, NC: University of North Carolina Press.

Rowe, G., Lingren, H., Van Zandt, S., Williams, R., DeFrain, J., & Stinnett, N. (Eds.). (1984). *Family strengths (Vol. 5): Continuity and diversity*. Lincoln: University of Nebraska Press.

Rubin, A. (1987). Case management. *Encyclopedia of Social Work* (pp. 212-222). Silver Spring, MD: National Association of Social Workers.

Sanborn, C. J. (1983). *Case management in mental health services*. New York: Haworth Press.

Sanford, N. (1972). Is the concept of prevention necessary or useful? In S. E. Golamn & C. Eisdorfer (Eds.), *Handbook of community mental health* (pp. 269-278). New York: Appleton-Century-Crofts.

Sarason, S. B., Carroll, C., Maton, K., Cohen, S., & Lorentz, E. (1977). *Human services and resource networks: Rationale, possibilities, and public policy*. Cambridge, MA: Brookline Books.

Satir, V. (1972). *Peoplemaking*. Palo Alto, CA: Science and Behavior Books.

Schulz, J. (1987). *Parents and professionals in special education*. Boston: Allyn & Bacon.

Schwartz, S. R., Goldman, H. H., & Churgin, S. (1982). Case management for the chronic mentally ill: Models and dimensions. *Hospital and Community Psychiatry, 33*, 1006-1009.

Seeman, J. (1989). Toward a model of positive health. *American Psychologist, 44*, 1099-1109.

Segal, S., & Aviram, V. (1978). *The mentally ill in community-based sheltered care*. New York: John Wiley & Sons.

Shelton, T. L., Jeppson, E. S., & Johnson, B. H. (1987). *Family-centered care for children with special health care needs*. Washington, DC: Association for the Care of Children's Health.

Sigel, I. (Ed.). (1985). *Parental belief systems: The psychological consequences for children*. Hillsdale, NJ: Lawrence Erlbaum.

Sigel, I.E., McGillicuddy-DeLisi, A.V., & Goodnow, J.J. (Eds.). (1992). *Parental belief systems: The psychological consequences for children*. Hillsdale, NJ: Lawrence Erlbaum.

Singer, G.H.S., & Irvin, L.K. (Eds.). (1989). *Support*

for caregiving families: Enabling positive adaptation to disability. Baltimore, MD: Paul H. Brookes.

Skinner, B. F. (1978). The ethics of helping people. In L. Wispe (Ed.), Sympathy, altruism and helping behavior (pp. 249-262). New York: Academic Press.

Slater, M. A., & Wikler, L. (1986). "Normalized" family resources for families with a developmentally disabled child. Social Work, 31, 385-390.

Smith, F. (1987). UCPA "Think Tank" identifies essential components of family support. Family Support Bulletin, 1(1), 4.

Smith, M. (1968). Schools and home: Focus on achievement. In A. Passow (Ed.), Developing programs for the educationally disadvantaged. New York: Teachers College Press.

Solomon, B. B. (1985). How do we really empower families? New strategies for social work practitioners. Family Resource Coalition Report, 3, 2-3.

Southard, E. E. (1918). The kingdom of evil: Advantages of an orderly approach in social case analysis. Proceedings, National Conference of Social Work, 337.

Stanley, M. A., & Maddux, J. E. (1986). Cognitive processes in health enhancement: Investigation of a combined protection motivation and self-efficacy model. Basic and Applied Social Psychology, 7, 101-113.

Stein, L. I., & Test, M. A. (1980). Alternative to mental hospital treatment I: Conceptual, model, treatment program, and clinical evaluation. Archives of General Psychiatry, 37, 392-397.

Steinberg, R. M., & Carter, G. W. (1983). Case management and the elderly. Lexington, MA: Lexington Books.

Stern, W. (1930). Psychology of early childhood (2nd ed.). New York: Holt.

Stinnett, N. (1979). Strengthening families. Family Perspective, 13, 3-9.

Stinnett, N. (1985). Research on strong families. In G. A. Rekers (Ed.), National leadership forum on strong families. Ventura, CA: Regal Books.

Stinnett, N., Chesser, B., & DeFrain, J. (Eds.). (1979a). Building family strengths (Vol. 1): Blueprints for action. Lincoln: University of Nebraska Press.

Stinnett, N., Chesser, B., DeFrain, J., & Knaub, P. (Eds.). (1979b). Family strengths (Vol. 2): Positive models for family life. Lincoln: University of Nebraska Press.

Stinnett, N., & DeFrain, J. (1985a). Family Strengths Inventory. In N. Stinnett & J. DeFrain (Eds.), Secrets of strong families (pp. 180-182). New York: Berkley Books.

Stinnett, N., & DeFrain, J. (Eds.). (1985b). Secrets of strong families. New York: Berkley Books.

Stinnett, N., DeFrain, J., King, K., Knaub, P., & Rowe, G. (Eds). (1981). Family strengths (Vol. 3): Roots of well-being. Lincoln: University of Nebraska Press.

Stinnett, N., DeFrain, J., King, K., Lingren, H., Van Zandt, S., & Williams, R. (Eds.). (1982). Family strengths (Vol. 4): Positive support systems. Lincoln: University of Nebraska Press.

Stinnett, N., Knorr, B., DeFrain, J., & Rowe, G. (1981). How strong families cope with crisis. Family Perspective, 15(4), 159-166.

Stinnett, N., Lynn, D., Kimmons, L., Fuenning, S., & DeFrain, J. (1984). Family strengths and personal wellness. Wellness Perspectives, 1, 25-31.

Stinnett, N., Tucker, D. M., & Shell, D. F. (1985). Executive families: Strengths, stress, & loneliness. Wellness Perspectives, 2(1), 21-29.

Stoneman, Z. (1985). Family involvement in early childhood special education programs. In N. H. Fallen & W. Umansky (Eds.), Young children with special needs (2nd ed., pp. 442-469). Columbus, OH: Charles E. Merrill.

Surgeon General. (1979). Healthy people: The Surgeon General's report on health promotion and disease prevention. Washington, DC: U.S. Department of Health, Education, and Welfare.

Swift, C. (1984). Empowerment: An antidote for folly. In J. Rappaport, C. Swift, & R. Hess (Eds.), Studies in empowerment: Steps toward understanding and action (pp. xi-xv). New York: Haworth Press.

Swift, C., & Levin, G. (1987). Empowerment: An emerging mental health technology. *Journal of Primary Prevention, 8* (1/2), 71-94.

Taylor, S. E. (1979). Hospital patient behavior: Reactance, helplessness or control? *Journal of Social Issues, 35*(1), 156-184.

Taylor, S. J., Knoll, J. A., Lehr, S., & Walker, P.M. (1989). Families for all children: Value-based services for children with disabilities and their families. In G. H. S. Singer & L. K. Irvin (Eds.), *Support for caregiving families: Enabling positive adaptation to disability* (pp. 27-40). Baltimore: Paul H. Brookes Publishing Co.

Thomas, K. W., & Velthouse, B. A. (1990). Cognitive elements of empowerment: An "interpretive" model of intrinsic task motivation. *Academy of Management Review, 15,* 666-681.

Thornton, J. (1990). Team teaching: A relationship based on trust and communication. *Young Children, 45,* 40-43.

Thurman, S.K. (1993). Some perspective on the continuing challenges in early intervention. In W. Brown, S.K. Thurman, & L. Pearl (Eds.), *Family-centered early intervention with infants and toddlers* (pp. 303-316)

Tolsdorf, C. C. (1976). Social networks, support, and coping: An exploratory study. *Family Process, 15,* 407-417.

Trivette, C. M., Deal, A., & Dunst, C. J. (1986). Family needs, sources of support, and professional roles: Critical elements of family systems assessment and intervention. *Diagnostique, 11,* 246-267.

Trivette, C. M., & Dunst, C. J. (1987). Proactive influences of social support in families of handicapped children. In H. G. Lingren, L. Kimmons, P. Lee, G. Rowe, L. Rottman, L. Schwab, & R. Williams (Eds.), *Family strengths Vol. 8-9: Pathways to well-being* (pp. 391-405). Lincoln: University of Nebraska Press.

Trivette, C. M., & Dunst, C. J. (1990). *Professional Helpers Characteristics Scale.* Unpublished scale, Center for Family Studies, Western Carolina Center, Morganton, NC.

Trivette, C. M., & Dunst, C. J. (1992). Characteristics and influences of role division and social support among mothers of handicapped preschoolers. *Topics in Early Childhood Special Education, 12*(3), 367-385.

Trivette, C. M., Dunst, C. J., Deal, A. G., Hamer, W., & Propst, S. (1990). Assessing family strengths and family functioning style. *Topics in Early Childhood Special Education, 101,* 16-35.

Trivette, C.M., Dunst, C.J., LaPointe, N., & Hamby, D. (1993). *Relationship between key elements of the empowerment construct.* Manuscript submitted for publication.

Trivette, C. M., Dunst, C. J., Morrow, J. B., Jodry, W. L., & Hamer, A. W. (1988). *Personal Assessment of Life Events Scale.* Unpublished scale, Center for Family Studies, Western Carolina Center, Morganton, NC.

Turnbull, A. P., Summers, J. A., & Brotherson, M. J. (1986). Family life cycle: Theoretical and empirical implications and future directions for families with mentally retarded members. In J. J. Gallagher & P. M. Vietze (Eds.), *Families of handicapped persons: Research, programs, and policy issues* (pp. 45-66). Baltimore, MD: Paul H. Brookes.

Uniform Partnership Act. (1941). Reprinted in *Martindalu-Hubbell Law Digests,* 1990 (pp. 177-181). Chicago: National Conference of Commissioners.

van Eys, J. (1984). The child as participant. In B. F. Brooks (Eds.), *Controversies in pediatric surgery* (pp. 221-225). Austin, TX: University of Texas Press.

van Eys, J. (1985). Caring toward care. *Children's Health Care, 13*(4), 160-166.

Van Zandt, S., Lingren, H., Rowe, G., Zeece, P., Kimmons, L., Lee, P., Shell, D., & Stinnett, N. (Eds.). (1986). *Family Strengths (Vol. 7): Vital connections.* Lincoln: University of Nebraska Press.

Vohs, J. (1987). Family-centered case management. In J. Gittler & M. Colton (Ed.), *Proceedings of the National Conference of Future Directions of Case Management Services for Children with Special Health Care Needs* (pp. 39-60). Iowa City, IA: National Maternal and Child Health Resource Center.

Vosler-Hunter, R. (1988). Elements of parent/professional collaboration. *Focal Point, 2*(2), 1-3. (Bulletin of the Research and Training Center, Portland State University.)

Walker, B. (1989). Strategies for improving parent-professional cooperation. In G. Singer & T. Irvin (Ed.), *Support for caregiving families: Enabling positive adaptation to disability* (pp. 103-119). Baltimore, MD: Brookes Publishing Co.

Walsh, F. (Ed.). (1982). *Normal family processes.* New York: Guilford Press.

Wandersman, A., & Florin, P. (Eds.). (1990). Citizen participation, voluntary organizations and community development: Insights for empowerment through research. *American Journal of Community Psychology, 18,* 49-177.

Warr, P., Barter, J., & Brownbridge, G. (1983). On the independence of positive and negative affect. *Journal of Personality and Social Psychology, 44,* 644-651.

Watson, D., & Pennebaker, J. W. (1989). Health complaints, stress, and distress: Exploring the central role of negative affectivity. *Psychological Review, 96,* 234-254.

Weil, M., & Karls, J. M. (1985). *Case management in human service practice: A systematic approach to mobilizing resources for clients.* San Francisco: Jossey-Bass.

Weiss, H. (1989). State family support and education programs: Lessons from the pioneers. *American Journal of Orthopsychiatry, 59,* 32-48.

Weiss, H. (1990). The challenges of empowerment in the family supports movement. *Networking Bulletin: Empowerment and Family Support, 2*(1), 3-8.

Weiss, H., & Jacobs, F. (Eds.). (1988a). *Evaluating family support programs.* Hawthorne, NJ: Aldine de Gruyter.

Weiss, H., & Jacobs, F. (1988b). Introduction: Family support and education programs–Challenges and opportunities. In H. Weiss & F. Jacobs (Eds.), *Evaluating family support programs* (pp. xix-xxix). Hawthorne, NJ: Aldine de Gruyter.

Weiss, R. (1974). The provisions of social relationships. In Z. Rubin (Ed.), *Doing unto others.* Englewood Cliffs, NJ: Prentice-Hall.

Weissbourd, B. (1987a). A brief history of family support programs. In S. L. Kagan, D. R. Powell, B. Weissbourd, & E. Zigler (Eds.), *America's family support programs* (pp. 38-56). New Haven, CT: Yale University Press.

Weissbourd, B. (1987b). Design, staffing, and funding of family support programs. In S. Kagan, D. Powell, B. Weissbourd, & E. Zigler (Eds.), *America's family support programs* (pp. 245-268). New Haven, CT: Yale University Press.

Weissbourd, B. (1990). Family resource and support programs: Changes and challenges in human services. *Prevention in Human Services, 99*(1), 69-85.

Weissbourd, B., & Kagan, S. L. (1989). Family support programs: Catalyst for change. *American Journal of Orthopsychiatry, 59,* 20-31.

Whaley, K., & Swadener, E. (1990). Multicultural education in infant and toddler setting. *Childhood Education, 66,* 238-240.

Whitmore, E. (1991). Evaluation and empowerment: It's the process that counts. *Networking Bulletin: Empowerment and Family Support, 2*(2), 1-7.

Whitmore, E., & Kerans, P. (1988). Participation, empowerment and welfare. *Canadian Review of Social Policy, 22,* 51-60.

Williams, R., Lingren, H., Rowe, G., Van Zandt, S., & Stinnett, N. (Eds.). (1985). *Family strengths (Vol. 6): Enhancement of interaction.* Lincoln, NE: Department of Human Development and the Family, University of Nebraska.

Wills, T. A. (1985). Supportive functions of interpersonal relationships. In S. Cohen & S. Syme (Eds.), *Social support and health* (pp. 61-82). New York: Academic Press.

Wolcott, I. (1989). *Family support services: A review of the literature and selected annotated bibliography.* Melbourne: Australian Institute of Family Studies.

World Health Organization. (1964). *Basic documents* (15th ed.). Geneva, Switzerland, WHO.

Yin, R. (1984). *Case study research: Design and methods.* Beverly Hills, CA: Sage Publishers.

Zautra, A., & Sandler, I. (1983). Life event needs assessments: Two models for measuring preventable mental health problems. In A. Zautra,

K. Bachrach, & R. Hess (Eds.), *Strategies for needs assessment in prevention* (pp. 35-58). New York: Haworth Press.

Zigler, E. (1986). The family resource movement: No longer the country's best kept secret. *Family Resource Coalition, 3*, 9-12.

Zigler, E., & Berman, W. (1983). Discerning the future of early childhood intervention. *American Psychologist, 38*, 894-906.

Zigler, E., & Black, K. B. (1989). America's family support movement: Strengths and limitations. *American Journal of Orthopsychiatry, 59*, 6-19.

Zigler, E., & Weiss, H. (1985). Family support system: An ecological approach to child development. In R. Rappaport (Eds.), *Children, youth, and families* (pp. 166-205). New York, NY: Cambridge University Press.

Zimmerman, M. A. (1990a). Toward a theory of learned hopefulness: A structural model analysis of participation and empowerment. *Journal of Research in Personality, 24*, 71-86.

Zimmerman, M. A. (1990b). Taking aim on empowerment research: On the distinction between individual and psychological concepts. *American Journal of Community Psychology, 18*, 169-177.

Zimmerman, M. A., Israel, B., Schulz, A., & Checkoway, B. (1992). Further explorations in empowerment theory: An empirical analysis of psychological empowerment. *American Journal of Community Psychology, 20*, 707-727.

Zimmerman, M. A., & Rappaport, J. (1988). Citizen participation, perceived control, and psychological empowerment. *American Journal of Community Psychology, 16*, 725-750.

Zola, I. K. (1966). Culture and symptoms: An analysis of patients presenting complaints. *American Sociological Review, 31*, 615-630.

INDEX

ABOUT THE EDITORS

Carl J. Dunst (Ph.D., Developmental Psychology, Vanderbilt University, George Peabody College, Nashville, TN) is Professor of Psychiatry, Medical College of Pennsylvania (Allegheny Campus); and Senior Research Scientist, Child and Family Studies Program, Allegheny General Hospital and Allegheny-Singer Research Institute, Pittsburgh, Pennsylvania. Dr. Dunst is a fellow of the American Psychological Association and recipient of several research and services awards. He is author of four books and numerous articles on supporting and strengthening family functioning. Dr. Dunst's research has focused on the environmental conditions that enhance and promote child, parent, and family development.

Carol M. Trivette (Ph.D., Child Development and Family Relations, University of North Carolina at Greensboro) is Director of the Family, Infant and Preschool Program and the Center for Family Studies located at Western Carolina Center in Morganton, North Carolina. She is co-author of three books and numerous articles on topics addressing issues of early intervention, family functioning, family support and empowerment. As the director of the Family, Infant and Preschool Program, she has responsibility for the development of a family support, early intervention model which includes the development of several family resource programs. Through the Center for Family Studies, her research interests have focused primarily on social support networks, helping relationships, empowerment, and social policy analyses.

Angela G. Deal (M.S.W., University of North Carolina at Chapel Hill) is the Executive Director of the Burke Partnership for Children, a non-profit, community based collaboration supporting young children and their families. She was previously Senior Coordinator of Child and Family Resources, Family, Infant and Preschool Program, at Western Carolina Center and she was responsible for four teams of professionals providing home-based intervention services. She also was direct administrator for four county-based family resource programs. Ms. Deal's other responsibilities included training of staff and interns, presenting at state and national conferences and producing products and publications on the program. She currently coordinates the Family Enablement Project, a national outreach training project funded through the U.S. Department of Education, and is actively involved in the development and refinement of the Enablement Model of working with families. Ms. Deal has eighteen years of social work experience with children and families.